Hey! You're Reading in the Wrong Direction!

This is the end of this graphic novel!

To properly enjoy this VIZ graphic novel, please turn it around and begin reading from right to left. Unlike English, Japanese is read right to left, so Japanese comics are read in reverse order from the way English comics are typically read.

This book has been printed in the original Japanese format in order to preserve the orientation of the original artwork. Have fun with it!

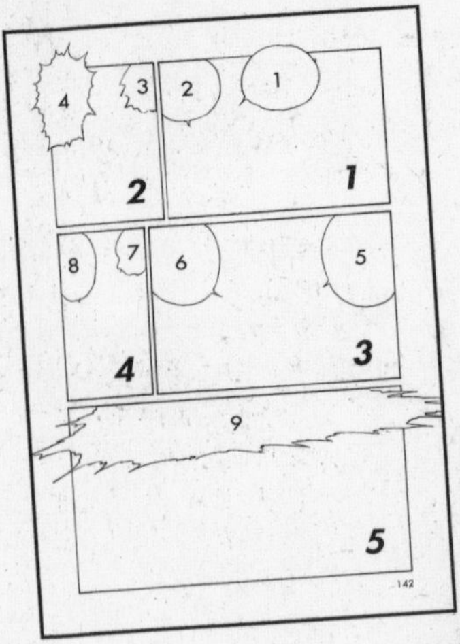

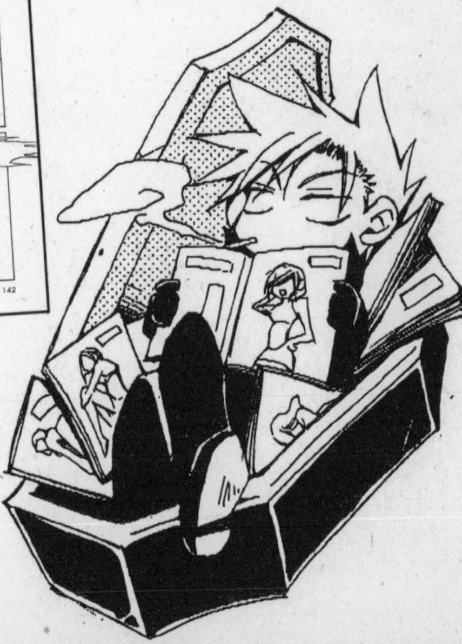

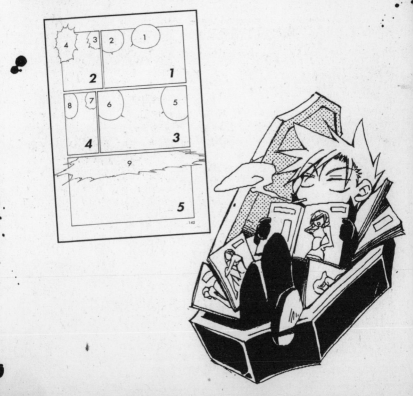

Natsume's
BOOK of FRIENDS

STORY and ART by
Yuki Midorikawa

Make Some Unusual New Friends

The power to see hidden spirits has always felt like a curse to troubled high schooler Takashi Natsume. But he's about to discover he inherited a lot more than just the Sight from his mysterious grandmother!

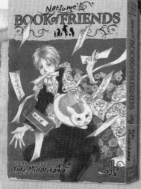

$9.99 USA / $12.99 CAN *
ISBN: 978-1-4215-3243-1

On sale at store.viz.com
Also available at your local bookstore or comic store

www.shojobeat.com

Natsume Yujincho © Yuki Midorikawa 2005/HAKUSENSHA, Inc.
* Price subject to change

RATED
FOR
TEEN
ratings.viz.com

www.viz.com

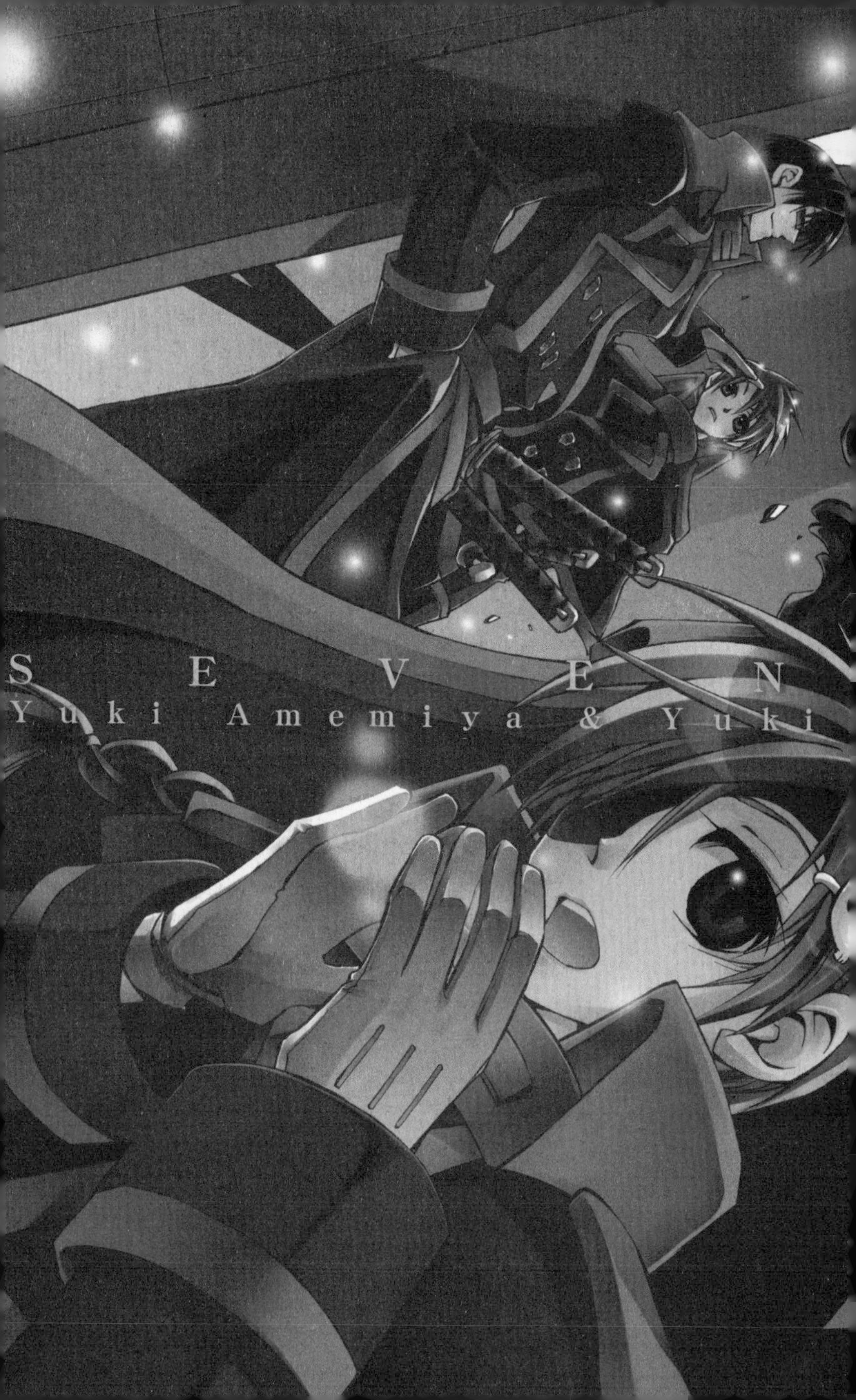
S E V E N
Yuki Amemiya & Yuki

C O N T E N T S

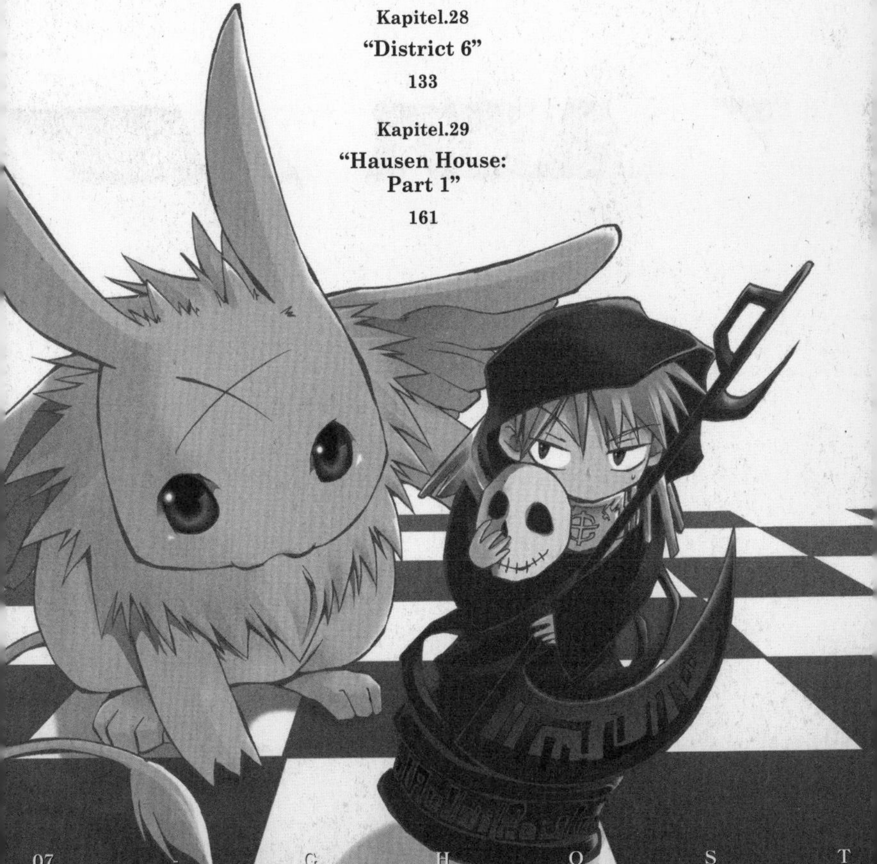

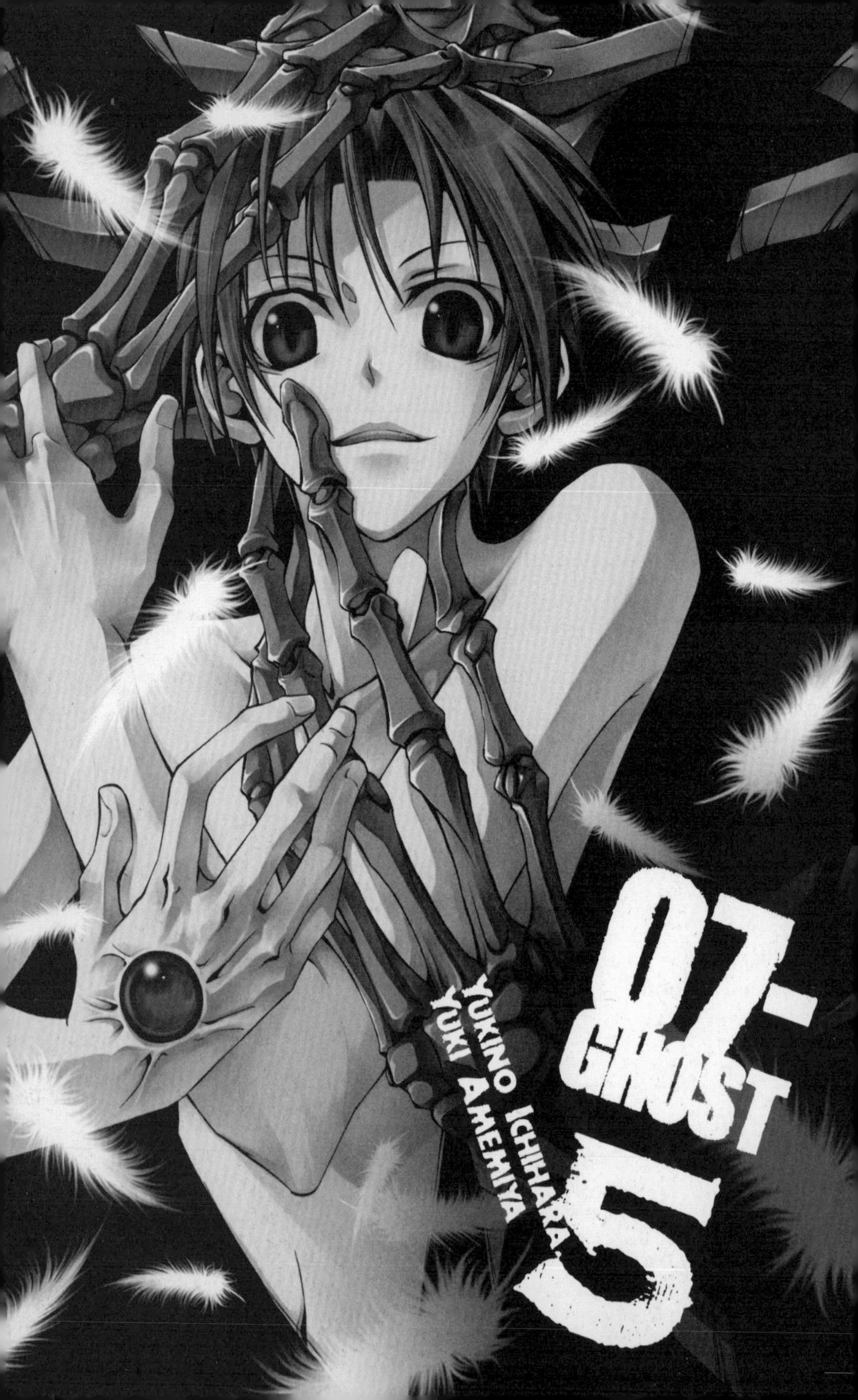
07-GHOST
5
YUKINO ICHIHARA
YUKI AMEMIYA

07 GHOST

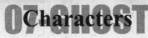

Characters

One thousand years ago, two equally powerful nations coexisted. One was the Barsburg Empire, protected by the Eye of Rafael. The other was the Raggs Kingdom, protected by the Eye of Mikael. Now that the Raggs Kingdom has been destroyed, things have changed...

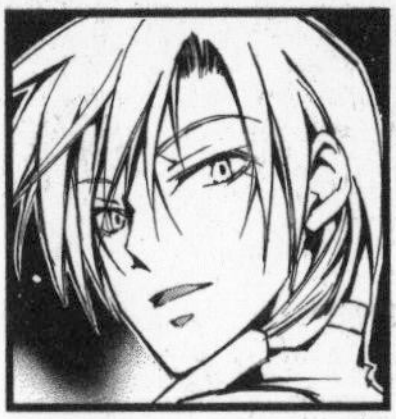

Hakuren

A bishop examinee from the prestigious Oak family. He's Teito's roommate and an ardent admirer of Frau.

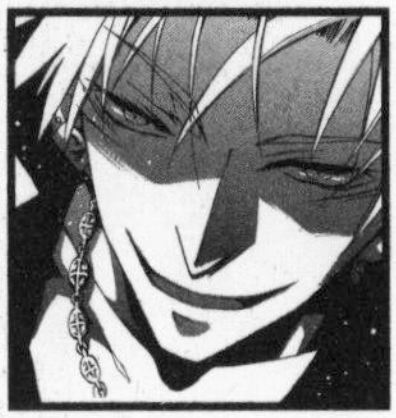

Frau

Bishop who saved Teito when he was fleeing from the academy. He is Zehel of the Seven Ghosts.

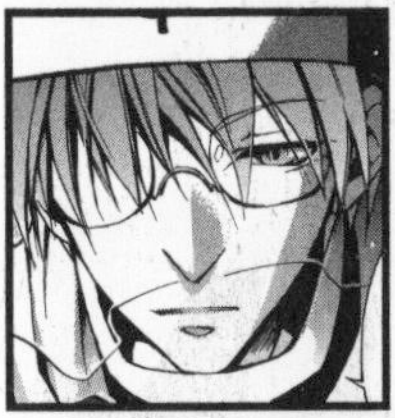

Castor

Bishop who can manipulate puppets. Along with Frau, he shelters Teito and is one of the Seven Ghosts.

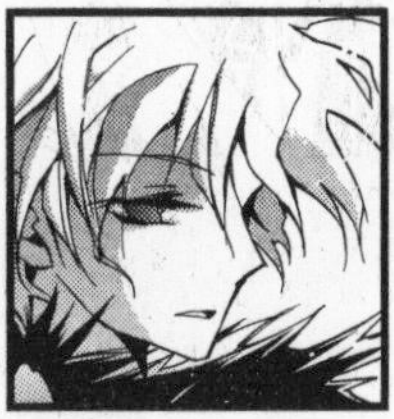

Labrador

Quiet bishop with the power of prophecy. One of the Seven Ghosts.

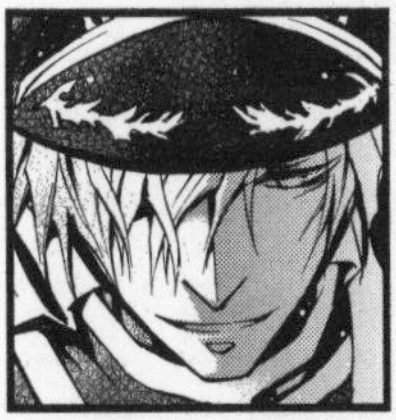

Ayanami

Imperial Army's Chief of Staff. Seeks the Eye of Mikael, and may be responsible for the king of Raggs' death.

Black Hawks

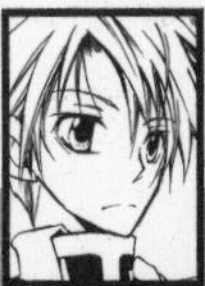

Hyuga's Begleiter: Konatsu

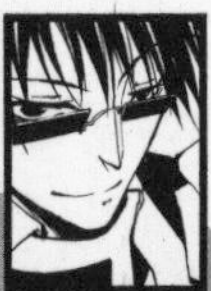

Major Hyuga

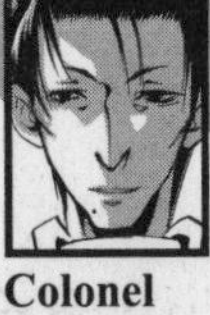

Colonel Katsuragi

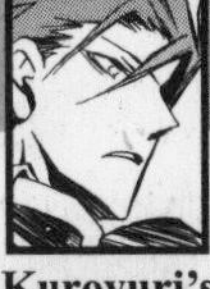

Kuroyuri's Begleiter: Haruse

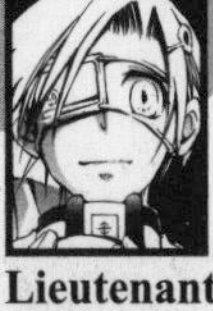

Lieutenant-Colonel Kuroyuri

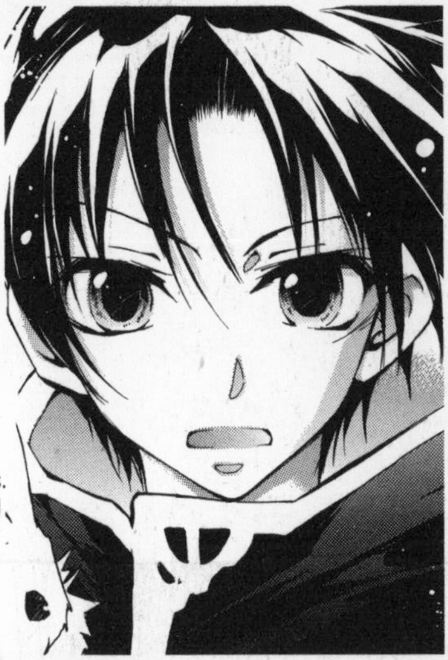

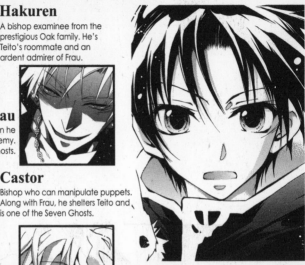

Teito Klein

Born a prince of Raggs, Teito was stripped of his memories and raised as a soldier by the military academy's chairman. He harbored the Eye of Mikael in his right hand until Ayanami's Black Hawks stole it. Currently training for the Bishop Examination. A boy of small stature.

Story

Teito is a student at the Barsburg Empire's military academy until the day he discovers that his father was the king of Raggs, the ruler of a kingdom the Barsburg Empire destroyed. Teito receives sanctuary from the Barsburg Church, but loses his best friend Mikage, who Ayanami controls like a puppet to get at Teito. To avenge Mikage's death, Teito, decides to become a bishop to obtain travel privileges to enter District 1 without inspection. But during the examination a most unwelcome adversary appears!

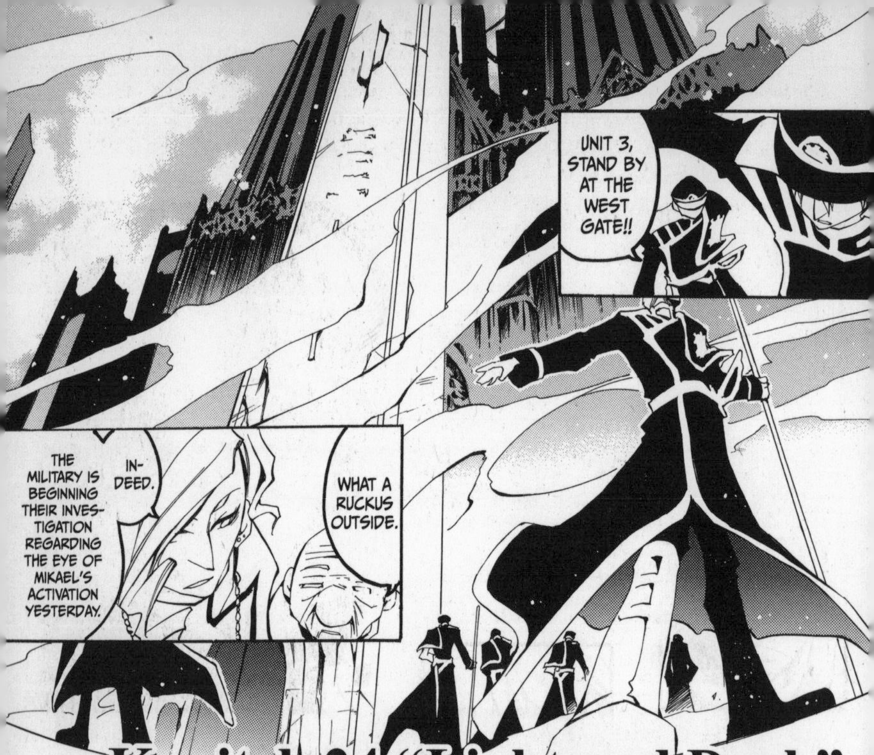
UNIT 3, STAND BY AT THE WEST GATE!!
WHAT A RUCKUS OUTSIDE.
IN-DEED.
THE MILITARY IS BEGINNING THEIR INVES-TIGATION REGARDING THE EYE OF MIKAEL'S ACTIVATION YESTERDAY.

Kapitel. 24 "Light and Dark"

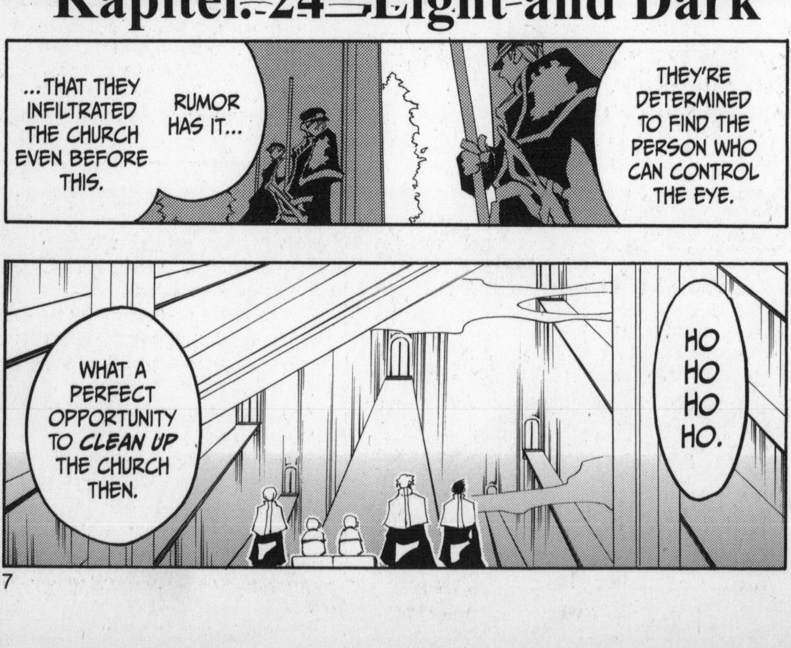
THEY'RE DETERMINED TO FIND THE PERSON WHO CAN CONTROL THE EYE.
RUMOR HAS IT...
...THAT THEY INFILTRATED THE CHURCH EVEN BEFORE THIS.
HO HO HO HO.
WHAT A PERFECT OPPORTUNITY TO *CLEAN UP* THE CHURCH THEN.

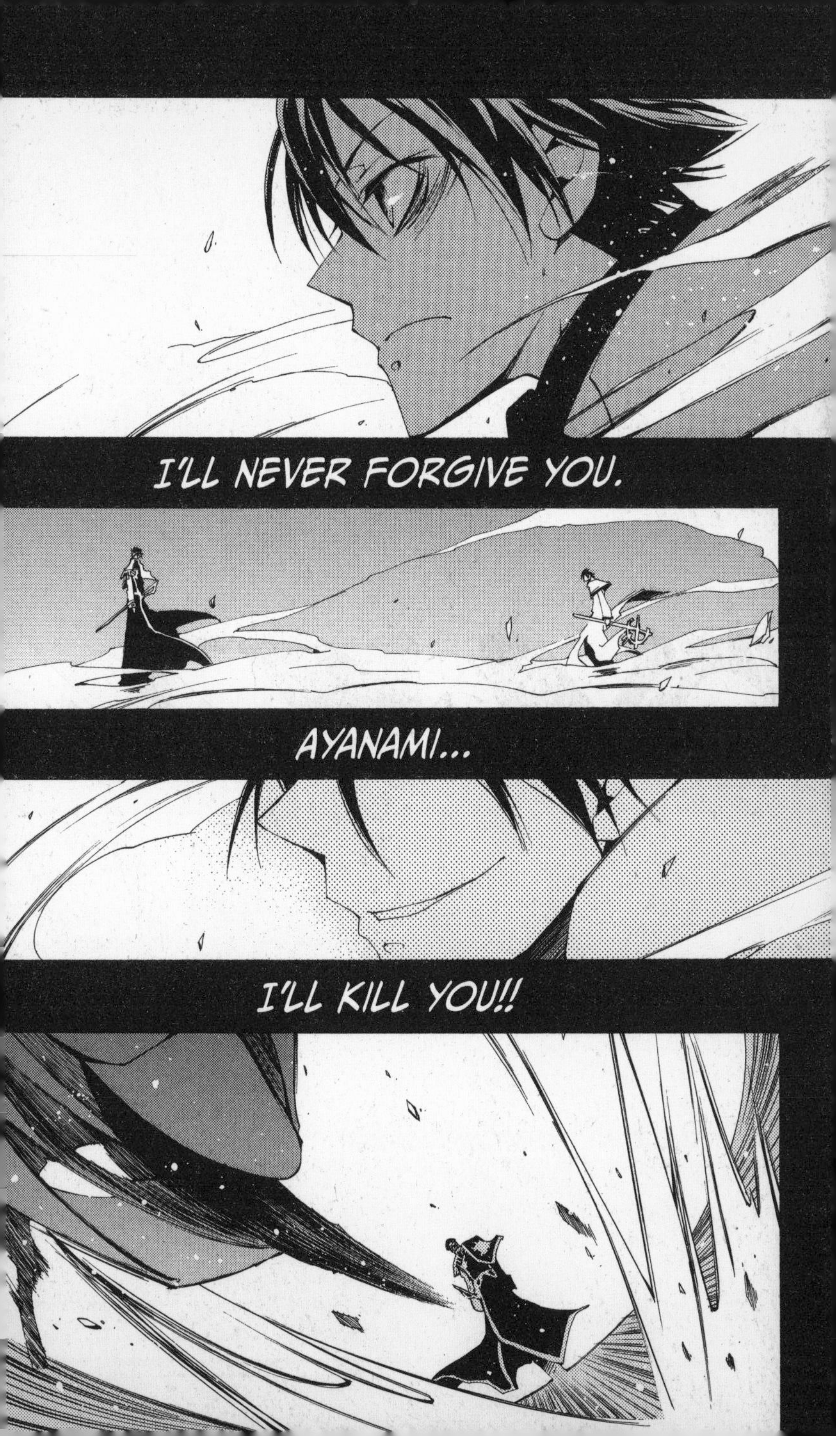
I'LL NEVER FORGIVE YOU.
AYANAMI...
I'LL KILL YOU!!

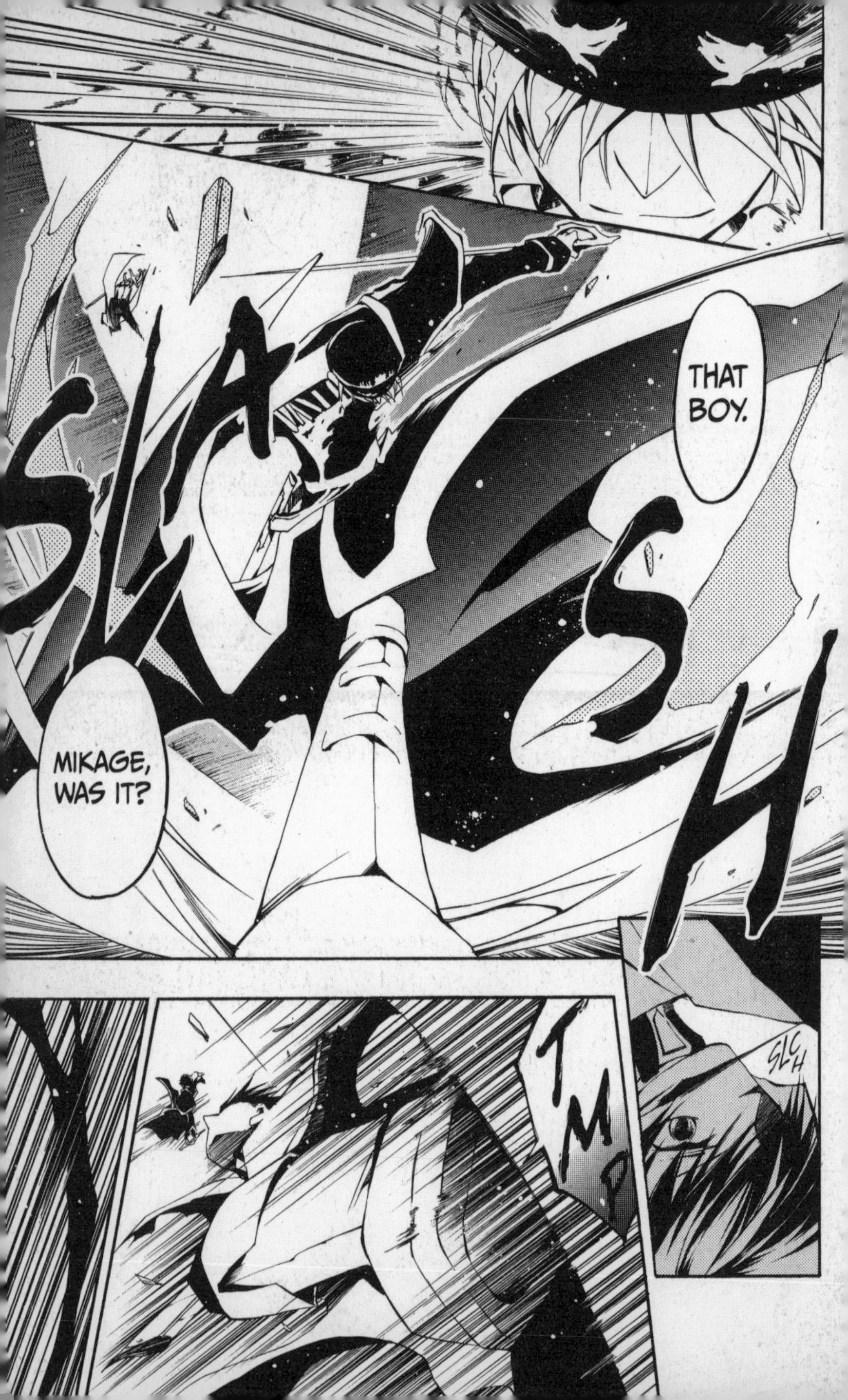
THAT BOY.
MIKAGE, WAS IT?
SLASH
SLCH
TMP

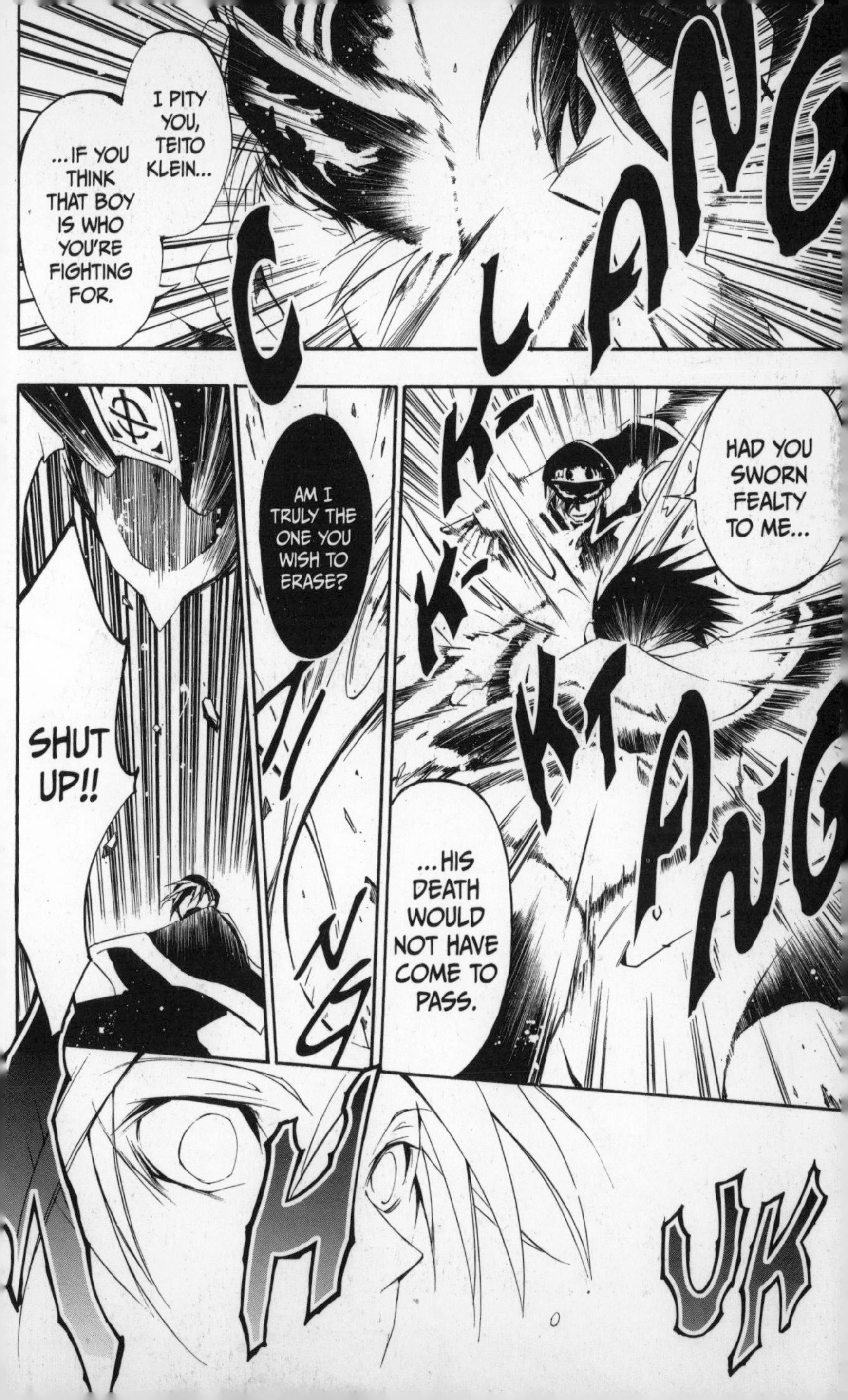
I PITY YOU, TEITO KLEIN...
...IF YOU THINK THAT BOY IS WHO YOU'RE FIGHTING FOR.
CLANG
HAD YOU SWORN FEALTY TO ME...
...HIS DEATH WOULD NOT HAVE COME TO PASS.
K-K-KLANG
AM I TRULY THE ONE YOU WISH TO ERASE?
SHUT UP!!
HUK

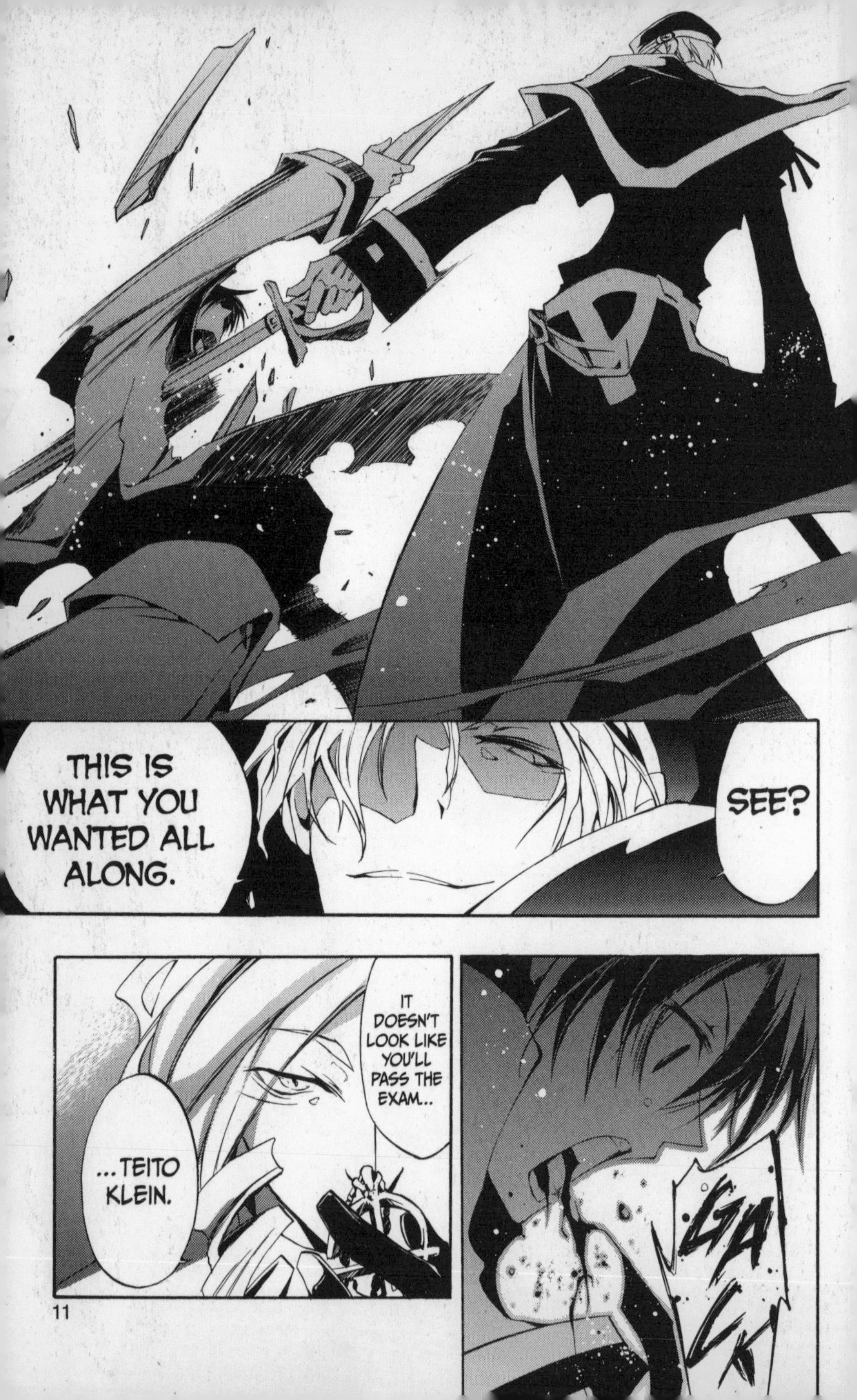
SEE?
THIS IS WHAT YOU WANTED ALL ALONG.
GACK
IT DOESN'T LOOK LIKE YOU'LL PASS THE EXAM..
...TEITO KLEIN.

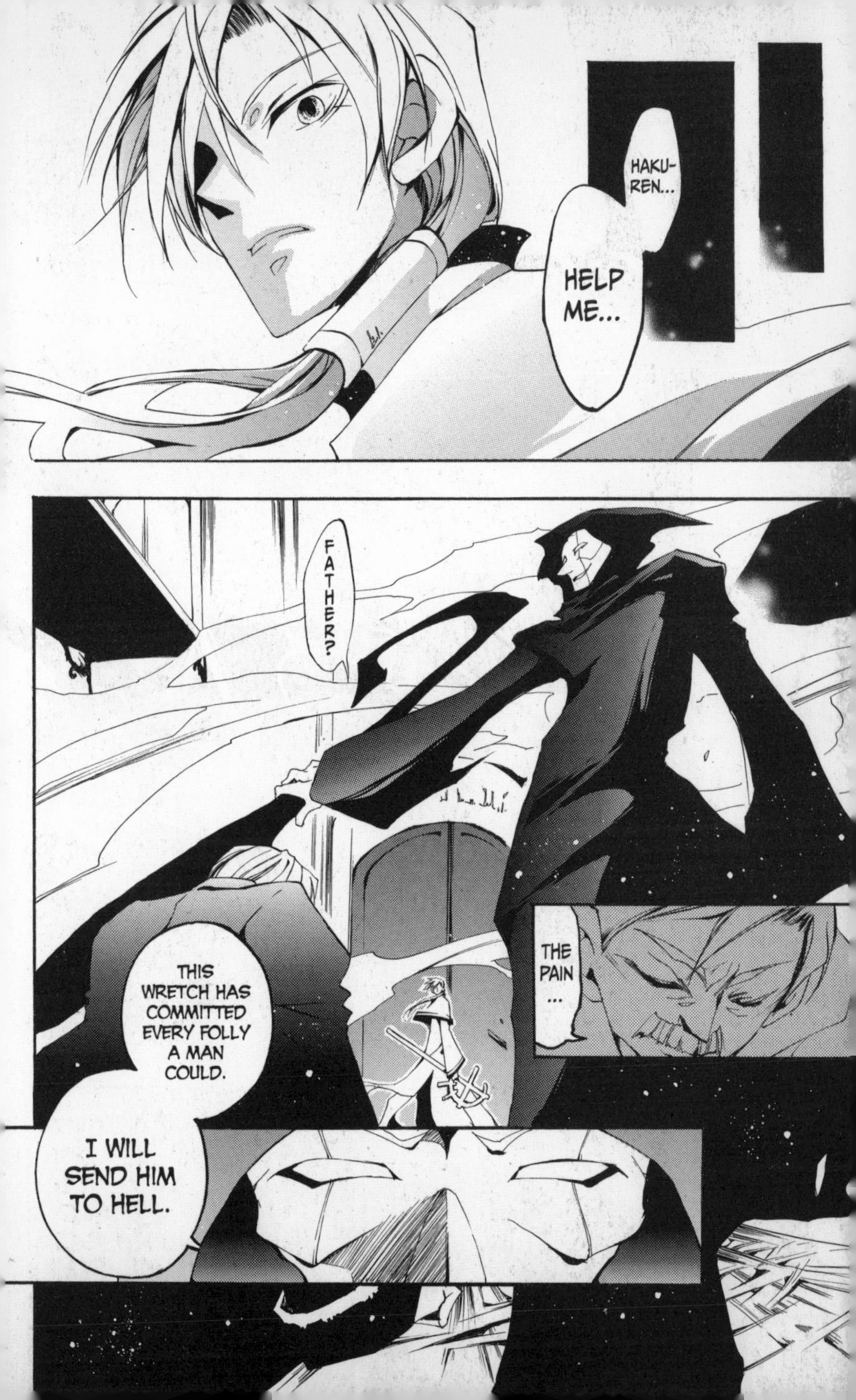
HAKU-REN...
HELP ME...
FATHER?
THE PAIN ...
THIS WRETCH HAS COMMITTED EVERY FOLLY A MAN COULD.
I WILL SEND HIM TO HELL.

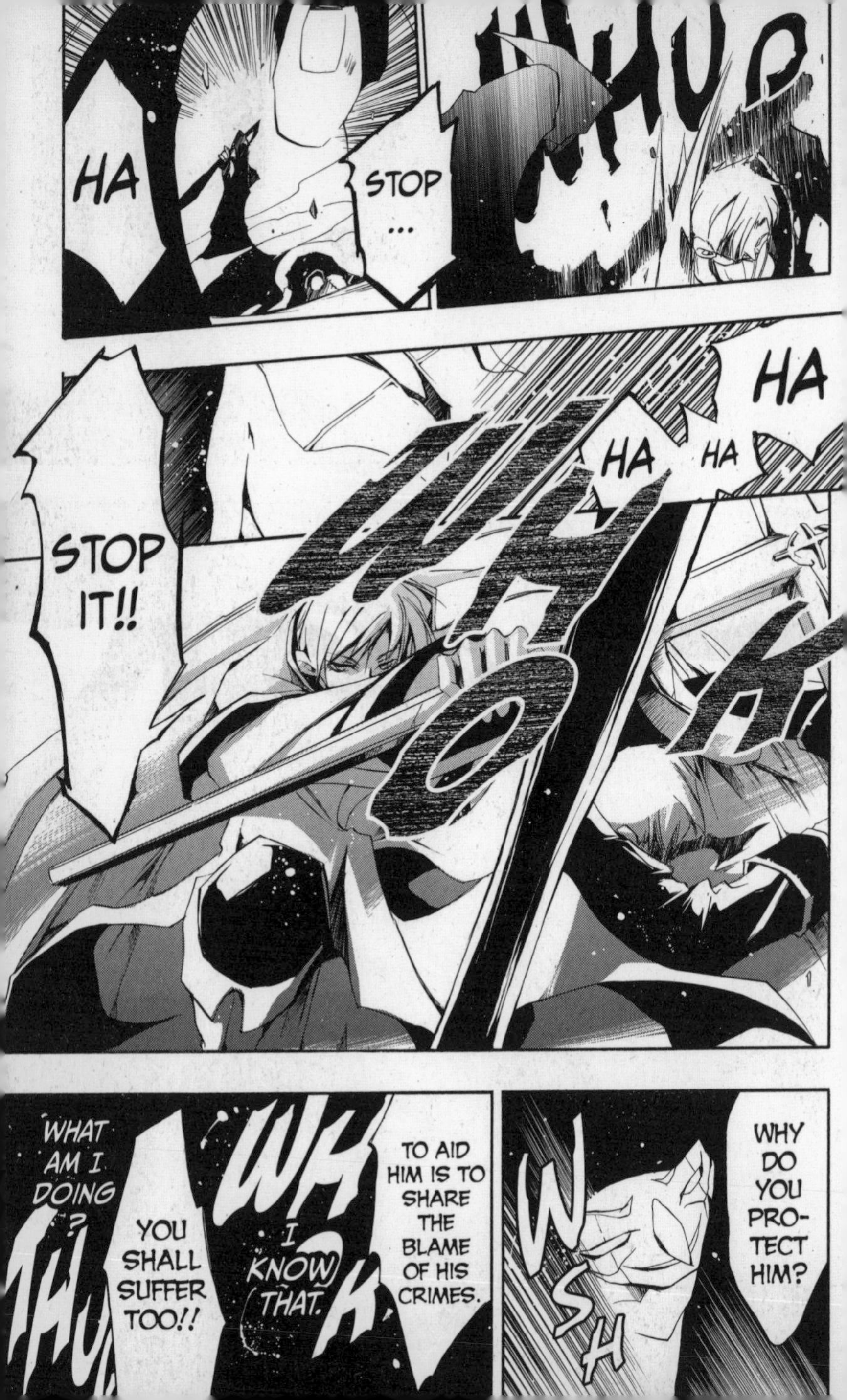
STOP ...
HA
HA
HA HA
STOP IT!!
WHY DO YOU PRO-TECT HIM?
TO AID HIM IS TO SHARE THE BLAME OF HIS CRIMES.
I KNOW THAT.
YOU SHALL SUFFER TOO!!
WHAT AM I DOING?

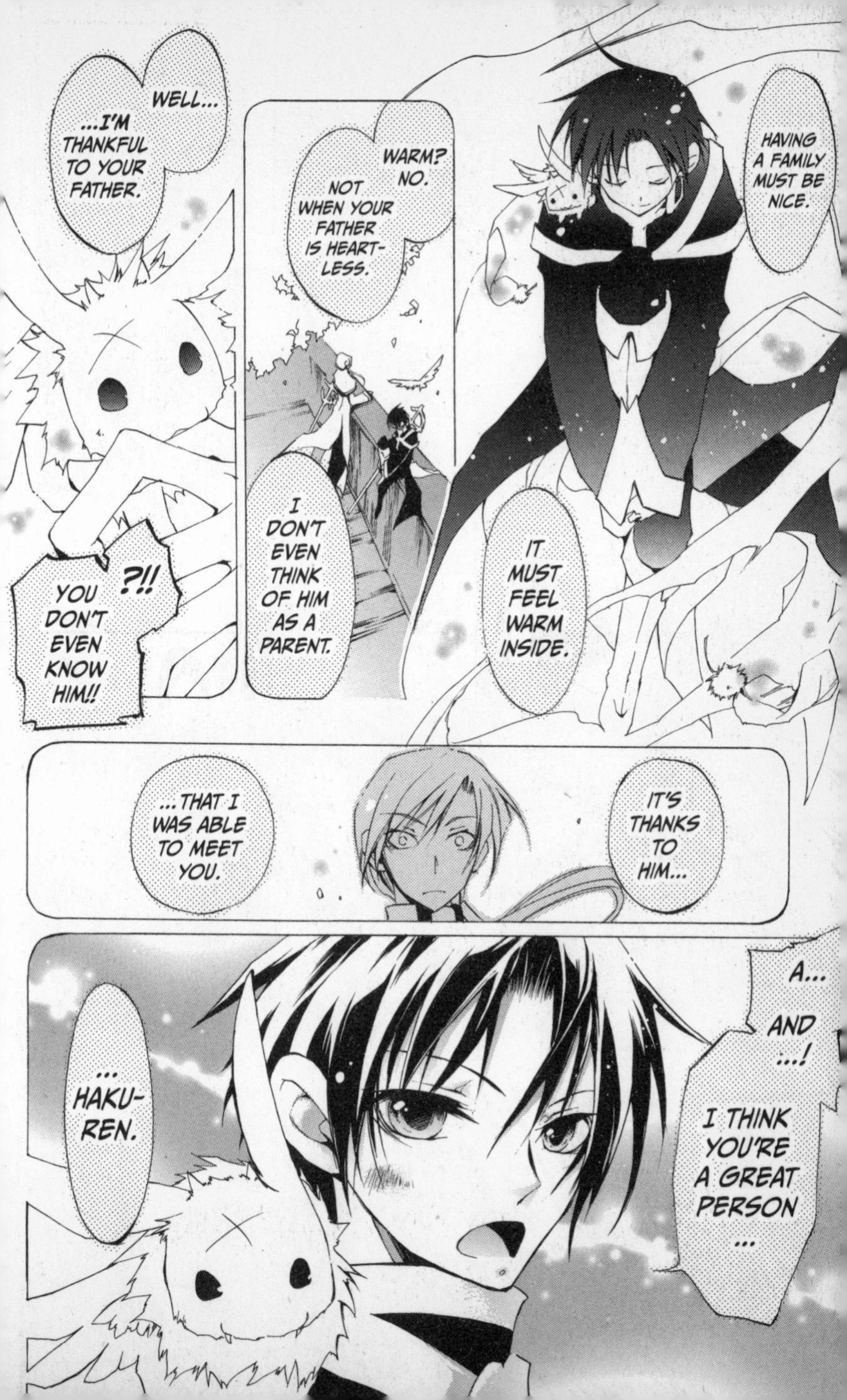
HAVING A FAMILY MUST BE NICE.
IT MUST FEEL WARM INSIDE.
WARM? NO.
NOT WHEN YOUR FATHER IS HEART-LESS.
I DON'T EVEN THINK OF HIM AS A PARENT.
WELL...
...I'M THANKFUL TO YOUR FATHER.
?!!
YOU DON'T EVEN KNOW HIM!!
IT'S THANKS TO HIM...
...THAT I WAS ABLE TO MEET YOU.
A... AND ...!
I THINK YOU'RE A GREAT PERSON ...
... HAKU-REN.

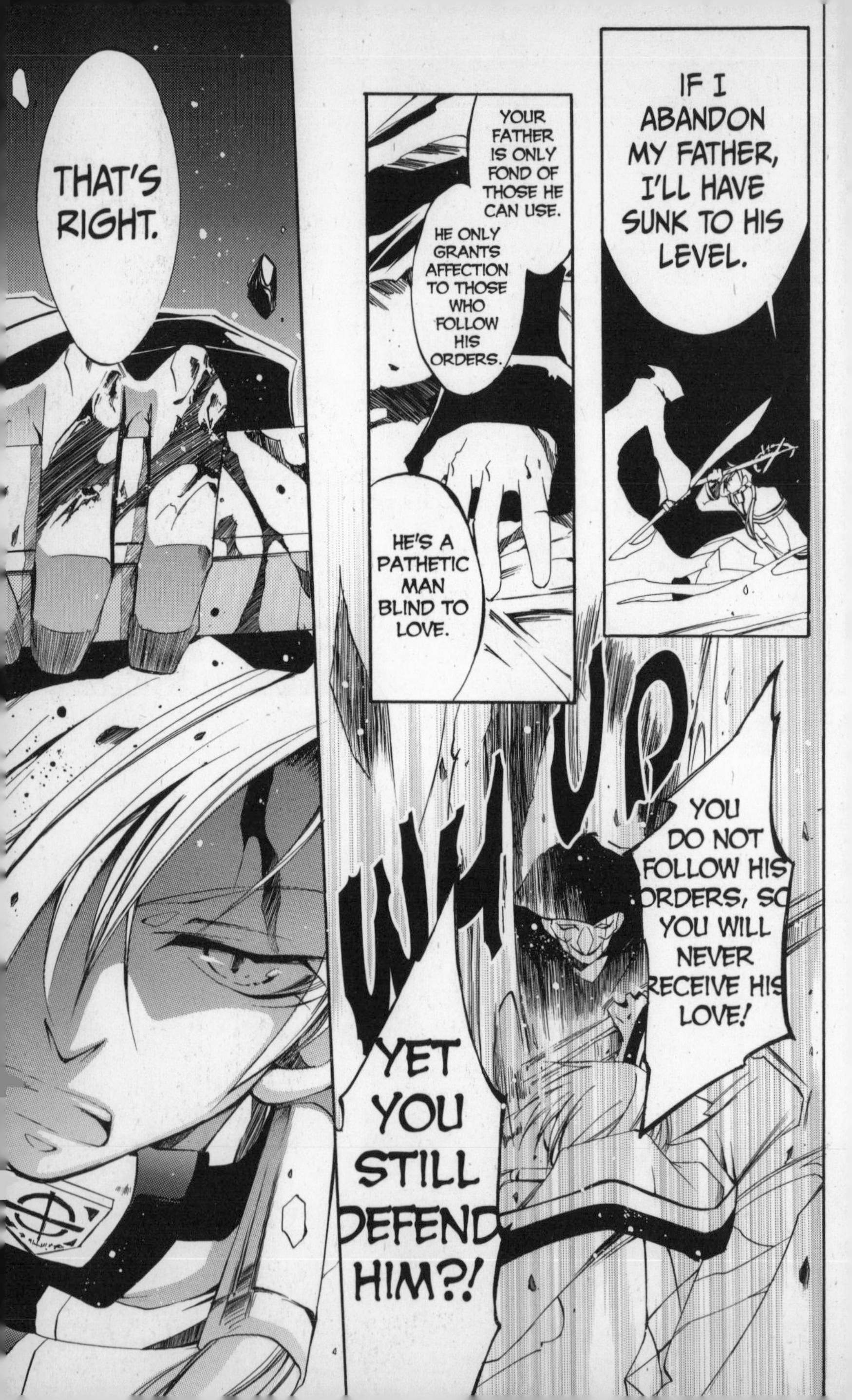
IF I ABANDON MY FATHER, I'LL HAVE SUNK TO HIS LEVEL.
YOUR FATHER IS ONLY FOND OF THOSE HE CAN USE.
HE ONLY GRANTS AFFECTION TO THOSE WHO FOLLOW HIS ORDERS.
HE'S A PATHETIC MAN BLIND TO LOVE.
WHUD
YOU DO NOT FOLLOW HIS ORDERS, SO YOU WILL NEVER RECEIVE HIS LOVE!
YET YOU STILL DEFEND HIM?!
THAT'S RIGHT.

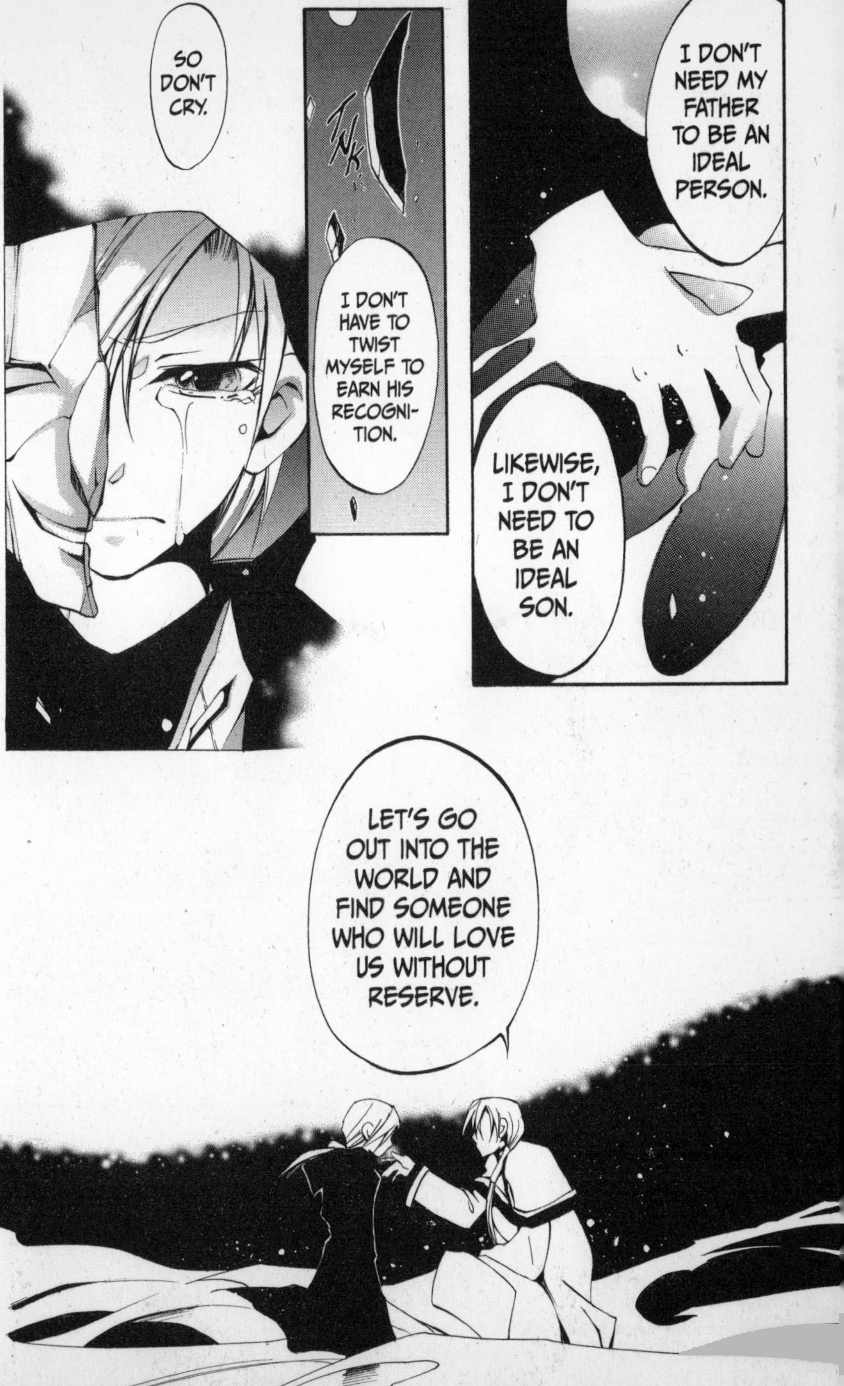
I DON'T NEED MY FATHER TO BE AN IDEAL PERSON.
LIKEWISE, I DON'T NEED TO BE AN IDEAL SON.
TINK
I DON'T HAVE TO TWIST MYSELF TO EARN HIS RECOGNITION.
SO DON'T CRY.
LET'S GO OUT INTO THE WORLD AND FIND SOMEONE WHO WILL LOVE US WITHOUT RESERVE.

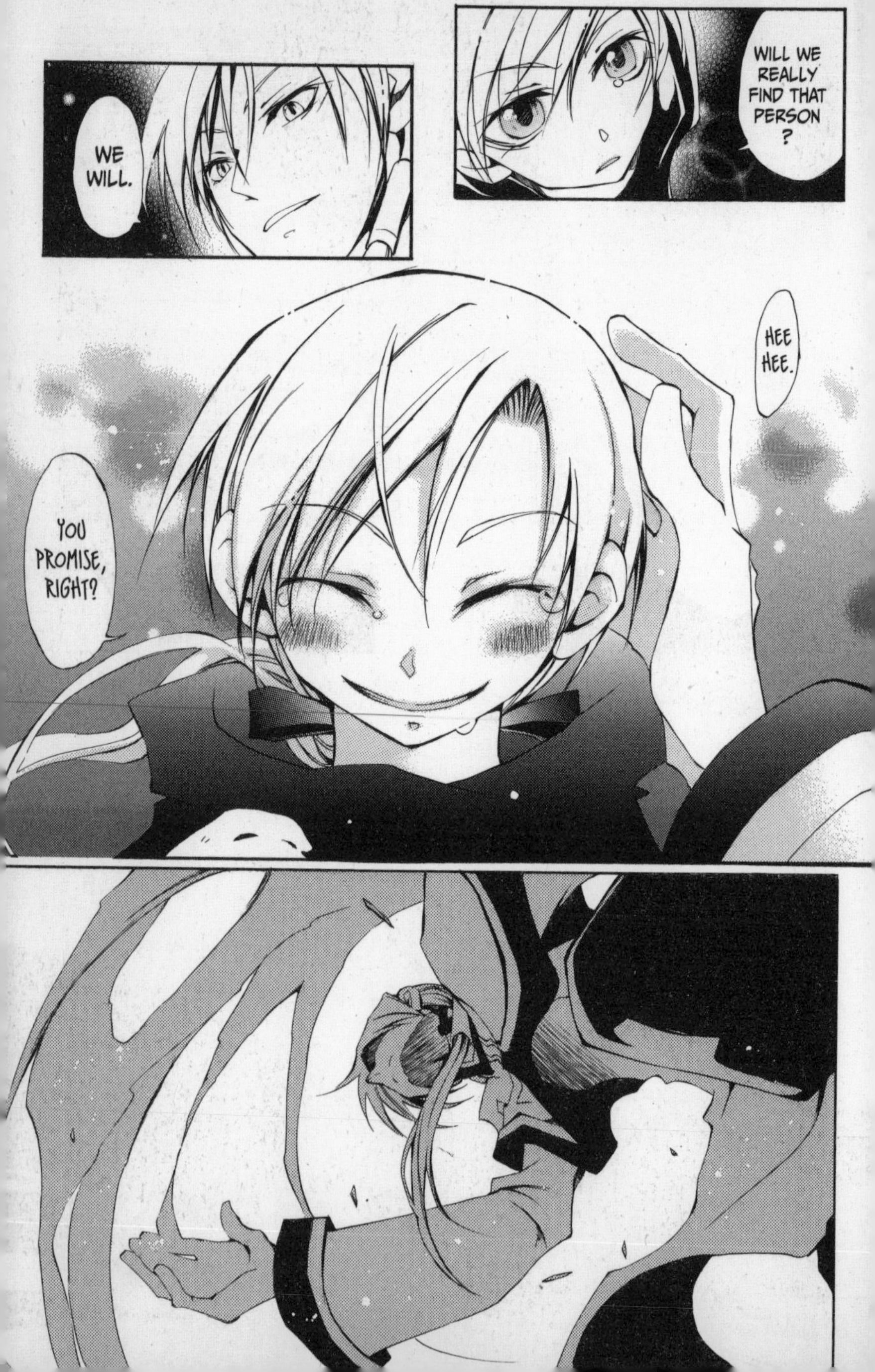
WILL WE REALLY FIND THAT PERSON?
WE WILL.
HEE HEE.
YOU PROMISE, RIGHT?

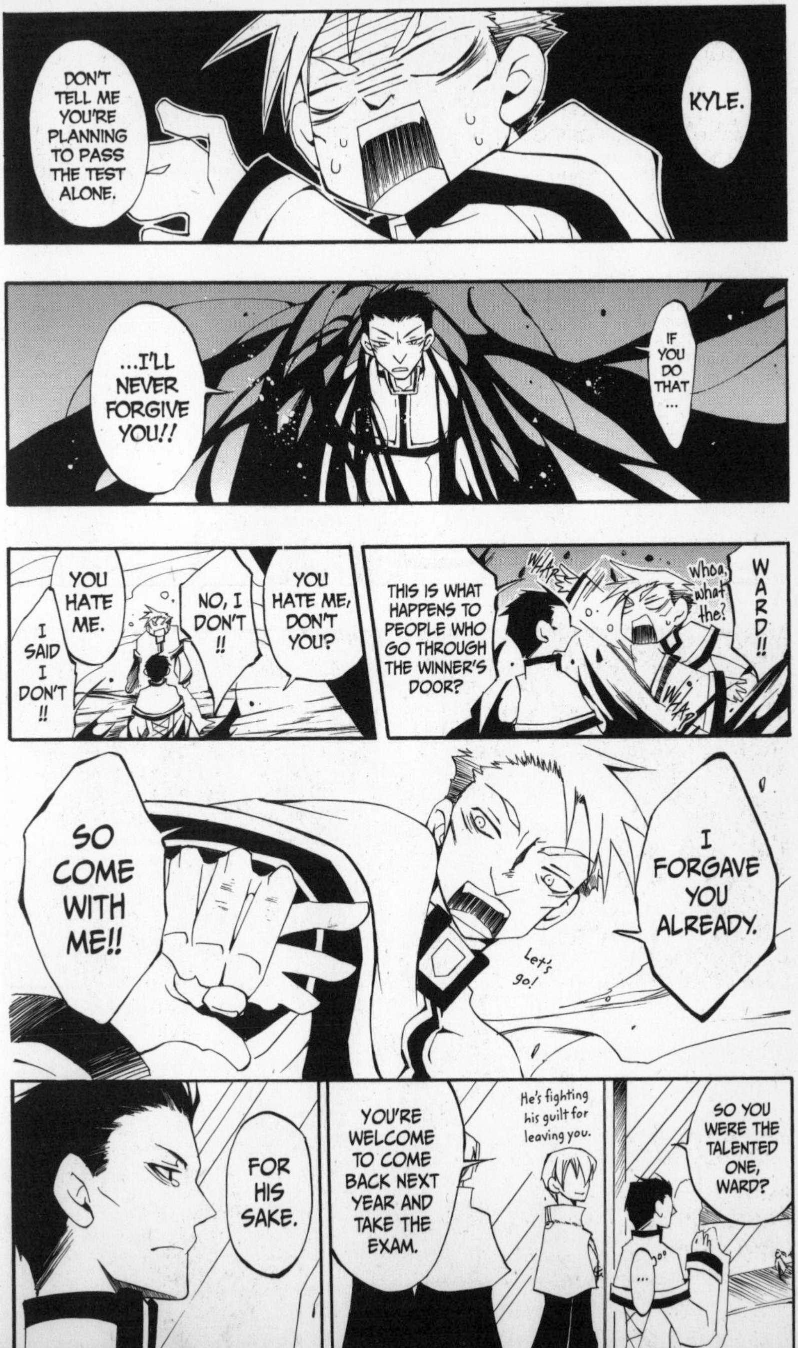
KYLE.
DON'T TELL ME YOU'RE PLANNING TO PASS THE TEST ALONE.
IF YOU DO THAT...
...I'LL NEVER FORGIVE YOU!!
WARD!!
Whoa, what the?
WHAP
WHAP
THIS IS WHAT HAPPENS TO PEOPLE WHO GO THROUGH THE WINNER'S DOOR?
YOU HATE ME, DON'T YOU?
NO, I DON'T!!
YOU HATE ME.
I SAID I DON'T!!
I FORGAVE YOU ALREADY.
Let's go!
SO COME WITH ME!!
SO YOU WERE THE TALENTED ONE, WARD?
...
He's fighting his guilt for leaving you.
YOU'RE WELCOME TO COME BACK NEXT YEAR AND TAKE THE EXAM.
FOR HIS SAKE.

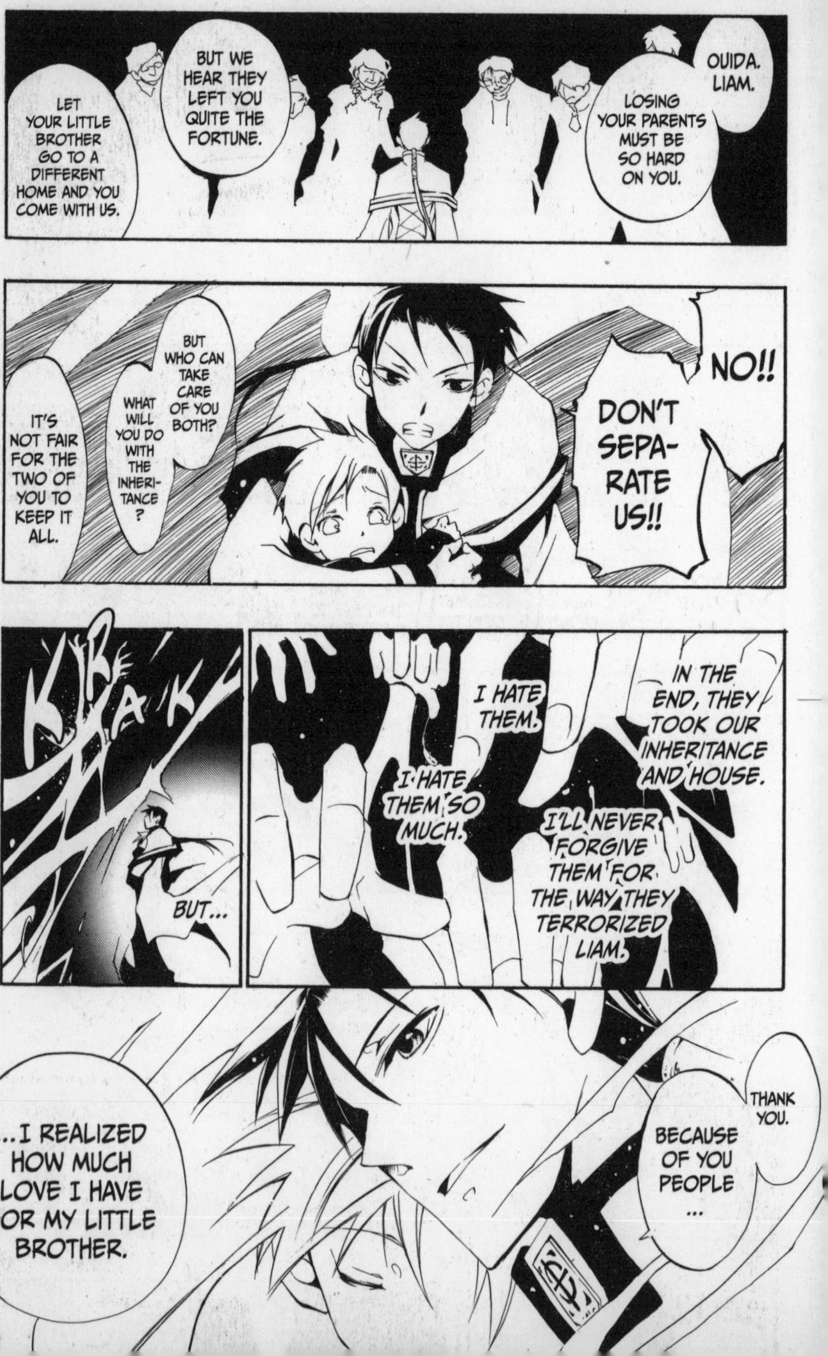
OUIDA. LIAM.
LOSING YOUR PARENTS MUST BE SO HARD ON YOU.
BUT WE HEAR THEY LEFT YOU QUITE THE FORTUNE.
LET YOUR LITTLE BROTHER GO TO A DIFFERENT HOME AND YOU COME WITH US.
NO!!
DON'T SEPA-RATE US!!
BUT WHO CAN TAKE CARE OF YOU BOTH?
WHAT WILL YOU DO WITH THE INHERI-TANCE?
IT'S NOT FAIR FOR THE TWO OF YOU TO KEEP IT ALL.
IN THE END, THEY TOOK OUR INHERITANCE AND HOUSE.
I HATE THEM.
I'LL NEVER FORGIVE THEM FOR THE WAY THEY TERRORIZED LIAM.
I HATE THEM SO MUCH.
KRAK
BUT...
THANK YOU.
BECAUSE OF YOU PEOPLE...
...I REALIZED HOW MUCH LOVE I HAVE FOR MY LITTLE BROTHER.

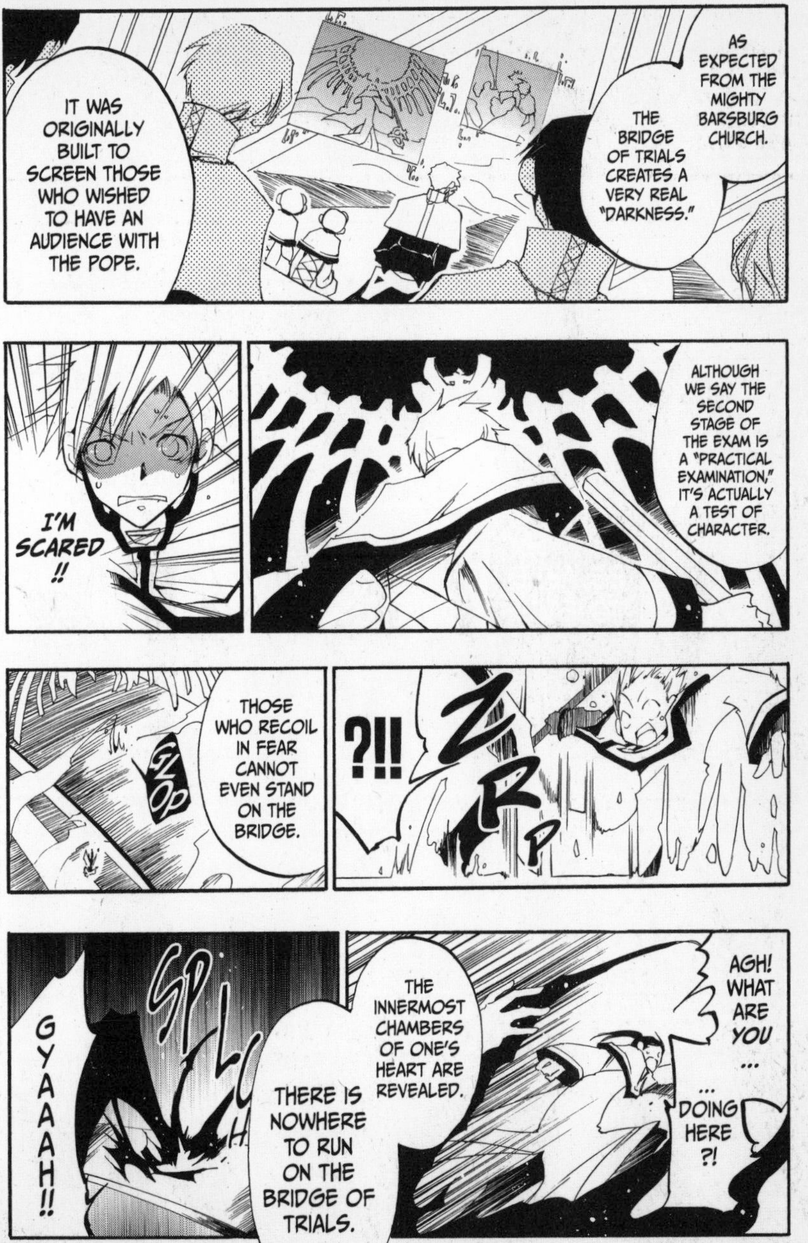
AS EXPECTED FROM THE MIGHTY BARSBURG CHURCH.
THE BRIDGE OF TRIALS CREATES A VERY REAL "DARKNESS."
IT WAS ORIGINALLY BUILT TO SCREEN THOSE WHO WISHED TO HAVE AN AUDIENCE WITH THE POPE.
ALTHOUGH WE SAY THE SECOND STAGE OF THE EXAM IS A "PRACTICAL EXAMINATION," IT'S ACTUALLY A TEST OF CHARACTER.
I'M SCARED!!
?!!
ZRP
THOSE WHO RECOIL IN FEAR CANNOT EVEN STAND ON THE BRIDGE.
GLOP
AGH! WHAT ARE YOU ...
... DOING HERE?!
THE INNERMOST CHAMBERS OF ONE'S HEART ARE REVEALED.
THERE IS NOWHERE TO RUN ON THE BRIDGE OF TRIALS.
GYAAAAH!!

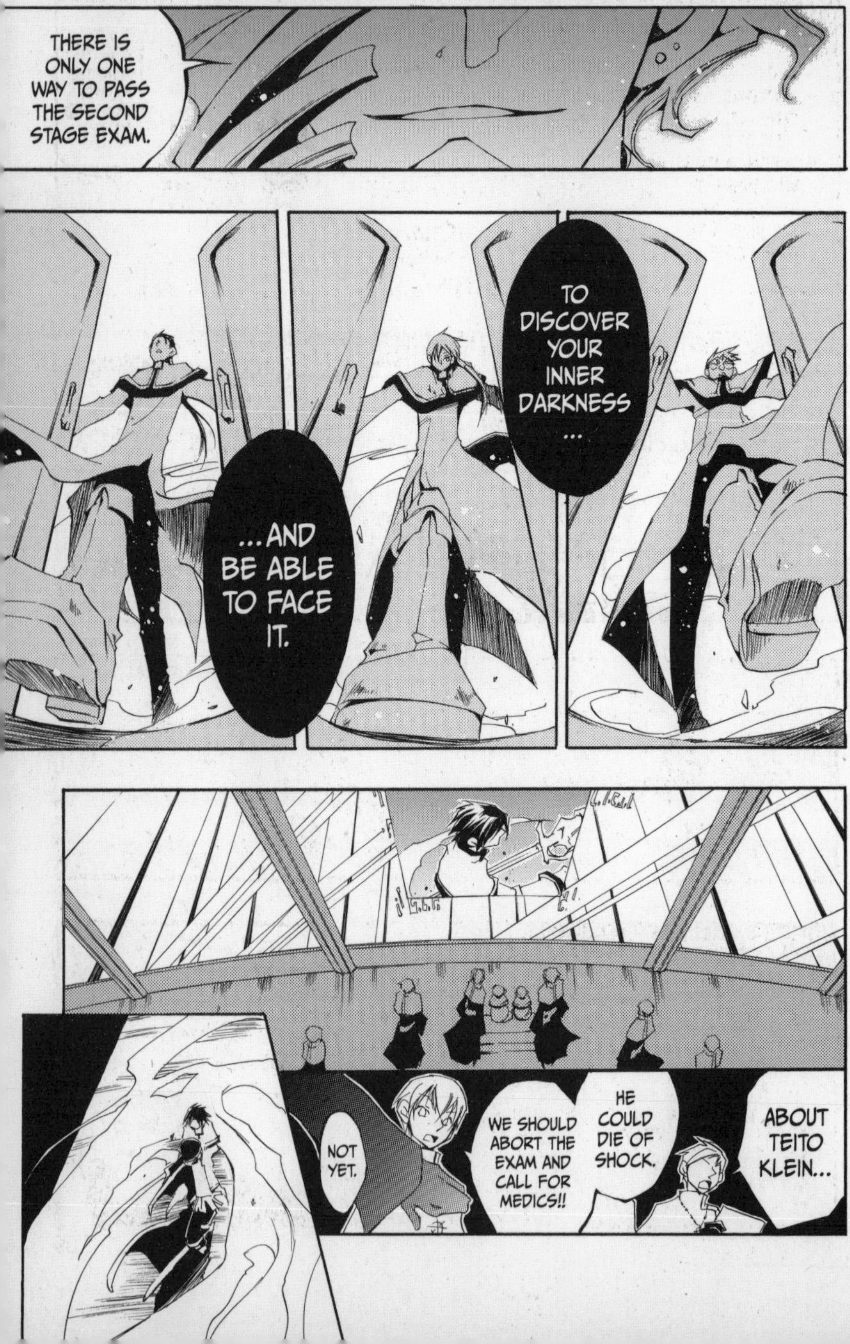
THERE IS ONLY ONE WAY TO PASS THE SECOND STAGE EXAM.
TO DISCOVER YOUR INNER DARKNESS ...
...AND BE ABLE TO FACE IT.
ABOUT TEITO KLEIN...
HE COULD DIE OF SHOCK.
WE SHOULD ABORT THE EXAM AND CALL FOR MEDICS!!
NOT YET.

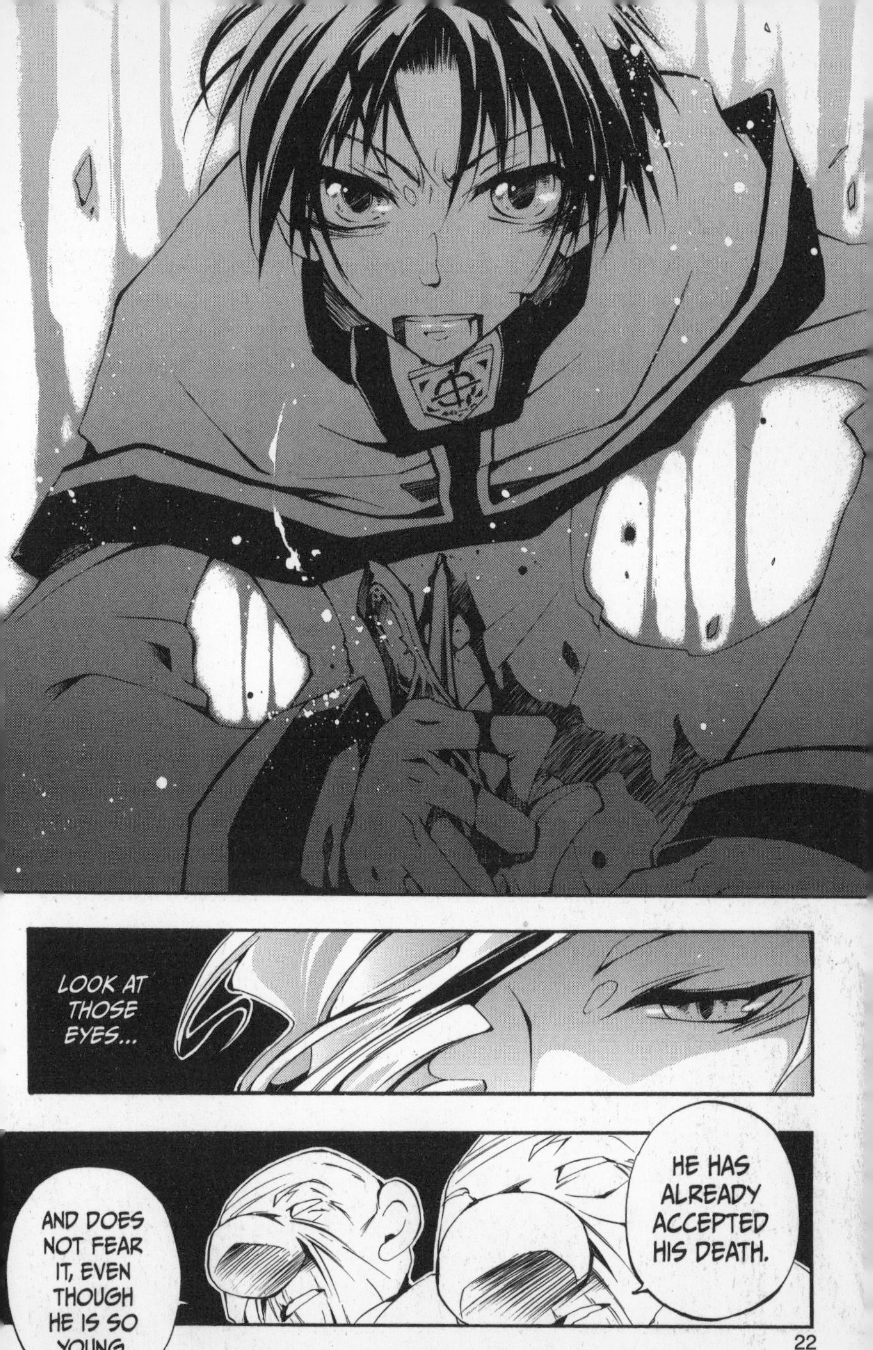
LOOK AT THOSE EYES...
HE HAS ALREADY ACCEPTED HIS DEATH.
AND DOES NOT FEAR IT, EVEN THOUGH HE IS SO YOUNG.

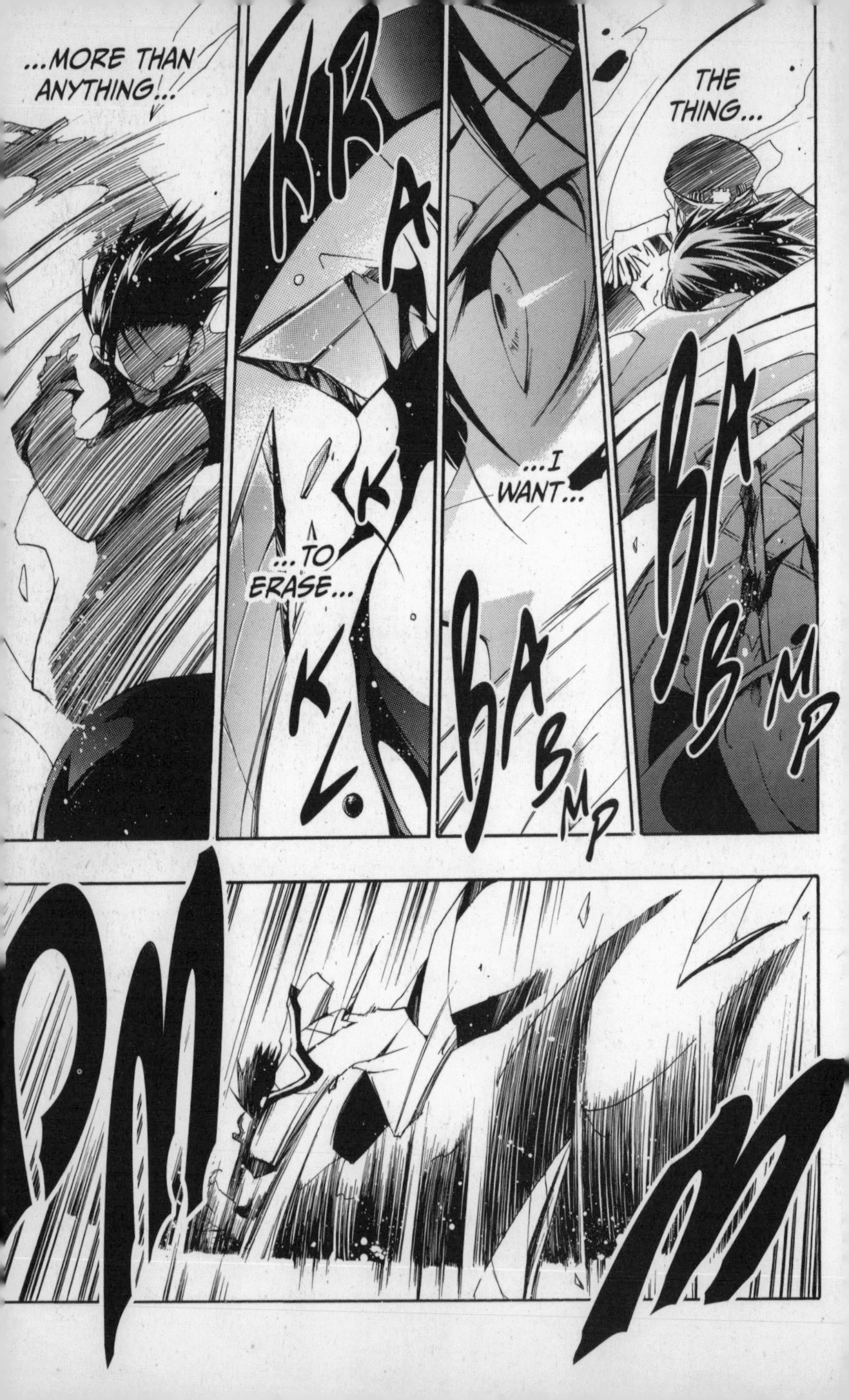
THE THING...
BABMP
...I WANT...
BABMP
KRAKKL
...TO ERASE...
...MORE THAN ANYTHING...

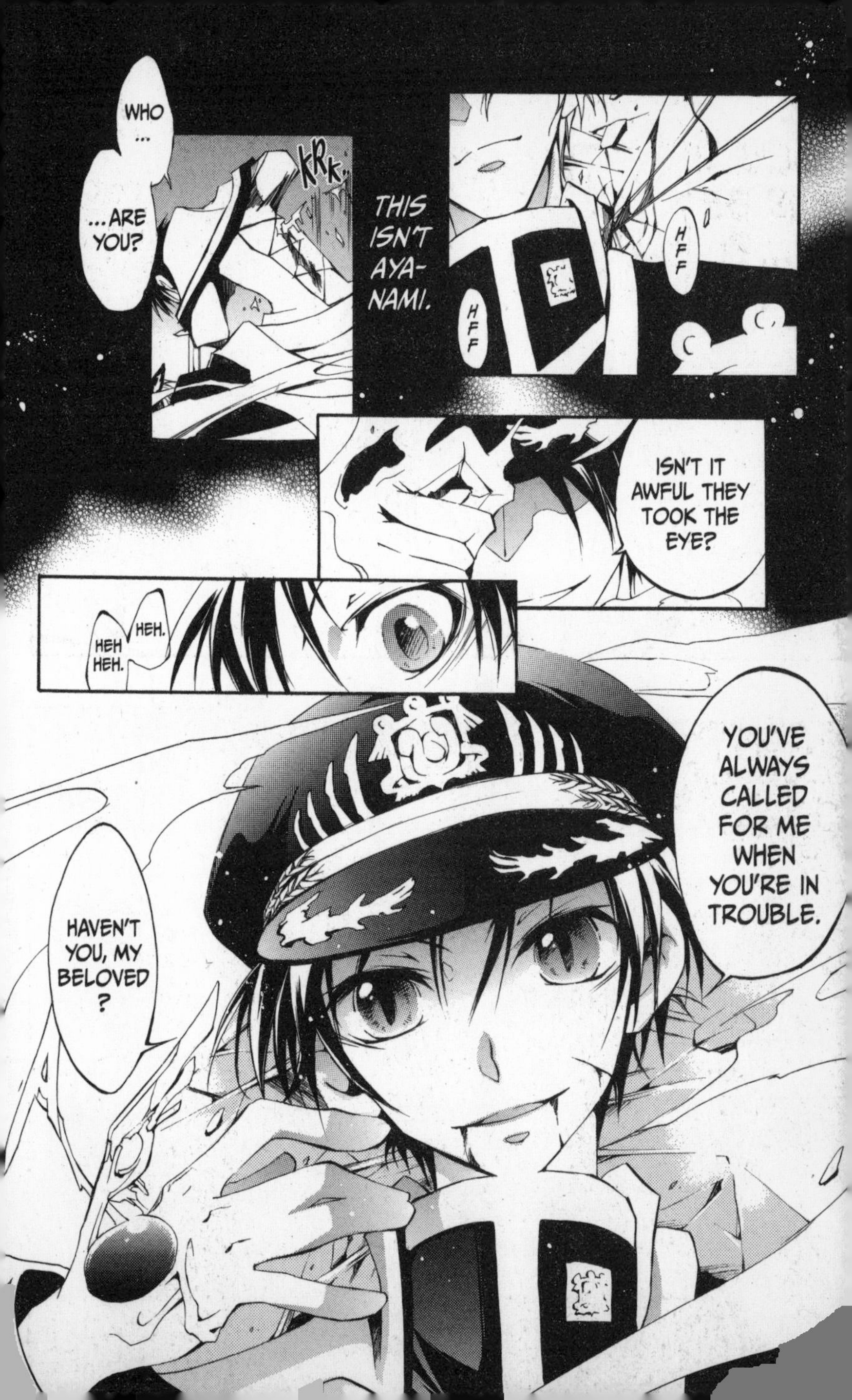
HFF
HFF
THIS ISN'T AYA-NAMI.
KRK..
WHO ...
...ARE YOU?
ISN'T IT AWFUL THEY TOOK THE EYE?
HEH.
HEH HEH.
YOU'VE ALWAYS CALLED FOR ME WHEN YOU'RE IN TROUBLE.
HAVEN'T YOU, MY BELOVED ?

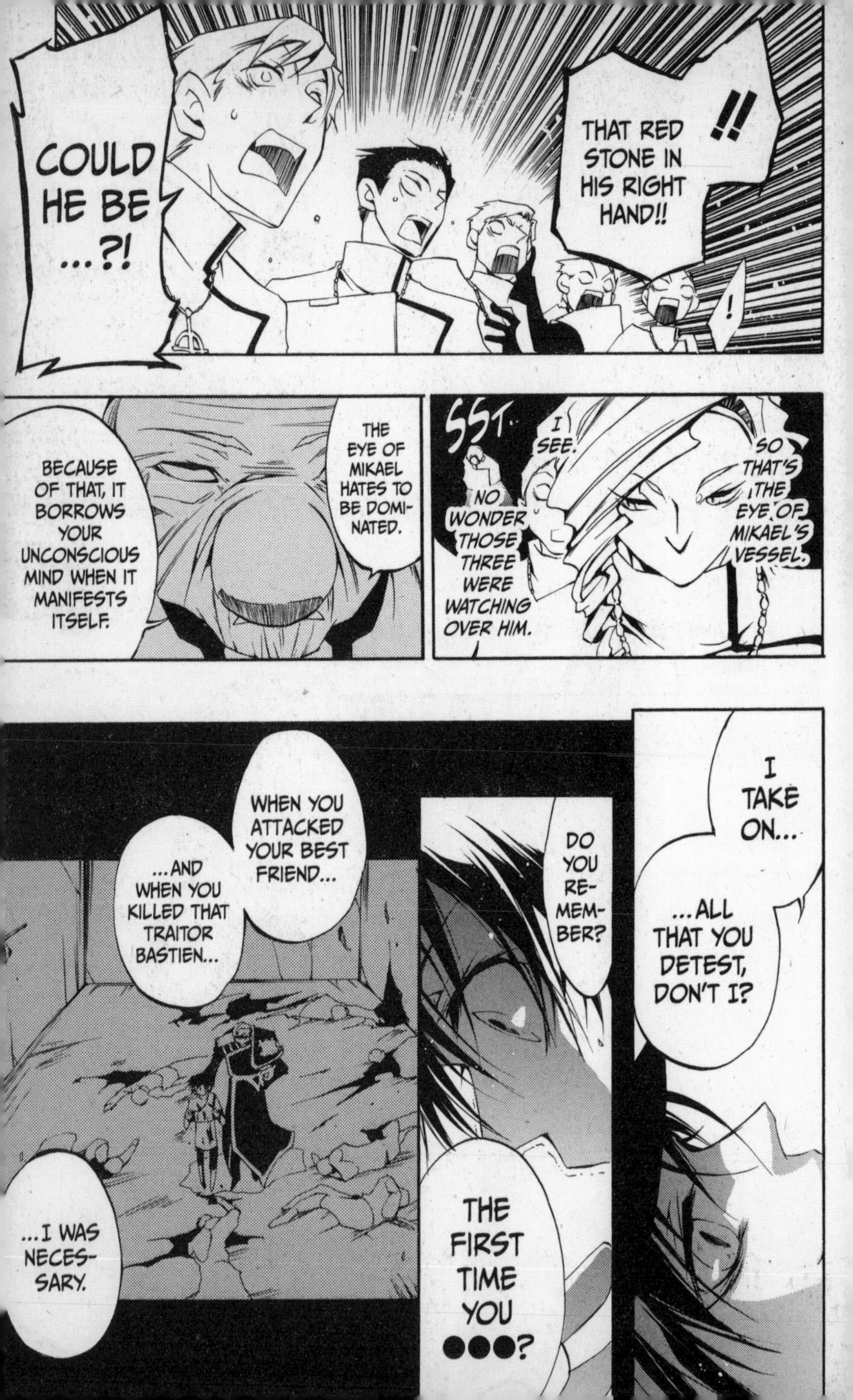
!!
THAT RED STONE IN HIS RIGHT HAND!!
!
COULD HE BE ...?!
SO THAT'S THE EYE OF MIKAEL'S VESSEL.
I SEE.
SST...
NO WONDER THOSE THREE WERE WATCHING OVER HIM.
THE EYE OF MIKAEL HATES TO BE DOMINATED.
BECAUSE OF THAT, IT BORROWS YOUR UNCONSCIOUS MIND WHEN IT MANIFESTS ITSELF.
I TAKE ON...
...ALL THAT YOU DETEST, DON'T I?
DO YOU REMEMBER?
THE FIRST TIME YOU ●●●?
WHEN YOU ATTACKED YOUR BEST FRIEND...
...AND WHEN YOU KILLED THAT TRAITOR BASTIEN...
...I WAS NECESSARY.

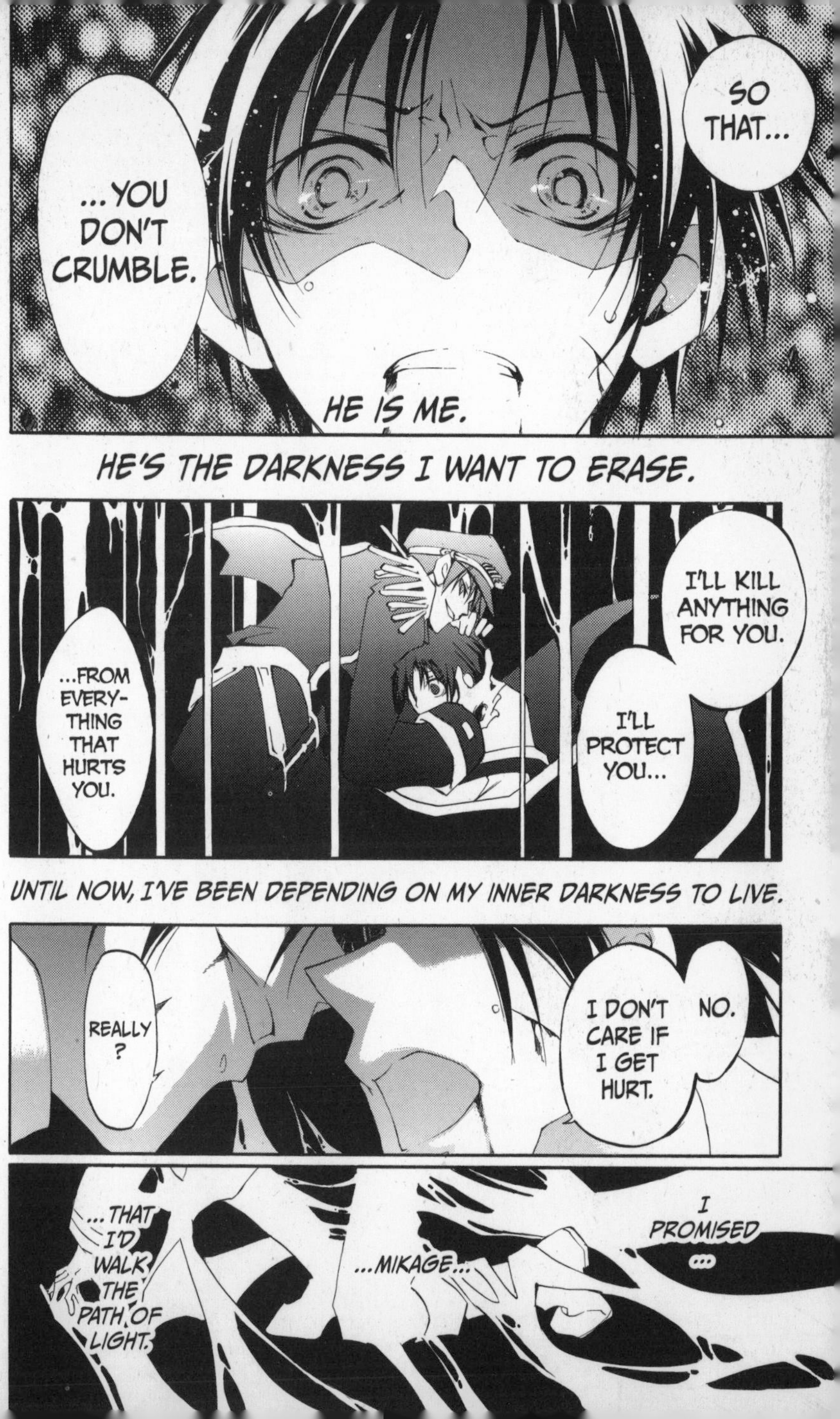
SO THAT...
...YOU DON'T CRUMBLE.
HE IS ME.
HE'S THE DARKNESS I WANT TO ERASE.
I'LL KILL ANYTHING FOR YOU.
I'LL PROTECT YOU...
...FROM EVERY-THING THAT HURTS YOU.
UNTIL NOW, I'VE BEEN DEPENDING ON MY INNER DARKNESS TO LIVE.
NO.
I DON'T CARE IF I GET HURT.
REALLY?
I PROMISED...
...MIKAGE...
...THAT I'D WALK THE PATH OF LIGHT.

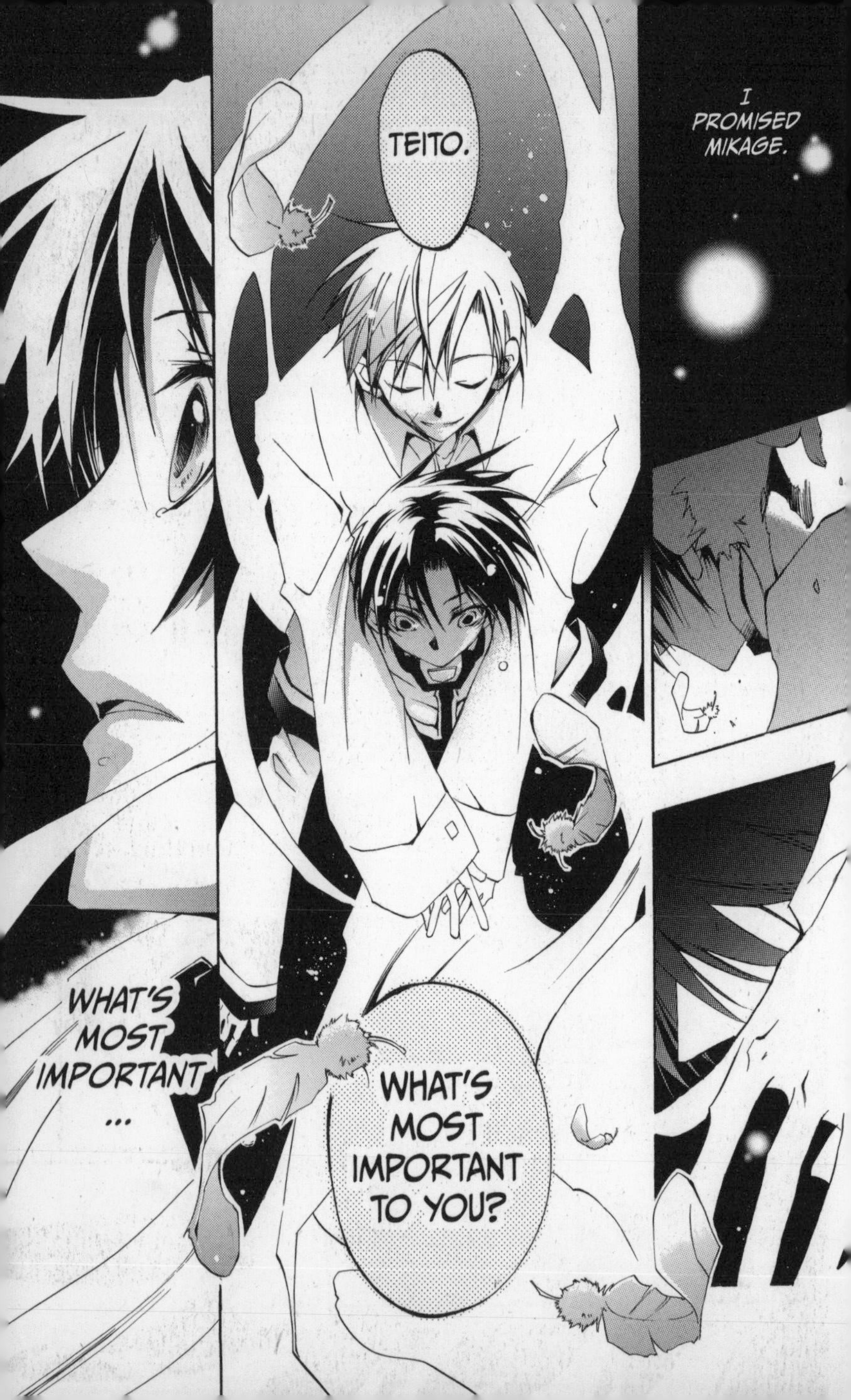

I PROMISED MIKAGE.
TEITO.
WHAT'S MOST IMPORTANT TO YOU?
WHAT'S MOST IMPORTANT ...

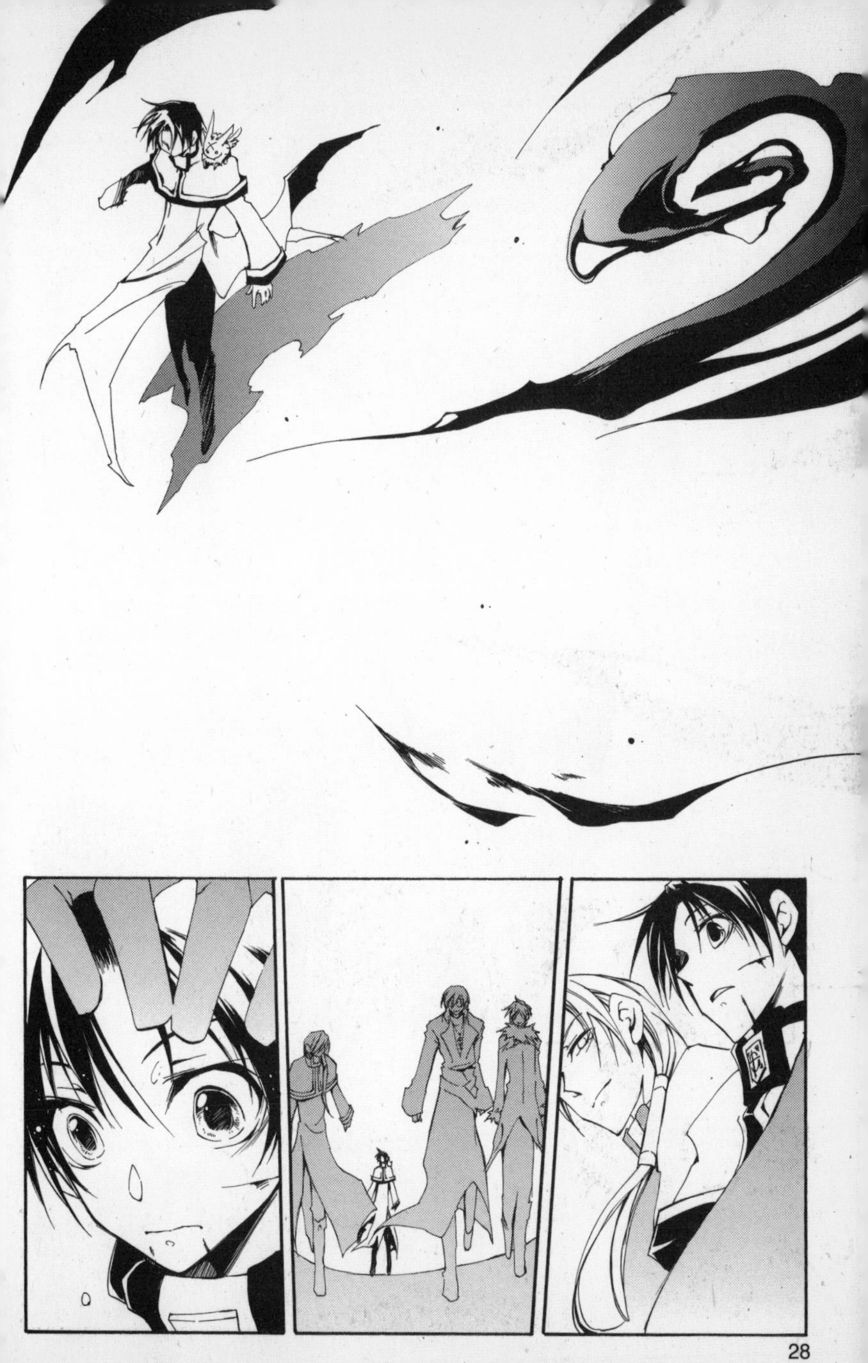

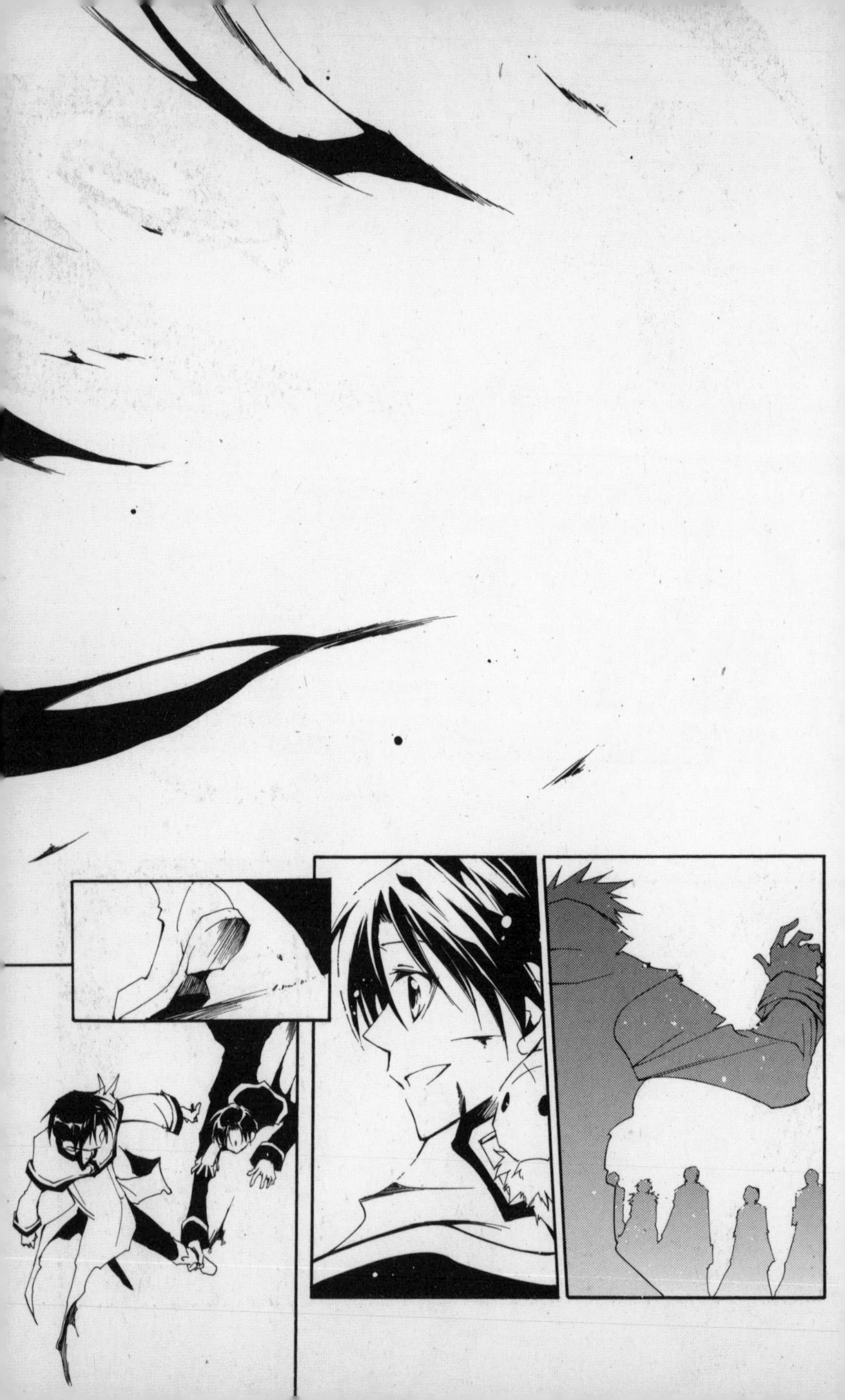

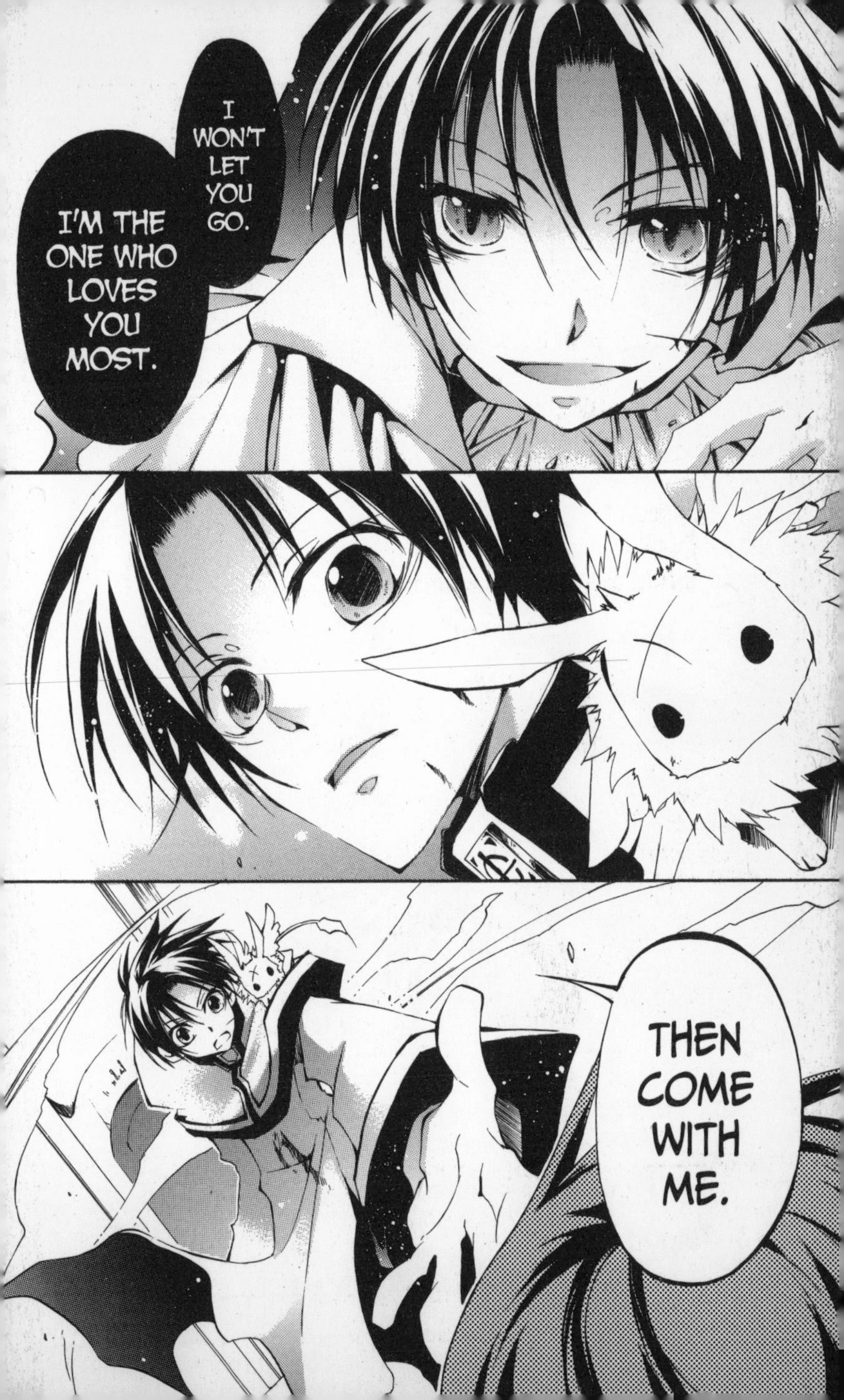
I WON'T LET YOU GO.
I'M THE ONE WHO LOVES YOU MOST.
THEN COME WITH ME.

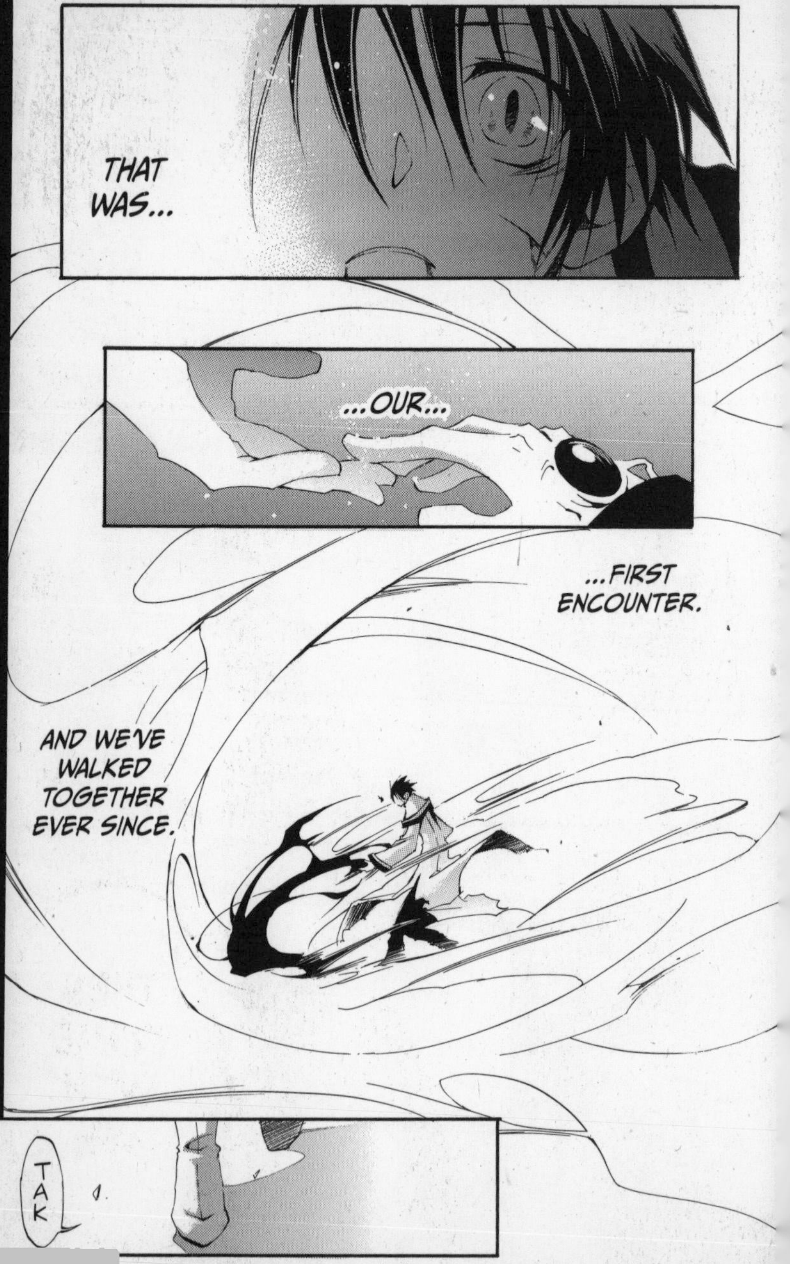
THAT WAS...
...OUR...
...FIRST ENCOUNTER.
AND WE'VE WALKED TOGETHER EVER SINCE.
TAK

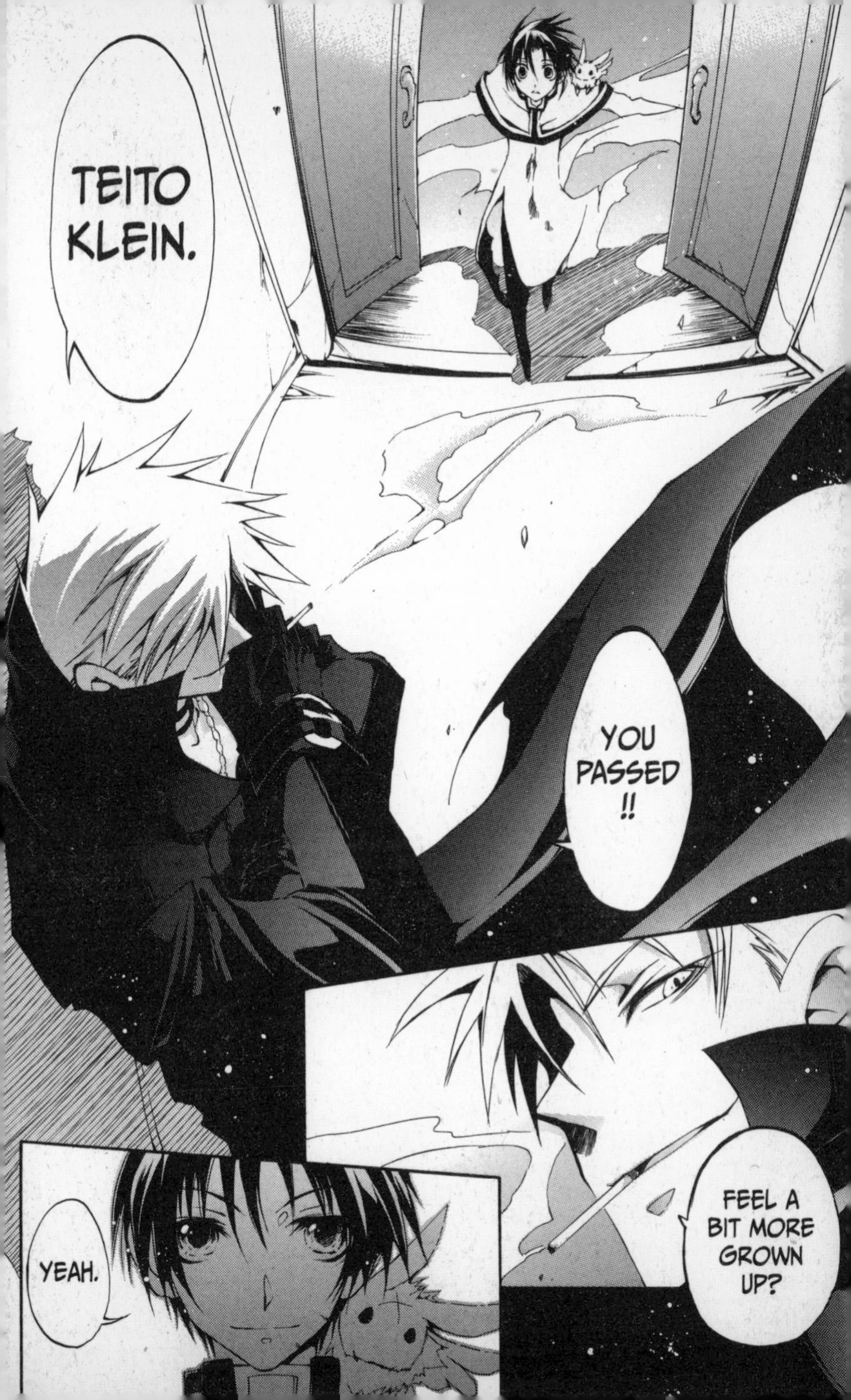
TEITO KLEIN.
YOU PASSED!!
FEEL A BIT MORE GROWN UP?
YEAH.

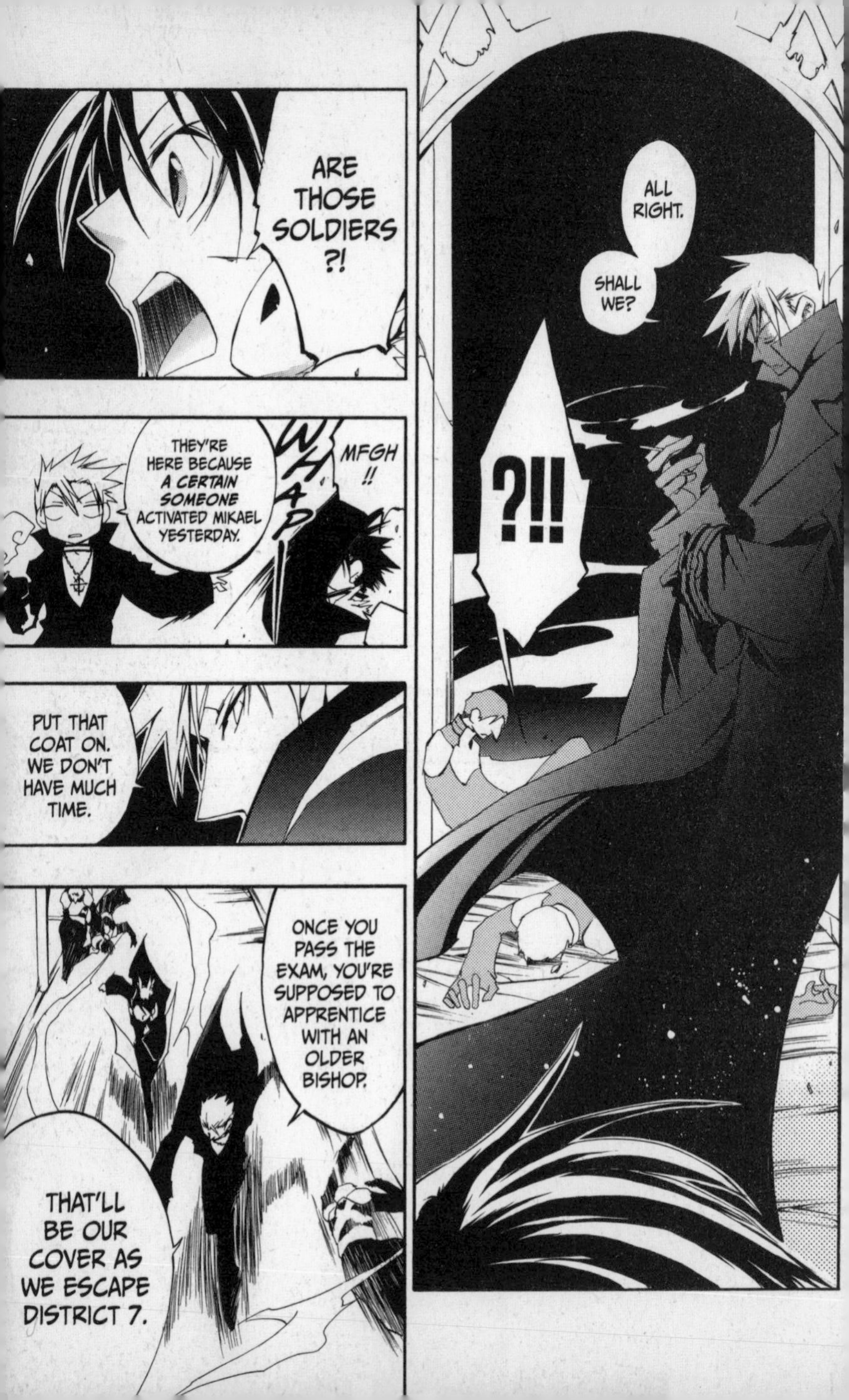
ALL RIGHT.
SHALL WE?
?!!
ARE THOSE SOLDIERS ?!
MFGH !!
WHAP
THEY'RE HERE BECAUSE *A CERTAIN SOMEONE* ACTIVATED MIKAEL YESTERDAY.
PUT THAT COAT ON. WE DON'T HAVE MUCH TIME.
ONCE YOU PASS THE EXAM, YOU'RE SUPPOSED TO APPRENTICE WITH AN OLDER BISHOP.
THAT'LL BE OUR COVER AS WE ESCAPE DISTRICT 7.

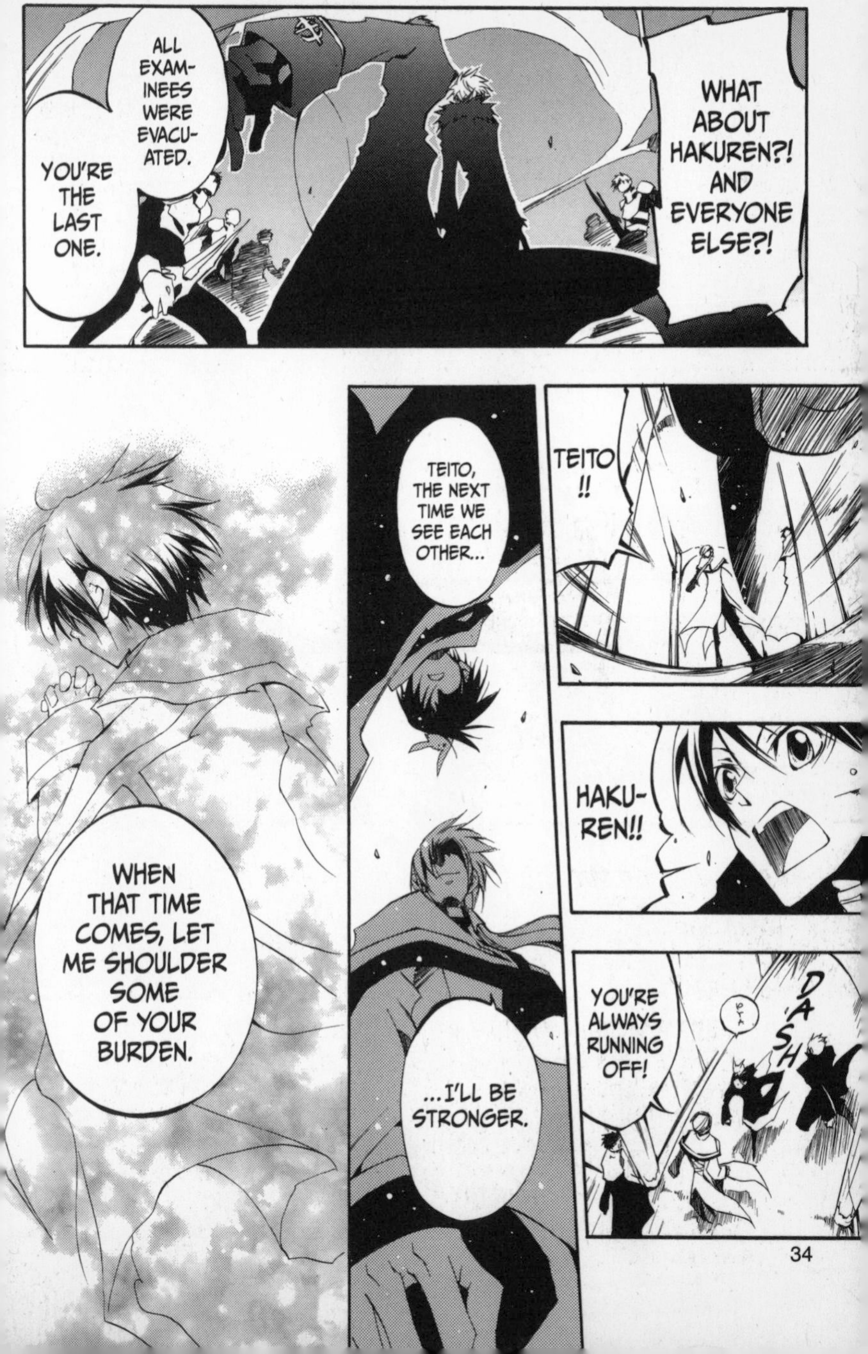
WHAT ABOUT HAKUREN?! AND EVERYONE ELSE?!
ALL EXAMINEES WERE EVACUATED.
YOU'RE THE LAST ONE.
TEITO!!
HAKUREN!!
YOU'RE ALWAYS RUNNING OFF!
DASH
TEITO, THE NEXT TIME WE SEE EACH OTHER...
...I'LL BE STRONGER.
WHEN THAT TIME COMES, LET ME SHOULDER SOME OF YOUR BURDEN.

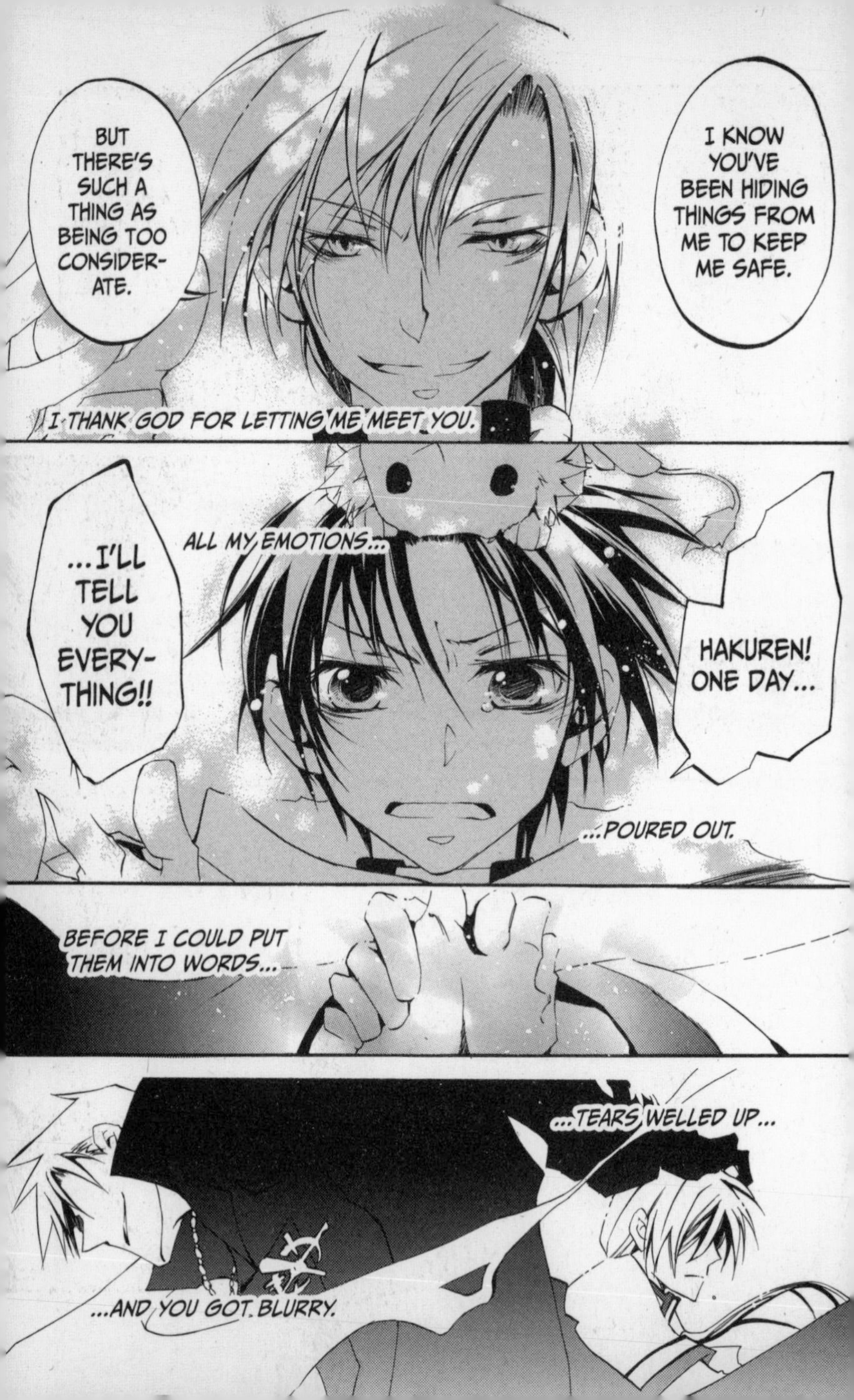
I KNOW YOU'VE BEEN HIDING THINGS FROM ME TO KEEP ME SAFE.
BUT THERE'S SUCH A THING AS BEING TOO CONSIDERATE.
I THANK GOD FOR LETTING ME MEET YOU.
HAKUREN! ONE DAY...
...I'LL TELL YOU EVERYTHING!!
ALL MY EMOTIONS...
...POURED OUT.
BEFORE I COULD PUT THEM INTO WORDS...
...TEARS WELLED UP...
...AND YOU GOT BLURRY.

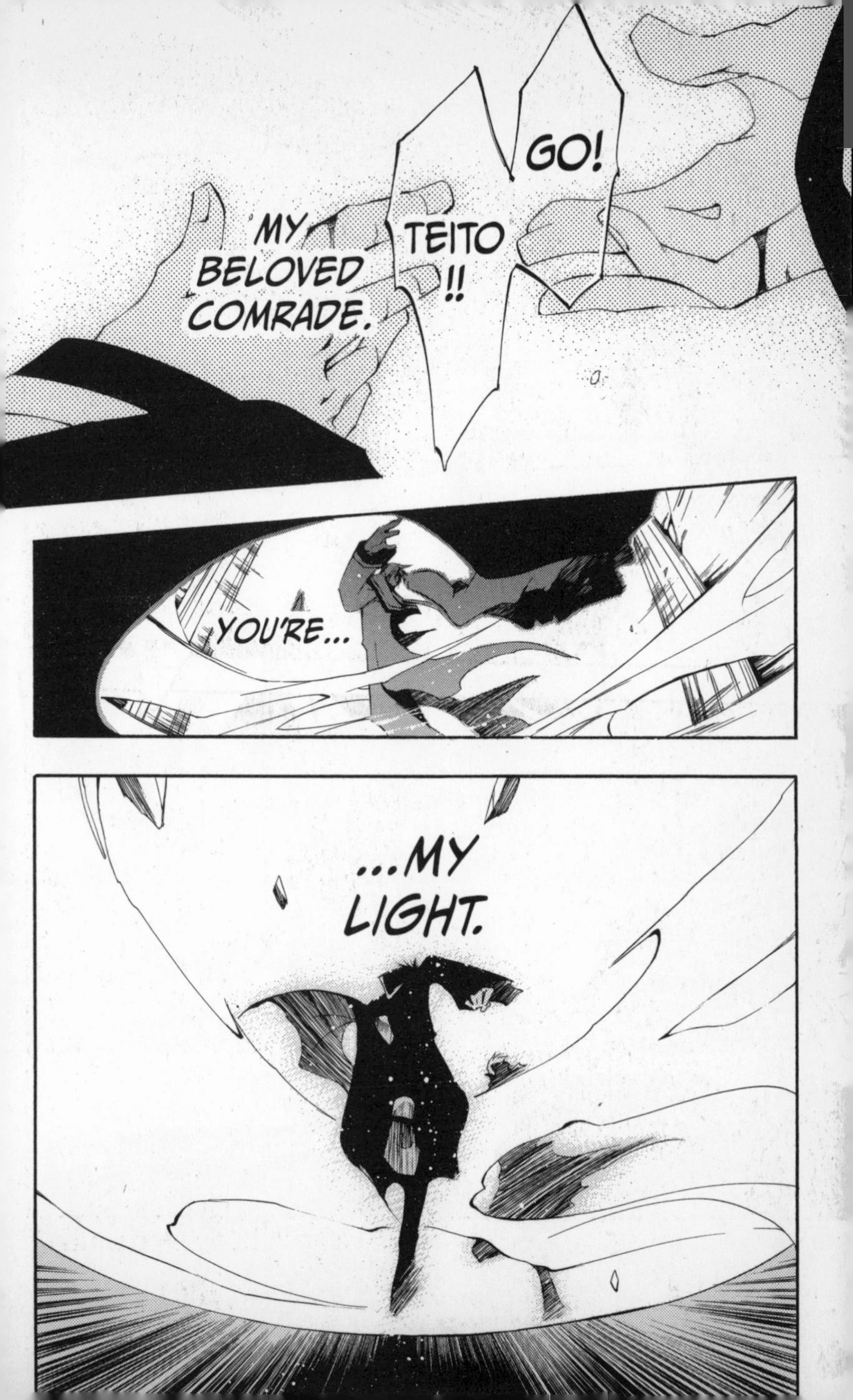
GO!
TEITO!!
MY BELOVED COMRADE.
YOU'RE...
...MY LIGHT.

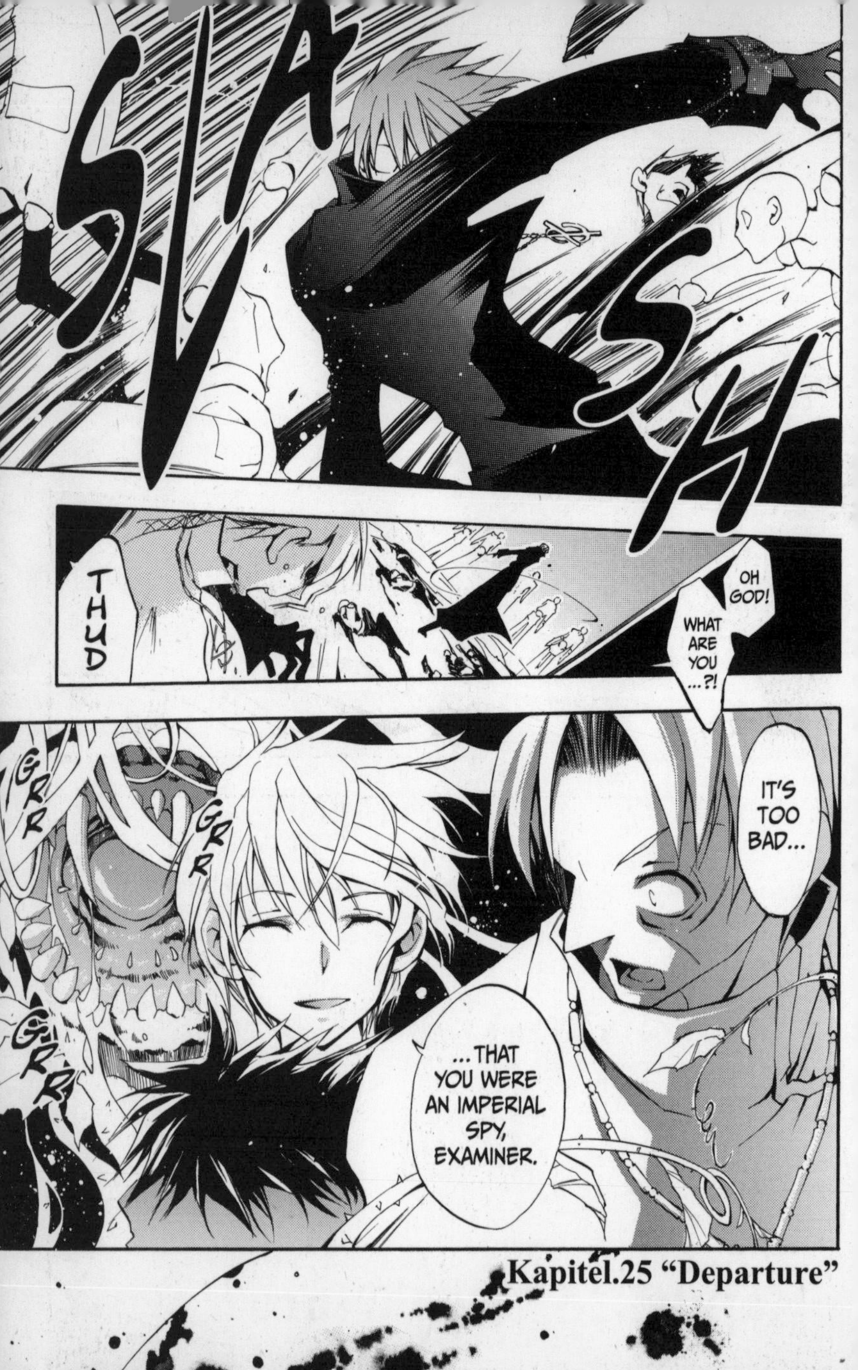
SLASH
OH GOD! WHAT ARE YOU ...?!
THUD
IT'S TOO BAD...
...THAT YOU WERE AN IMPERIAL SPY, EXAMINER.
GRR
GRR
GRR

Kapitel.25 "Departure"

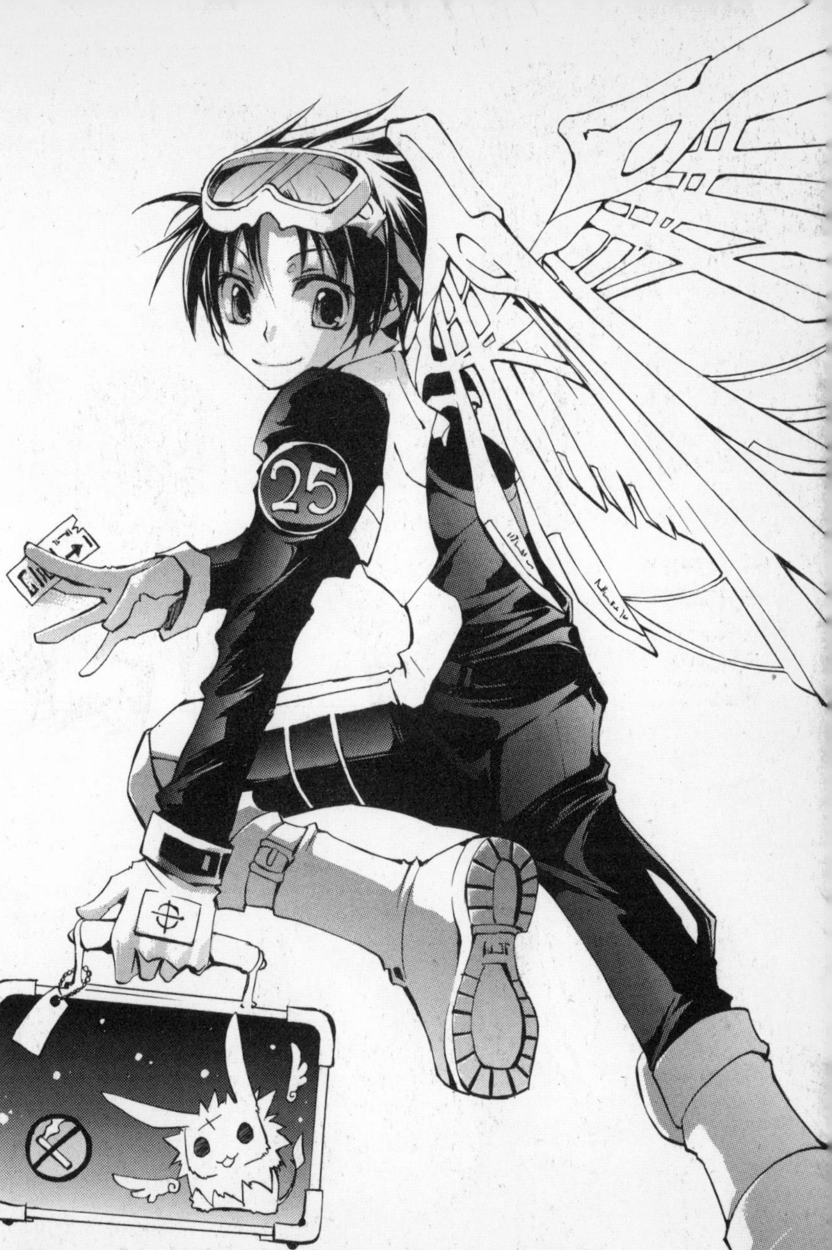
25

Kapitel.25 “Departure”

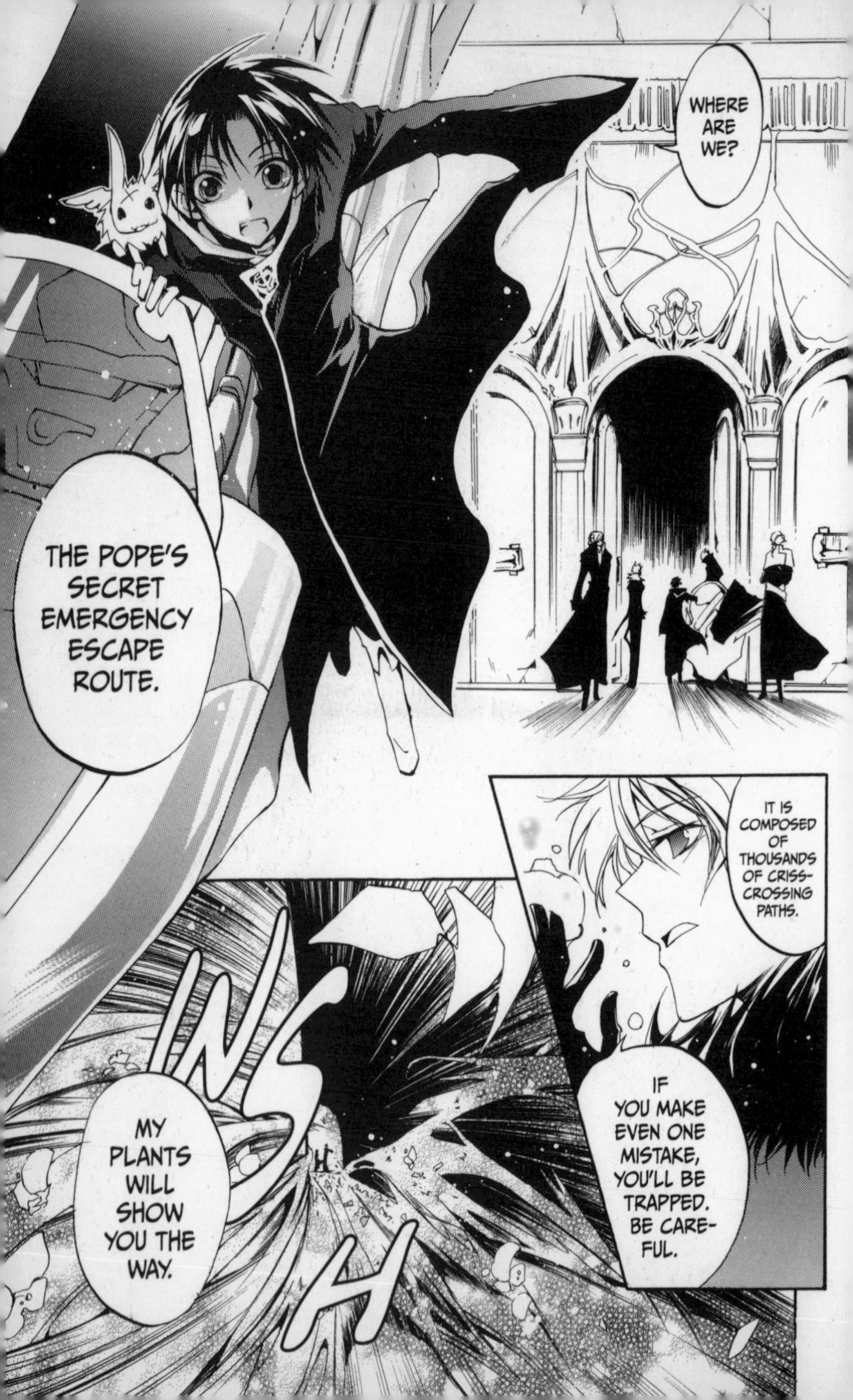
WHERE ARE WE?
THE POPE'S SECRET EMERGENCY ESCAPE ROUTE.
IT IS COMPOSED OF THOUSANDS OF CRISS-CROSSING PATHS.
IF YOU MAKE EVEN ONE MISTAKE, YOU'LL BE TRAPPED. BE CARE-FUL.
MY PLANTS WILL SHOW YOU THE WAY.

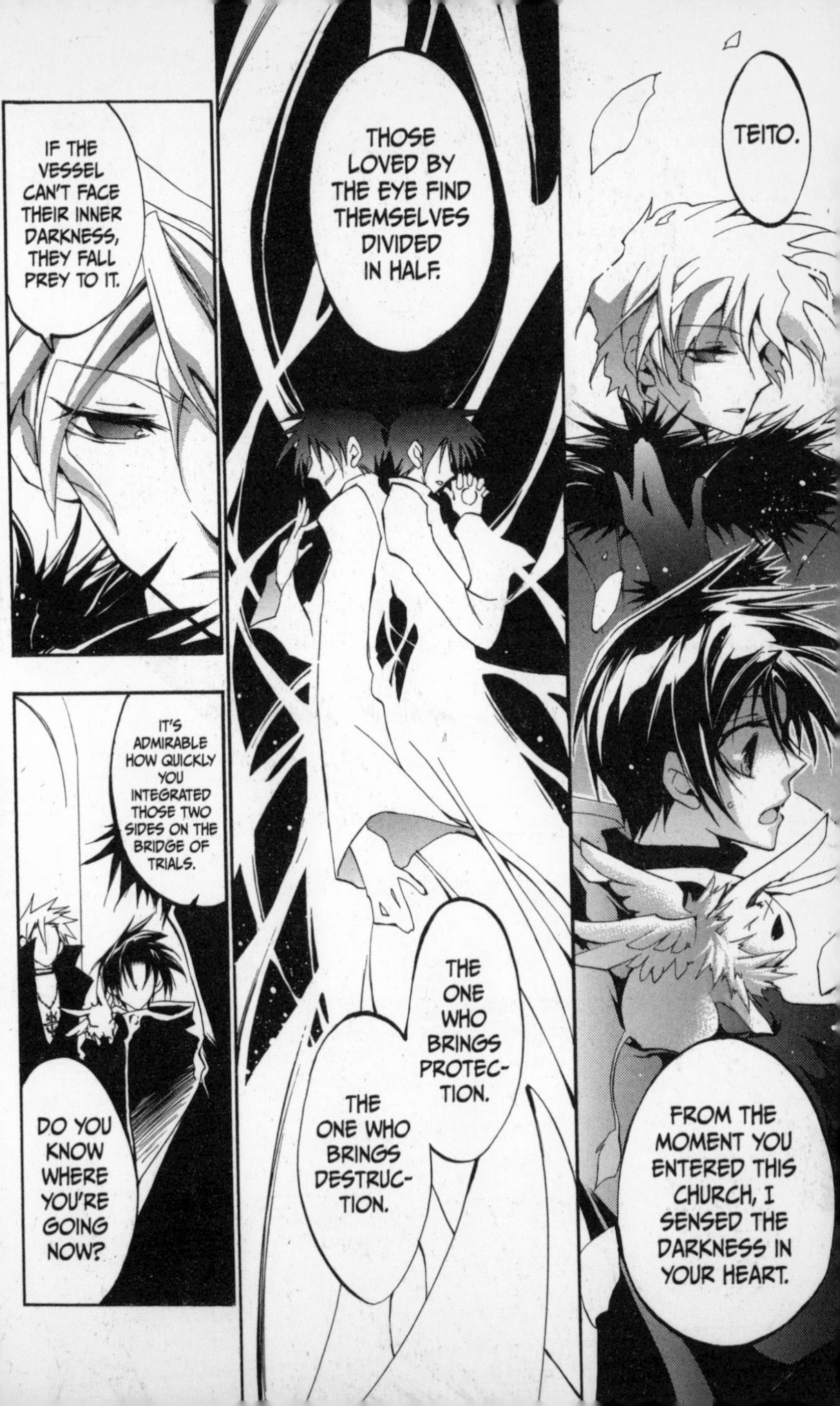
TEITO.
FROM THE MOMENT YOU ENTERED THIS CHURCH, I SENSED THE DARKNESS IN YOUR HEART.
THOSE LOVED BY THE EYE FIND THEMSELVES DIVIDED IN HALF.
THE ONE WHO BRINGS PROTEC-TION.
THE ONE WHO BRINGS DESTRUC-TION.
IF THE VESSEL CAN'T FACE THEIR INNER DARKNESS, THEY FALL PREY TO IT.
IT'S ADMIRABLE HOW QUICKLY YOU INTEGRATED THOSE TWO SIDES ON THE BRIDGE OF TRIALS.
DO YOU KNOW WHERE YOU'RE GOING NOW?

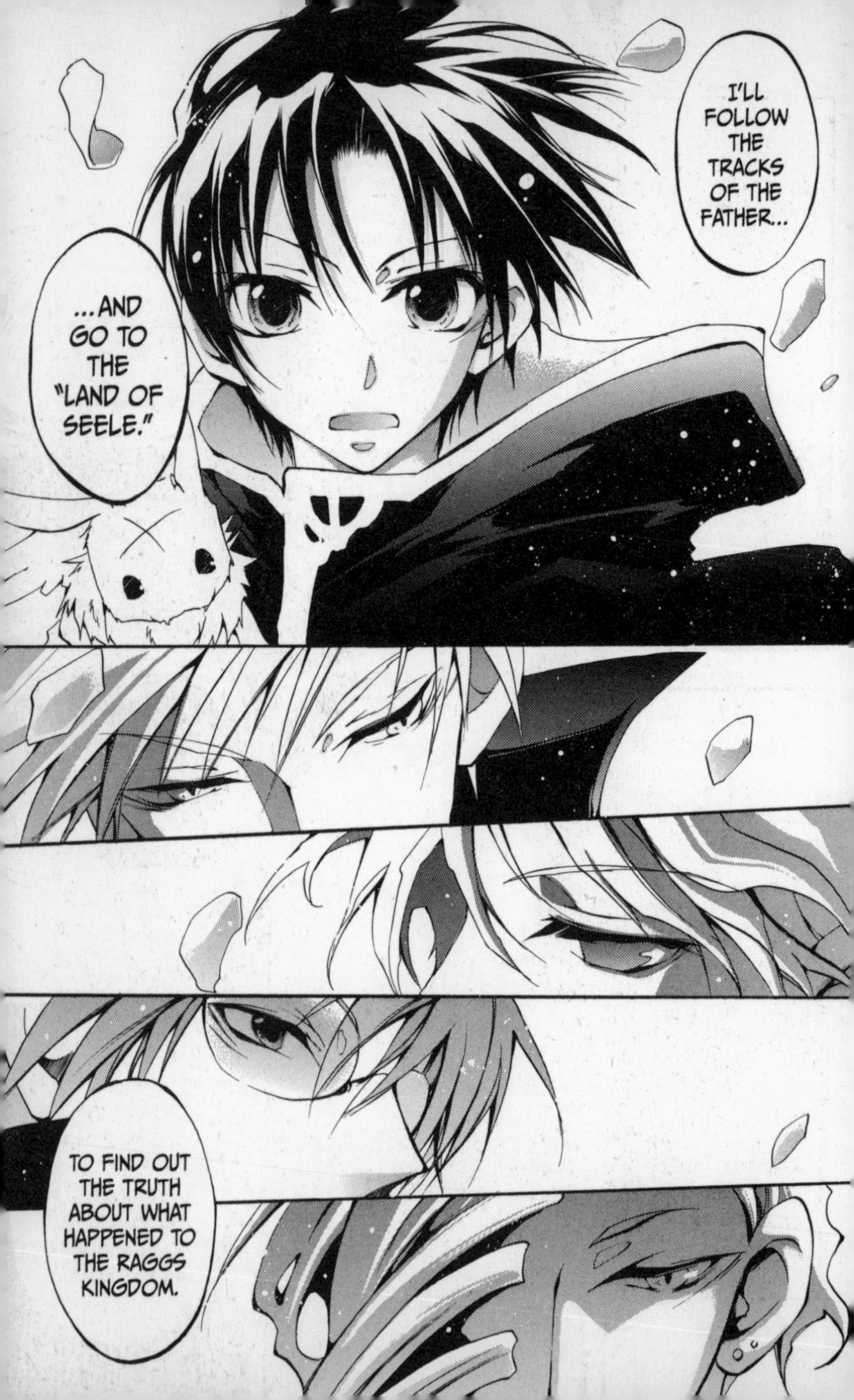
I'LL FOLLOW THE TRACKS OF THE FATHER...
...AND GO TO THE "LAND OF SEELE."
TO FIND OUT THE TRUTH ABOUT WHAT HAPPENED TO THE RAGGS KINGDOM.

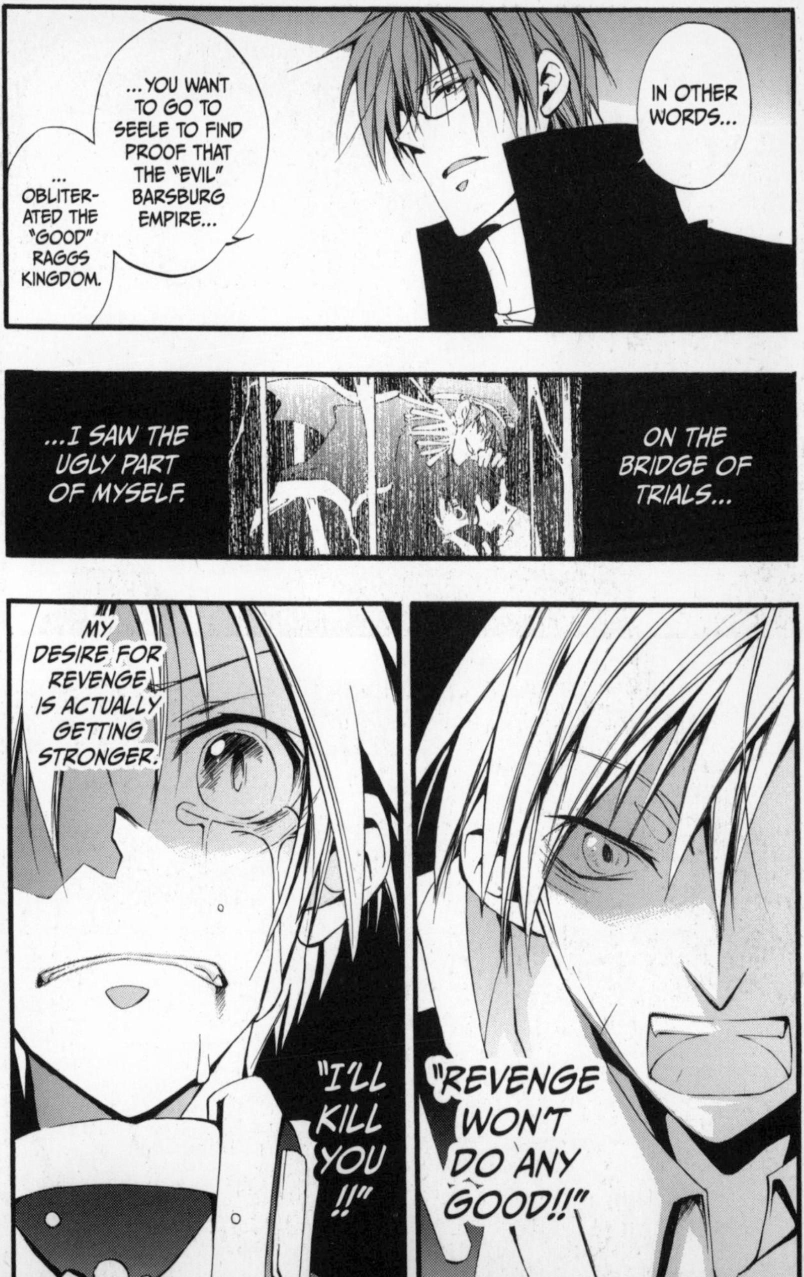
IN OTHER WORDS...
...YOU WANT TO GO TO SEELE TO FIND PROOF THAT THE "EVIL" BARSBURG EMPIRE...
...OBLITERATED THE "GOOD" RAGGS KINGDOM.
ON THE BRIDGE OF TRIALS...
...I SAW THE UGLY PART OF MYSELF.
"REVENGE WON'T DO ANY GOOD!!"
MY DESIRE FOR REVENGE IS ACTUALLY GETTING STRONGER.
"I'LL KILL YOU!!"

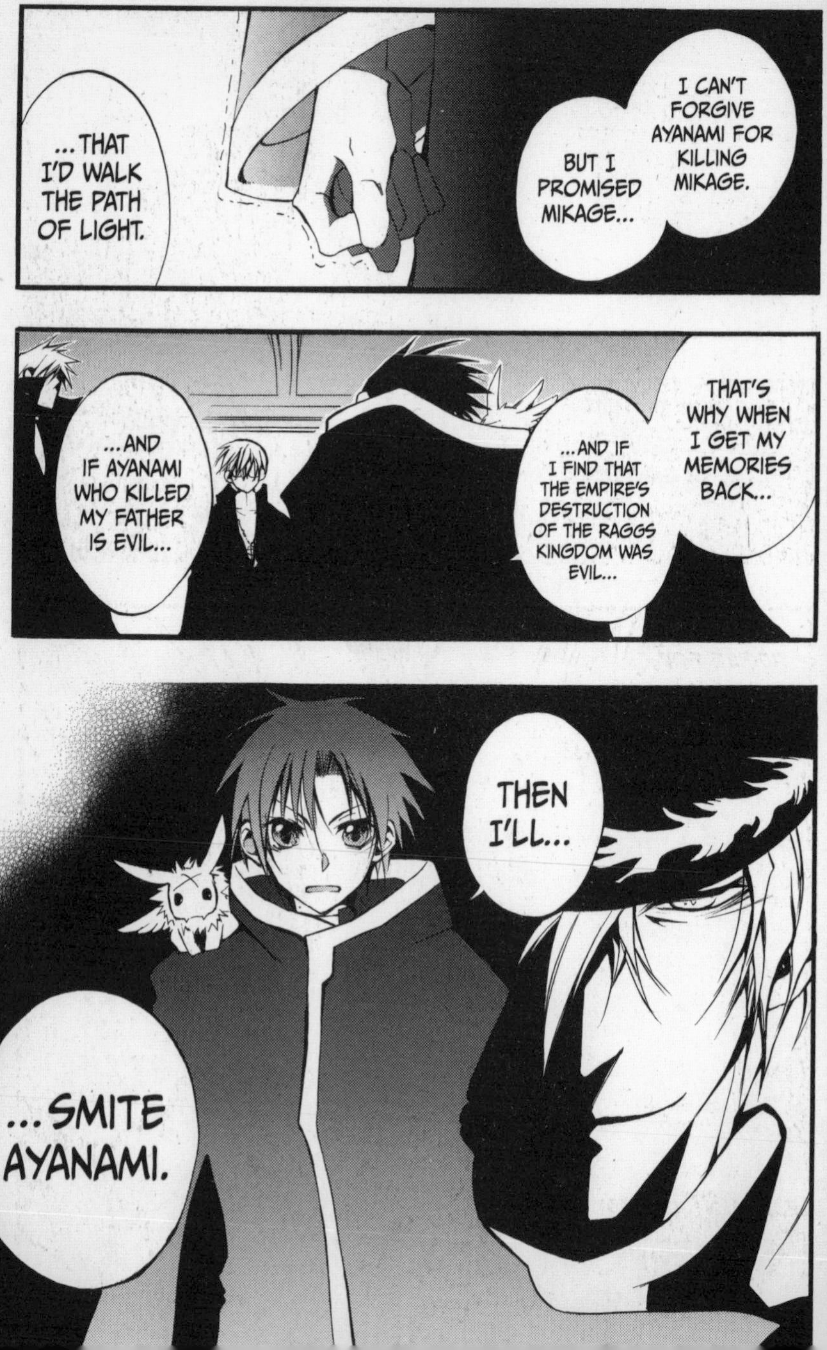
I CAN'T FORGIVE AYANAMI FOR KILLING MIKAGE.
BUT I PROMISED MIKAGE...
...THAT I'D WALK THE PATH OF LIGHT.
THAT'S WHY WHEN I GET MY MEMORIES BACK...
...AND IF I FIND THAT THE EMPIRE'S DESTRUCTION OF THE RAGGS KINGDOM WAS EVIL...
...AND IF AYANAMI WHO KILLED MY FATHER IS EVIL...
THEN I'LL...
...SMITE AYANAMI.

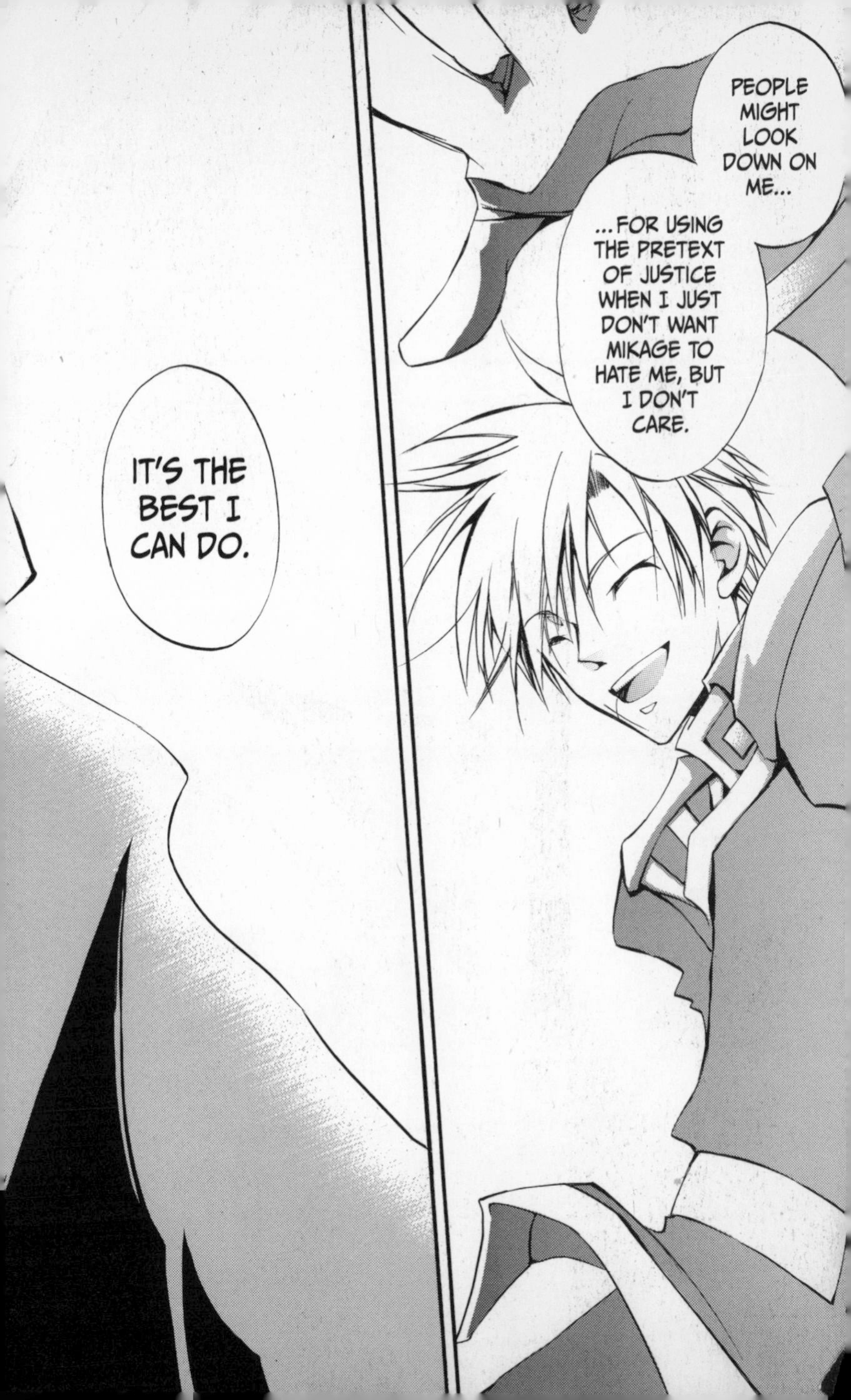
PEOPLE MIGHT LOOK DOWN ON ME...
...FOR USING THE PRETEXT OF JUSTICE WHEN I JUST DON'T WANT MIKAGE TO HATE ME, BUT I DON'T CARE.
IT'S THE BEST I CAN DO.

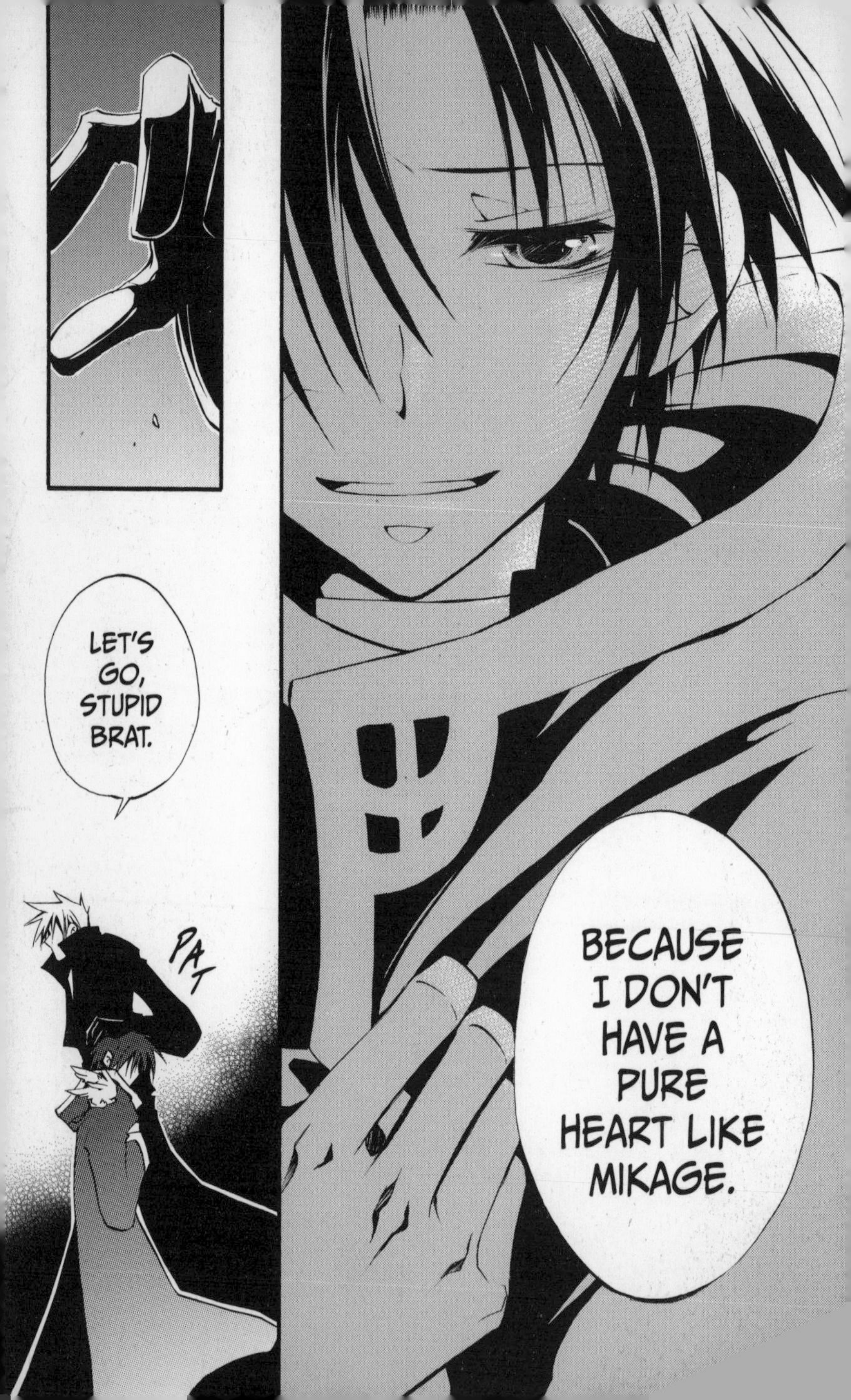
BECAUSE I DON'T HAVE A PURE HEART LIKE MIKAGE.
LET'S GO, STUPID BRAT.
PAT

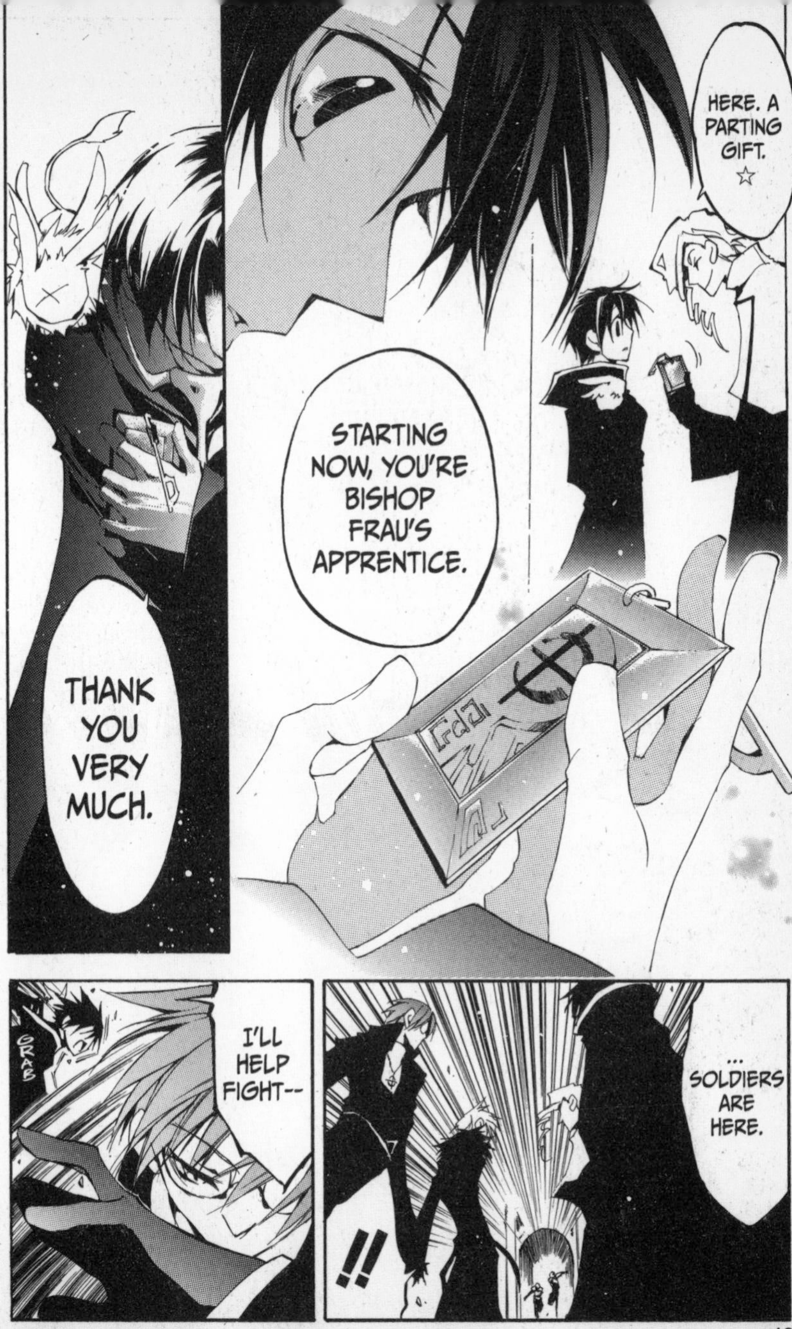
HERE. A PARTING GIFT. ☆
STARTING NOW, YOU'RE BISHOP FRAU'S APPRENTICE.
THANK YOU VERY MUCH.
... SOLDIERS ARE HERE.
!!
I'LL HELP FIGHT--
GRAB

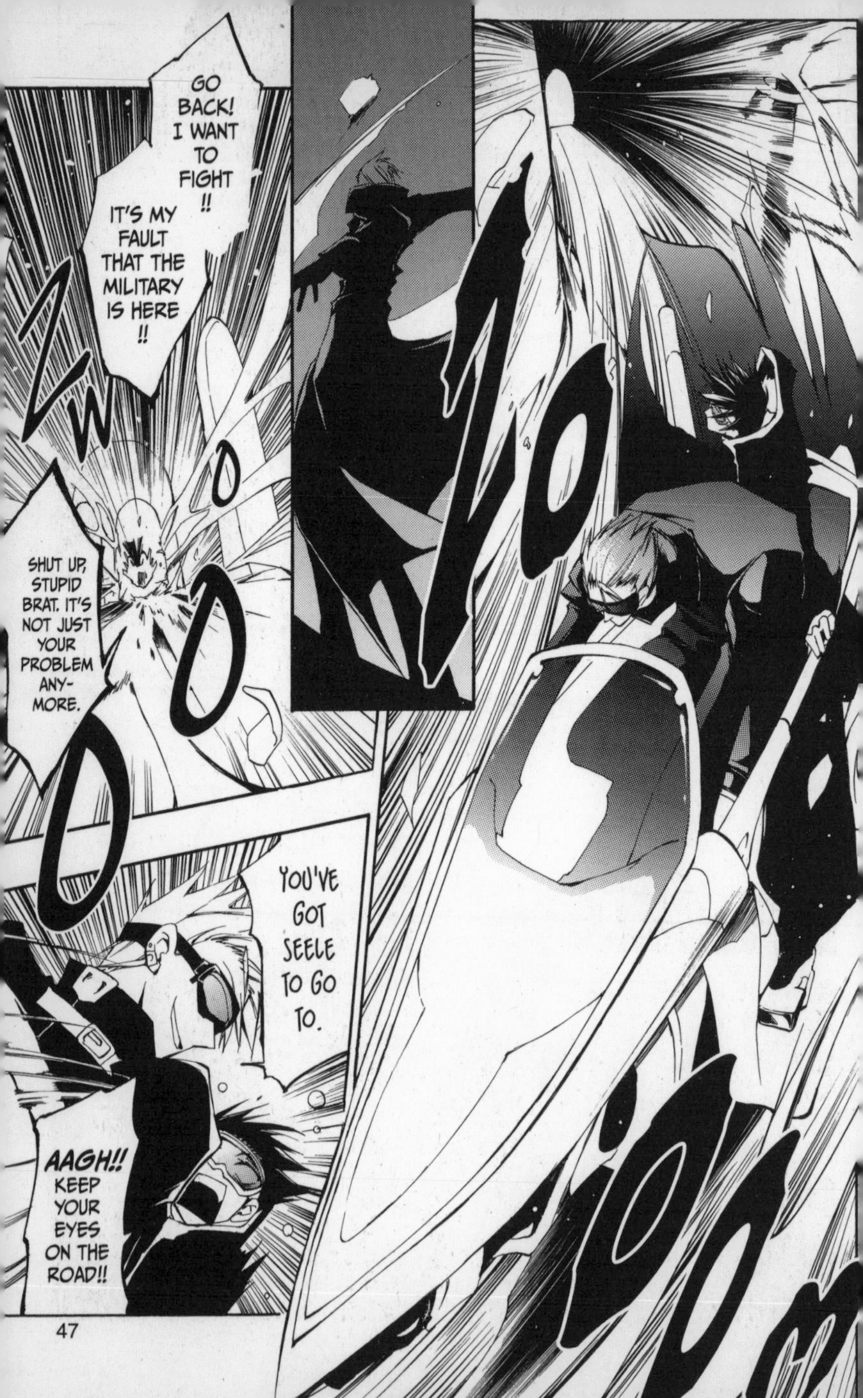
GO BACK! I WANT TO FIGHT!!
IT'S MY FAULT THAT THE MILITARY IS HERE!!
SHUT UP, STUPID BRAT. IT'S NOT JUST YOUR PROBLEM ANY-MORE.
YOU'VE GOT SEELE TO GO TO.
AAGH!! KEEP YOUR EYES ON THE ROAD!!

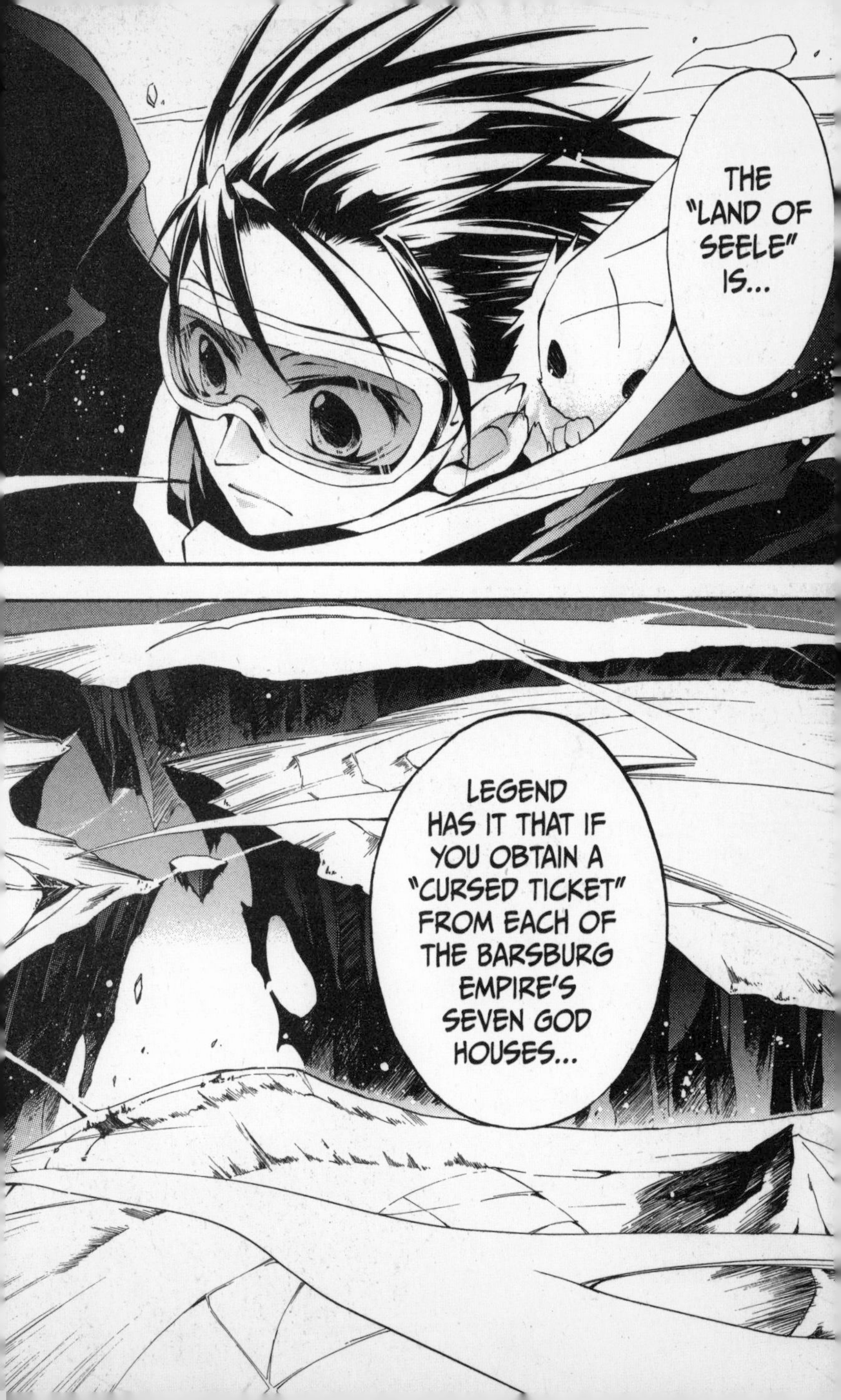
THE "LAND OF SEELE" IS...
LEGEND HAS IT THAT IF YOU OBTAIN A "CURSED TICKET" FROM EACH OF THE BARSBURG EMPIRE'S SEVEN GOD HOUSES...

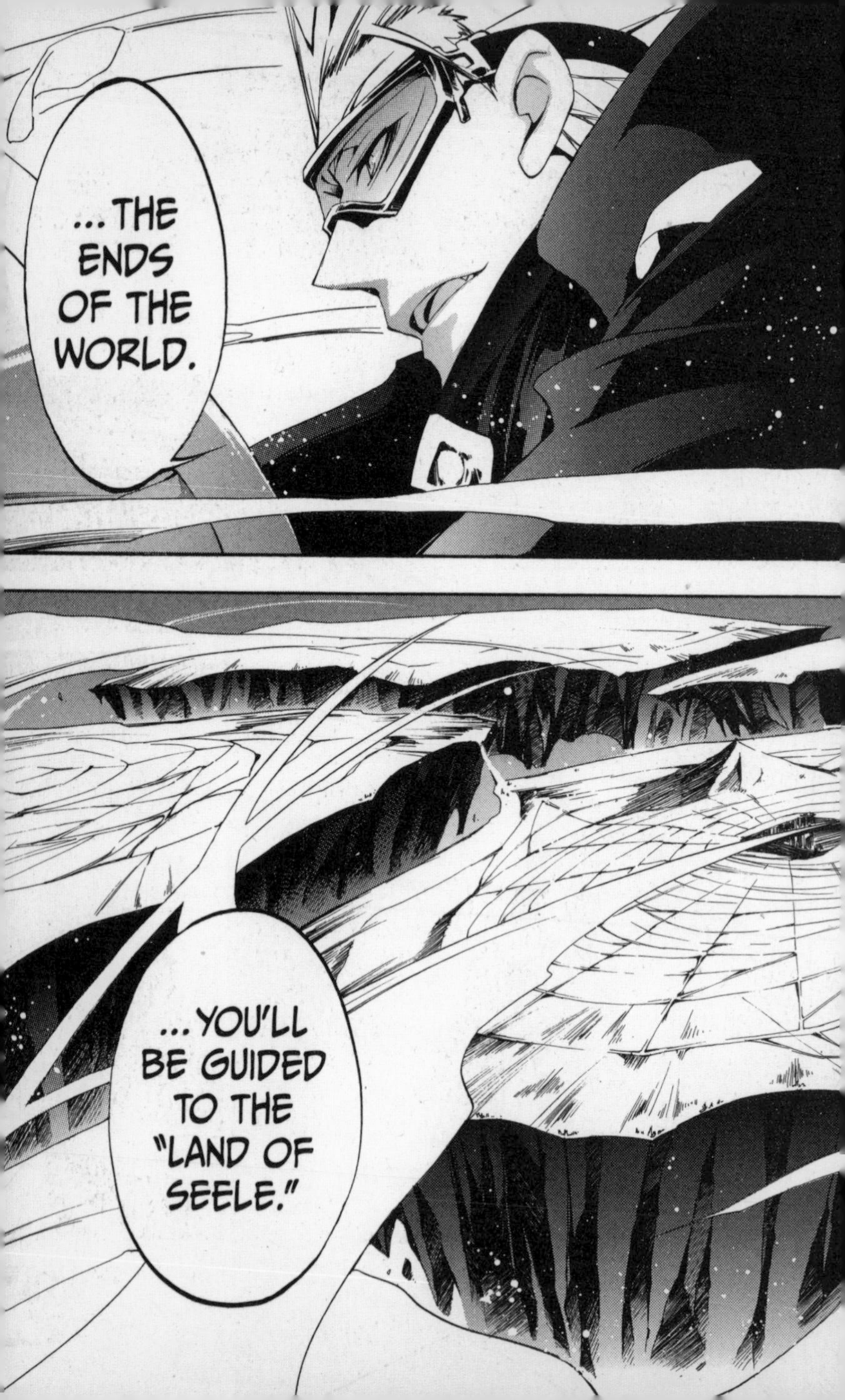
...THE ENDS OF THE WORLD.
...YOU'LL BE GUIDED TO THE "LAND OF SEELE."

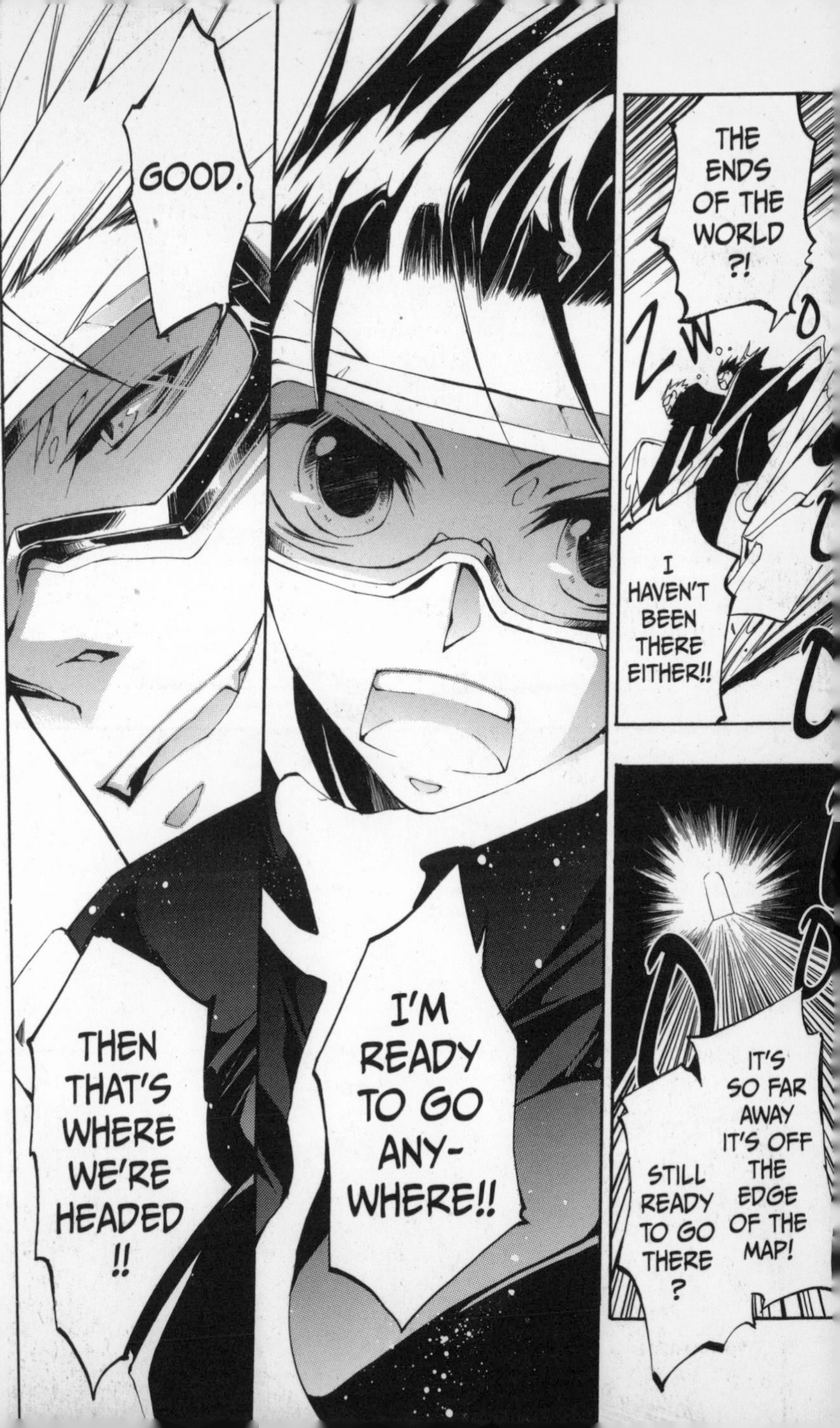
THE ENDS OF THE WORLD ?!
I HAVEN'T BEEN THERE EITHER!!
IT'S SO FAR AWAY IT'S OFF THE EDGE OF THE MAP!
STILL READY TO GO THERE ?
I'M READY TO GO ANY-WHERE!!
GOOD.
THEN THAT'S WHERE WE'RE HEADED !!

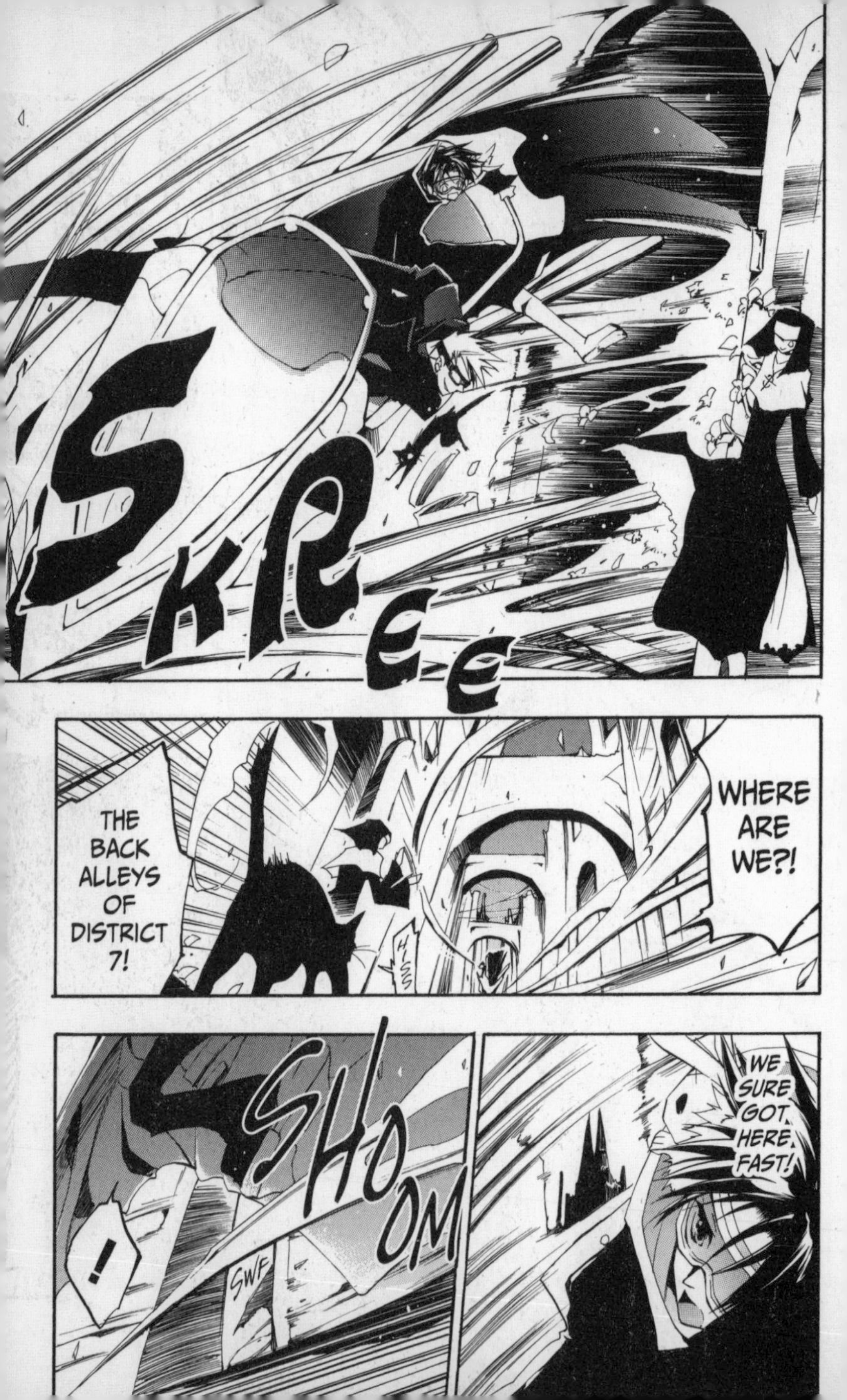
SKREEE
WHERE ARE WE?!
THE BACK ALLEYS OF DISTRICT 7!
HISS
WE SURE GOT HERE FAST!
SHOOM
!
SWF

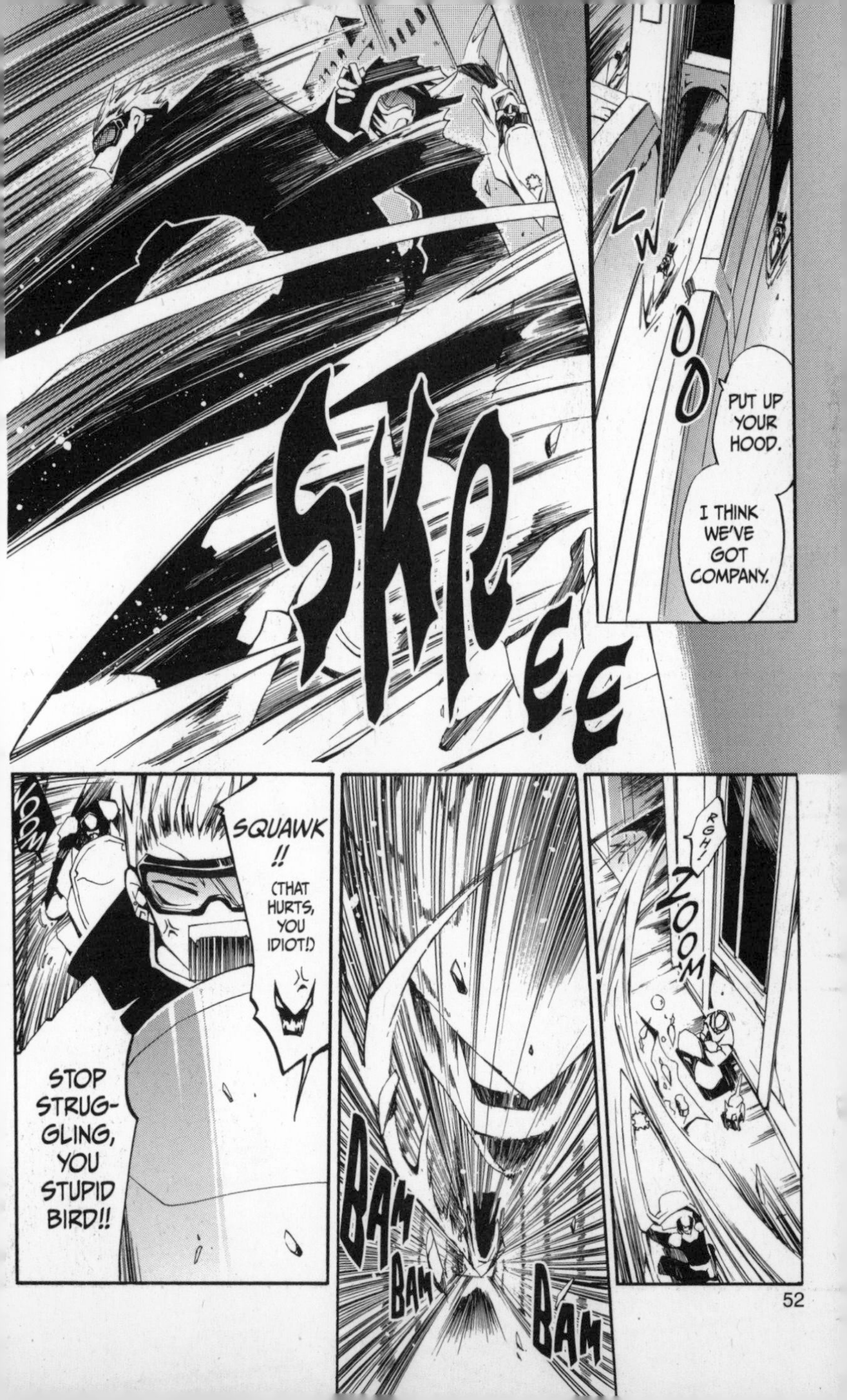
ZWOOD
PUT UP YOUR HOOD.
I THINK WE'VE GOT COMPANY.
SKREEE
RGH!
ZOOOM
BAM
BAM
BAM
BAM
SQUAWK!!
(THAT HURTS, YOU IDIOT!)
VOOOM
STOP STRUG-GLING, YOU STUPID BIRD!!

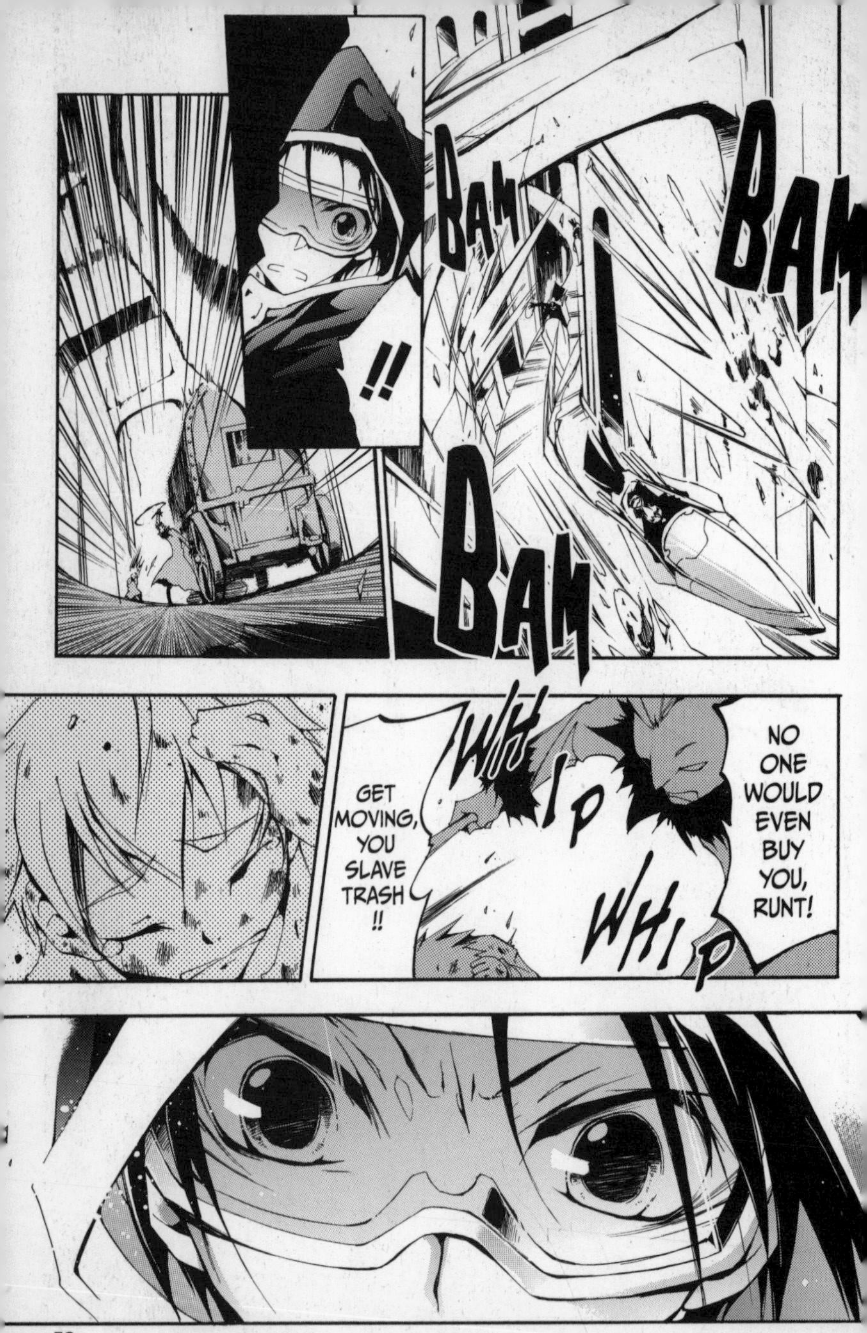
BAM
BAM
BAM
!!
NO ONE WOULD EVEN BUY YOU, RUNT!
WHIP
GET MOVING, YOU SLAVE TRASH!!
WHIP

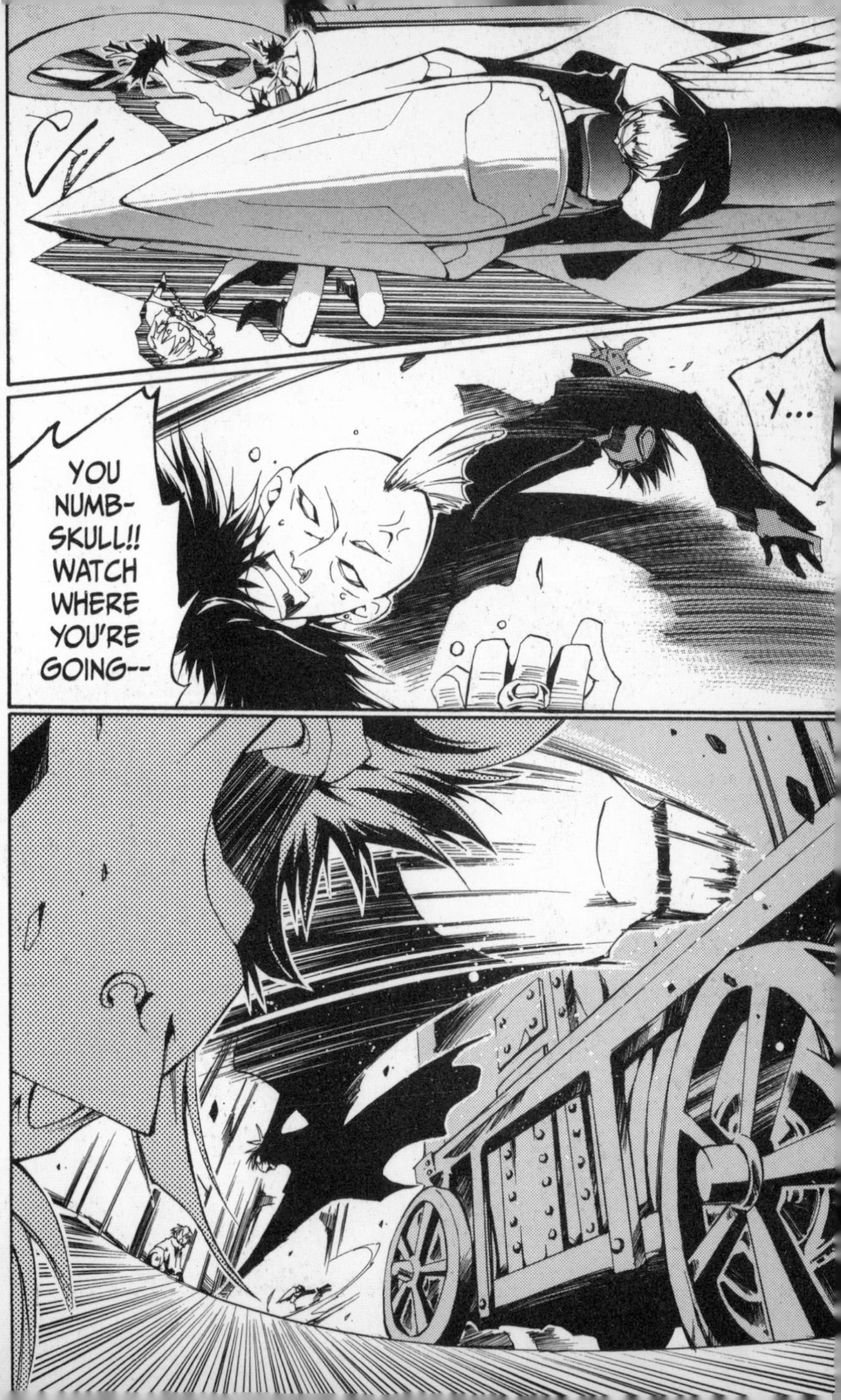
Y...
YOU NUMB-SKULL!! WATCH WHERE YOU'RE GOING--

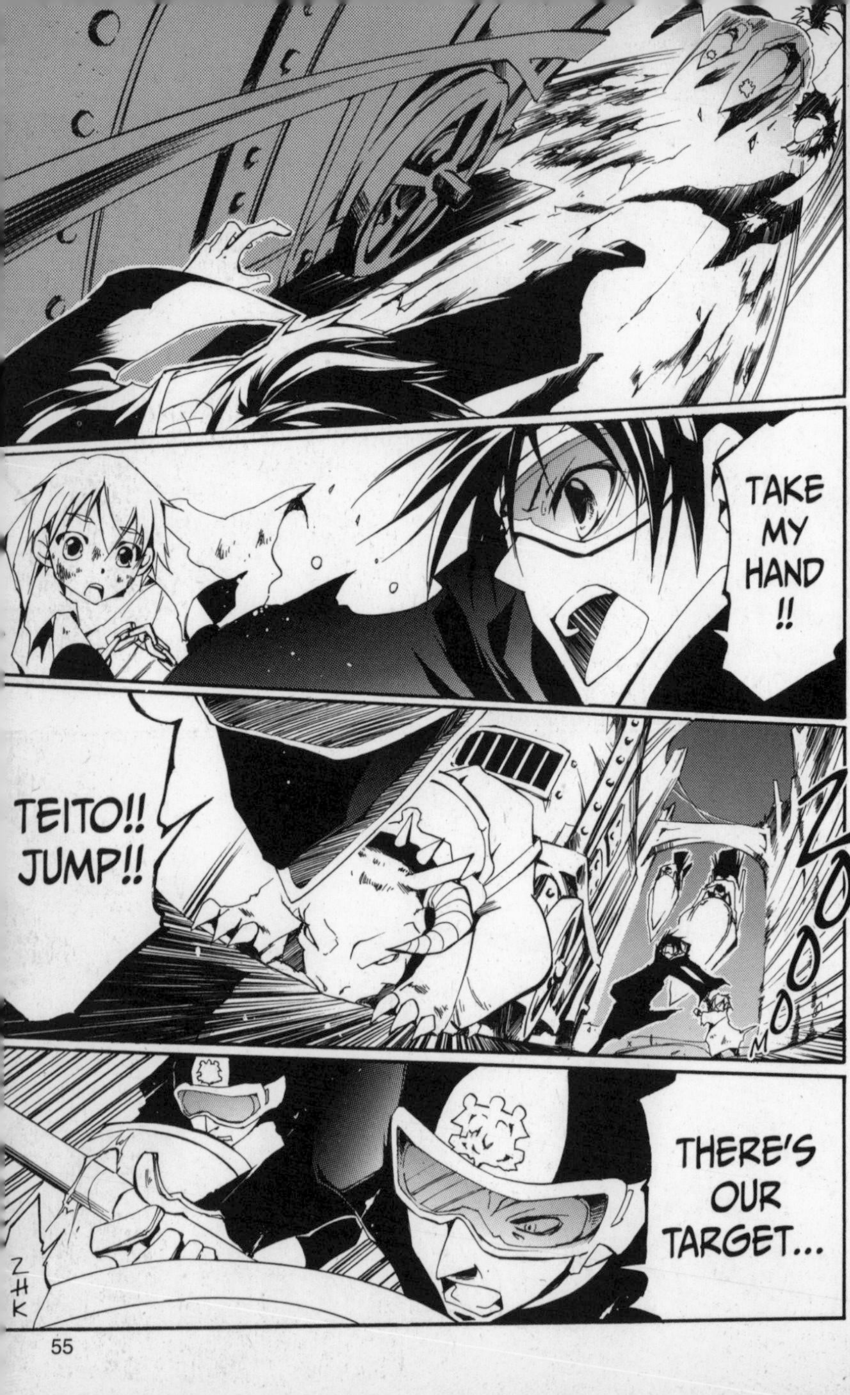
TAKE MY HAND!!
ZOOOOM
TEITO!! JUMP!!
THERE'S OUR TARGET...
ZHK

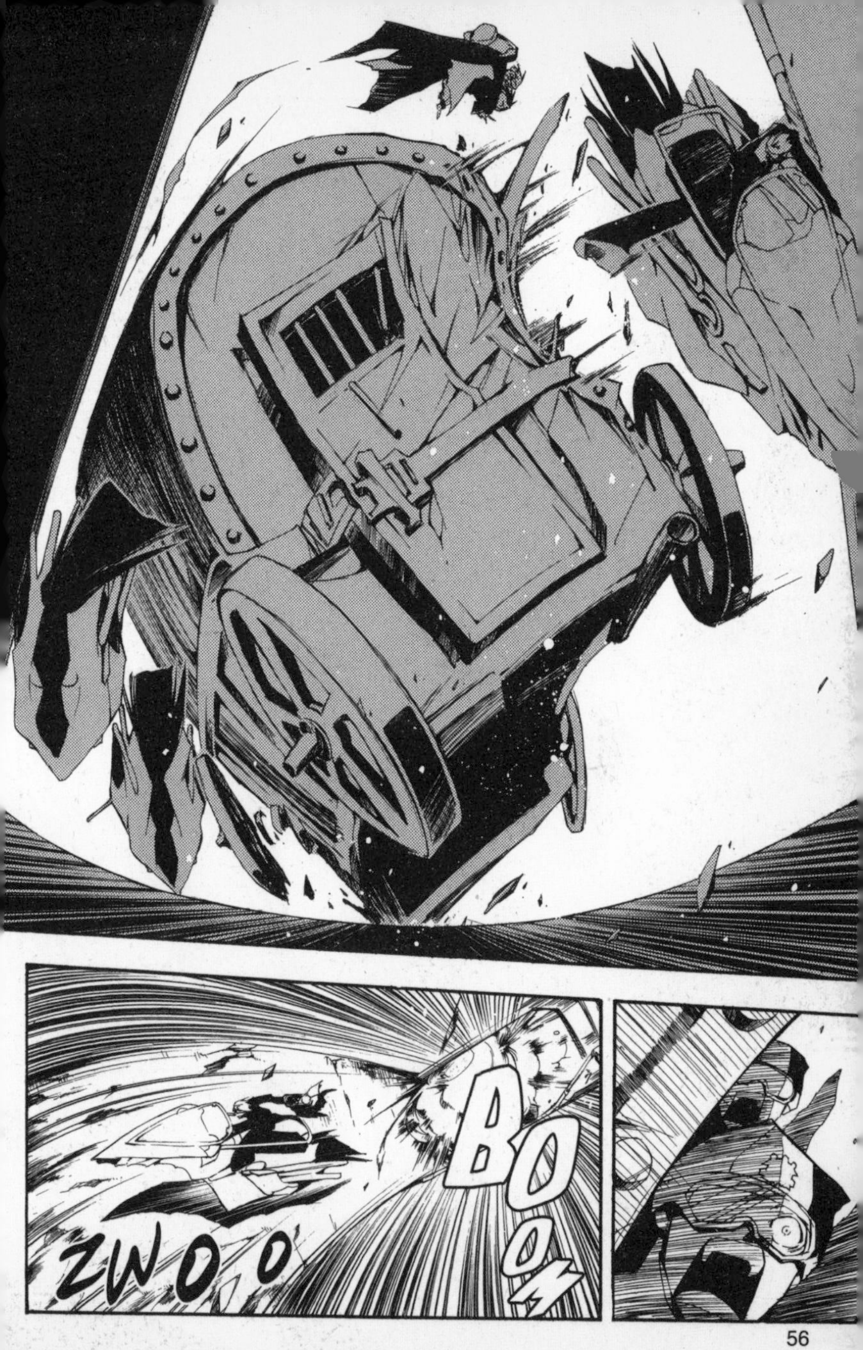
BOOM
ZWOO

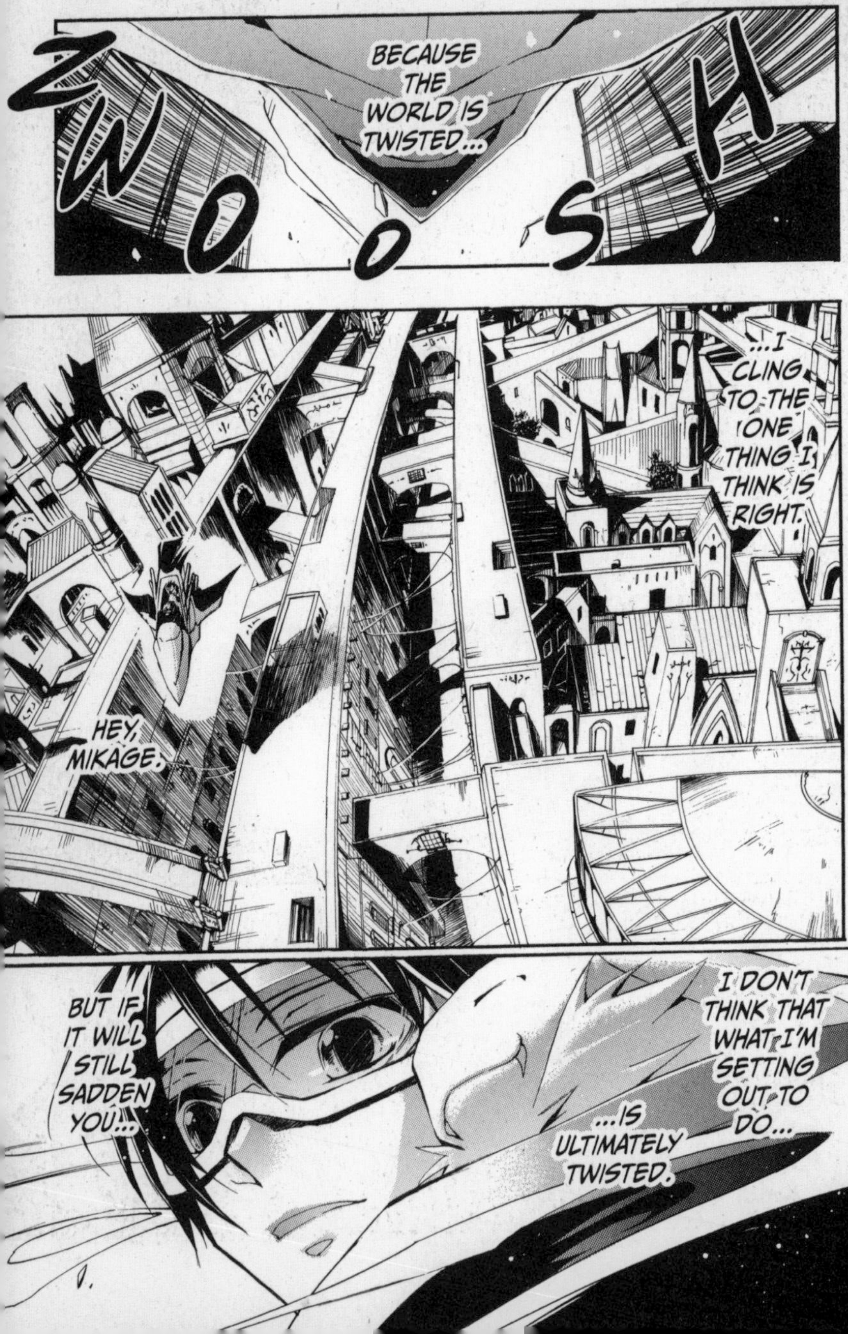
ZWOOSH
BECAUSE THE WORLD IS TWISTED...
...I CLING TO THE ONE THING I THINK IS RIGHT.
HEY, MIKAGE.
I DON'T THINK THAT WHAT I'M SETTING OUT TO DO...
...IS ULTIMATELY TWISTED.
BUT IF IT WILL STILL SADDEN YOU...

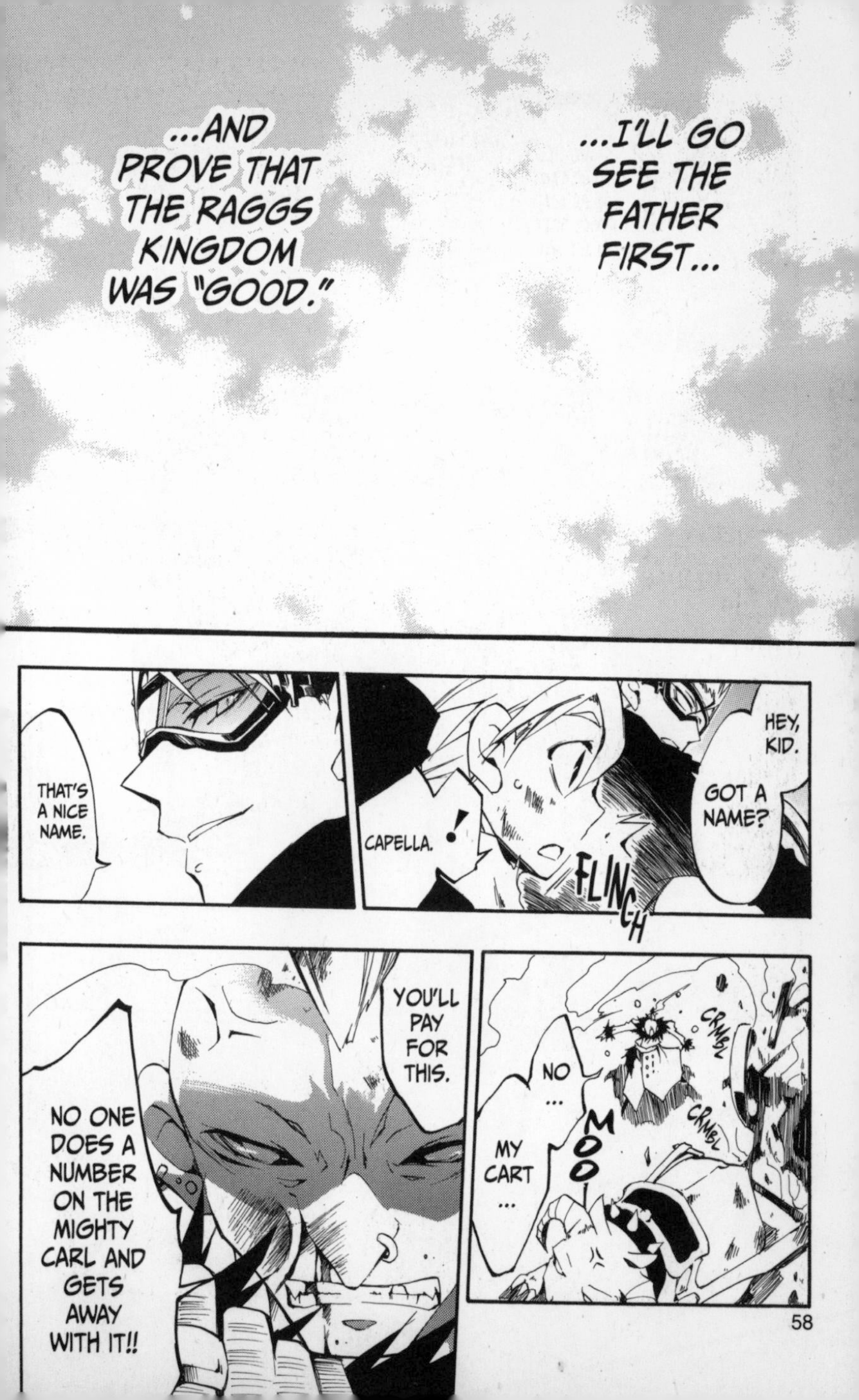
...I'LL GO SEE THE FATHER FIRST...
...AND PROVE THAT THE RAGGS KINGDOM WAS "GOOD."
HEY, KID.
GOT A NAME?
FLINCH
CAPELLA.
!
THAT'S A NICE NAME.
CRMBL
CRMBL
NO ...
MY CART ...
MOO
YOU'LL PAY FOR THIS.
NO ONE DOES A NUMBER ON THE MIGHTY CARL AND GETS AWAY WITH IT!!

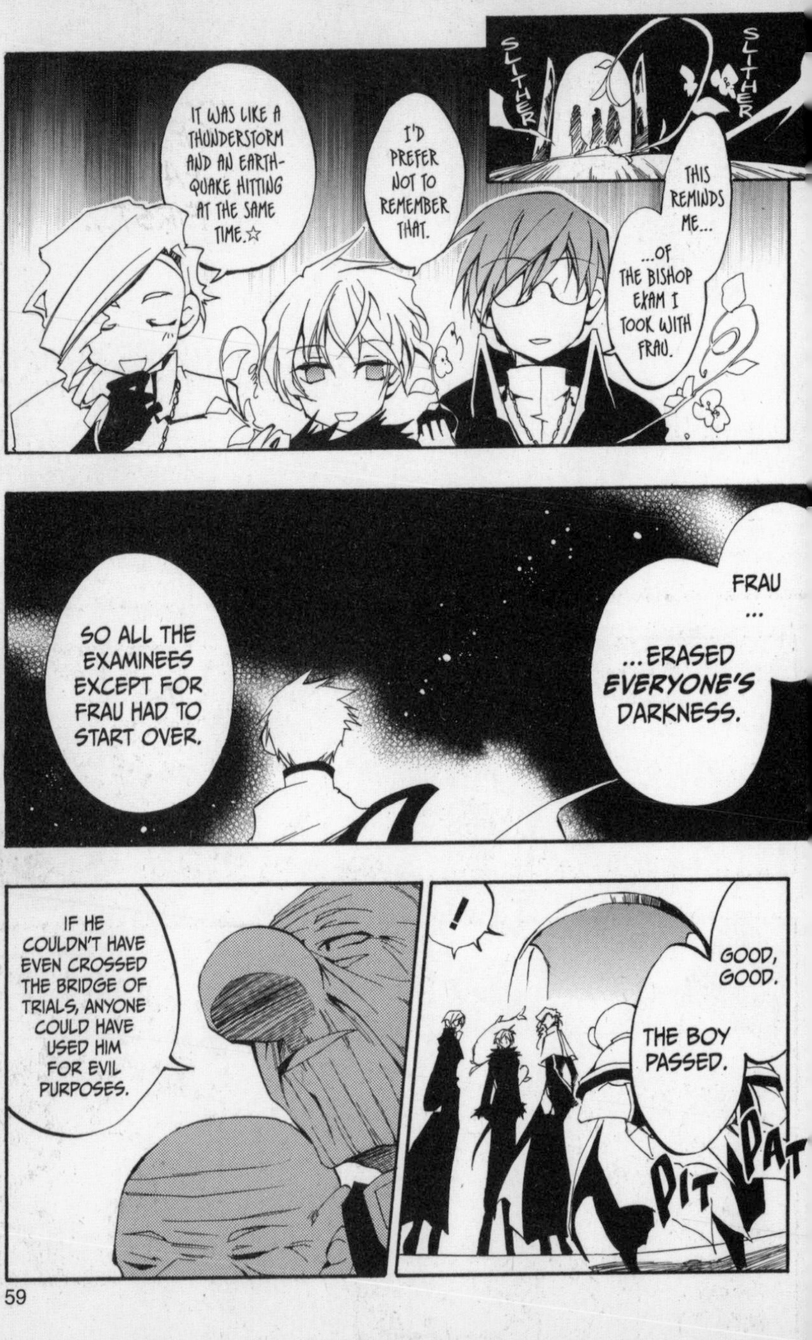
SLITHER
SLITHER
THIS REMINDS ME...
...OF THE BISHOP EXAM I TOOK WITH FRAU.
I'D PREFER NOT TO REMEMBER THAT.
IT WAS LIKE A THUNDERSTORM AND AN EARTH-QUAKE HITTING AT THE SAME TIME.☆
FRAU...
...ERASED EVERYONE'S DARKNESS.
SO ALL THE EXAMINEES EXCEPT FOR FRAU HAD TO START OVER.
GOOD, GOOD.
THE BOY PASSED.
!
PIT PAT
IF HE COULDN'T HAVE EVEN CROSSED THE BRIDGE OF TRIALS, ANYONE COULD HAVE USED HIM FOR EVIL PURPOSES.

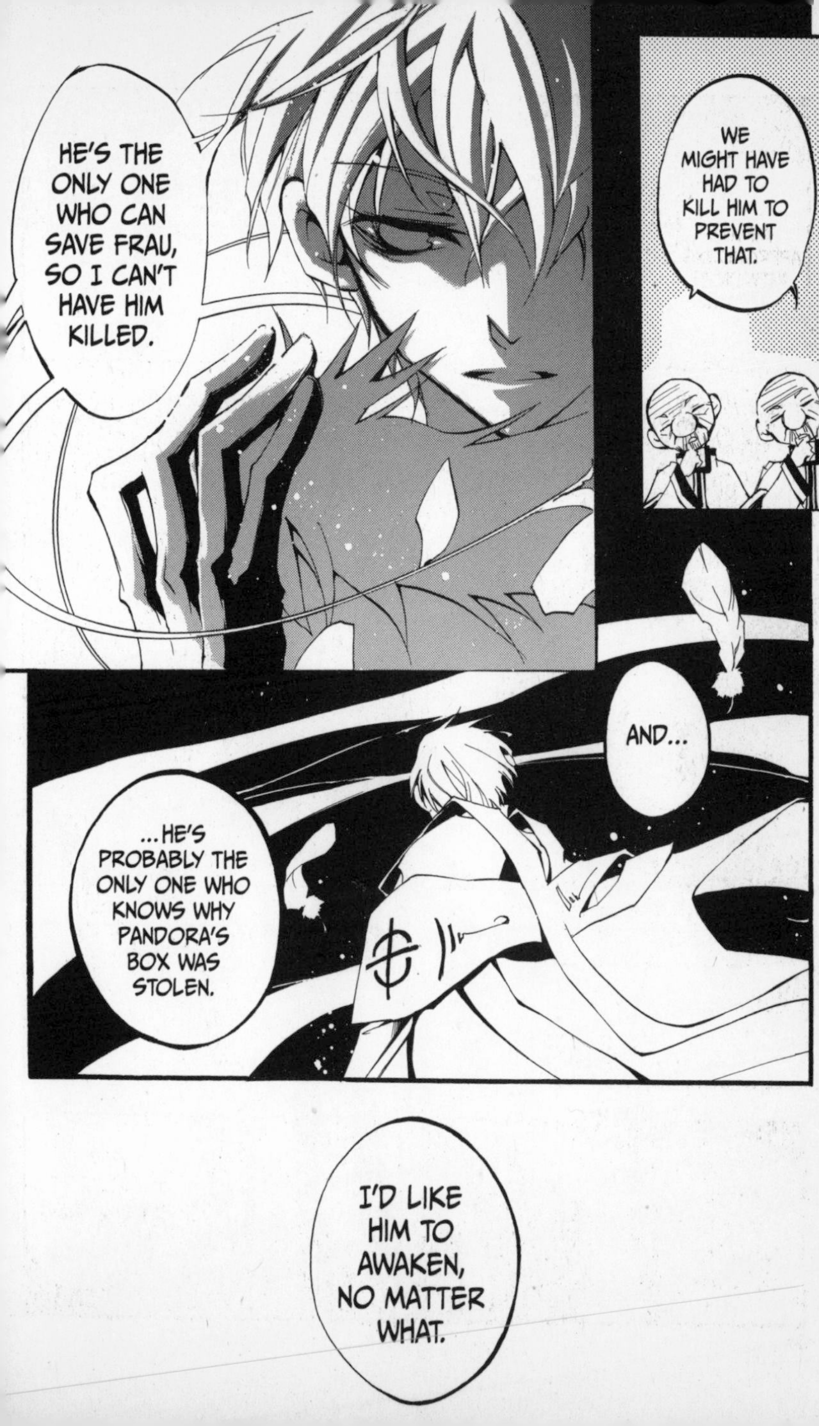
WE MIGHT HAVE HAD TO KILL HIM TO PREVENT THAT.
HE'S THE ONLY ONE WHO CAN SAVE FRAU, SO I CAN'T HAVE HIM KILLED.
AND...
...HE'S PROBABLY THE ONLY ONE WHO KNOWS WHY PANDORA'S BOX WAS STOLEN.
I'D LIKE HIM TO AWAKEN, NO MATTER WHAT.

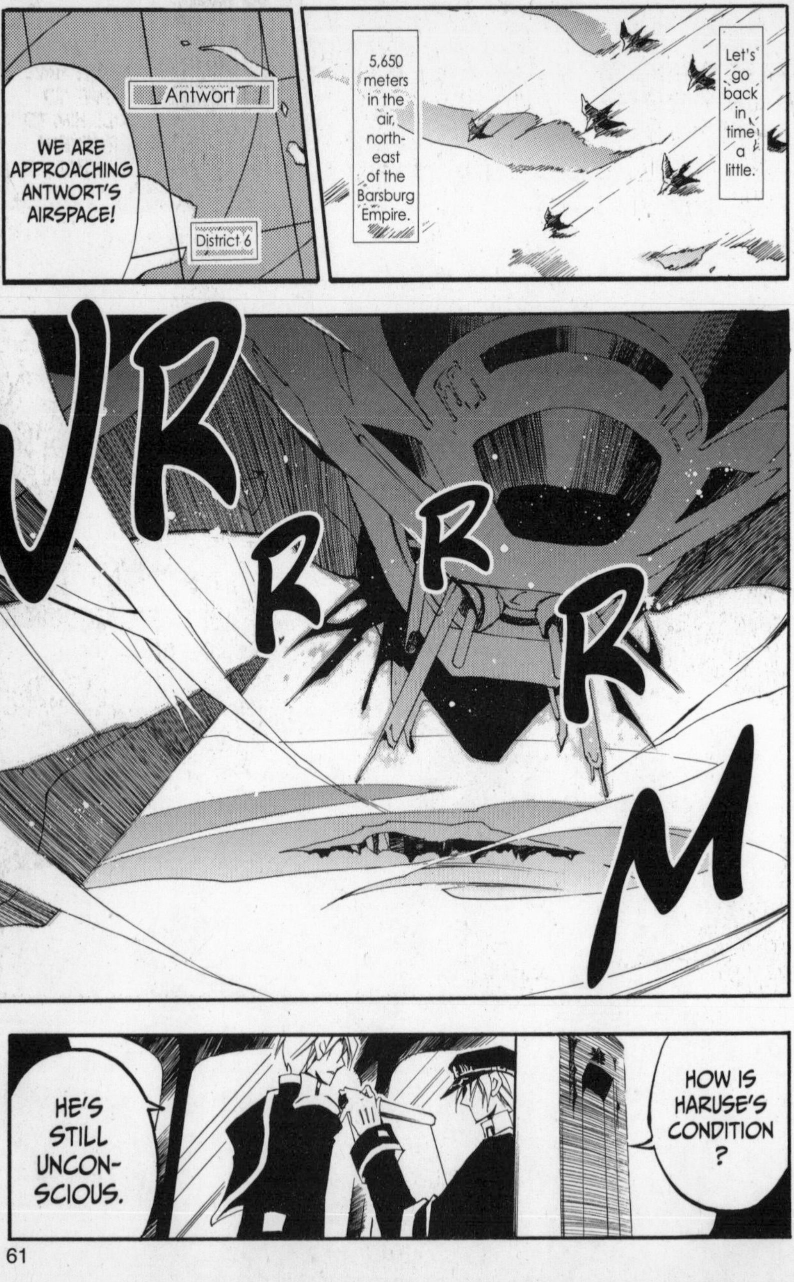
Let's go back in time a little.
5,650 meters in the air, northeast of the Barsburg Empire.
Antwort
WE ARE APPROACHING ANTWORT'S AIRSPACE!
District 6
VRRRRM
HOW IS HARUSE'S CONDITION?
HE'S STILL UNCON-SCIOUS.

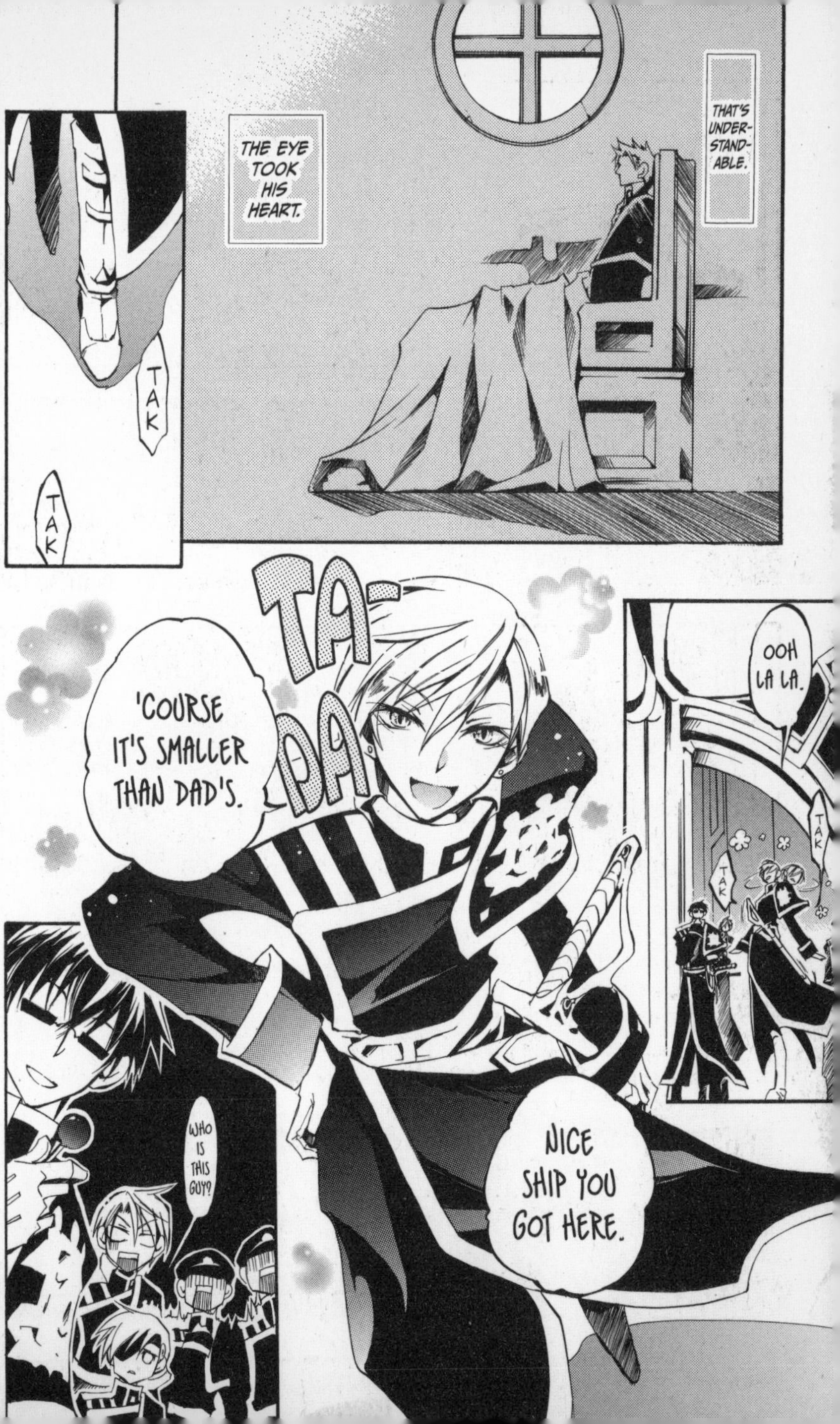
THAT'S UNDER-STAND-ABLE.
THE EYE TOOK HIS HEART.
TAK
TAK
OOH LA LA.
TAK
TAK
TA-DA
NICE SHIP YOU GOT HERE.
'COURSE IT'S SMALLER THAN DAD'S.
WHO IS THIS GUY?

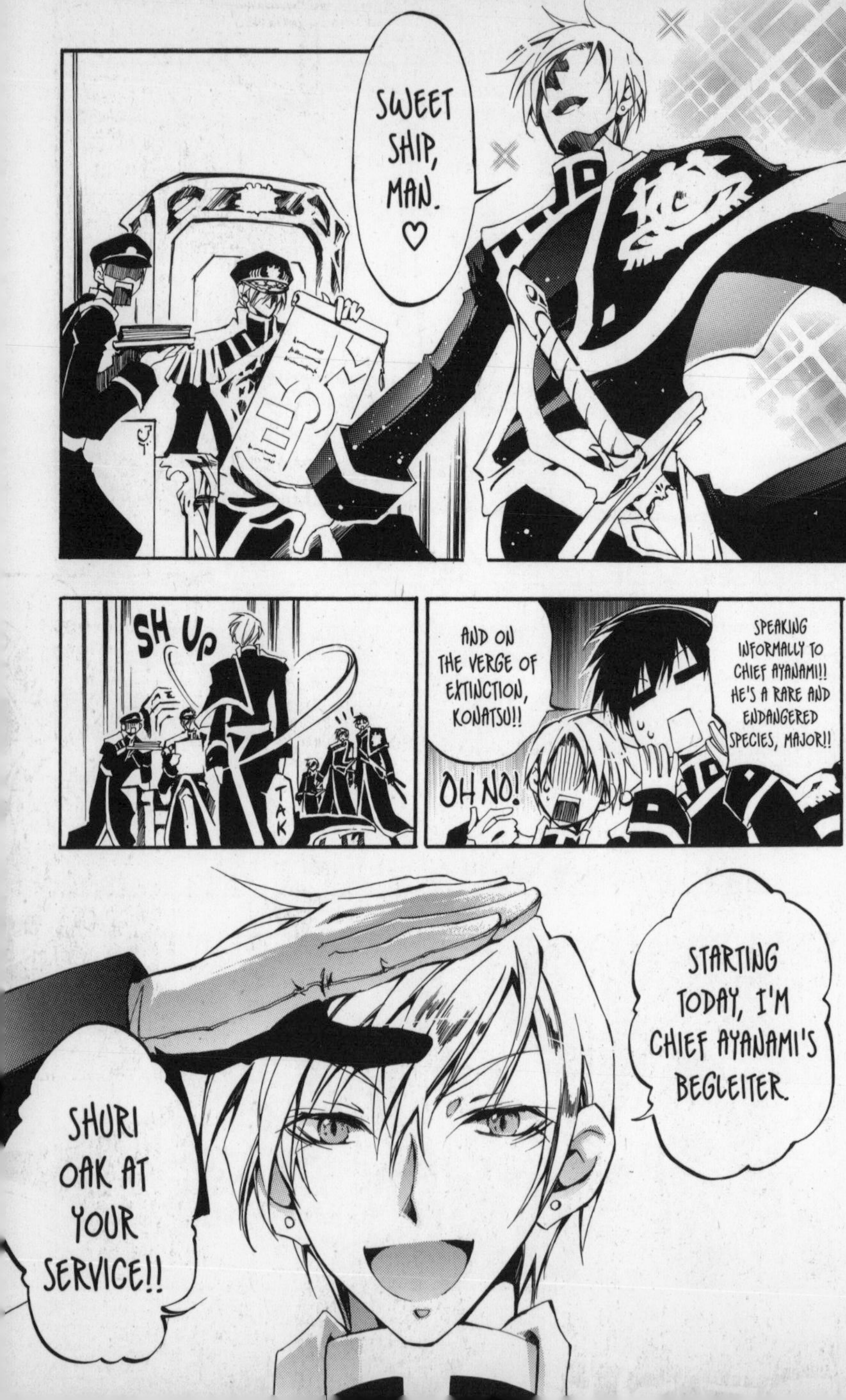
SWEET SHIP, MAN. ♡
SPEAKING INFORMALLY TO CHIEF AYANAMI!! HE'S A RARE AND ENDANGERED SPECIES, MAJOR!!
AND ON THE VERGE OF EXTINCTION, KONATSU!!
OH NO!
SH UP
TAK
STARTING TODAY, I'M CHIEF AYANAMI'S BEGLEITER.
SHURI OAK AT YOUR SERVICE!!

begleiter = assistant to an officer of high military rank

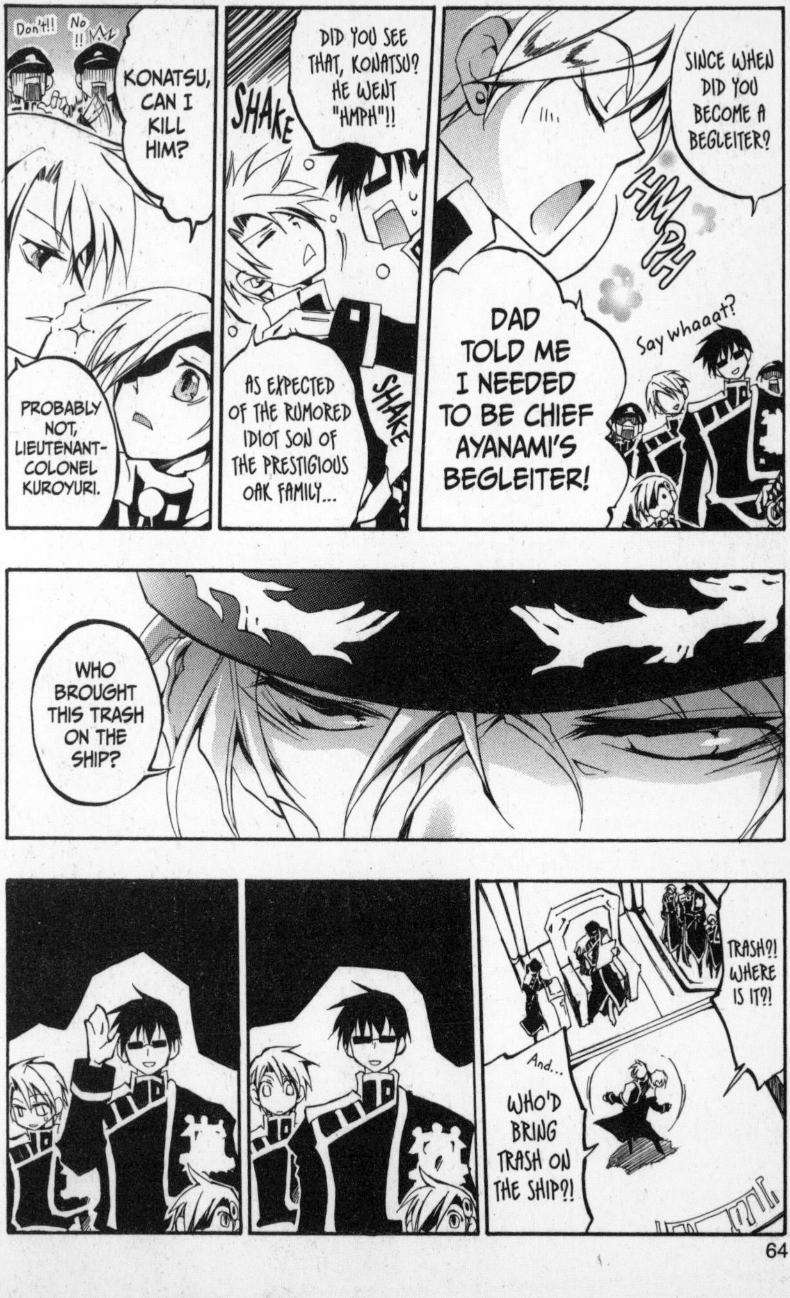
SINCE WHEN DID YOU BECOME A BEGLEITER?
HMPH
DAD TOLD ME I NEEDED TO BE CHIEF AYANAMI'S BEGLEITER!
Say whaaat?
SHAKE
DID YOU SEE THAT, KONATSU? HE WENT "HMPH"!!
SHAKE
AS EXPECTED OF THE RUMORED IDIOT SON OF THE PRESTIGIOUS OAK FAMILY...
KONATSU, CAN I KILL HIM?
Don't!!
No!!
PROBABLY NOT, LIEUTENANT-COLONEL KUROYURI.
WHO BROUGHT THIS TRASH ON THE SHIP?
TRASH?! WHERE IS IT?!
And...
WHO'D BRING TRASH ON THE SHIP?!

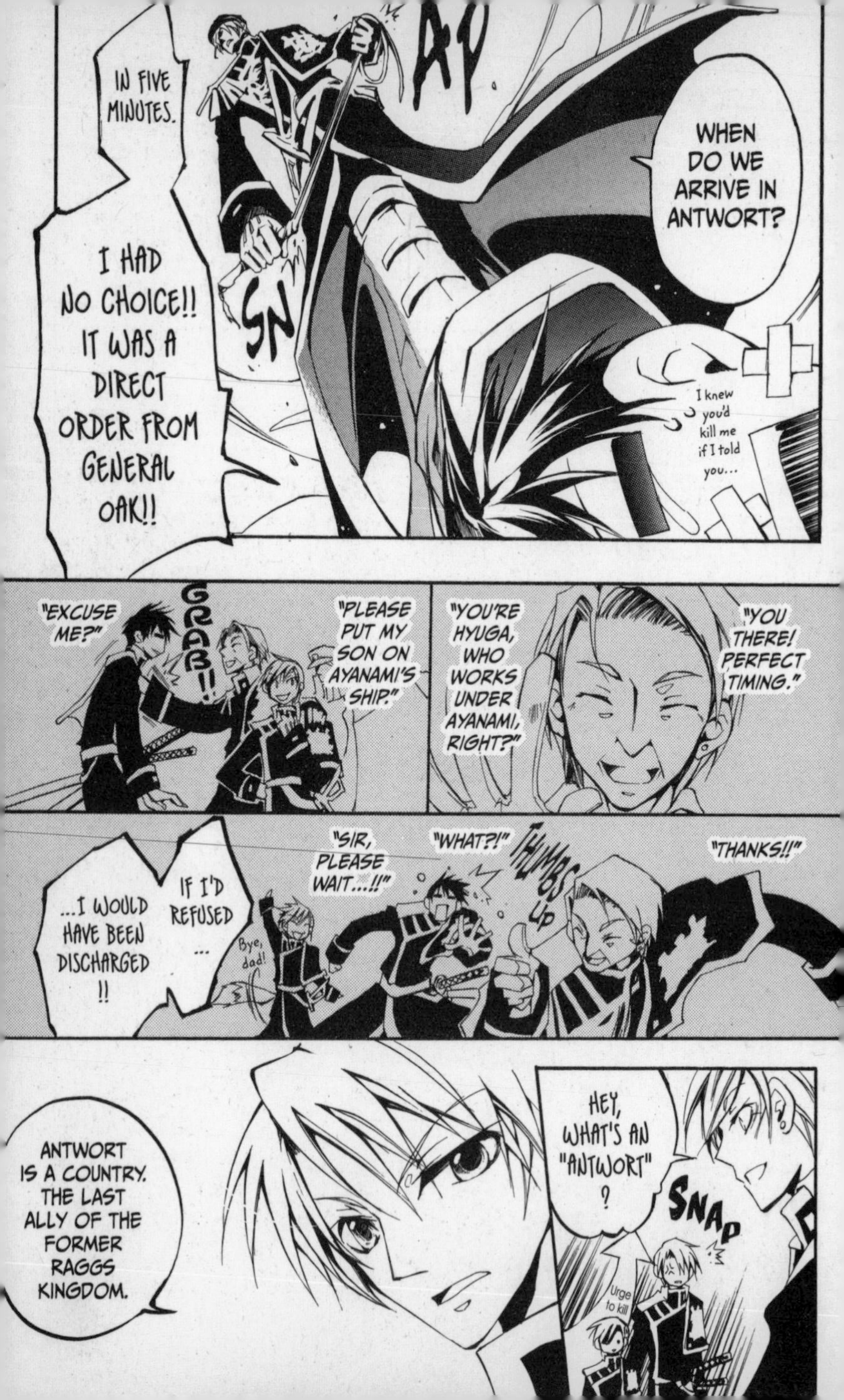
WHEN DO WE ARRIVE IN ANTWORT?
AP
IN FIVE MINUTES.
I knew you'd kill me if I told you...
SN
I HAD NO CHOICE!! IT WAS A DIRECT ORDER FROM GENERAL OAK!!
"YOU THERE! PERFECT TIMING."
"YOU'RE HYUGA, WHO WORKS UNDER AYANAMI, RIGHT?"
"PLEASE PUT MY SON ON AYANAMI'S SHIP."
GRAB!!
"EXCUSE ME?"
"THANKS!!"
THUMBS UP
"WHAT?!"
"SIR, PLEASE WAIT...!!"
Bye, dad!
IF I'D REFUSED...
...I WOULD HAVE BEEN DISCHARGED!!
HEY, WHAT'S AN "ANTWORT"?
SNAP
Urge to kill
ANTWORT IS A COUNTRY. THE LAST ALLY OF THE FORMER RAGGS KINGDOM.

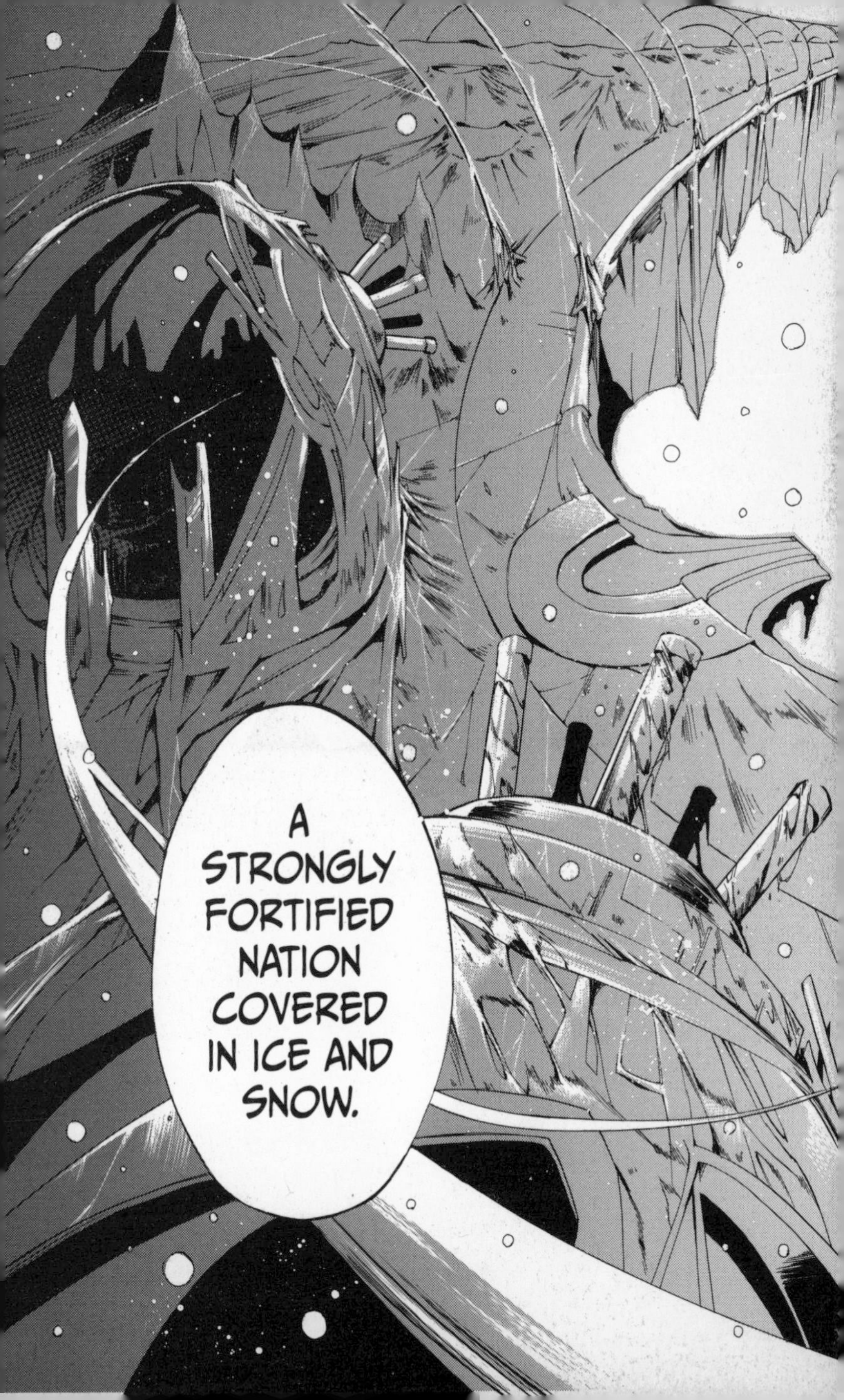
A STRONGLY FORTIFIED NATION COVERED IN ICE AND SNOW.

Kapitel.26 "Antwort"

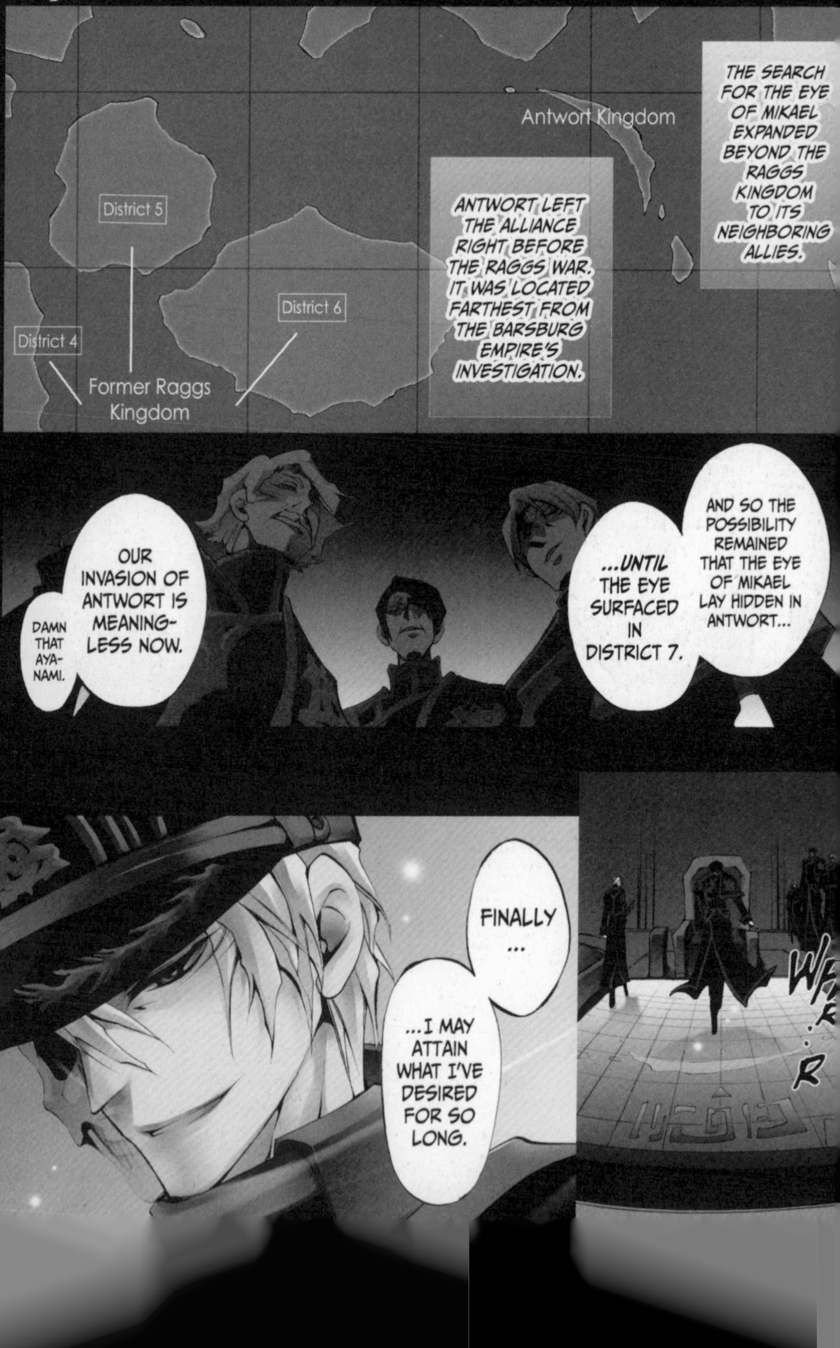
THE SEARCH FOR THE EYE OF MIKAEL EXPANDED BEYOND THE RAGGS KINGDOM TO ITS NEIGHBORING ALLIES.
Antwort Kingdom
ANTWORT LEFT THE ALLIANCE RIGHT BEFORE THE RAGGS WAR. IT WAS LOCATED FARTHEST FROM THE BARSBURG EMPIRE'S INVESTIGATION.
District 5
District 6
District 4
Former Raggs Kingdom
AND SO THE POSSIBILITY REMAINED THAT THE EYE OF MIKAEL LAY HIDDEN IN ANTWORT...
...UNTIL THE EYE SURFACED IN DISTRICT 7.
OUR INVASION OF ANTWORT IS MEANINGLESS NOW.
DAMN THAT AYANAMI.
FINALLY...
...I MAY ATTAIN WHAT I'VE DESIRED FOR SO LONG.

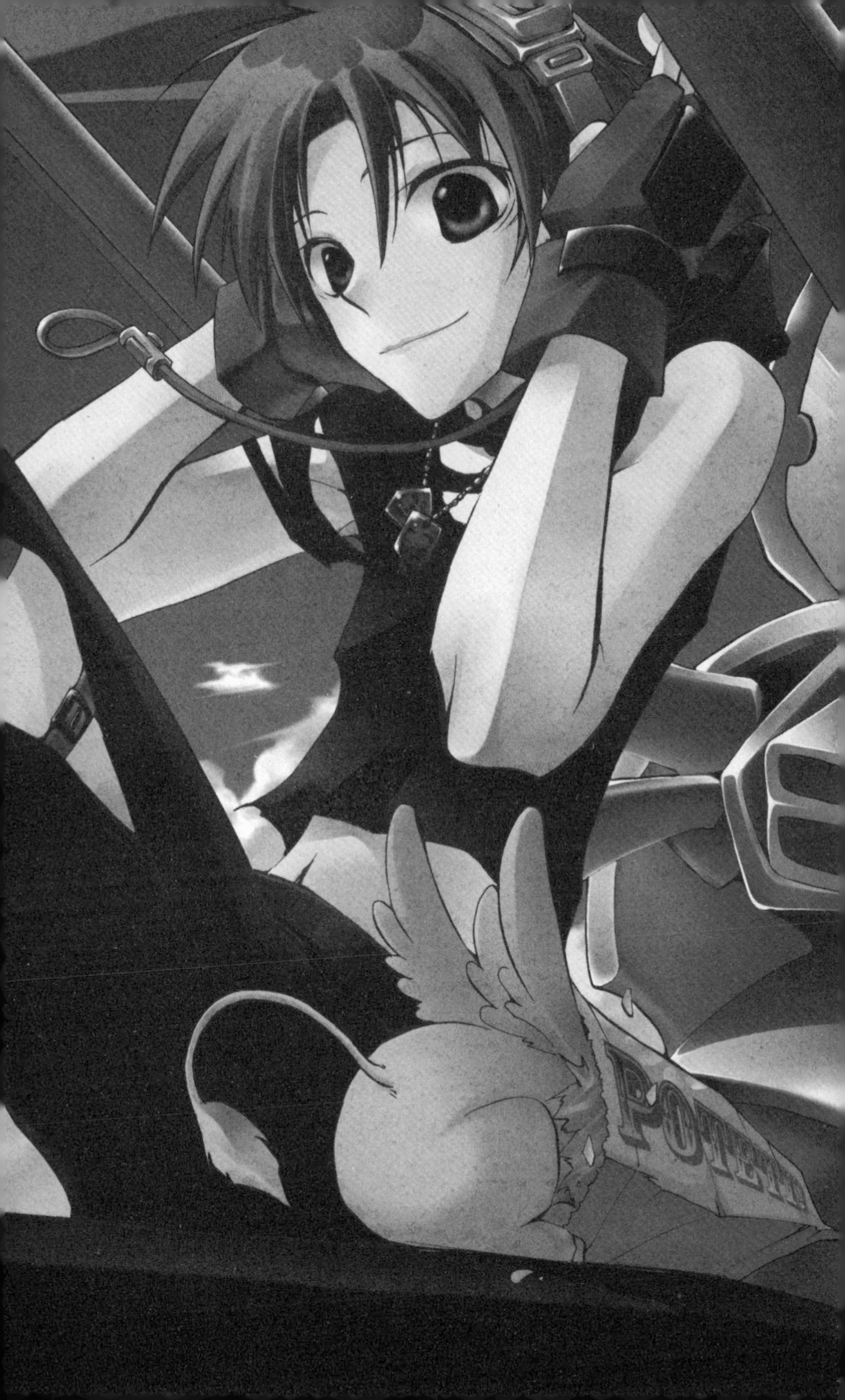

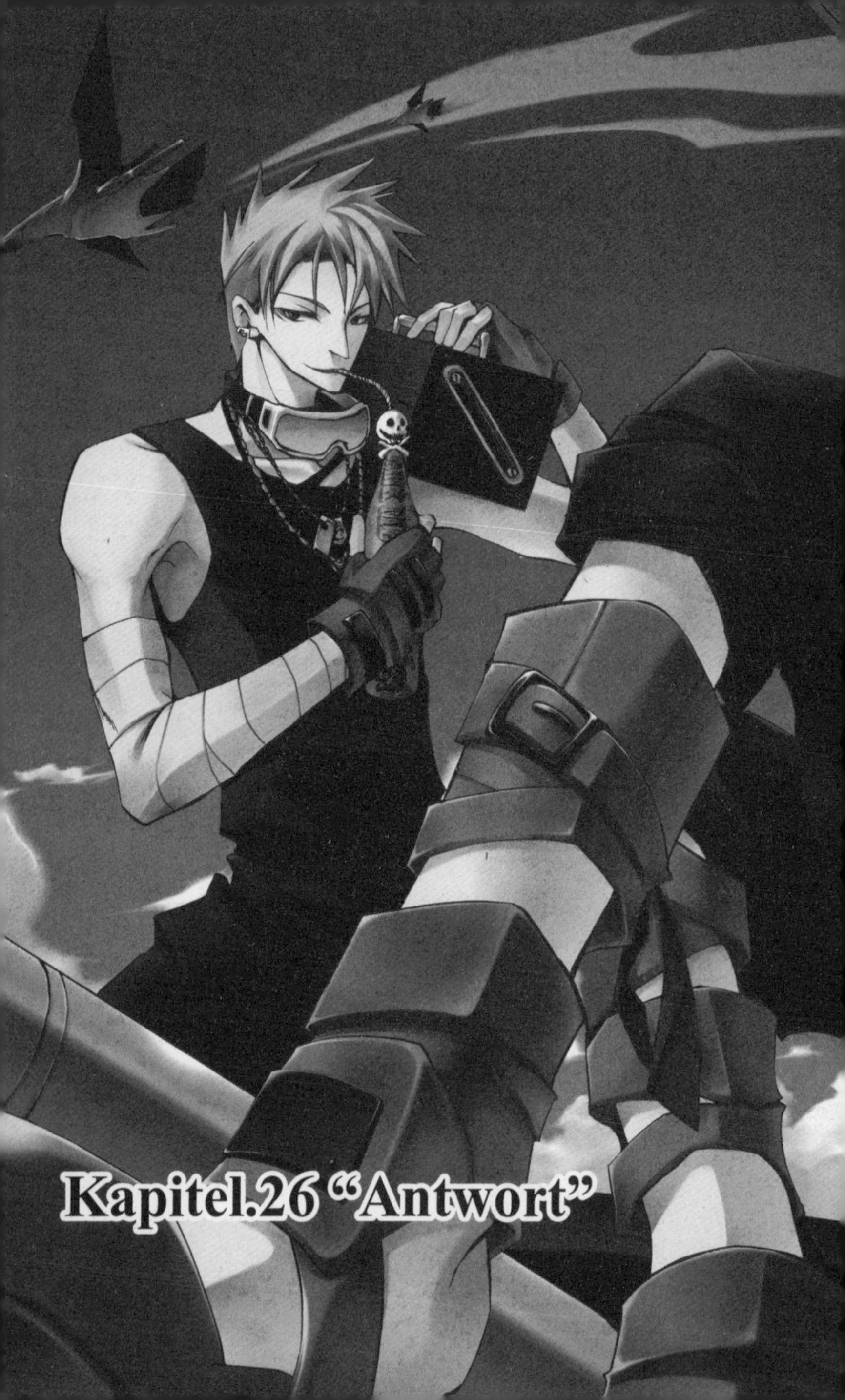
Kapitel.26 “Antwort”

♪ Mirror, Mirror

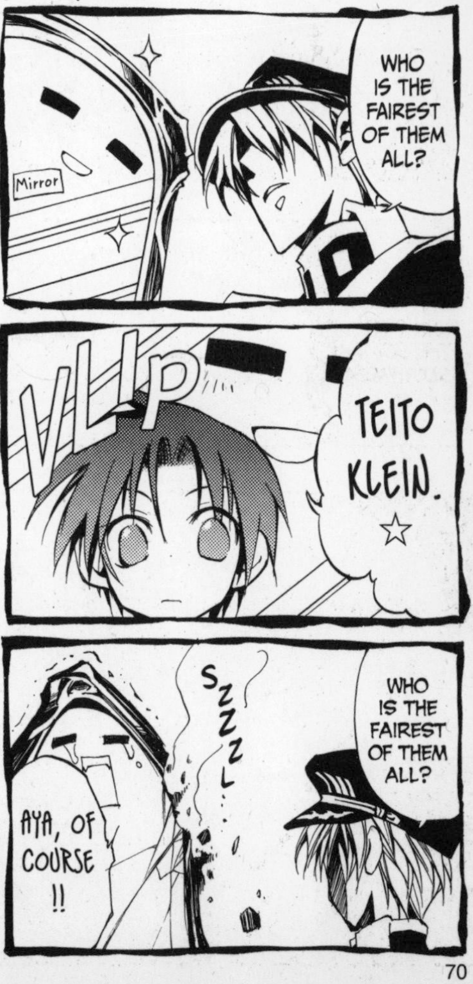
WHO IS THE FAIREST OF THEM ALL?
Mirror
VLIP
TEITO KLEIN. ☆
WHO IS THE FAIREST OF THEM ALL?
SZZZL...
AYA, OF COURSE !!

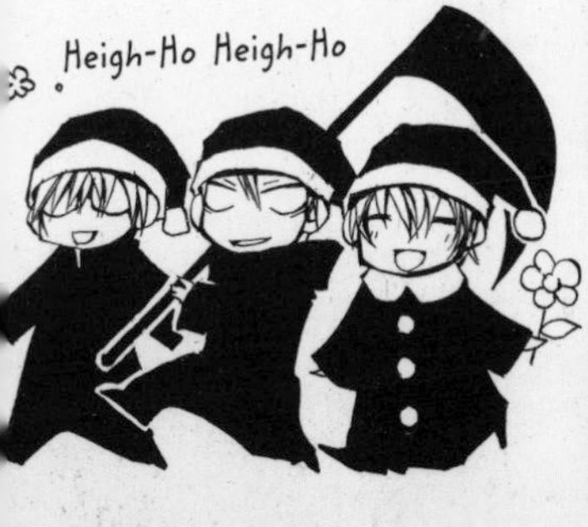
Heigh-Ho Heigh-Ho

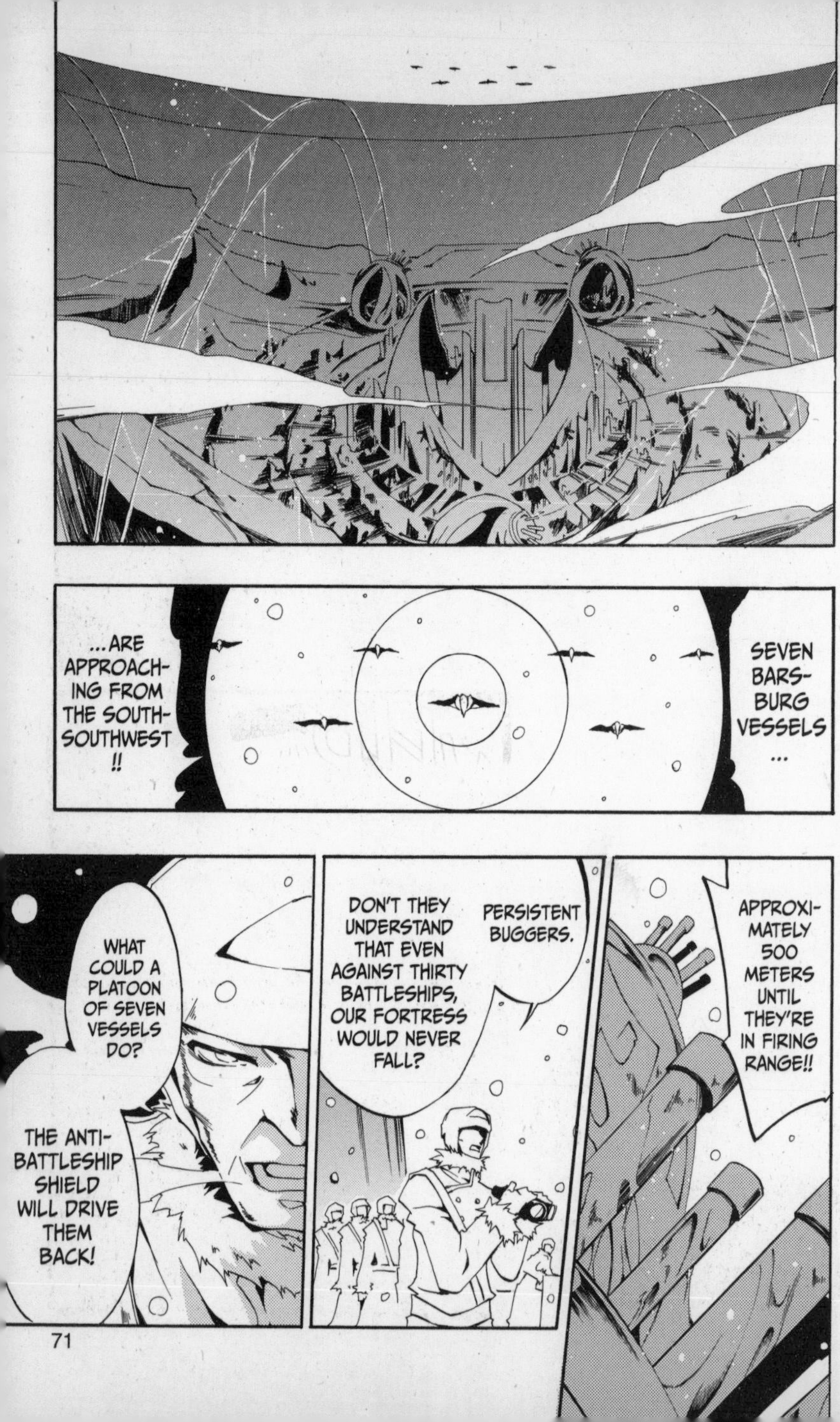
SEVEN BARSBURG VESSELS...
...ARE APPROACHING FROM THE SOUTH-SOUTHWEST!!
APPROXIMATELY 500 METERS UNTIL THEY'RE IN FIRING RANGE!!
PERSISTENT BUGGERS.
DON'T THEY UNDERSTAND THAT EVEN AGAINST THIRTY BATTLESHIPS, OUR FORTRESS WOULD NEVER FALL?
WHAT COULD A PLATOON OF SEVEN VESSELS DO?
THE ANTI-BATTLESHIP SHIELD WILL DRIVE THEM BACK!

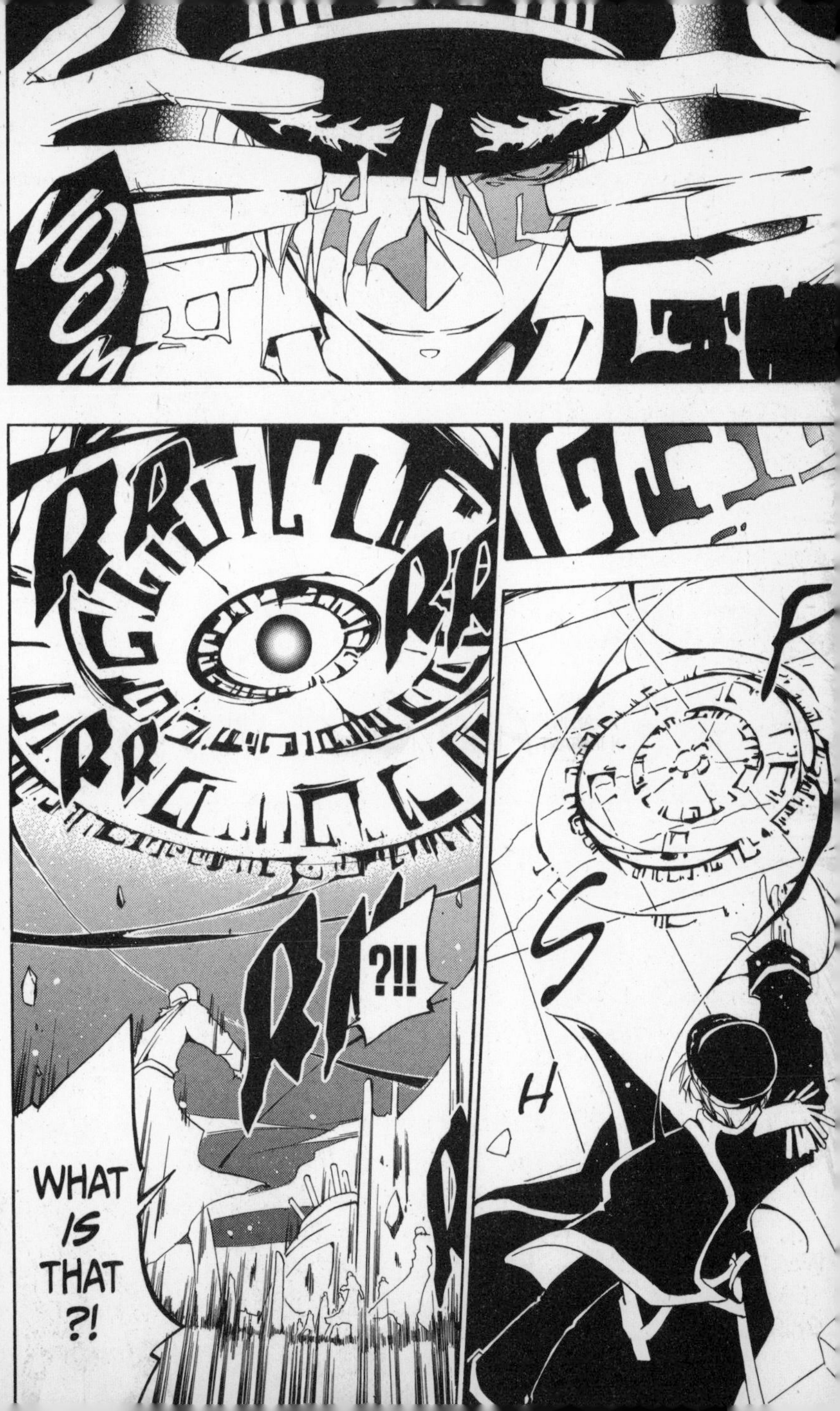
VOOM
?!!
WHAT IS THAT ?!

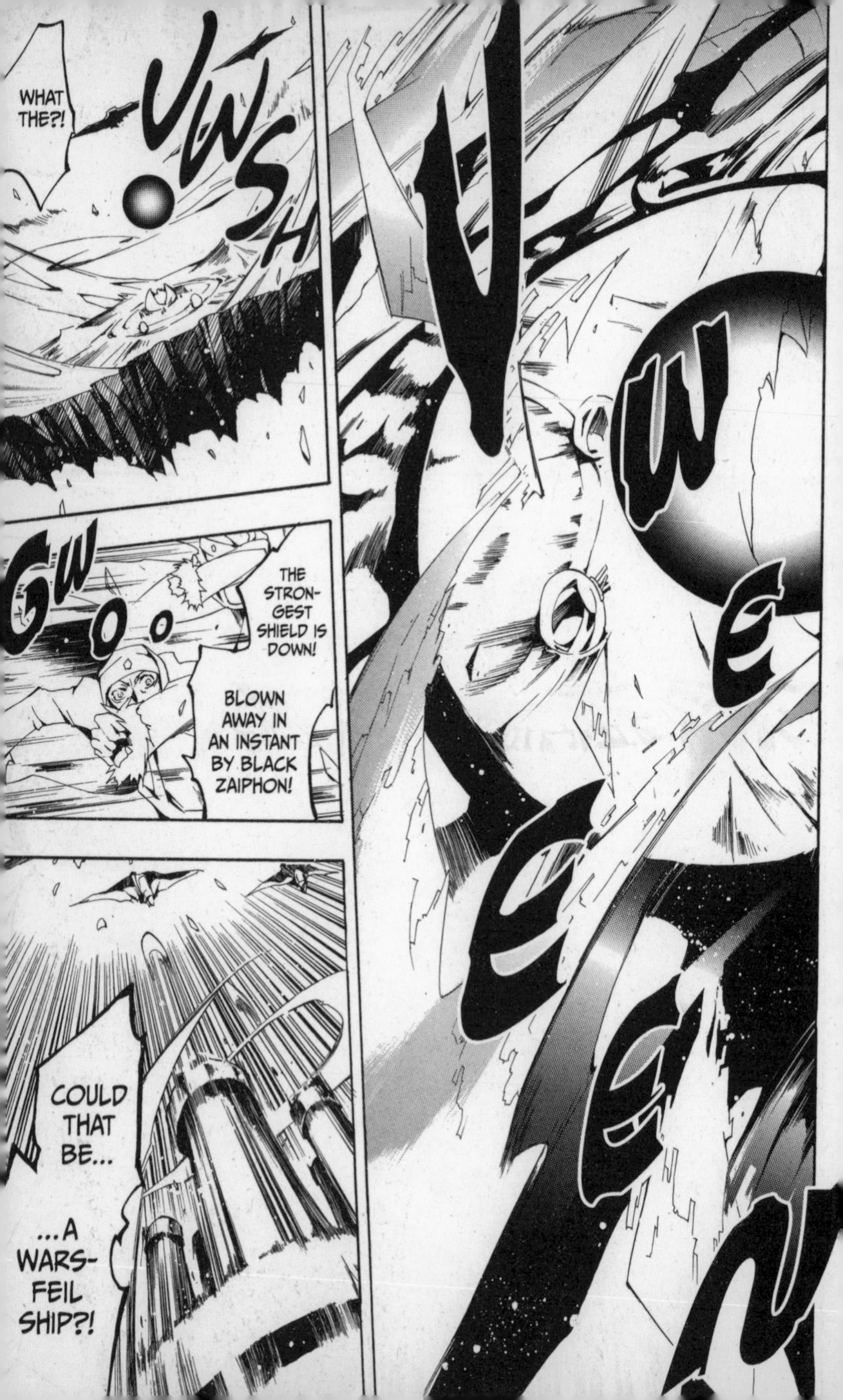
WHAT THE?!
GWOOO
THE STRONGEST SHIELD IS DOWN!
BLOWN AWAY IN AN INSTANT BY BLACK ZAIPHON!
COULD THAT BE...
...A WARSFEIL SHIP?!

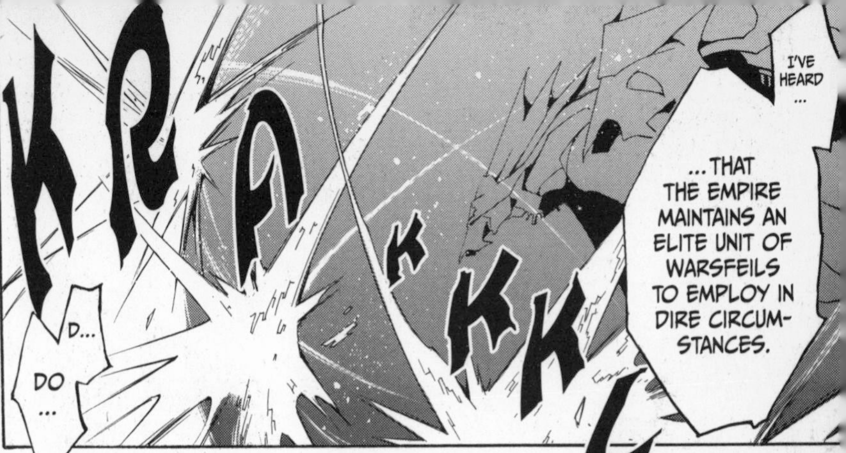
I'VE HEARD ...
...THAT THE EMPIRE MAINTAINS AN ELITE UNIT OF WARSFEILS TO EMPLOY IN DIRE CIRCUM-STANCES.
D... DO ...
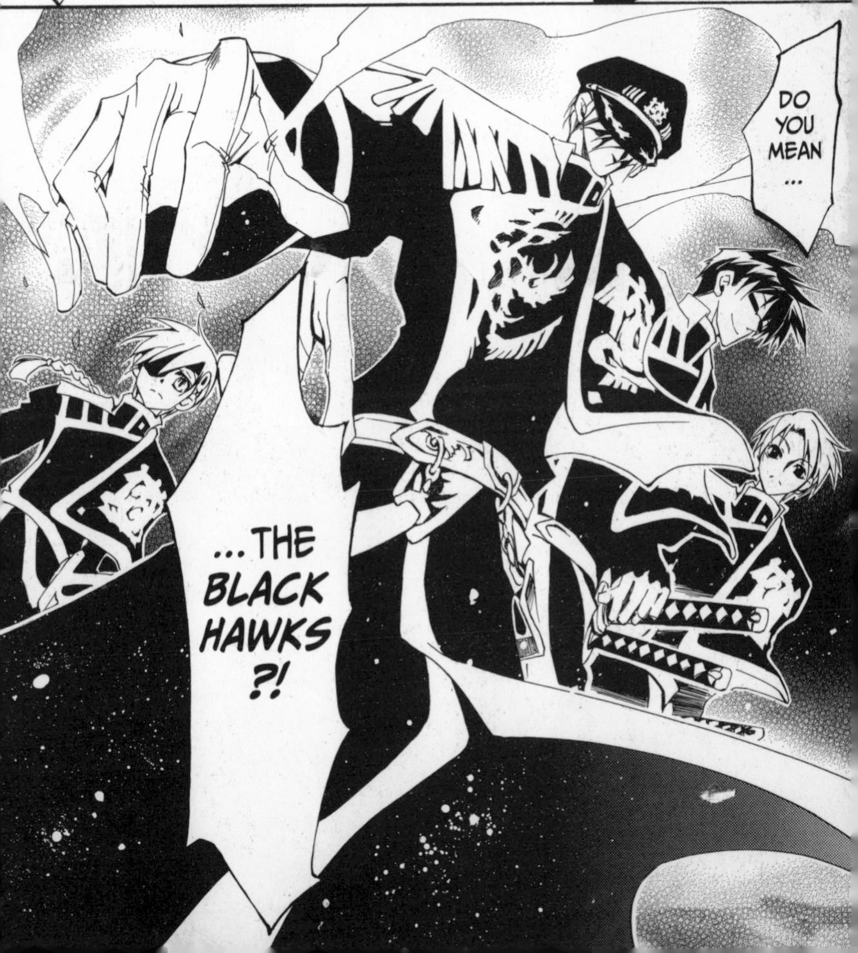
DO YOU MEAN ...
...THE BLACK HAWKS ?!

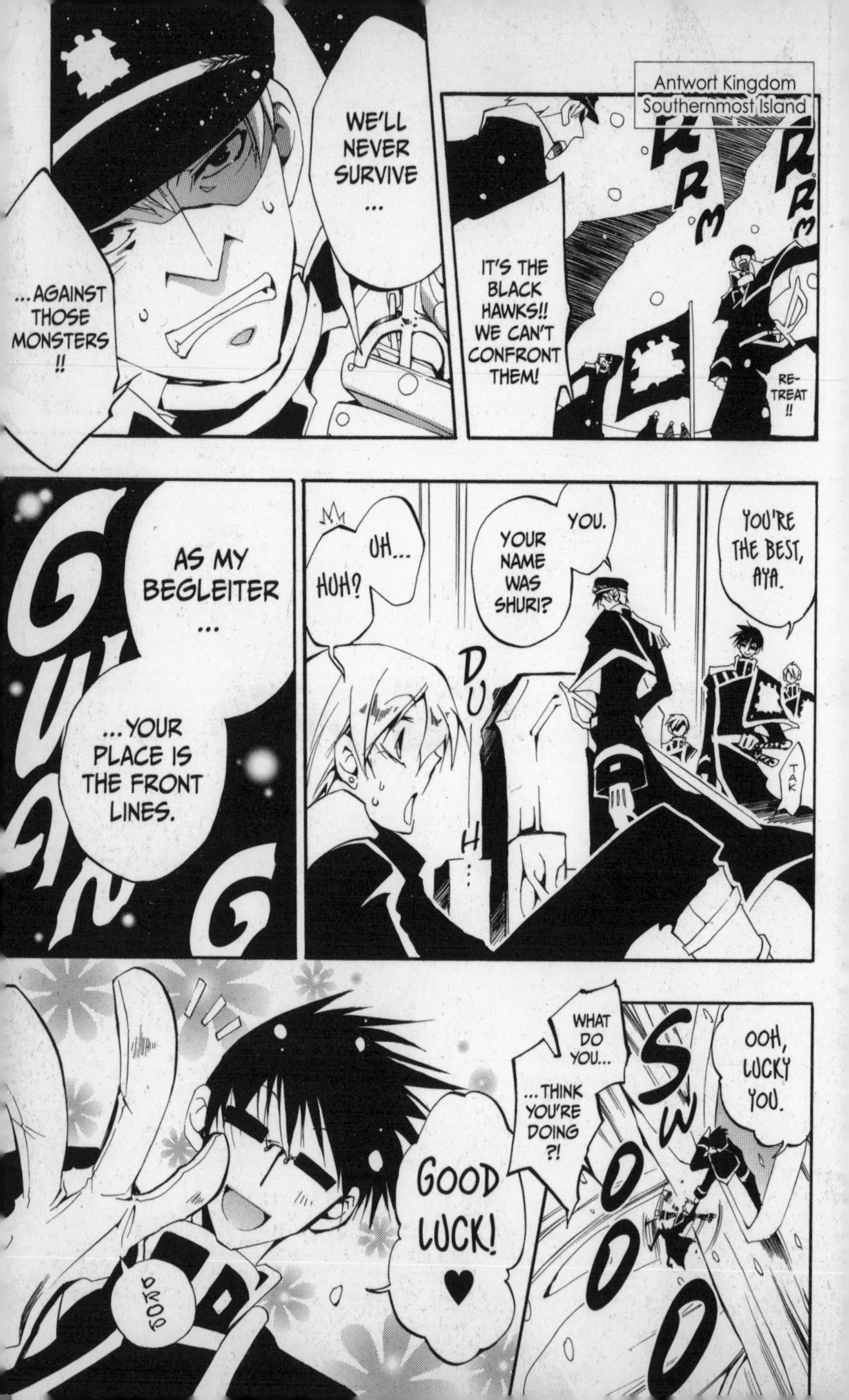
Antwort Kingdom
Southernmost Island
KRM
RRM
IT'S THE BLACK HAWKS!! WE CAN'T CONFRONT THEM!
RE-TREAT!!
WE'LL NEVER SURVIVE ...
...AGAINST THOSE MONSTERS !!
YOU'RE THE BEST, AYA.
YOU.
YOUR NAME WAS SHURI?
TAK
UH...
HUH?
DUH...
AS MY BEGLEITER ...
...YOUR PLACE IS THE FRONT LINES.
OOH, LUCKY YOU.
SWOOO
WHAT DO YOU...
...THINK YOU'RE DOING ?!
GOOD LUCK! ♥
DROP

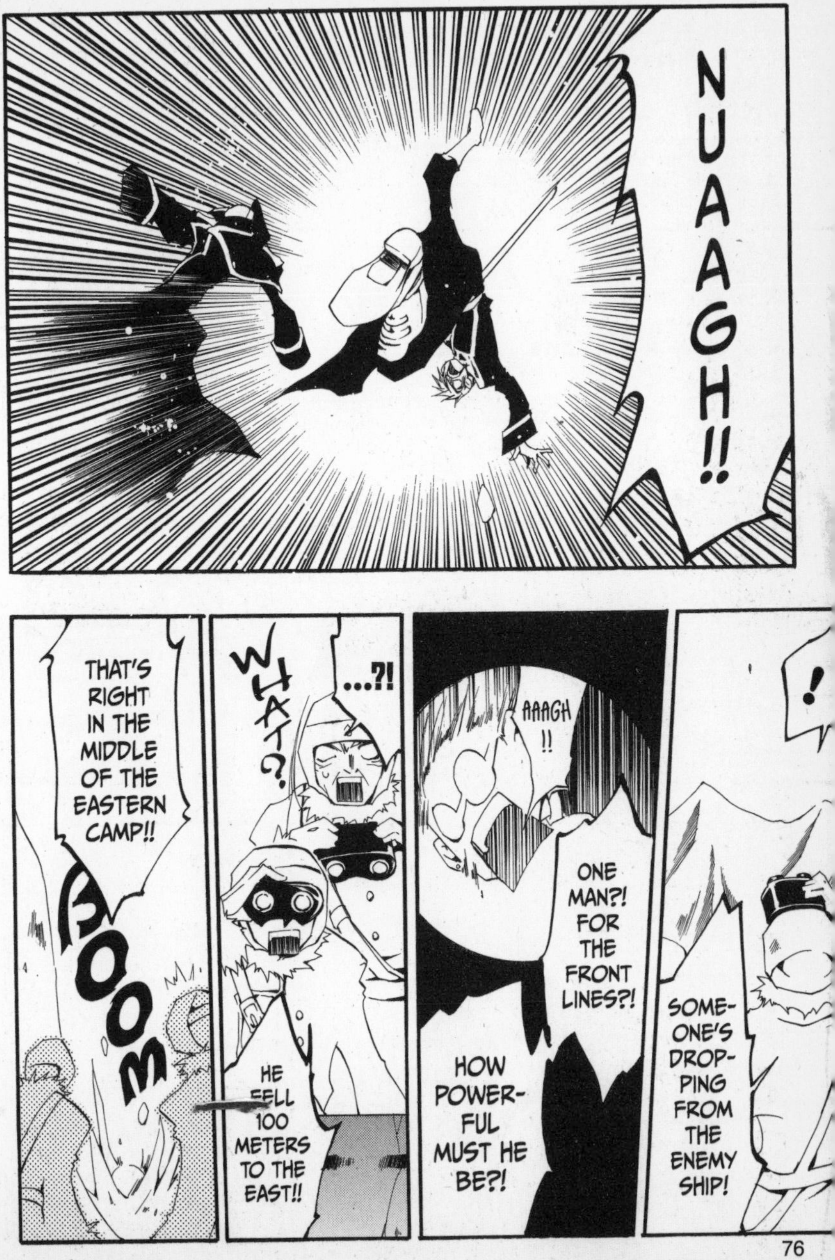
NUAAGH!!
!
SOME-ONE'S DROP-PING FROM THE ENEMY SHIP!
AAAGH !!
ONE MAN?! FOR THE FRONT LINES?!
HOW POWER-FUL MUST HE BE?!
...?!
WHAT?
HE FELL 100 METERS TO THE EAST!!
THAT'S RIGHT IN THE MIDDLE OF THE EASTERN CAMP!!
BOOM

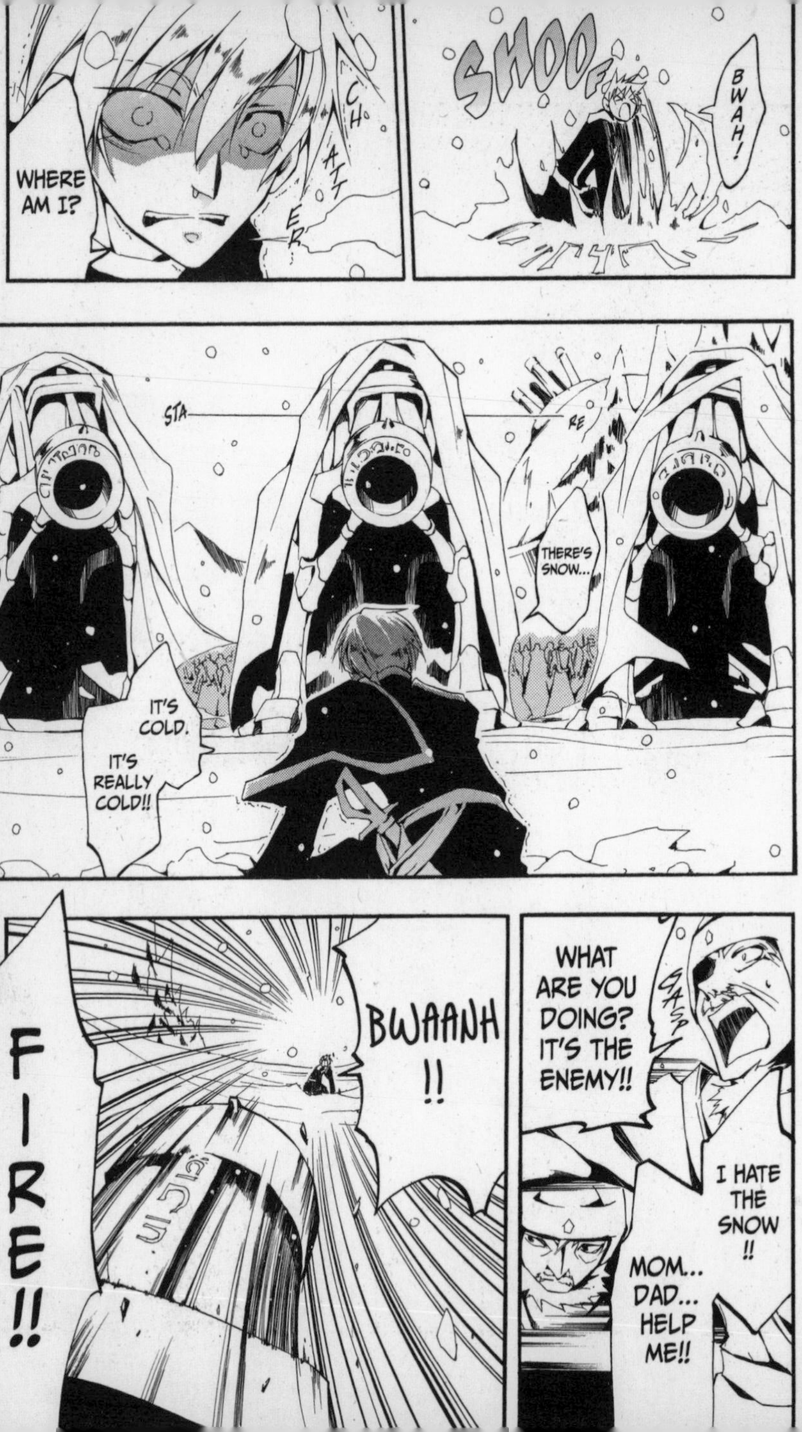
SHOOF
BWAH!
CHATTER
WHERE AM I?
STA RE
THERE'S SNOW...
IT'S COLD.
IT'S REALLY COLD!!
GASP
WHAT ARE YOU DOING? IT'S THE ENEMY!!
I HATE THE SNOW!!
MOM... DAD... HELP ME!!
BWAANH!!
FIRE!!

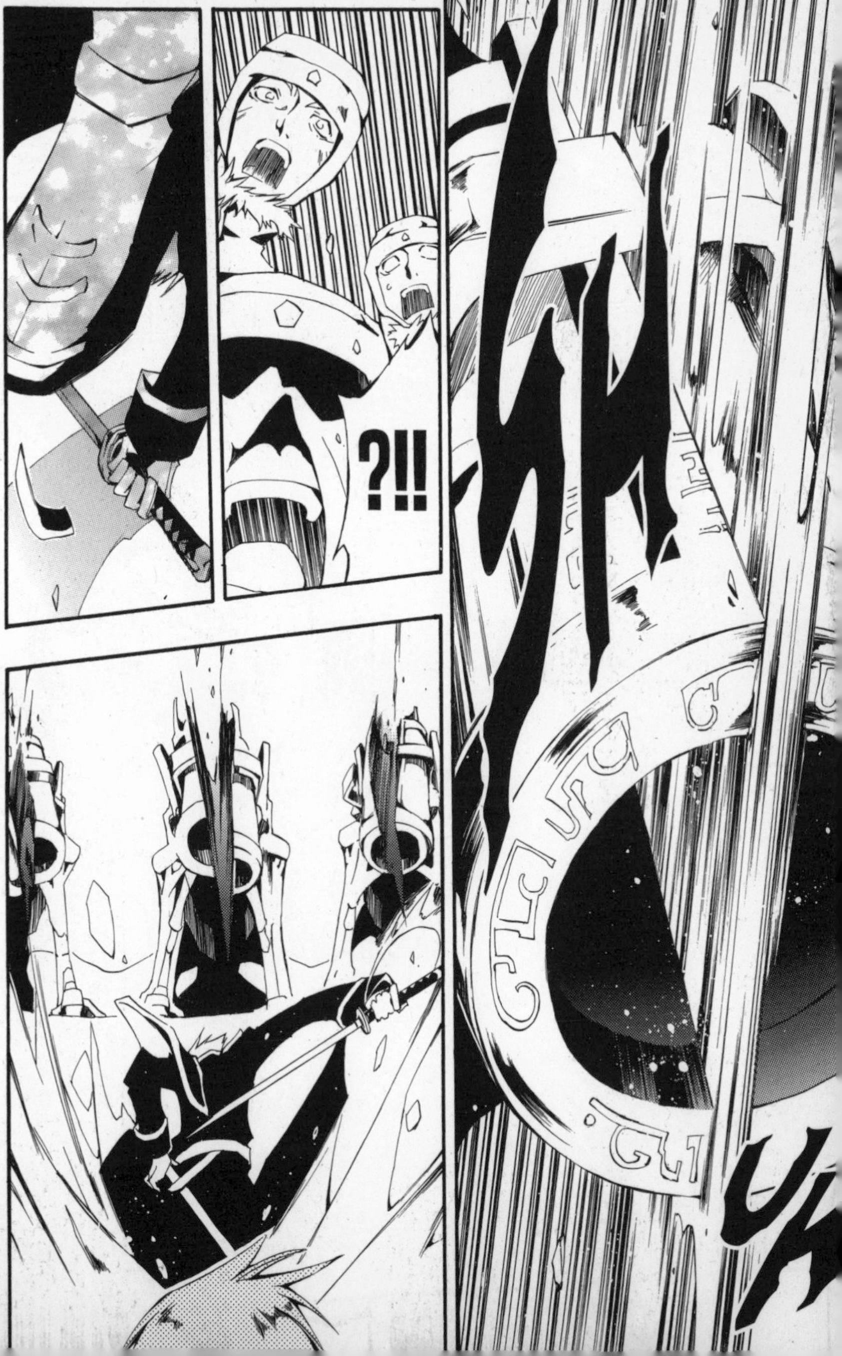
?!!

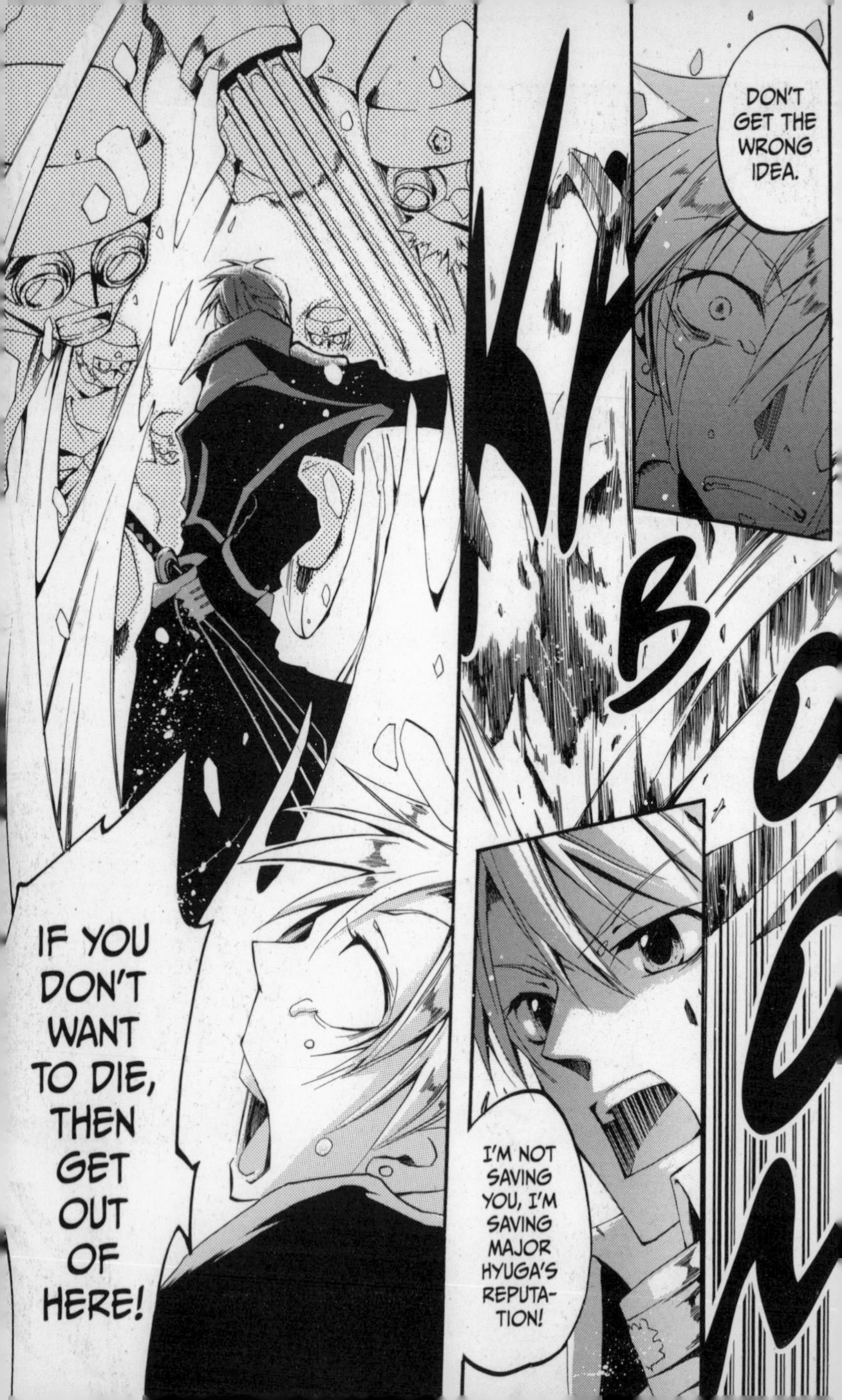
DON'T GET THE WRONG IDEA.
I'M NOT SAVING YOU, I'M SAVING MAJOR HYUGA'S REPUTATION!
IF YOU DON'T WANT TO DIE, THEN GET OUT OF HERE!

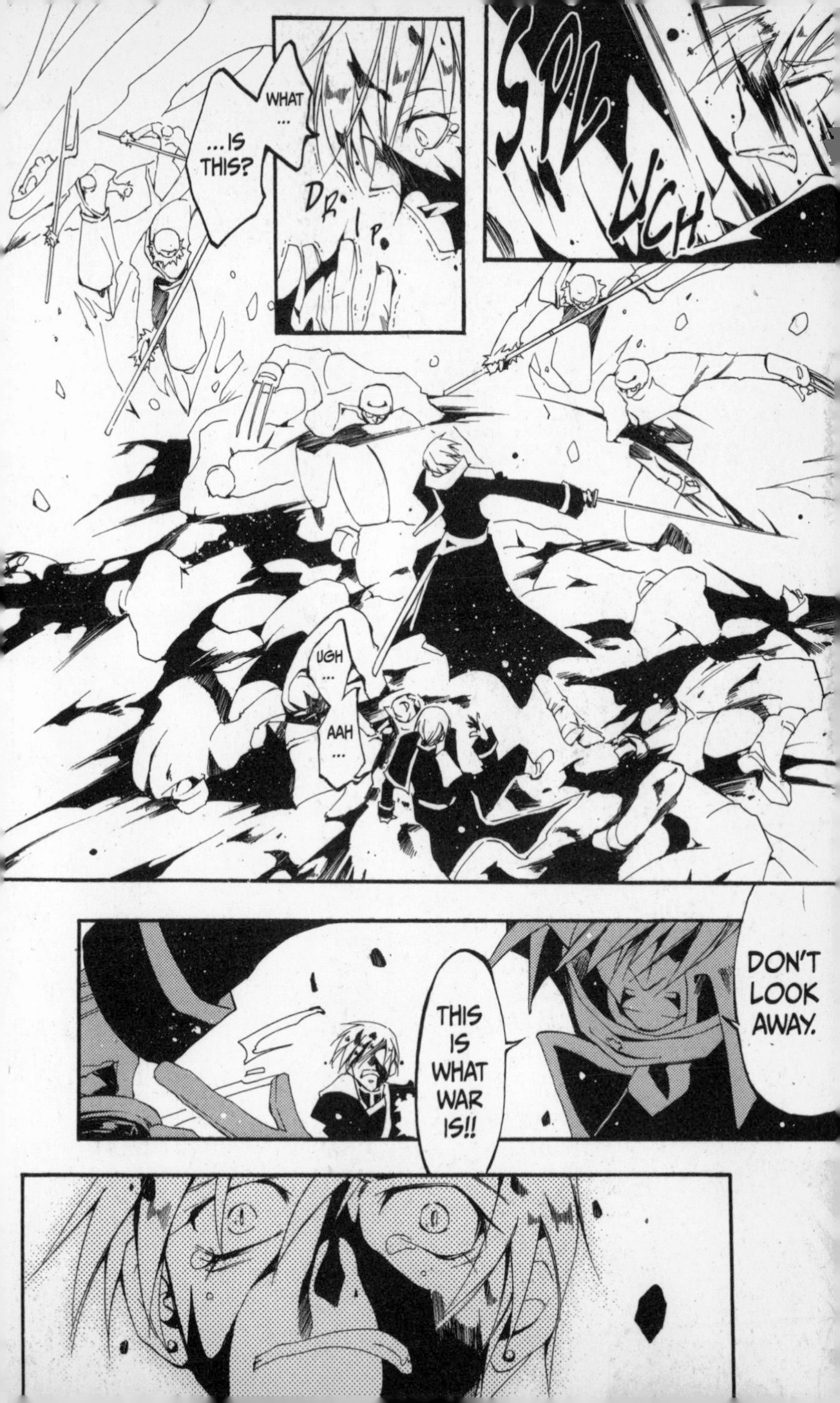
SPLUCH
WHAT ...
...IS THIS?
DRIP
UGH ...
AAH ...
DON'T LOOK AWAY.
THIS IS WHAT WAR IS!!

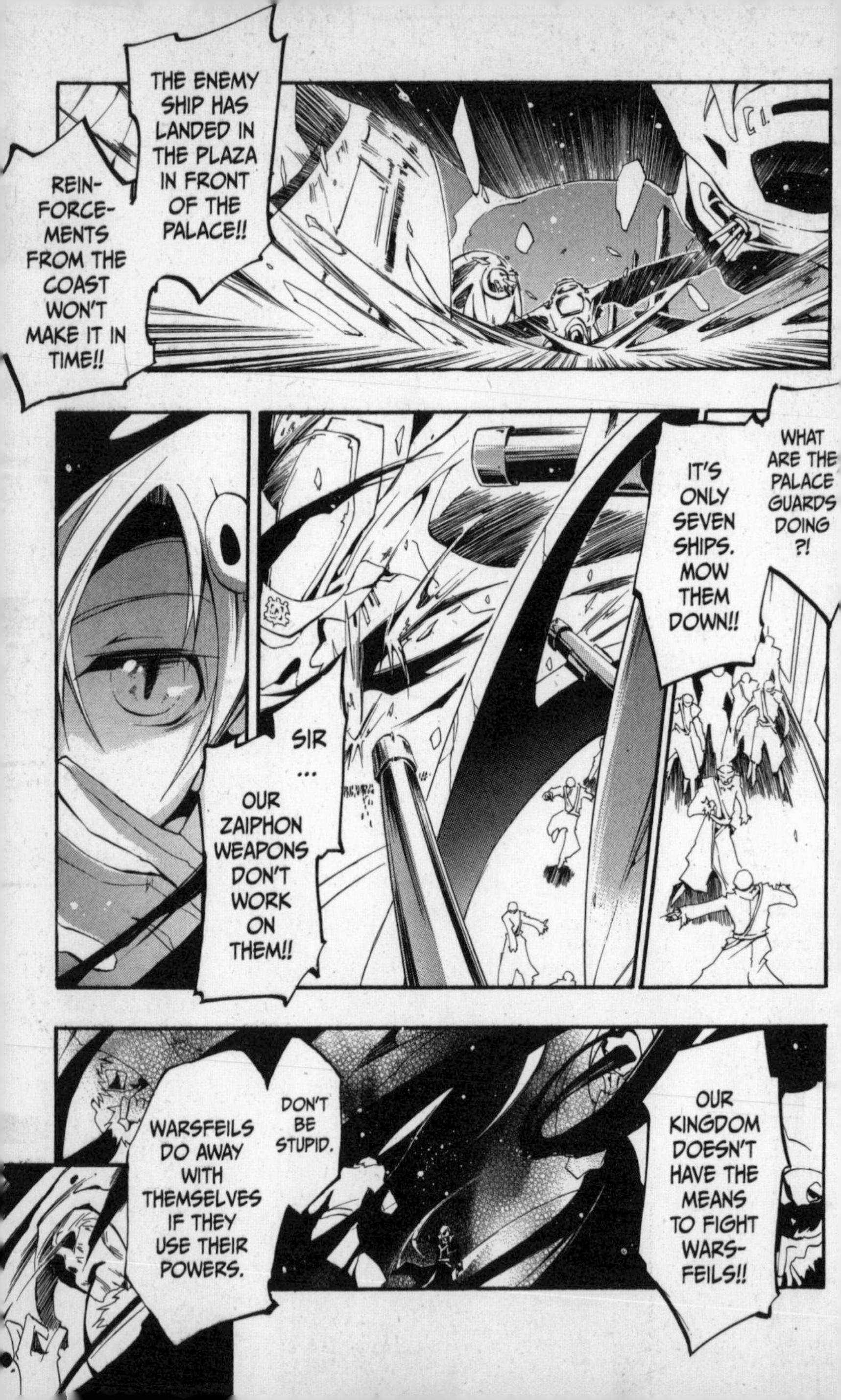
THE ENEMY SHIP HAS LANDED IN THE PLAZA IN FRONT OF THE PALACE!!
REIN-FORCE-MENTS FROM THE COAST WON'T MAKE IT IN TIME!!
WHAT ARE THE PALACE GUARDS DOING?!
IT'S ONLY SEVEN SHIPS. MOW THEM DOWN!!
SIR... OUR ZAIPHON WEAPONS DON'T WORK ON THEM!!
OUR KINGDOM DOESN'T HAVE THE MEANS TO FIGHT WARS-FEILS!!
DON'T BE STUPID.
WARSFEILS DO AWAY WITH THEMSELVES IF THEY USE THEIR POWERS.

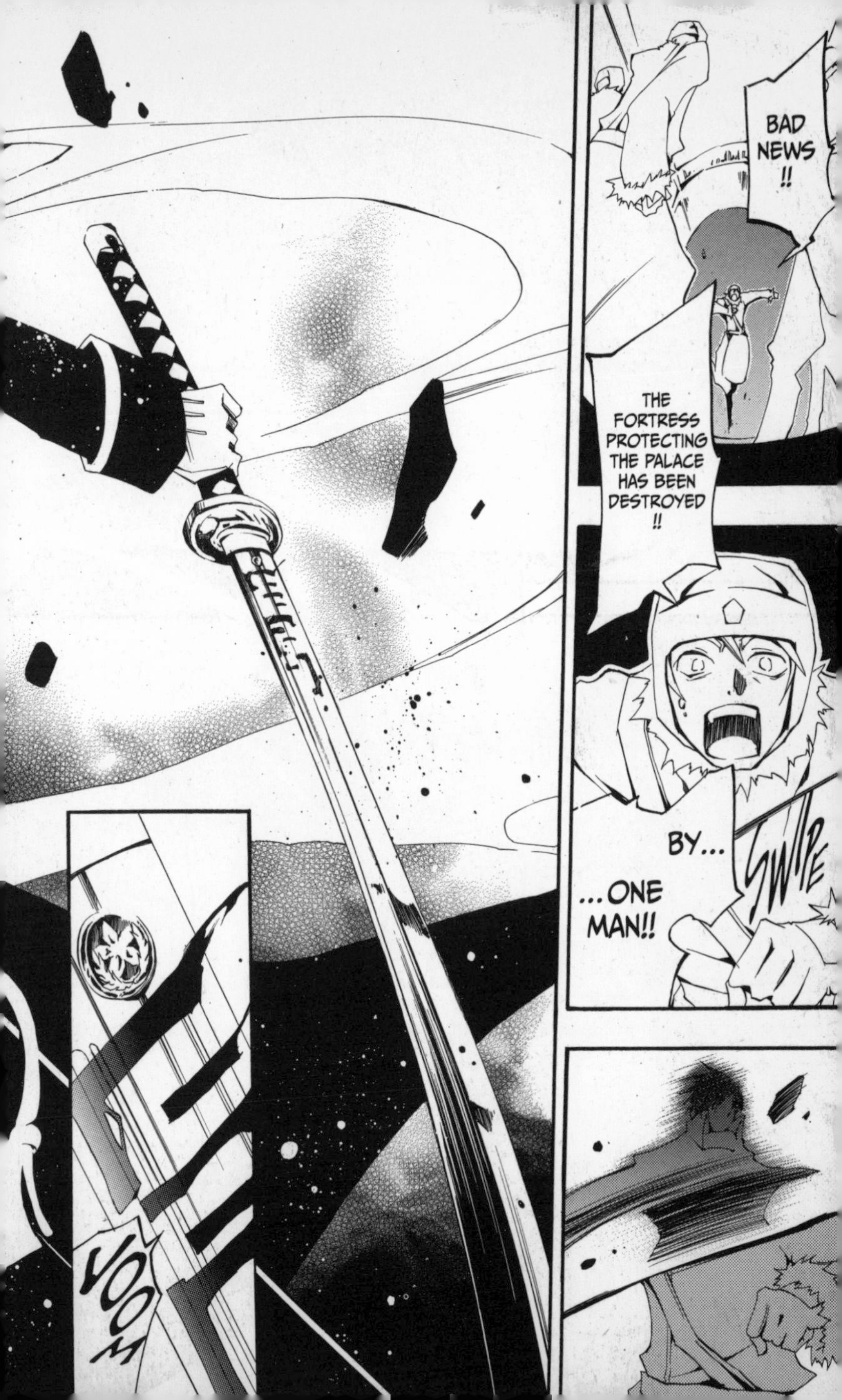
BAD NEWS!!
THE FORTRESS PROTECTING THE PALACE HAS BEEN DESTROYED!!
BY...
...ONE MAN!!
SWIPE
VOOM

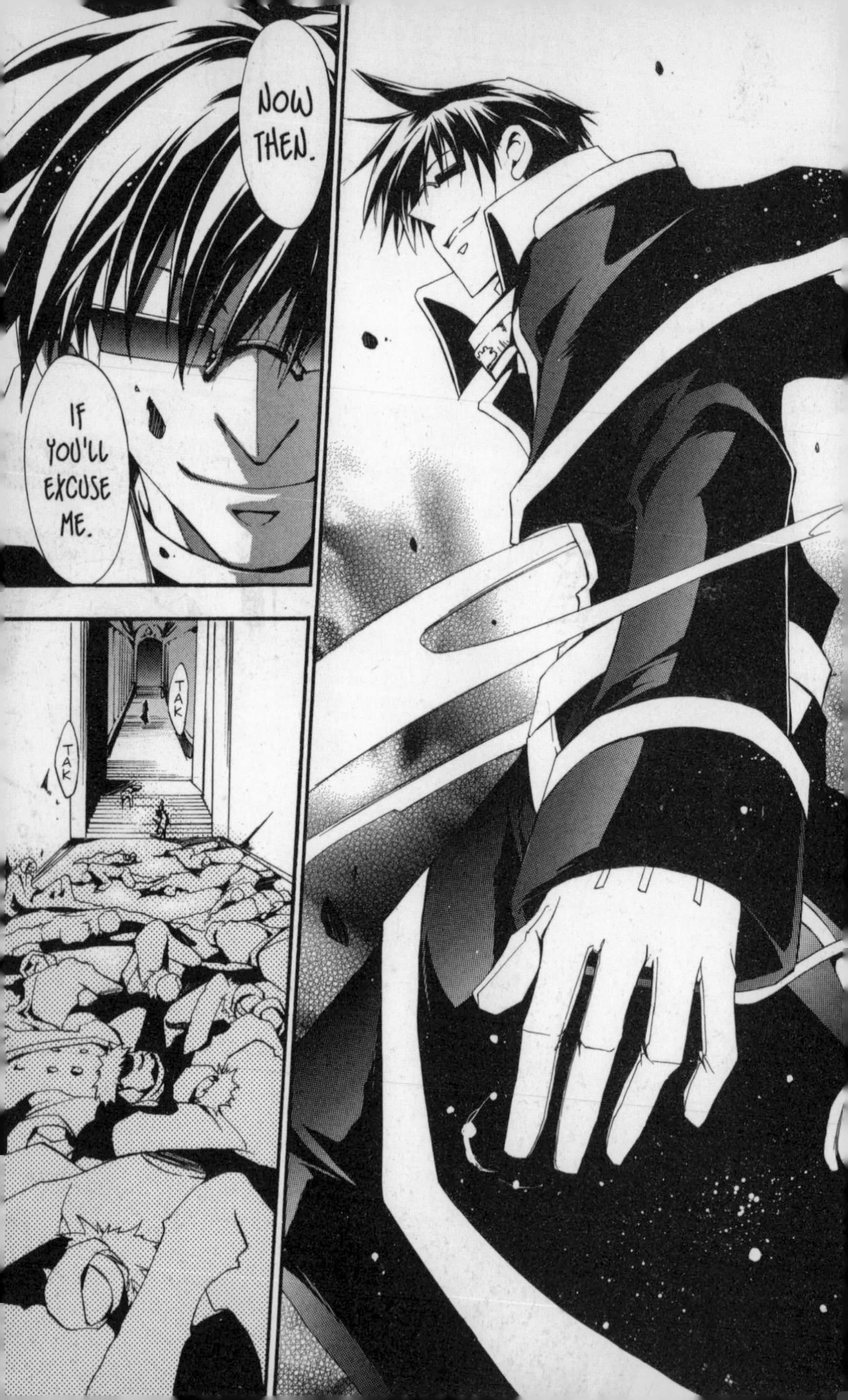
NOW THEN.
IF YOU'LL EXCUSE ME.
TAK
TAK

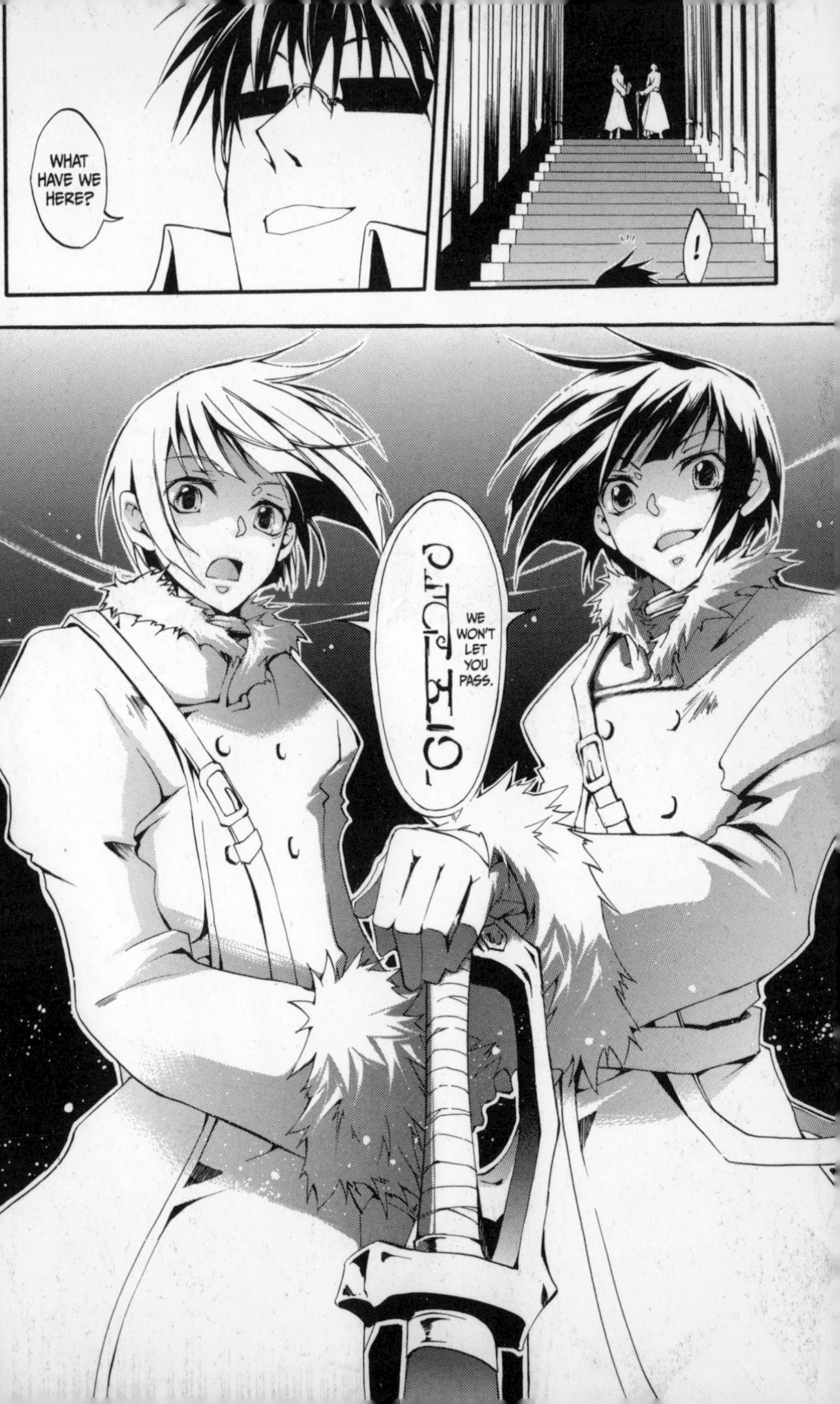
!
WHAT HAVE WE HERE?
WE WON'T LET YOU PASS.

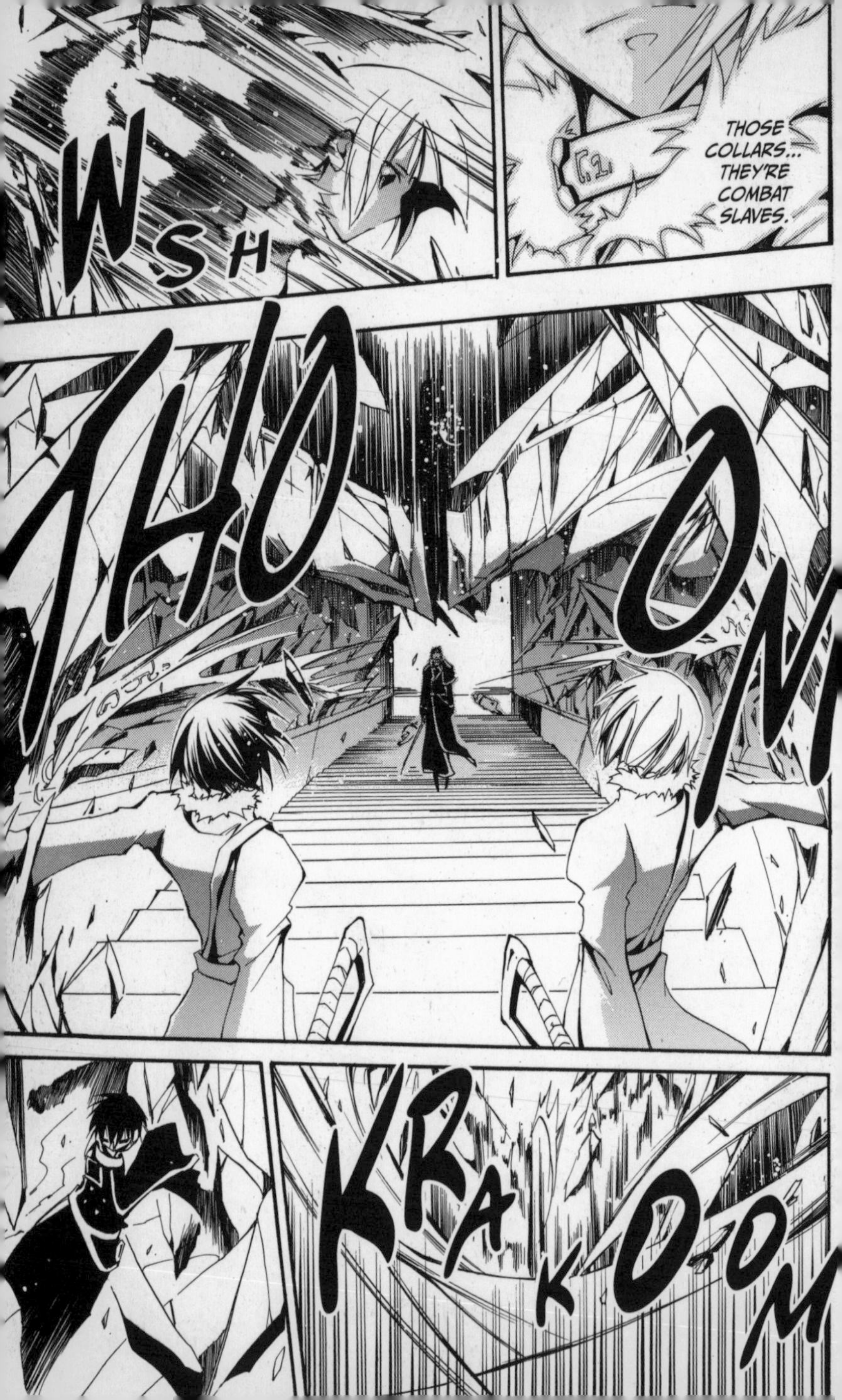
THOSE COLLARS... THEY'RE COMBAT SLAVES.
WSH
THOOM
KRAKOOM

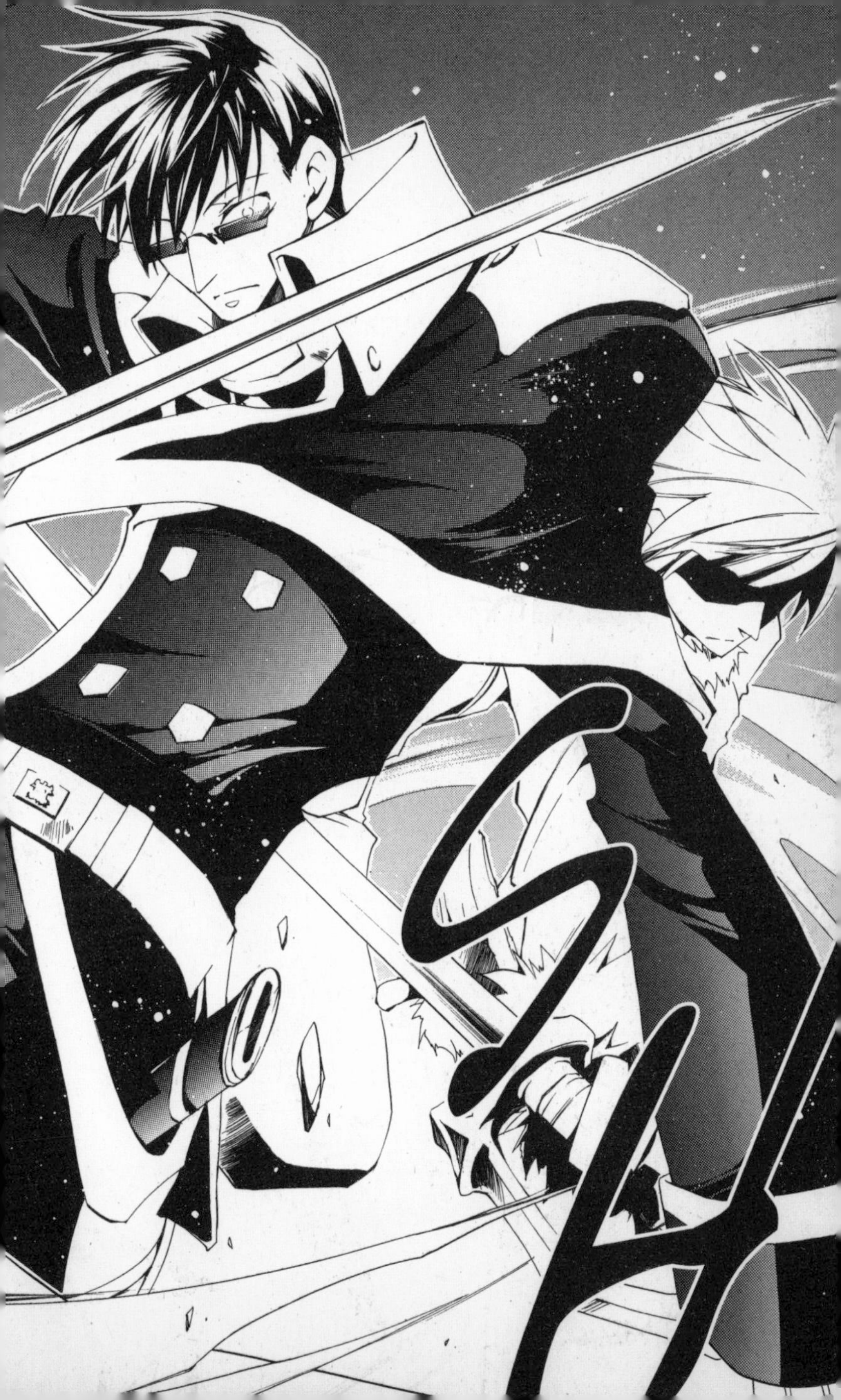

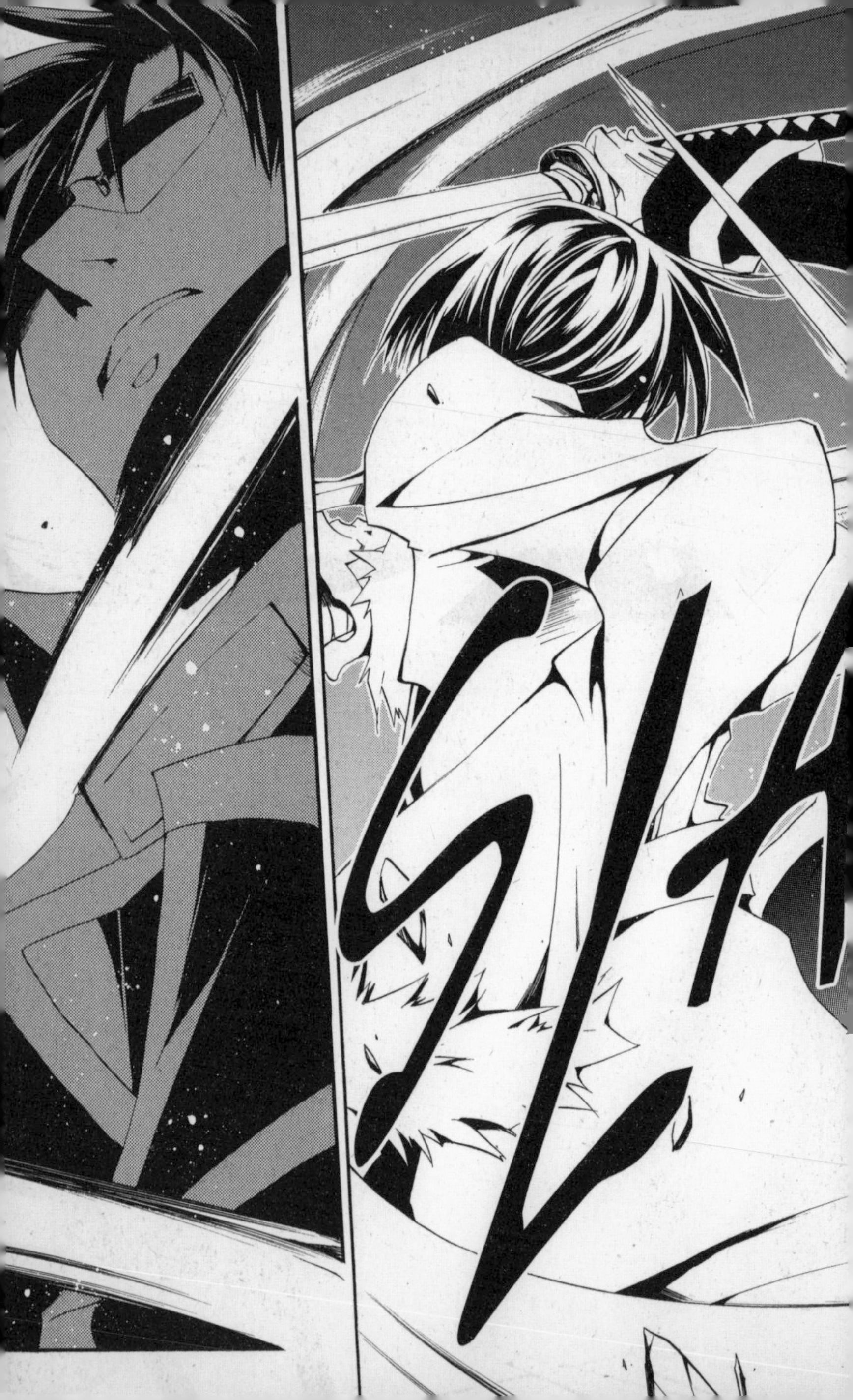

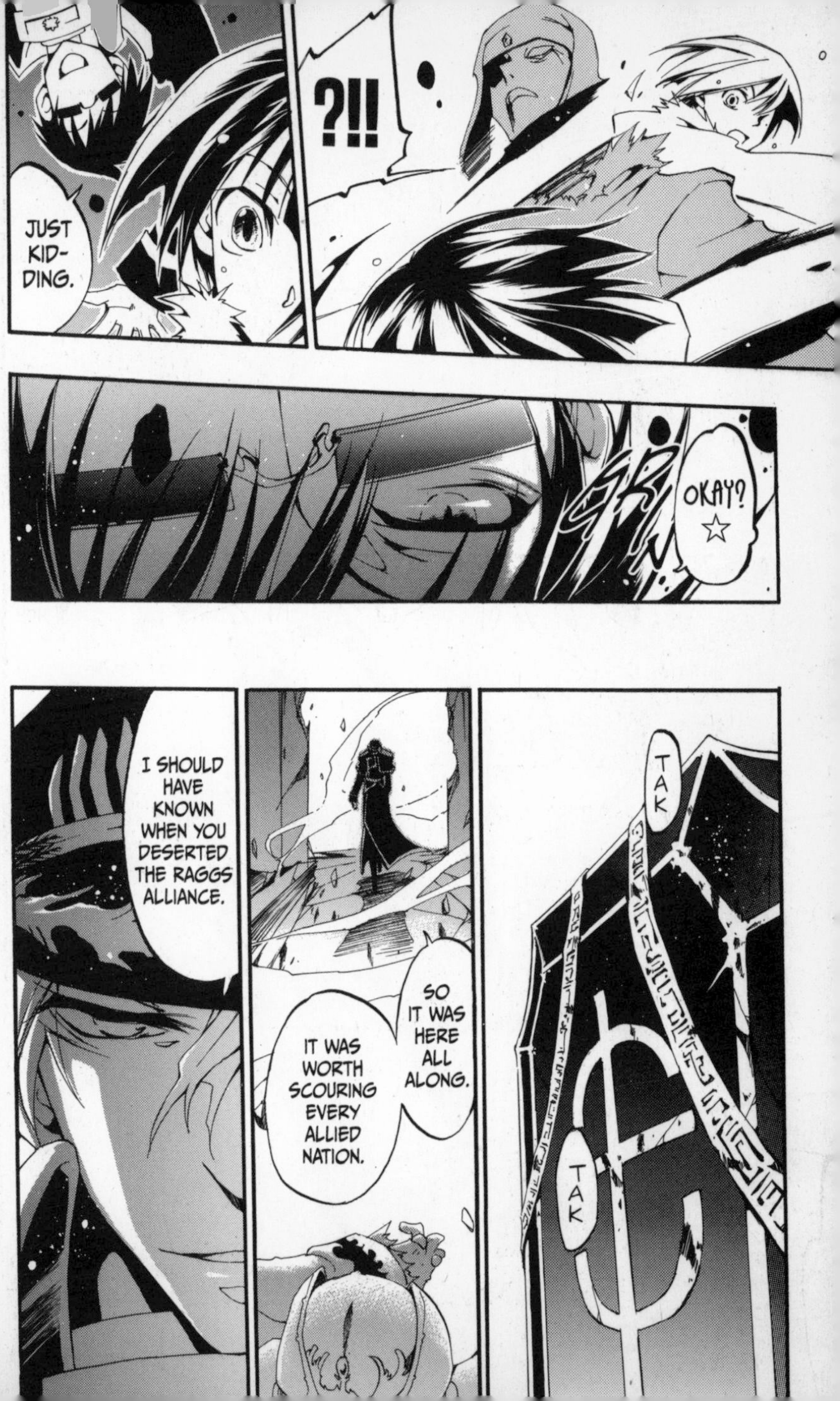
?!!
JUST KID-DING.
OKAY? ☆
TAK
TAK
SO IT WAS HERE ALL ALONG.
IT WAS WORTH SCOURING EVERY ALLIED NATION.
I SHOULD HAVE KNOWN WHEN YOU DESERTED THE RAGGS ALLIANCE.

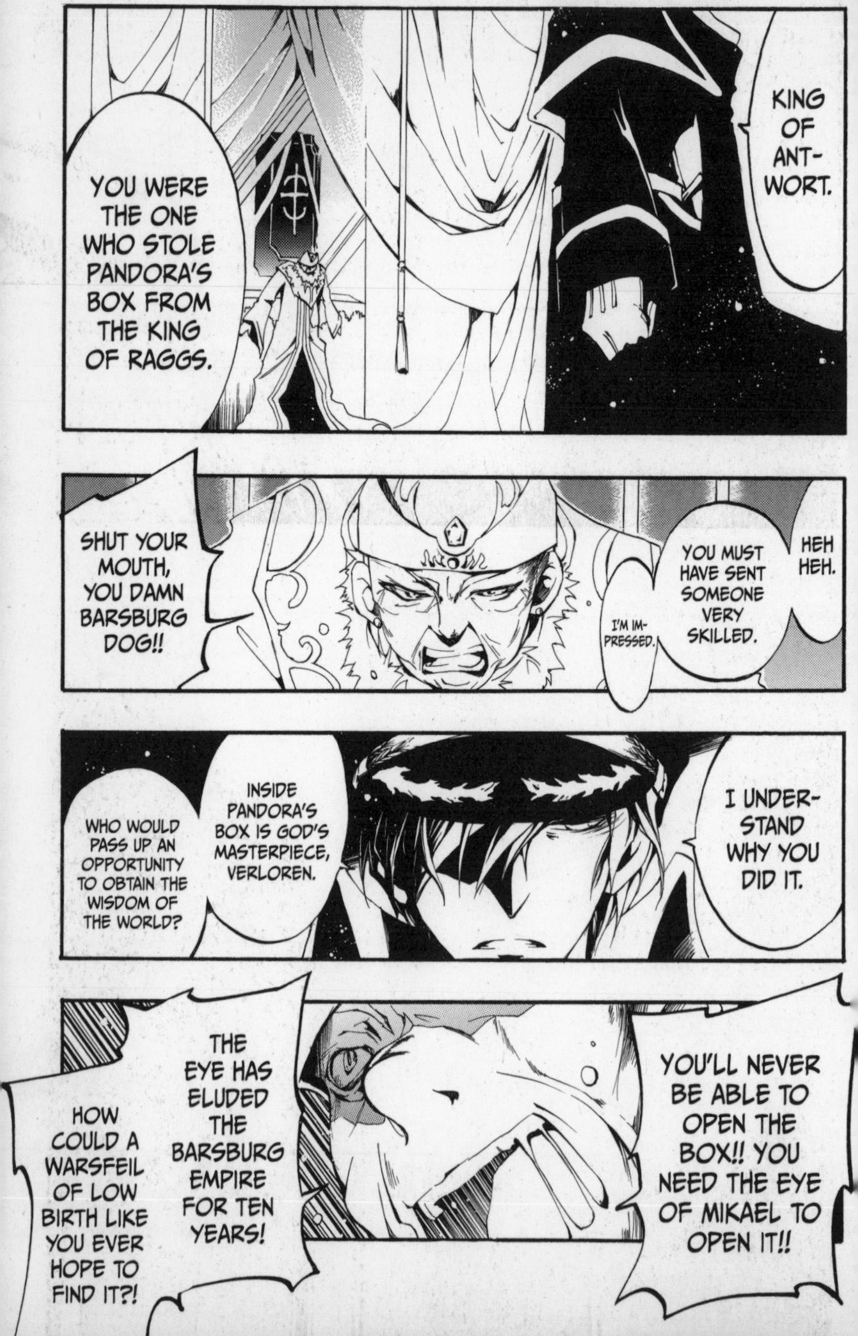
KING OF ANT-WORT.
YOU WERE THE ONE WHO STOLE PANDORA'S BOX FROM THE KING OF RAGGS.
HEH HEH.
YOU MUST HAVE SENT SOMEONE VERY SKILLED.
I'M IM-PRESSED.
SHUT YOUR MOUTH, YOU DAMN BARSBURG DOG!!
I UNDER-STAND WHY YOU DID IT.
INSIDE PANDORA'S BOX IS GOD'S MASTERPIECE, VERLOREN.
WHO WOULD PASS UP AN OPPORTUNITY TO OBTAIN THE WISDOM OF THE WORLD?
YOU'LL NEVER BE ABLE TO OPEN THE BOX!! YOU NEED THE EYE OF MIKAEL TO OPEN IT!!
THE EYE HAS ELUDED THE BARSBURG EMPIRE FOR TEN YEARS!
HOW COULD A WARSFEIL OF LOW BIRTH LIKE YOU EVER HOPE TO FIND IT?!

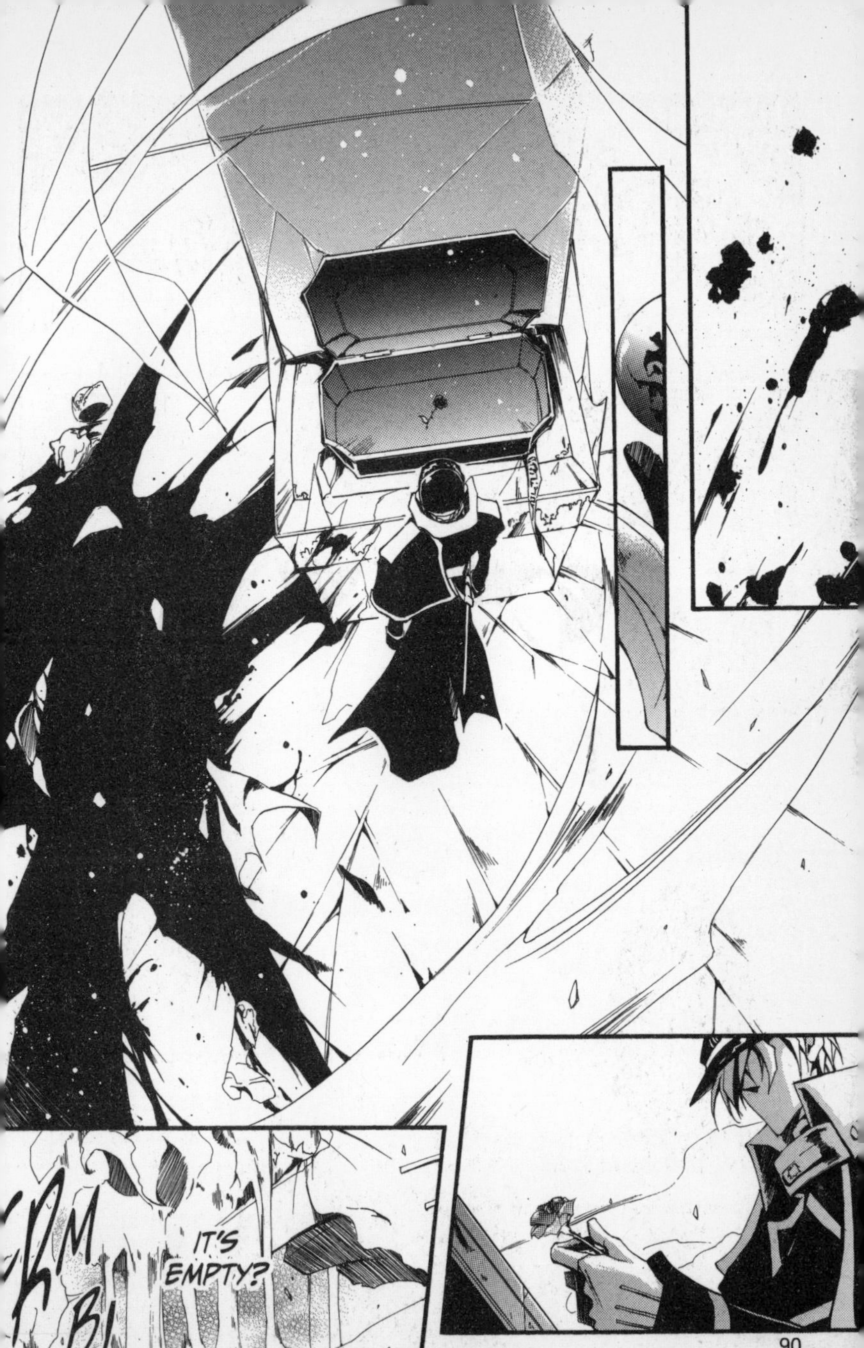
RMBL...
IT'S EMPTY?

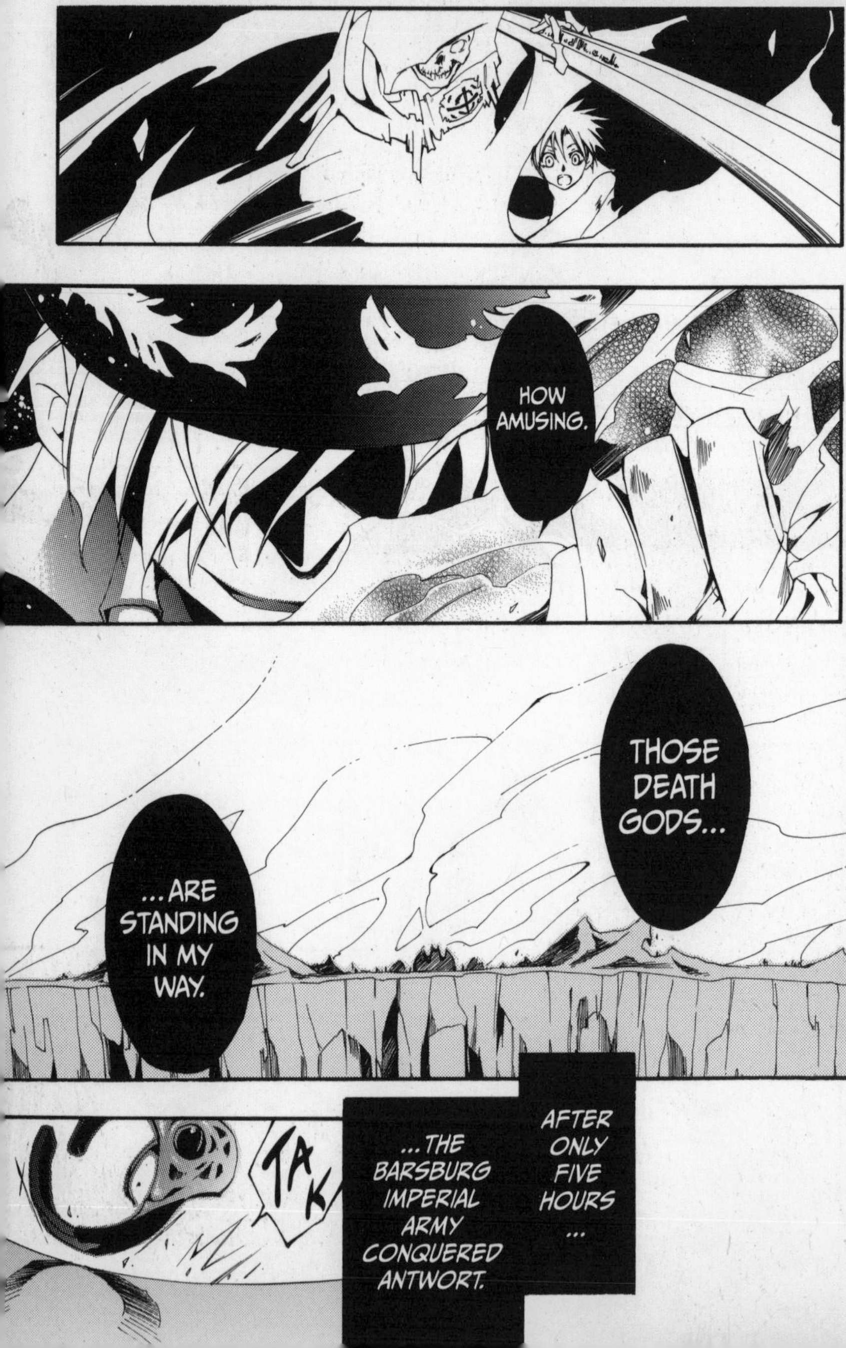
HOW AMUSING.
THOSE DEATH GODS...
...ARE STANDING IN MY WAY.
AFTER ONLY FIVE HOURS ...
...THE BARSBURG IMPERIAL ARMY CONQUERED ANTWORT.
TAK

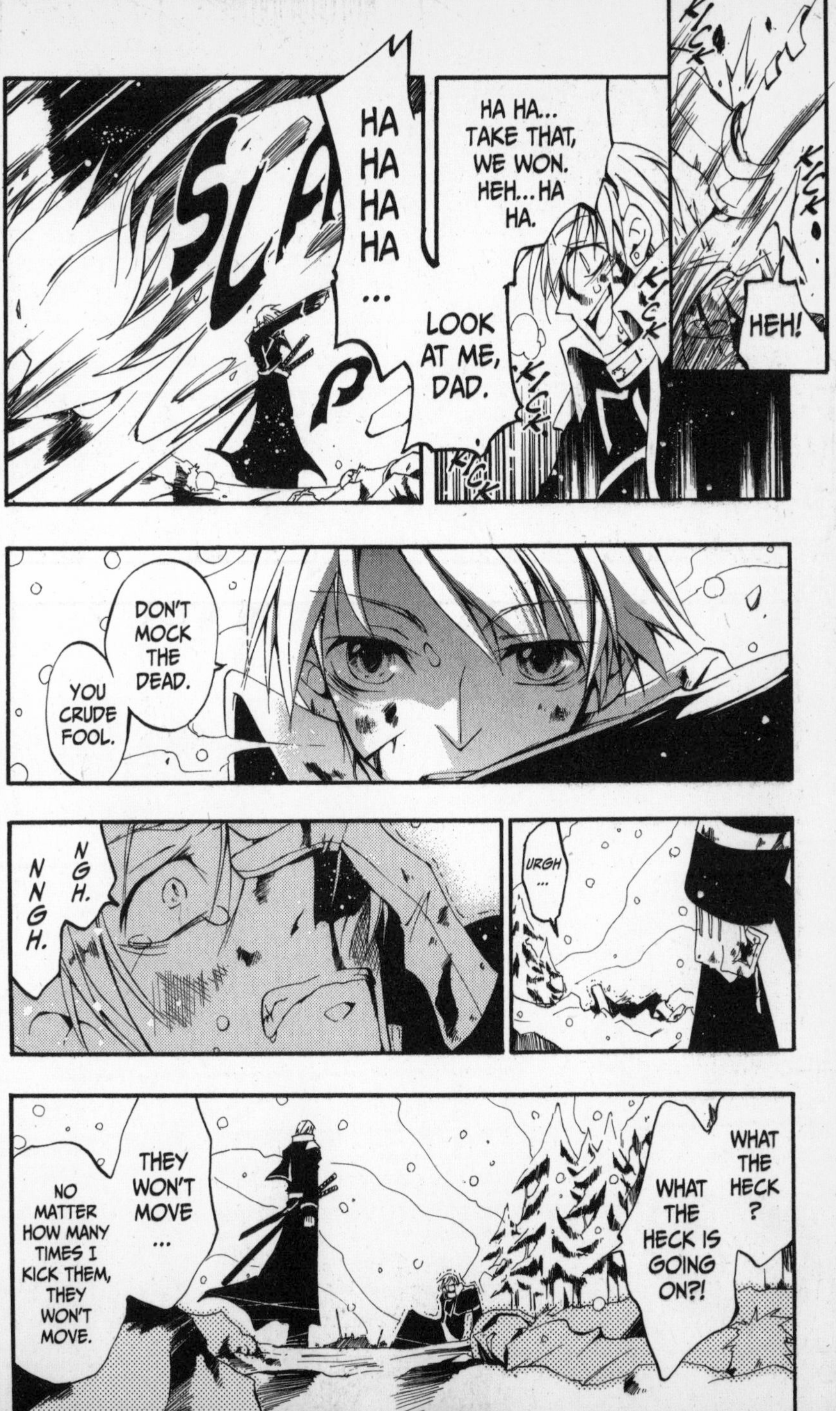
KICK
KICK
HEH!
HA HA... TAKE THAT, WE WON. HEH... HA HA.
LOOK AT ME, DAD.
KICK
KICK
KICK
KICK
SLA
HA HA HA HA ...
DON'T MOCK THE DEAD.
YOU CRUDE FOOL.
URGH ...
NGH.
NNGH.
WHAT THE HECK?
WHAT THE HECK IS GOING ON?!
THEY WON'T MOVE ...
NO MATTER HOW MANY TIMES I KICK THEM, THEY WON'T MOVE.

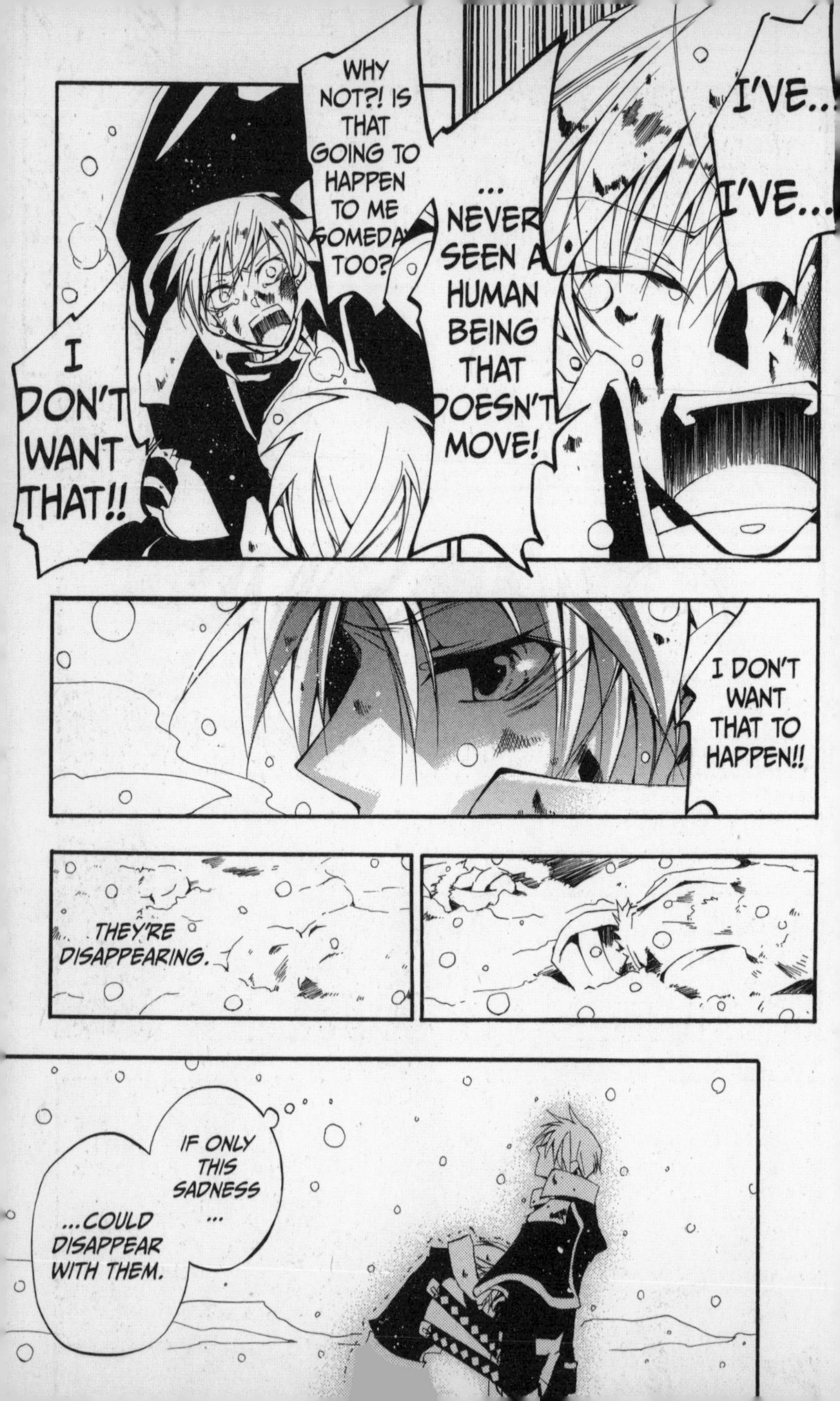
I'VE... I'VE...
...NEVER SEEN A HUMAN BEING THAT DOESN'T MOVE!
WHY NOT?! IS THAT GOING TO HAPPEN TO ME SOMEDAY TOO?
I DON'T WANT THAT!!
I DON'T WANT THAT TO HAPPEN!!
THEY'RE DISAPPEARING.
IF ONLY THIS SADNESS ...
...COULD DISAPPEAR WITH THEM.

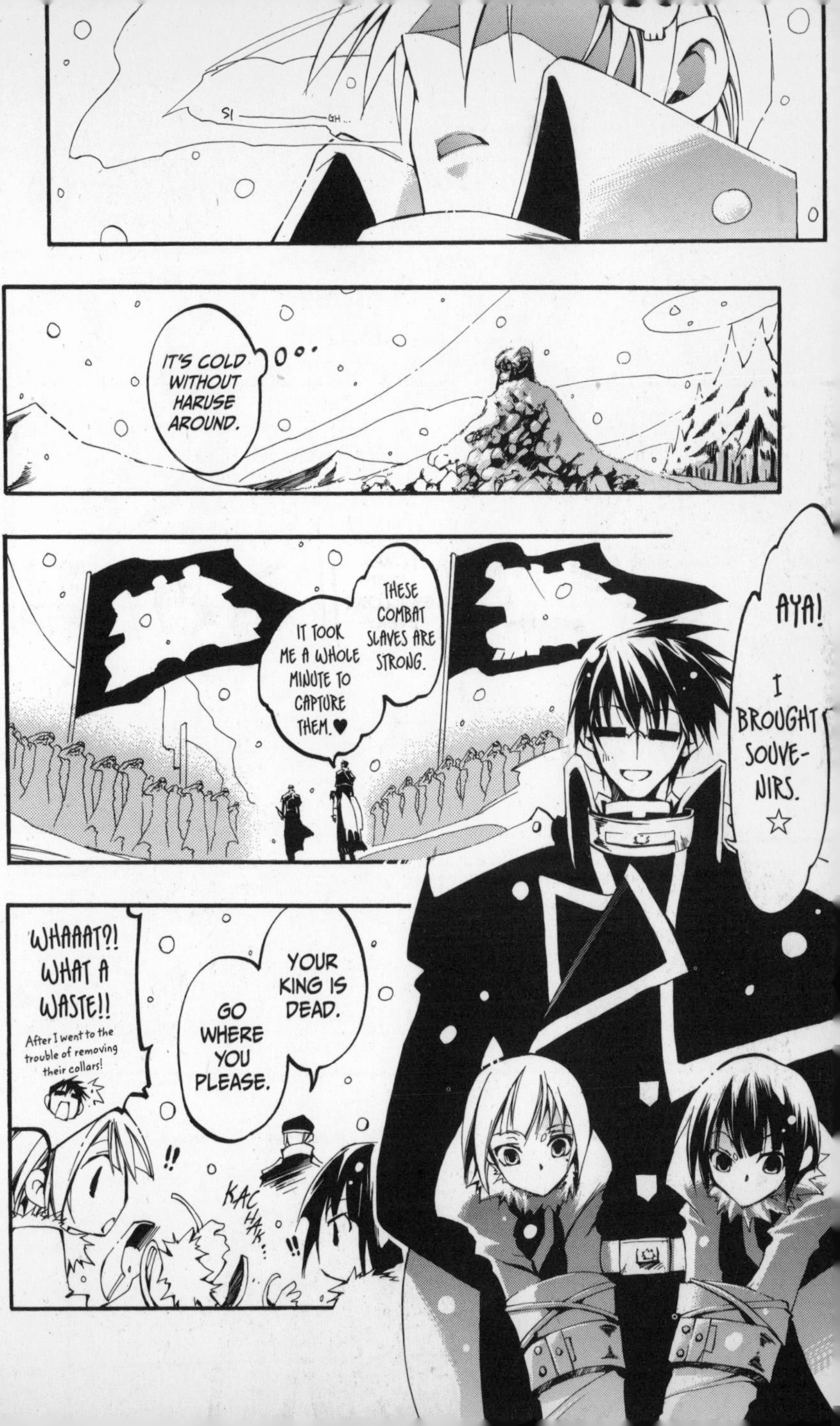

SI——GH...
IT'S COLD WITHOUT HARUSE AROUND.
AYA! I BROUGHT SOUVE-NIRS. ☆
THESE COMBAT SLAVES ARE STRONG.
IT TOOK ME A WHOLE MINUTE TO CAPTURE THEM.♥
YOUR KING IS DEAD.
GO WHERE YOU PLEASE.
WHAAAT?! WHAT A WASTE!!
After I went to the trouble of removing their collars!
!!
KACHAK...
!!

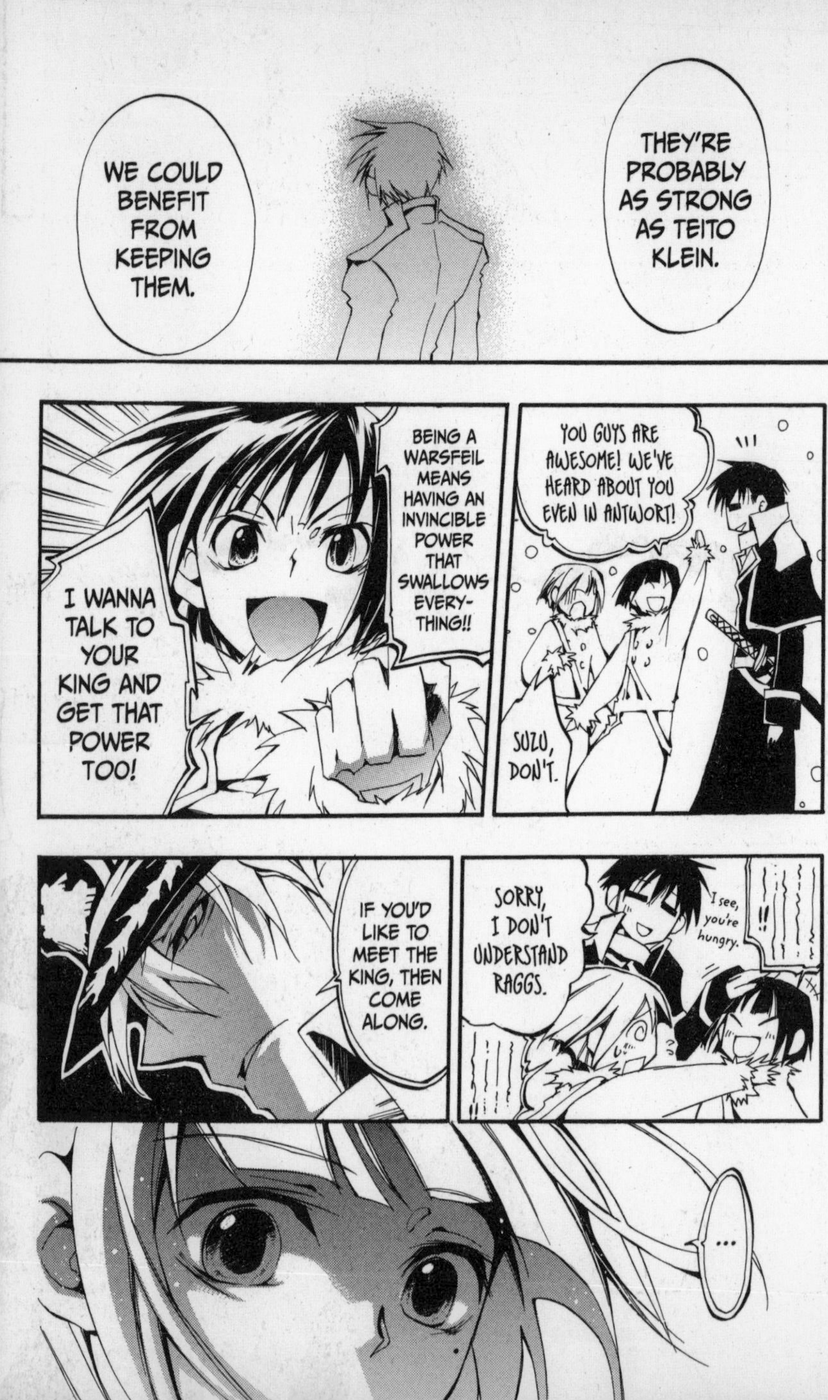
THEY'RE PROBABLY AS STRONG AS TEITO KLEIN.
WE COULD BENEFIT FROM KEEPING THEM.
YOU GUYS ARE AWESOME! WE'VE HEARD ABOUT YOU EVEN IN ANTWORT!
SUZU, DON'T.
BEING A WARSFEIL MEANS HAVING AN INVINCIBLE POWER THAT SWALLOWS EVERY-THING!!
I WANNA TALK TO YOUR KING AND GET THAT POWER TOO!
SORRY, I DON'T UNDERSTAND RAGGS.
I see, you're hungry.
IF YOU'D LIKE TO MEET THE KING, THEN COME ALONG.
...

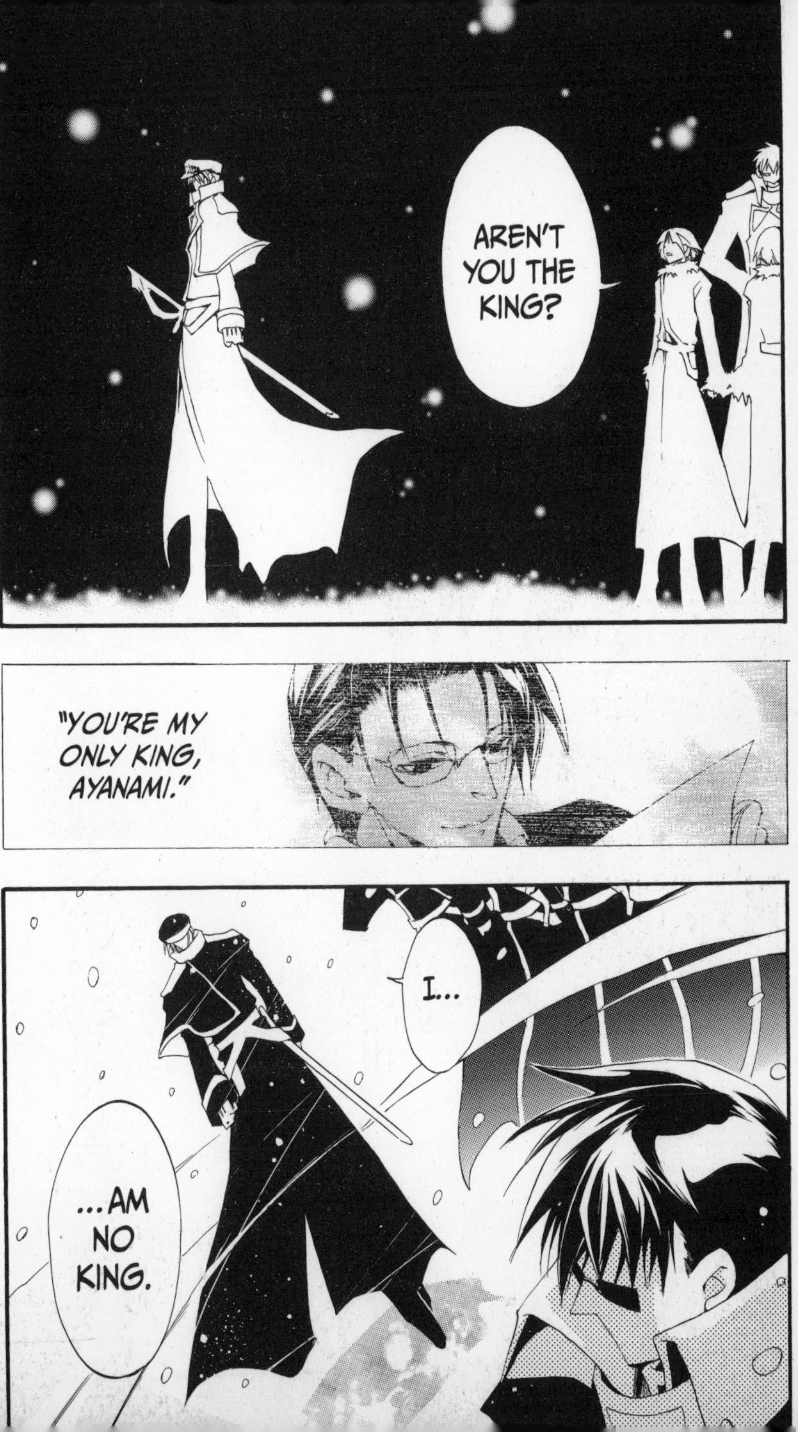
AREN'T YOU THE KING?
"YOU'RE MY ONLY KING, AYANAMI."
I...
...AM NO KING.

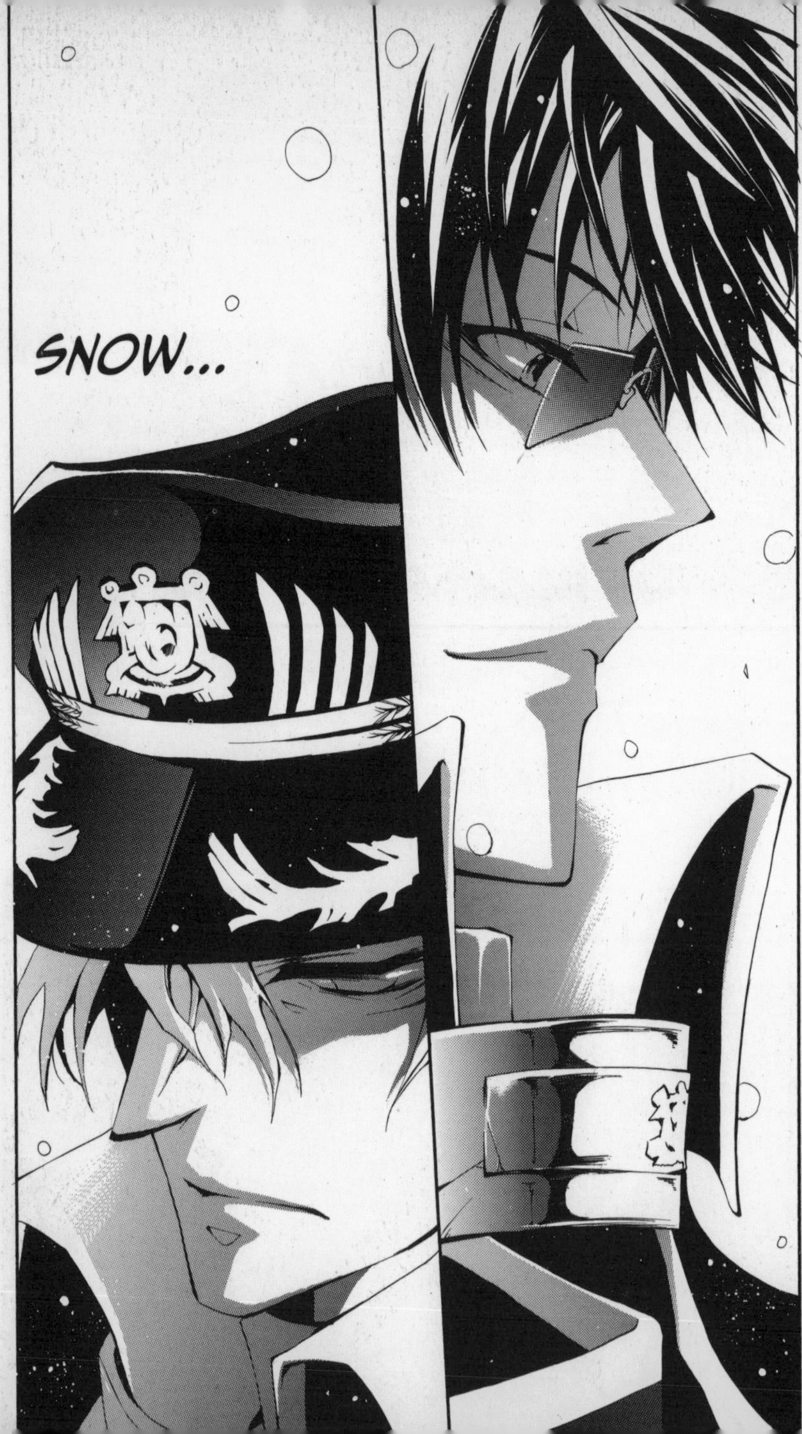
SNOW...

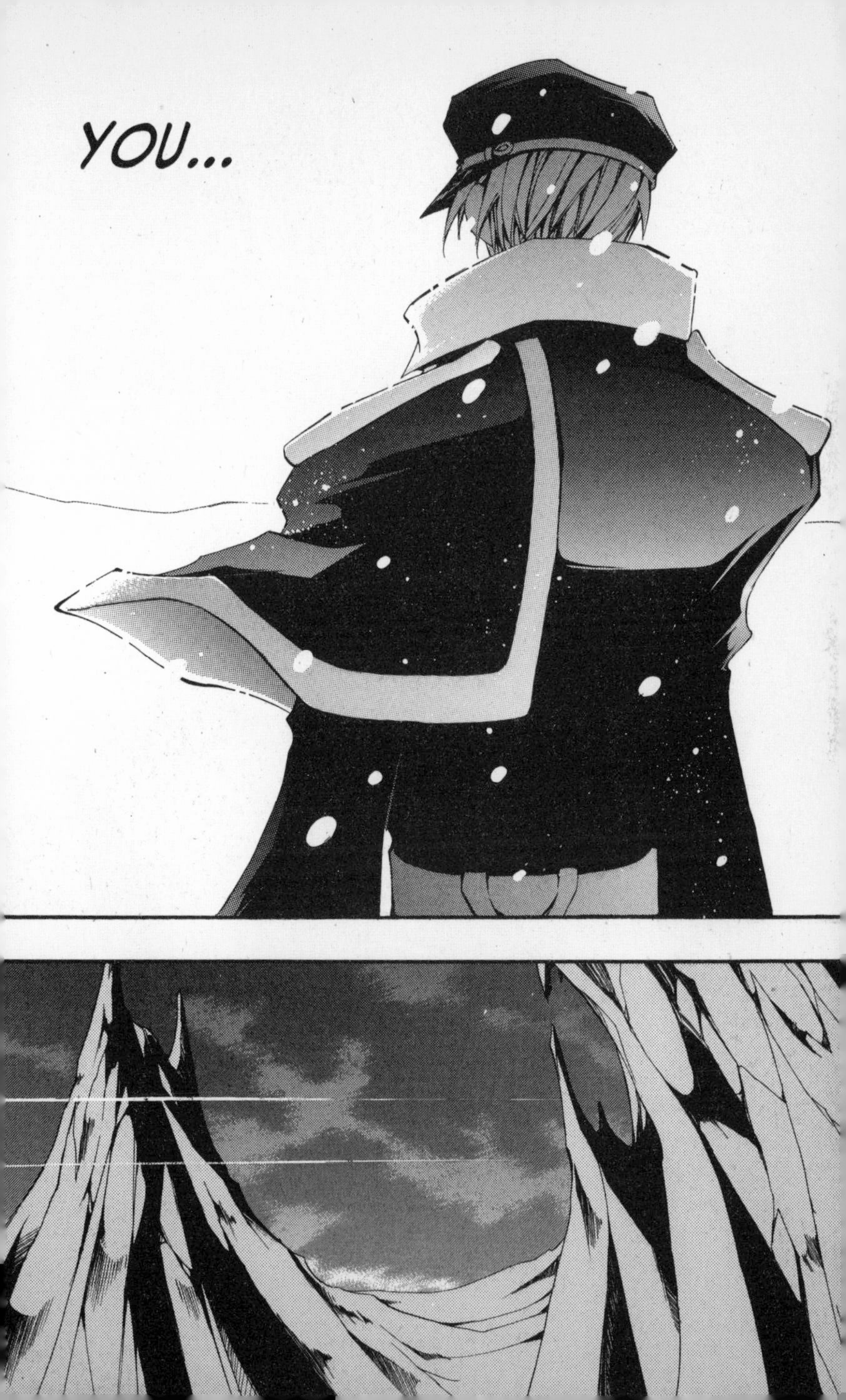
YOU...

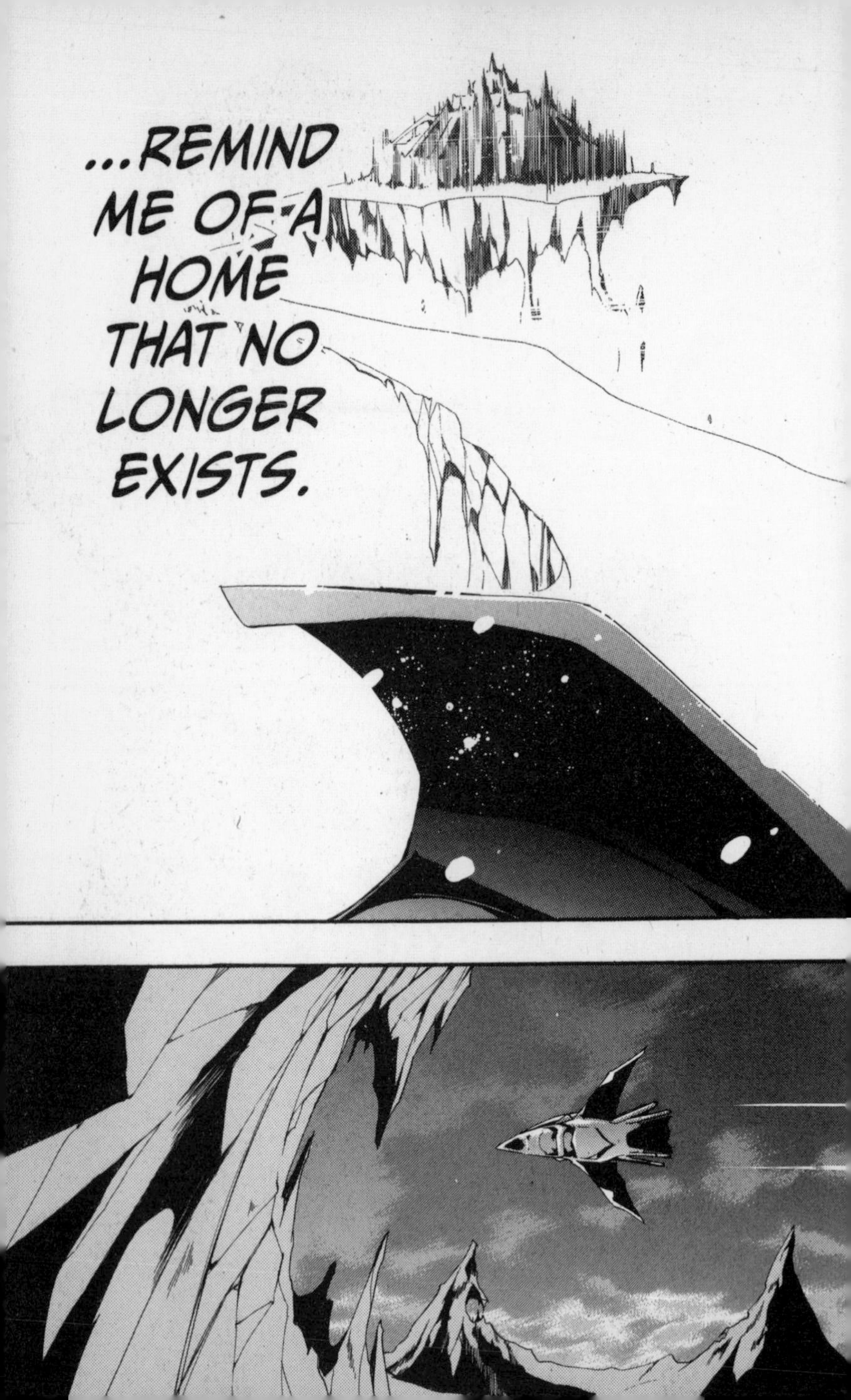
...REMIND ME OF A HOME THAT NO LONGER EXISTS.

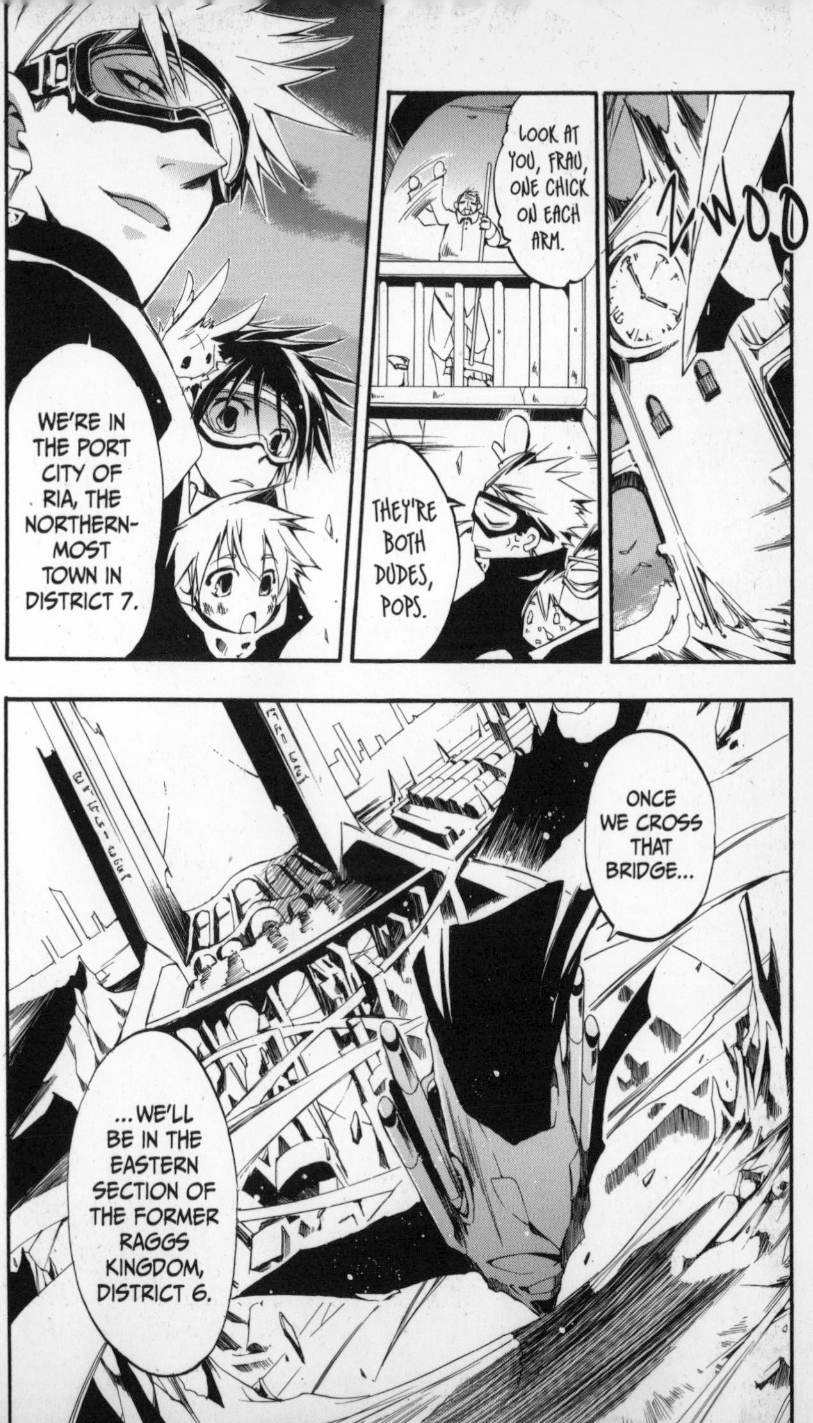
ZWOO
LOOK AT YOU, FRAU, ONE CHICK ON EACH ARM.
THEY'RE BOTH DUDES, POPS.
WE'RE IN THE PORT CITY OF RIA, THE NORTHERN-MOST TOWN IN DISTRICT 7.
ONCE WE CROSS THAT BRIDGE...
...WE'LL BE IN THE EASTERN SECTION OF THE FORMER RAGGS KINGDOM, DISTRICT 6.

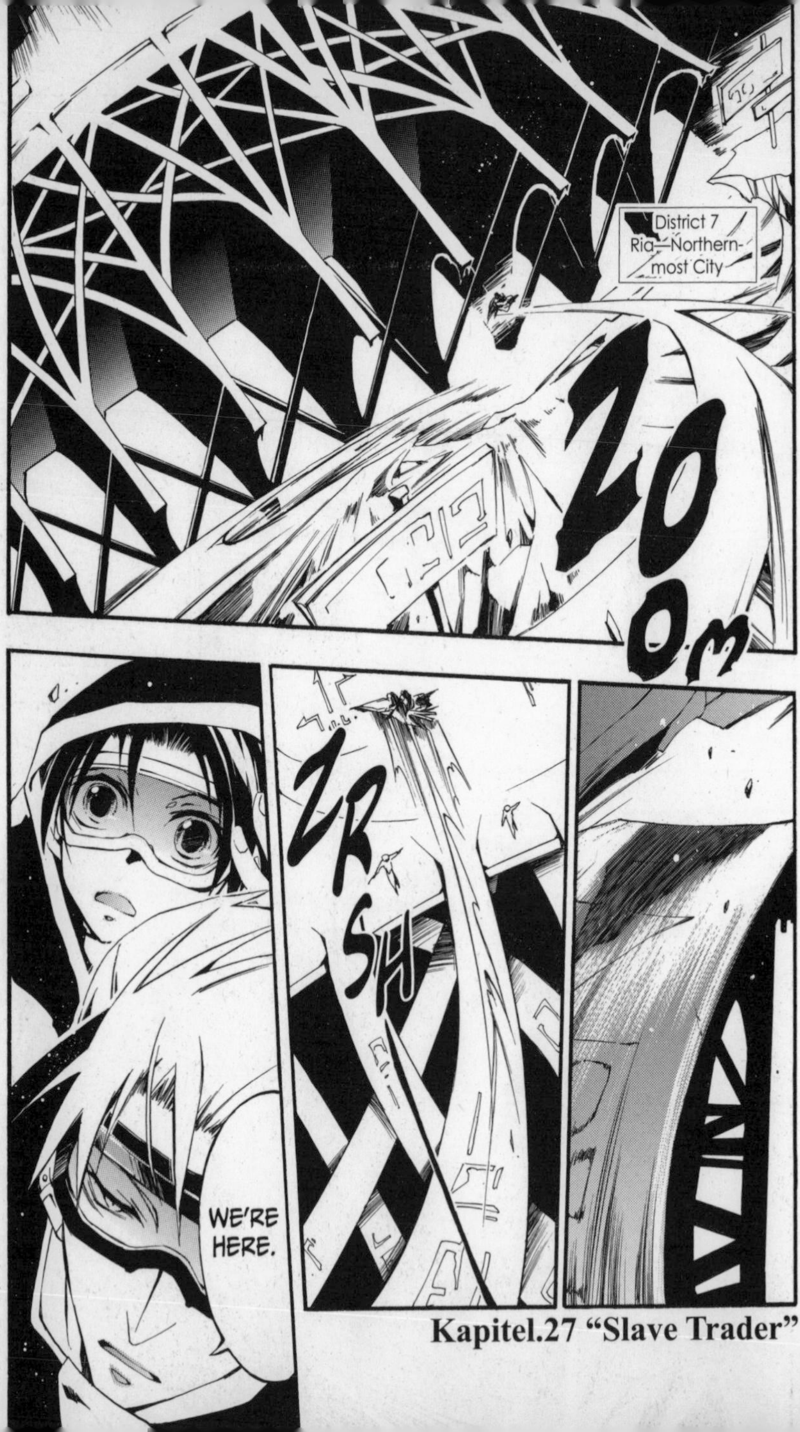
District 7 Ria—Northern-most City
ZOOM
ZRSH
WE'RE HERE.

Kapitel.27 "Slave Trader"

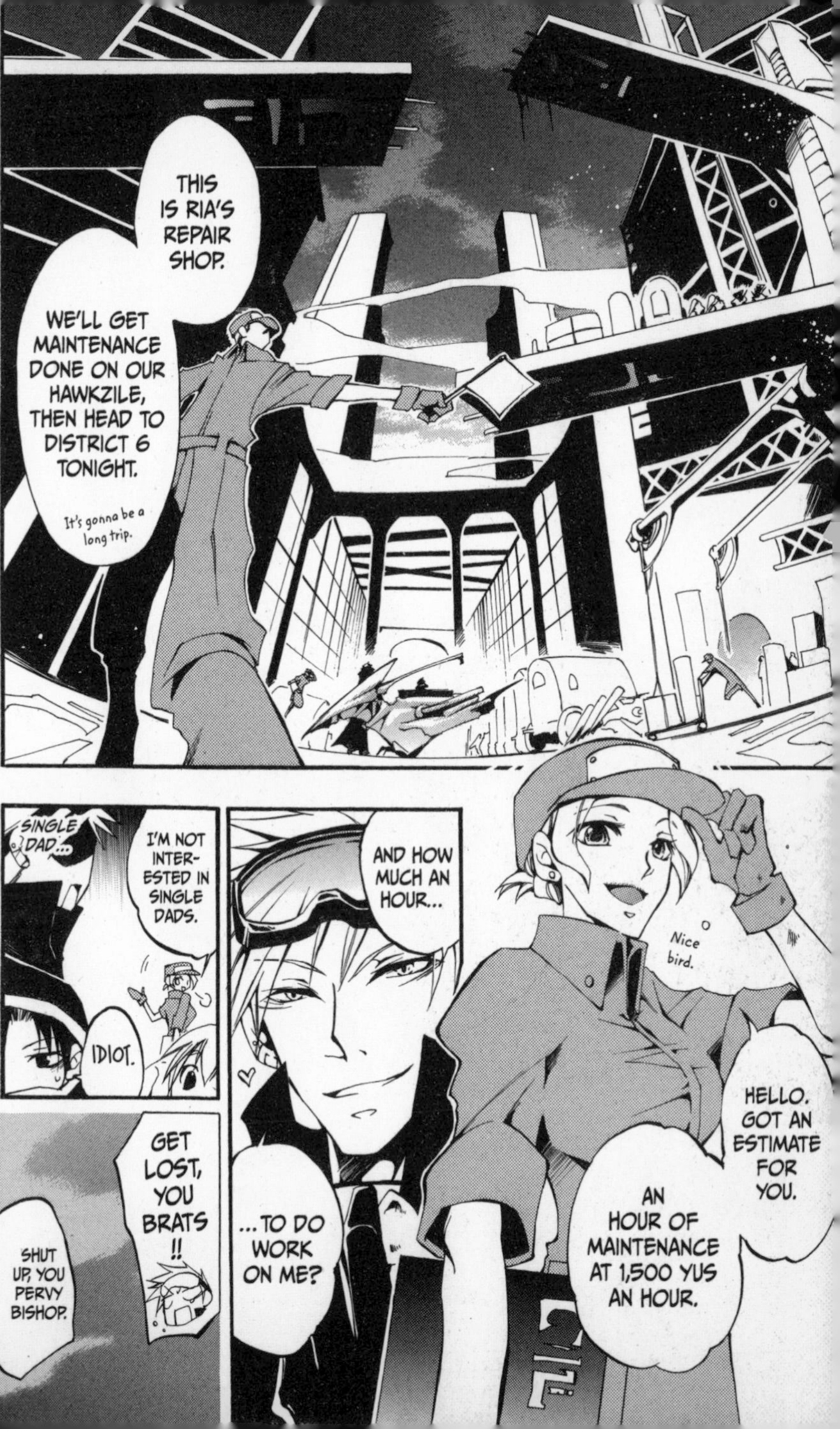
THIS IS RIA'S REPAIR SHOP.
WE'LL GET MAINTENANCE DONE ON OUR HAWKZILE, THEN HEAD TO DISTRICT 6 TONIGHT.
It's gonna be a long trip.
Nice bird.
HELLO. GOT AN ESTIMATE FOR YOU.
AN HOUR OF MAINTENANCE AT 1,500 YUS AN HOUR.
AND HOW MUCH AN HOUR...
...TO DO WORK ON ME?
I'M NOT INTER-ESTED IN SINGLE DADS.
SINGLE DAD...
IDIOT.
GET LOST, YOU BRATS!!
SHUT UP, YOU PERVY BISHOP.

Kapitel.27 “Slave Trader”

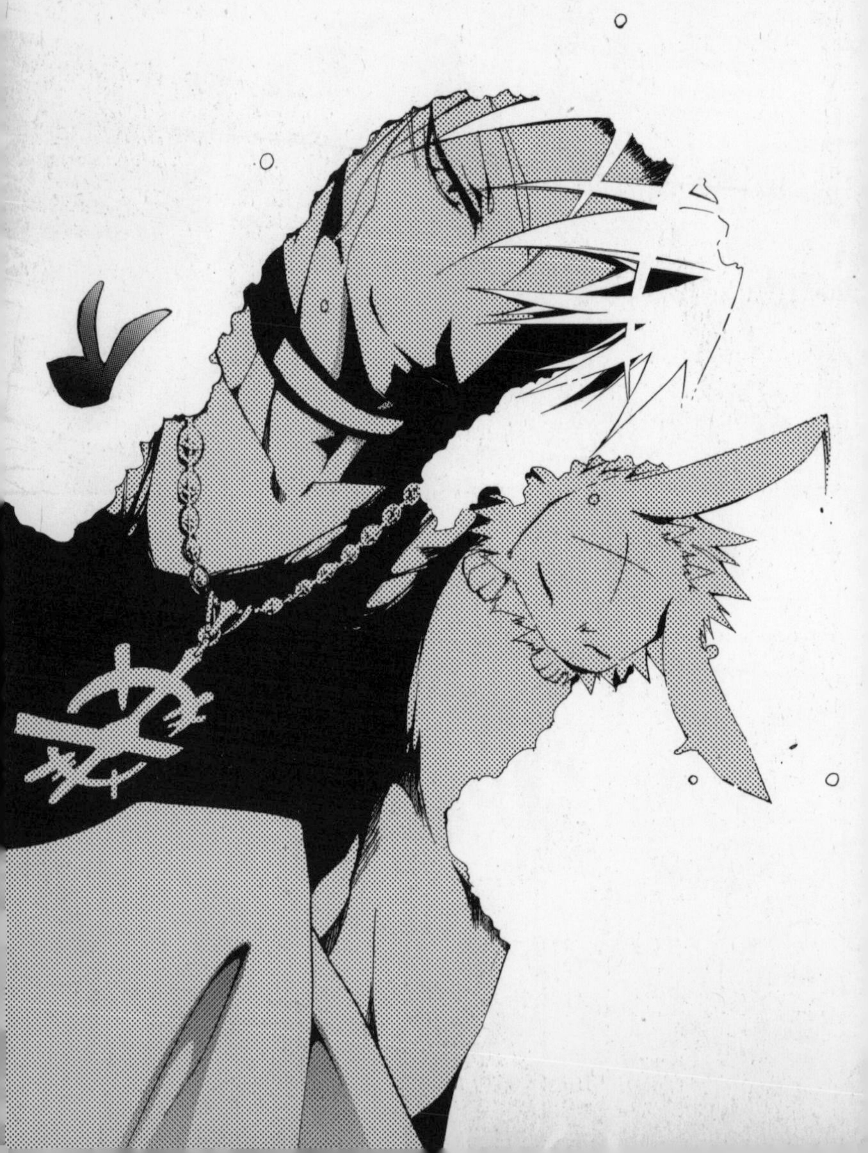

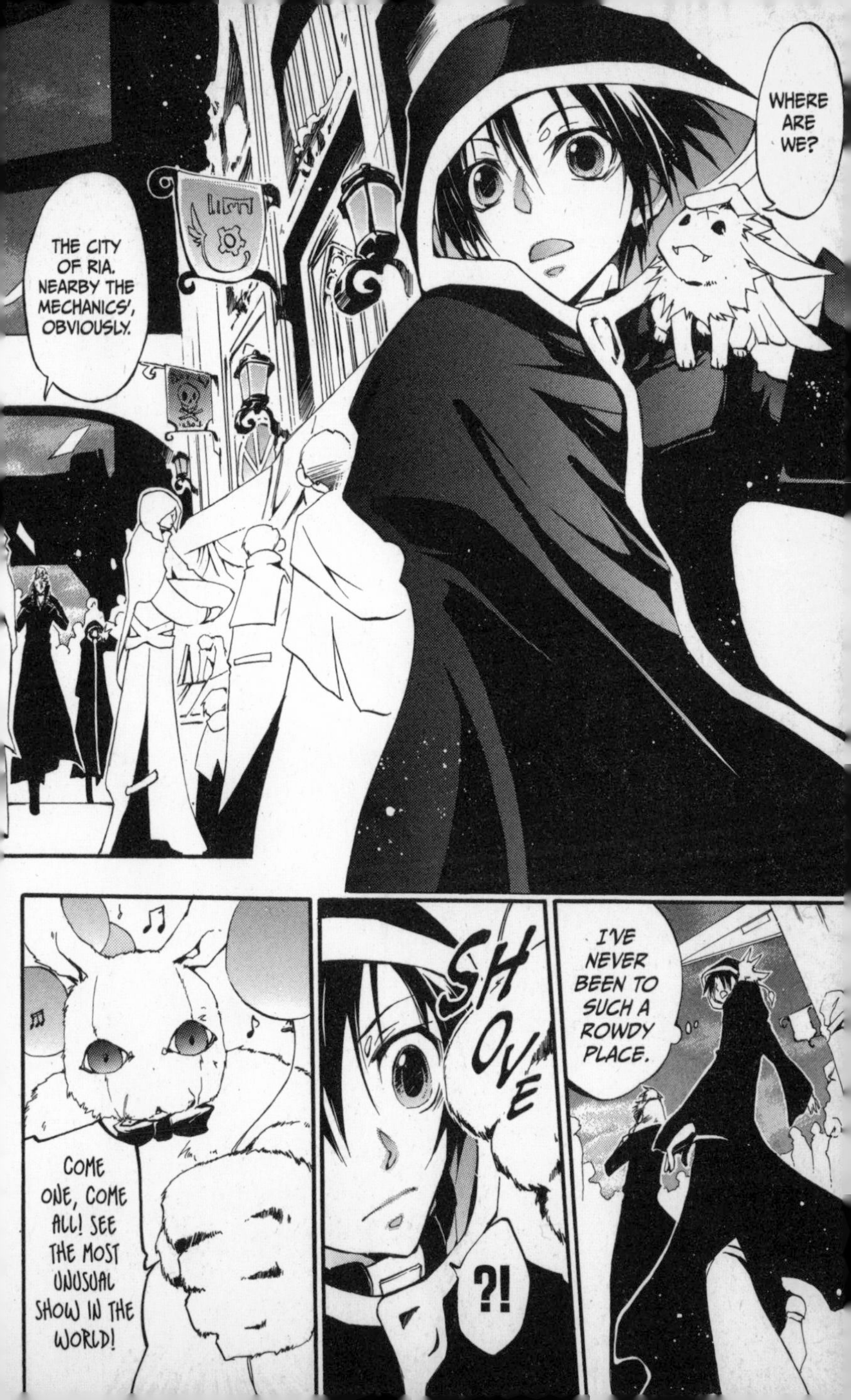
WHERE ARE WE?
THE CITY OF RIA. NEARBY THE MECHANICS', OBVIOUSLY.
I'VE NEVER BEEN TO SUCH A ROWDY PLACE.
SHOVE
?!
COME ONE, COME ALL! SEE THE MOST UNUSUAL SHOW IN THE WORLD!

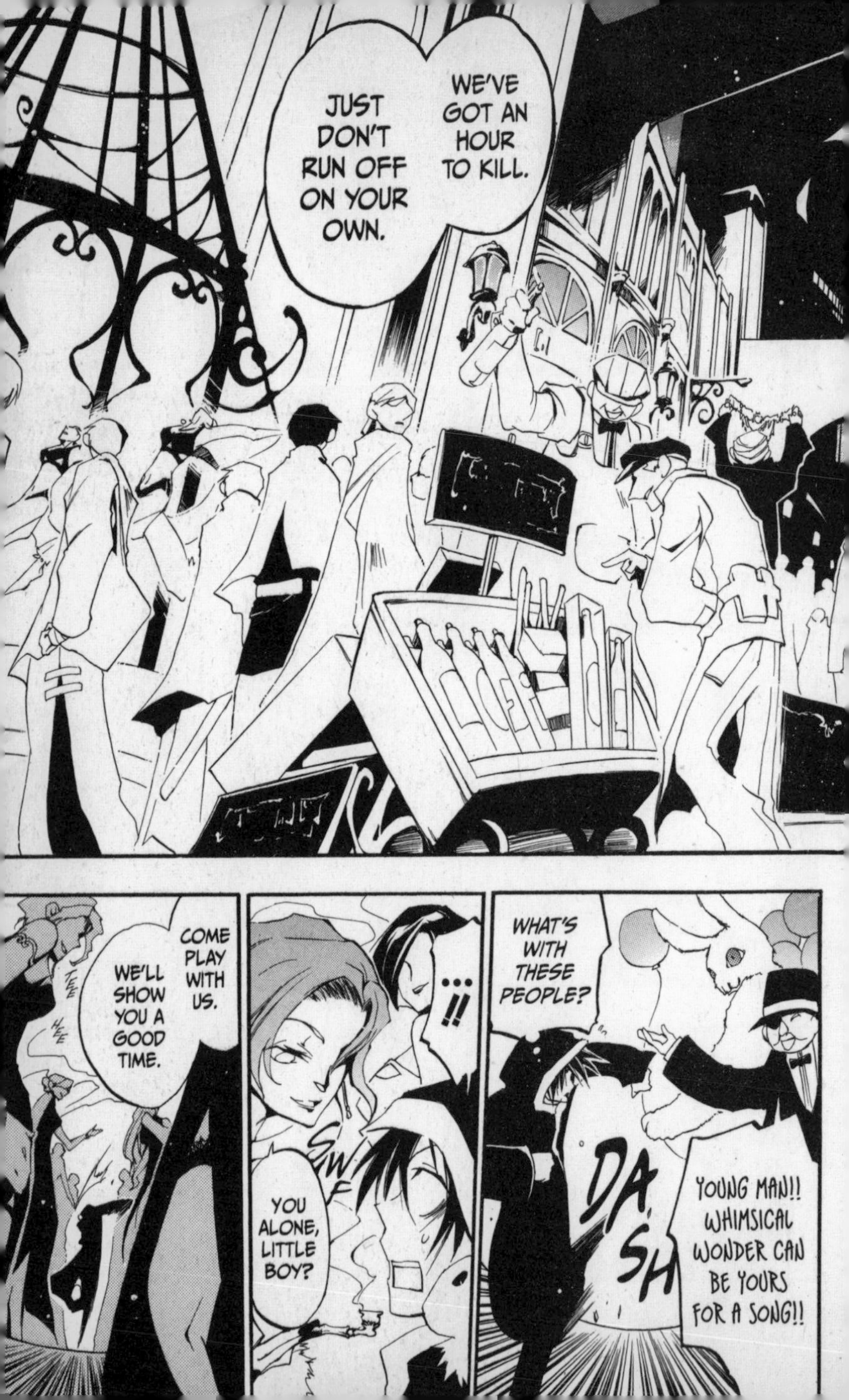
WE'VE GOT AN HOUR TO KILL.
JUST DON'T RUN OFF ON YOUR OWN.
WHAT'S WITH THESE PEOPLE?
DASH
YOUNG MAN!! WHIMSICAL WONDER CAN BE YOURS FOR A SONG!!
...!!
SWF
YOU ALONE, LITTLE BOY?
COME PLAY WITH US.
WE'LL SHOW YOU A GOOD TIME.
TEE HEE

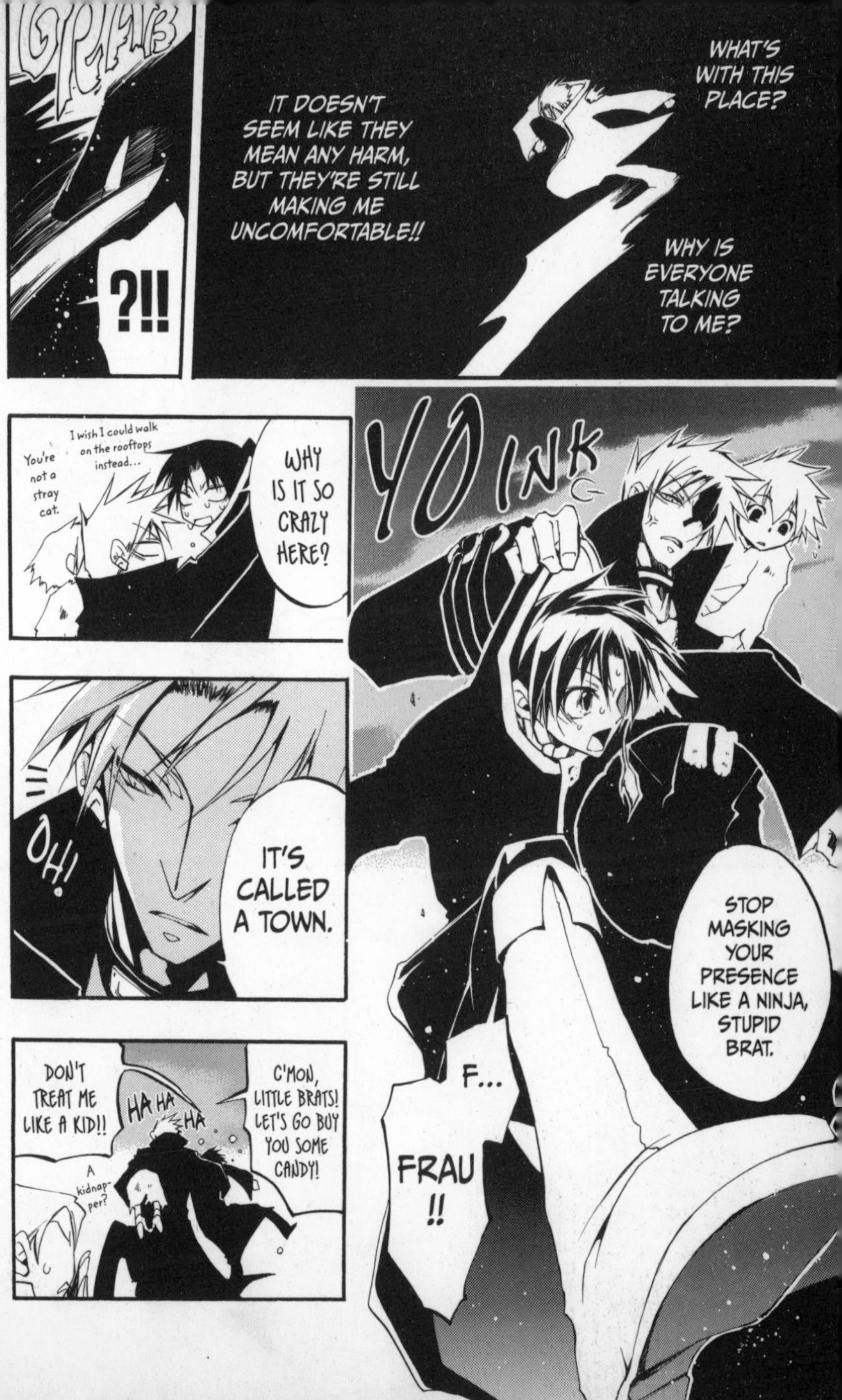
WHAT'S WITH THIS PLACE?
WHY IS EVERYONE TALKING TO ME?
IT DOESN'T SEEM LIKE THEY MEAN ANY HARM, BUT THEY'RE STILL MAKING ME UNCOMFORTABLE!!
?!!
YOINK
STOP MASKING YOUR PRESENCE LIKE A NINJA, STUPID BRAT.
F...
FRAU!!
WHY IS IT SO CRAZY HERE?
I wish I could walk on the rooftops instead...
You're not a stray cat.
OH!
IT'S CALLED A TOWN.
C'MON, LITTLE BRATS! LET'S GO BUY YOU SOME CANDY!
HA HA HA
DON'T TREAT ME LIKE A KID!!
A kidnapper?

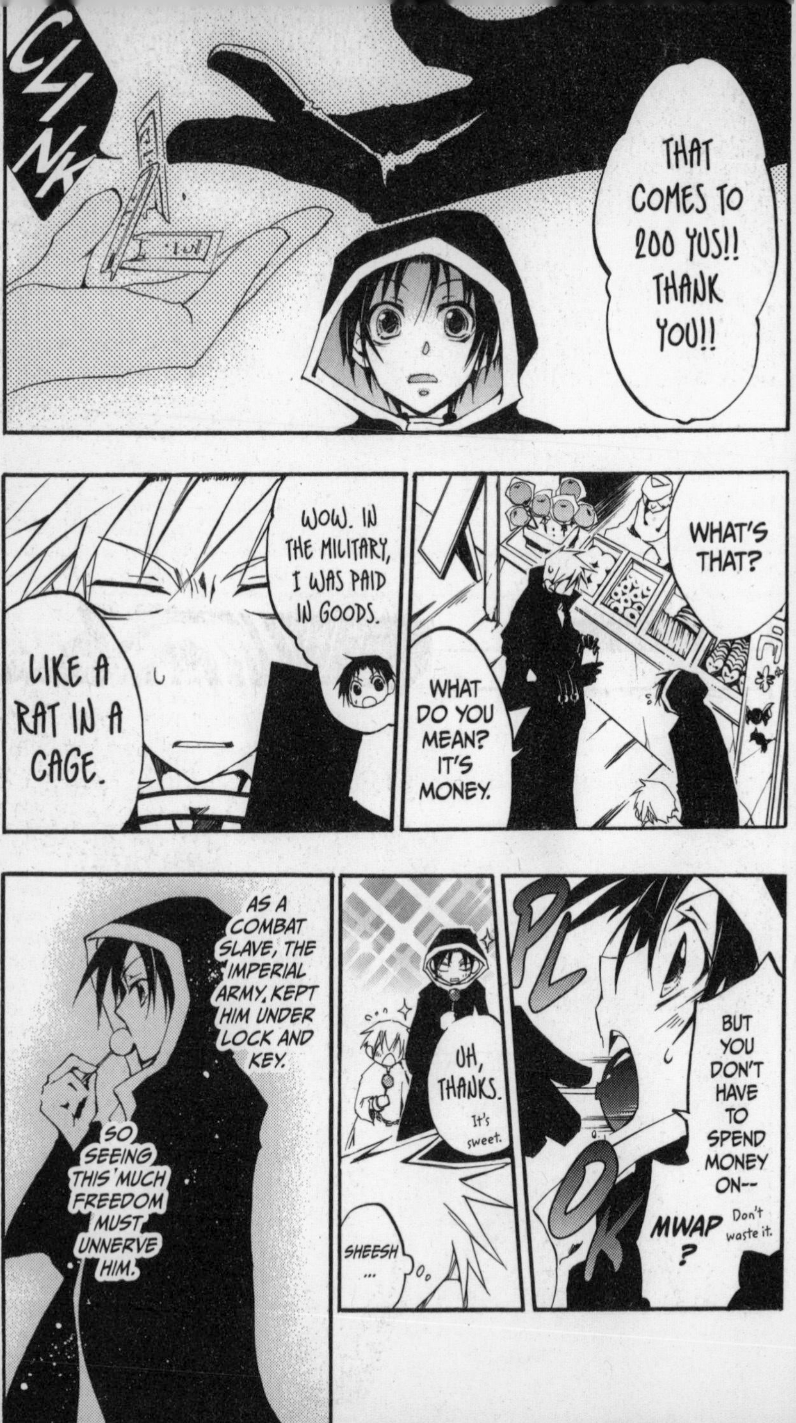
THAT COMES TO 200 YUS!! THANK YOU!!
CLINK
WHAT'S THAT?
WHAT DO YOU MEAN? IT'S MONEY.
WOW. IN THE MILITARY, I WAS PAID IN GOODS.
LIKE A RAT IN A CAGE.
PLOOK
BUT YOU DON'T HAVE TO SPEND MONEY ON--
Don't waste it.
MWAP ?
UH, THANKS.
It's sweet.
SHEESH ...
AS A COMBAT SLAVE, THE IMPERIAL ARMY KEPT HIM UNDER LOCK AND KEY.
SO SEEING THIS MUCH FREEDOM MUST UNNERVE HIM.

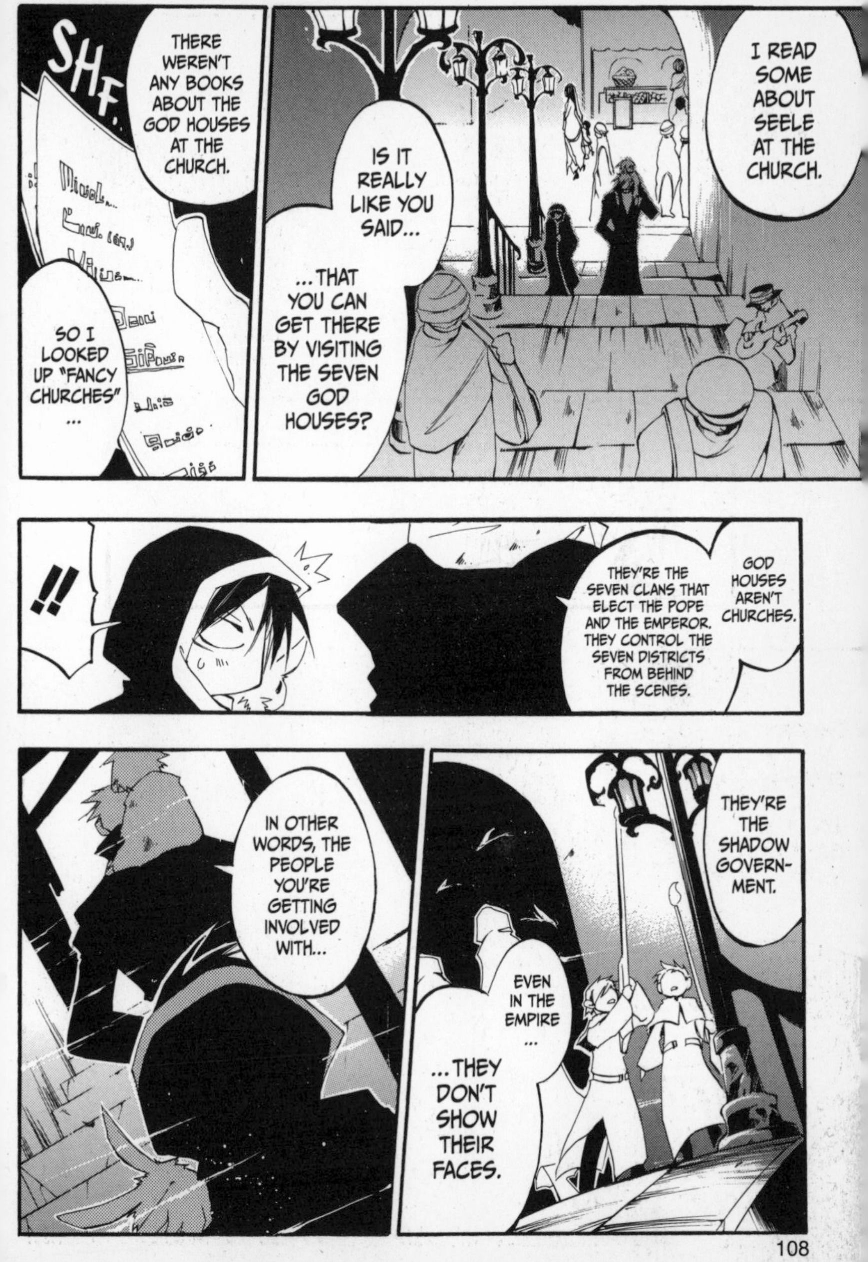
I READ SOME ABOUT SEELE AT THE CHURCH.
IS IT REALLY LIKE YOU SAID...
...THAT YOU CAN GET THERE BY VISITING THE SEVEN GOD HOUSES?
SHF.
THERE WEREN'T ANY BOOKS ABOUT THE GOD HOUSES AT THE CHURCH.
SO I LOOKED UP "FANCY CHURCHES"...
GOD HOUSES AREN'T CHURCHES.
THEY'RE THE SEVEN CLANS THAT ELECT THE POPE AND THE EMPEROR. THEY CONTROL THE SEVEN DISTRICTS FROM BEHIND THE SCENES.
!!
THEY'RE THE SHADOW GOVERN-MENT.
EVEN IN THE EMPIRE...
...THEY DON'T SHOW THEIR FACES.
IN OTHER WORDS, THE PEOPLE YOU'RE GETTING INVOLVED WITH...

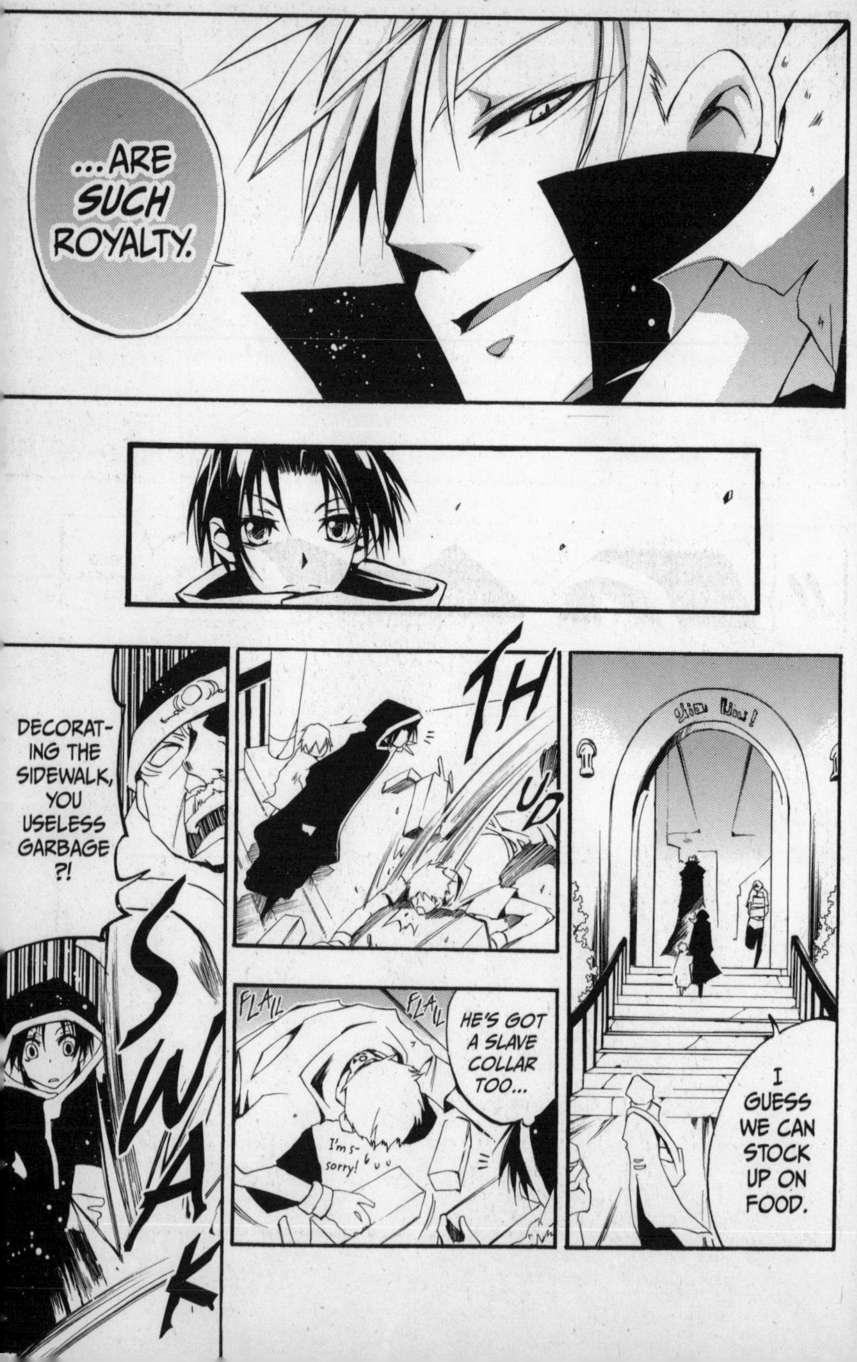
...ARE SUCH ROYALTY.
I GUESS WE CAN STOCK UP ON FOOD.
THUD
FLAIL FLAIL
HE'S GOT A SLAVE COLLAR TOO...
I'm s-sorry!
DECORAT-ING THE SIDEWALK, YOU USELESS GARBAGE?!
SWAK

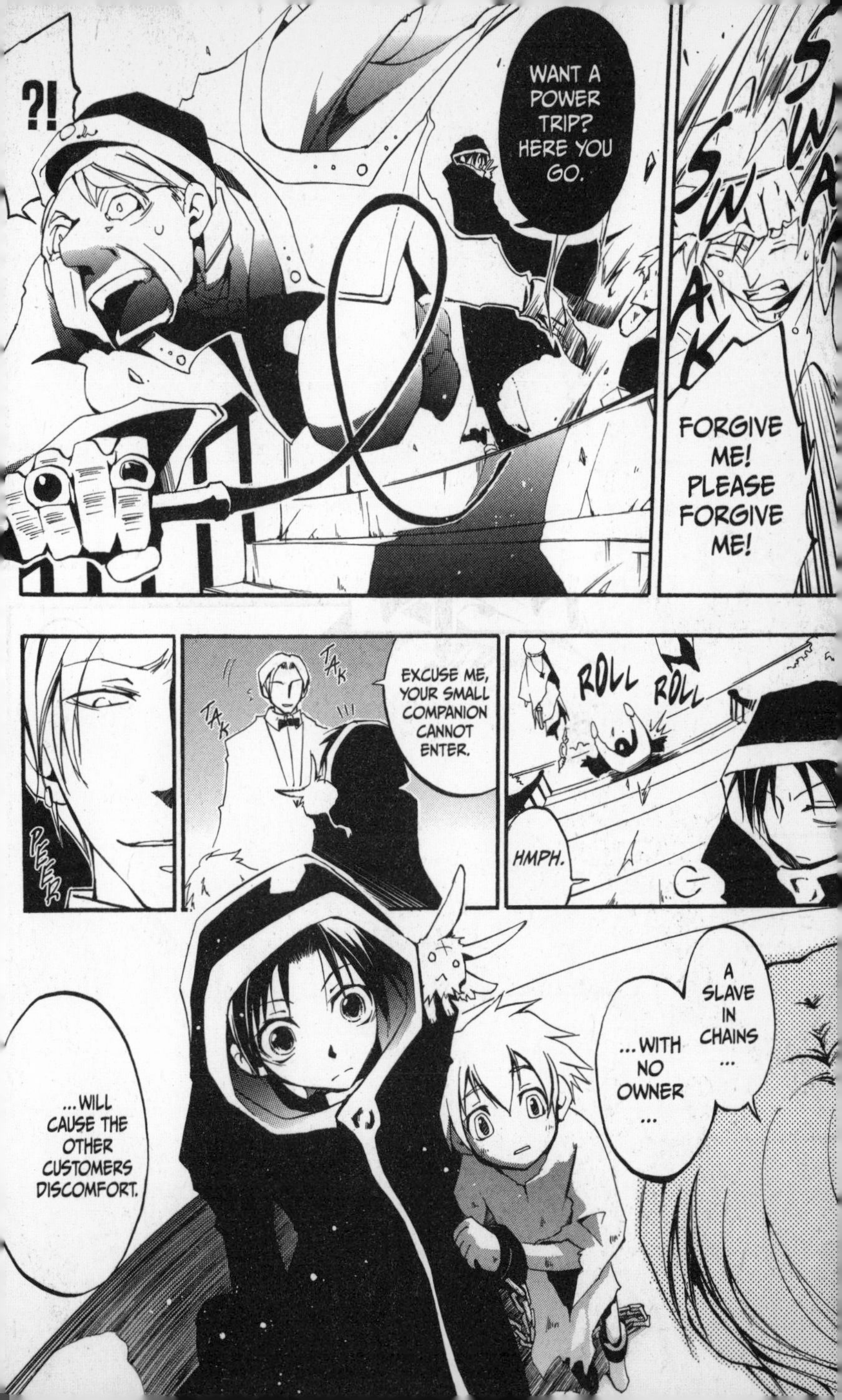
SWAK
SWAK
FORGIVE ME! PLEASE FORGIVE ME!
WANT A POWER TRIP? HERE YOU GO.
?!
ROLL
ROLL
HMPH.
TAK
TAK
EXCUSE ME, YOUR SMALL COMPANION CANNOT ENTER.
PEEER
A SLAVE IN CHAINS ...
... WITH NO OWNER ...
... WILL CAUSE THE OTHER CUSTOMERS DISCOMFORT.

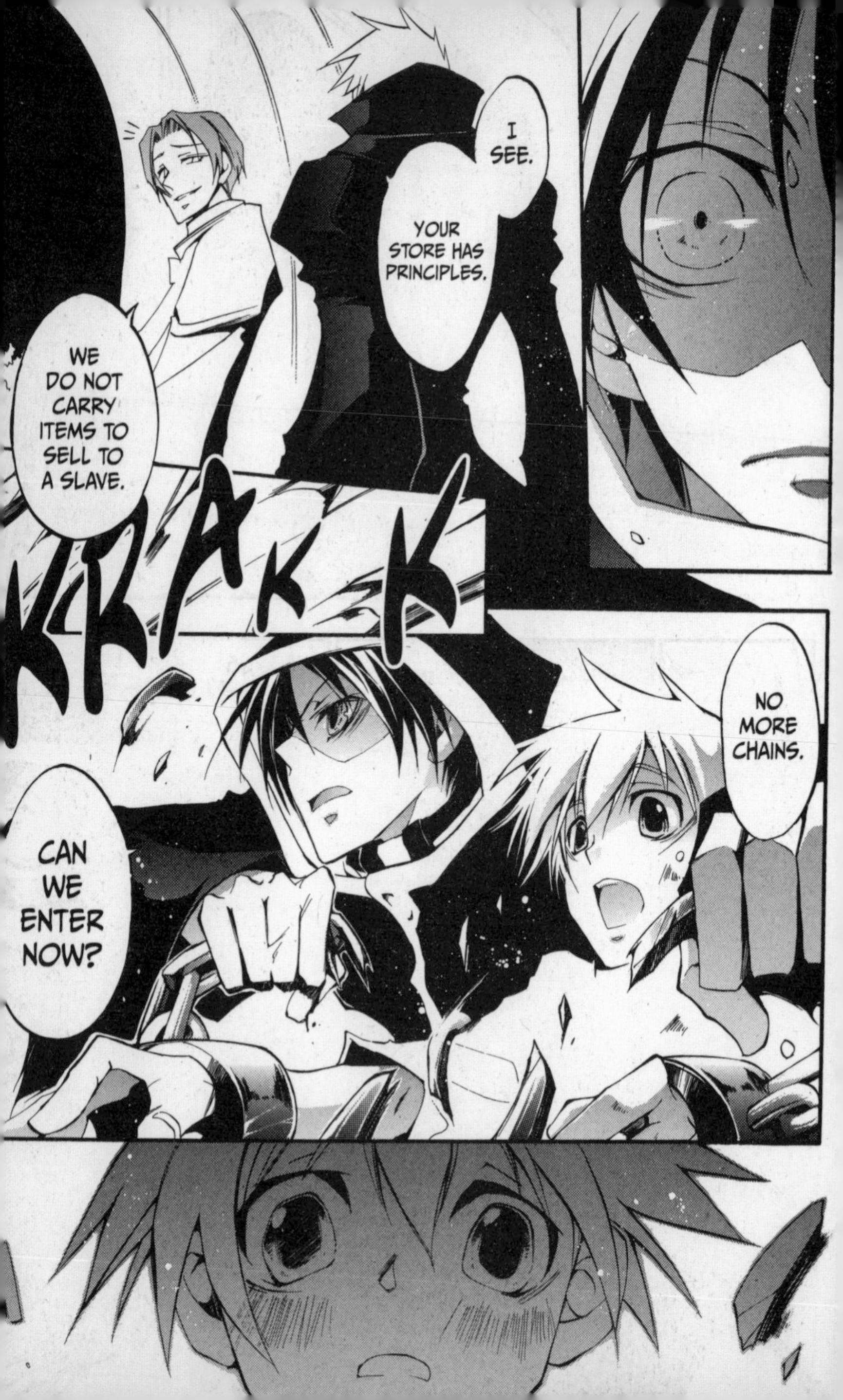
I SEE.
YOUR STORE HAS PRINCIPLES.
WE DO NOT CARRY ITEMS TO SELL TO A SLAVE.
KRAKK
NO MORE CHAINS.
CAN WE ENTER NOW?

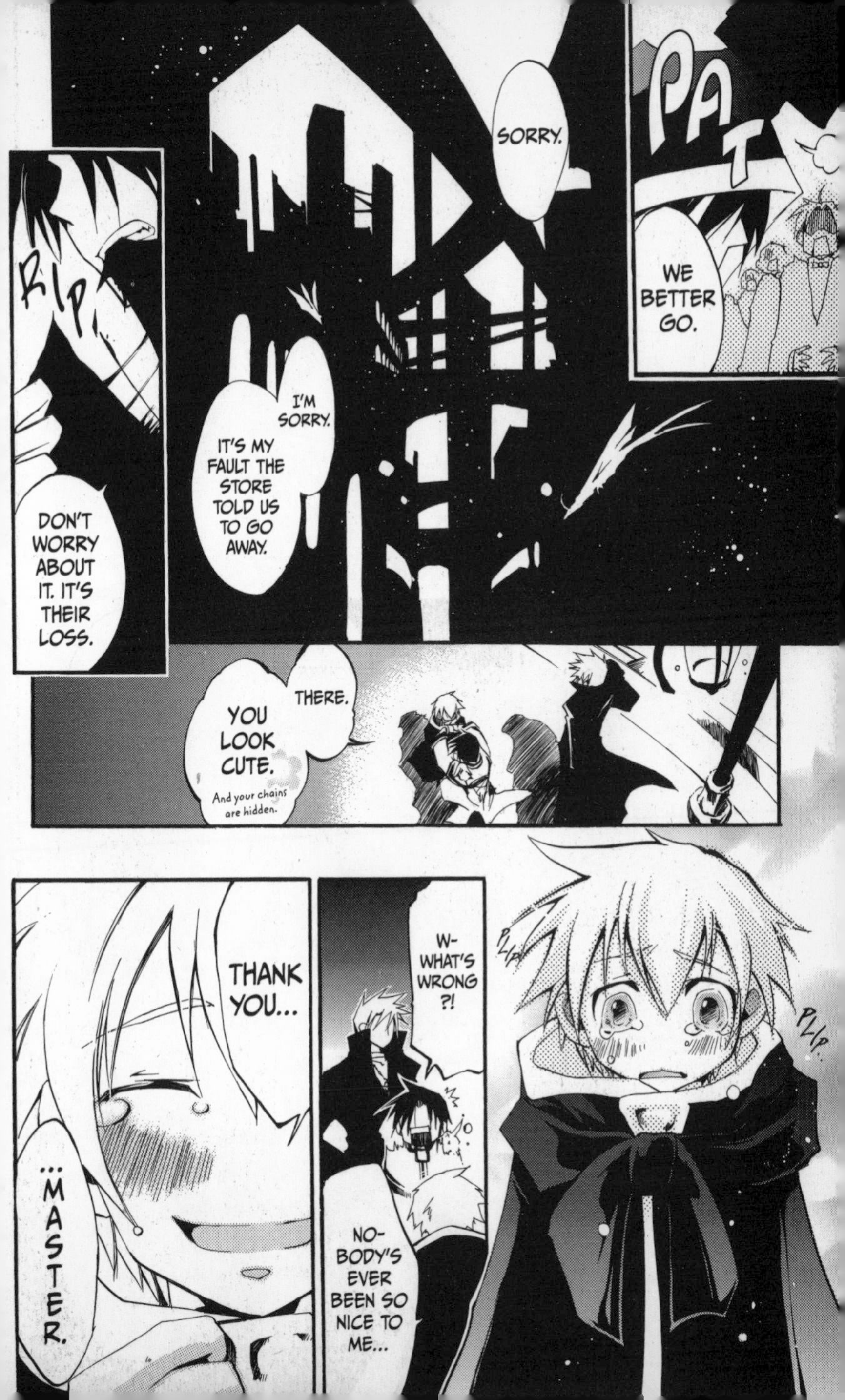
PAT
WE BETTER GO.
SORRY.
I'M SORRY.
IT'S MY FAULT THE STORE TOLD US TO GO AWAY.
RIP
DON'T WORRY ABOUT IT. IT'S THEIR LOSS.
THERE.
YOU LOOK CUTE.
And your chains are hidden.
PLIP
PLIP.
W-WHAT'S WRONG?!
NO-BODY'S EVER BEEN SO NICE TO ME...
THANK YOU...
...MASTER.

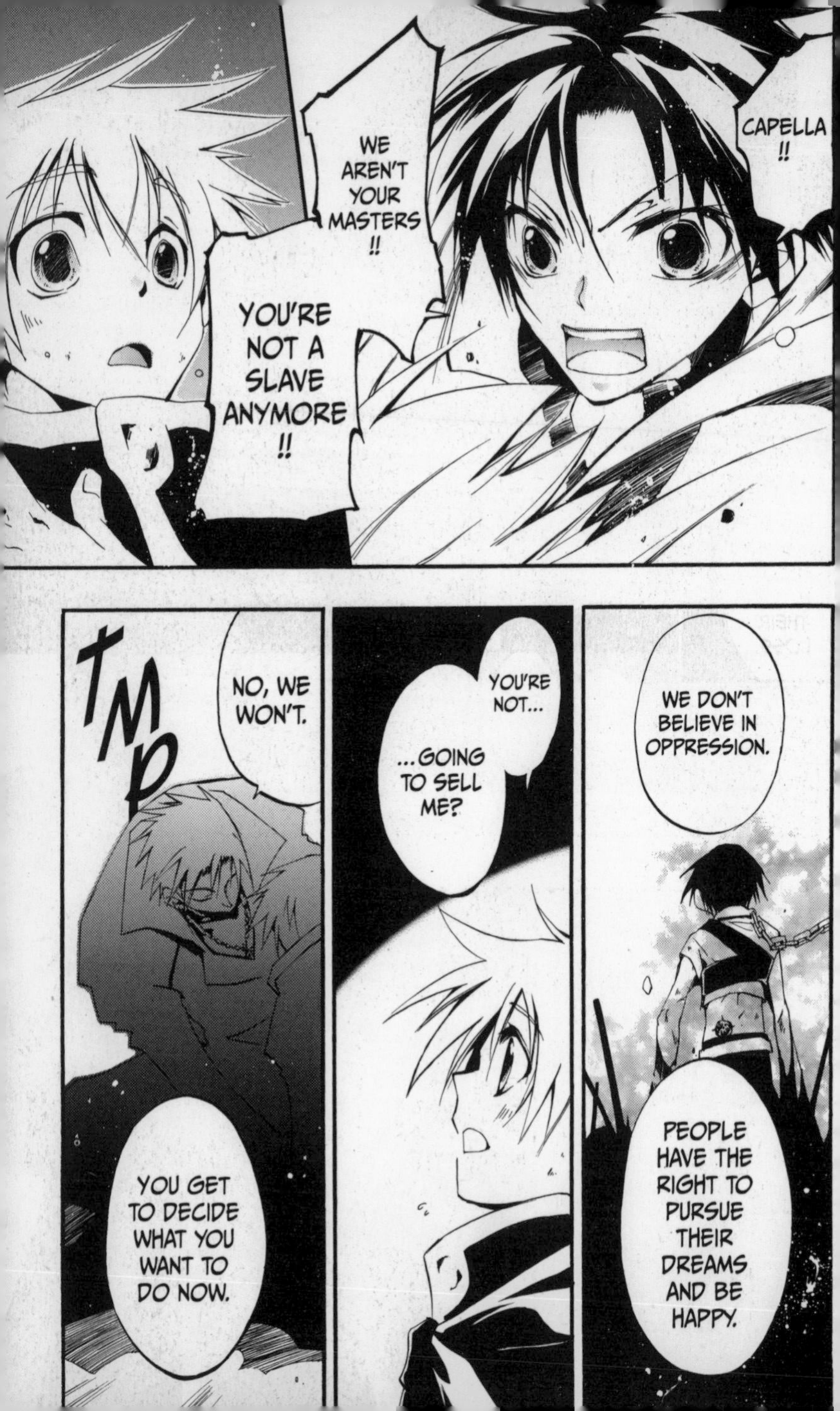
CAPELLA !!
WE AREN'T YOUR MASTERS !!
YOU'RE NOT A SLAVE ANYMORE !!
WE DON'T BELIEVE IN OPPRESSION.
PEOPLE HAVE THE RIGHT TO PURSUE THEIR DREAMS AND BE HAPPY.
YOU'RE NOT...
...GOING TO SELL ME?
NO, WE WON'T.
TMP
YOU GET TO DECIDE WHAT YOU WANT TO DO NOW.

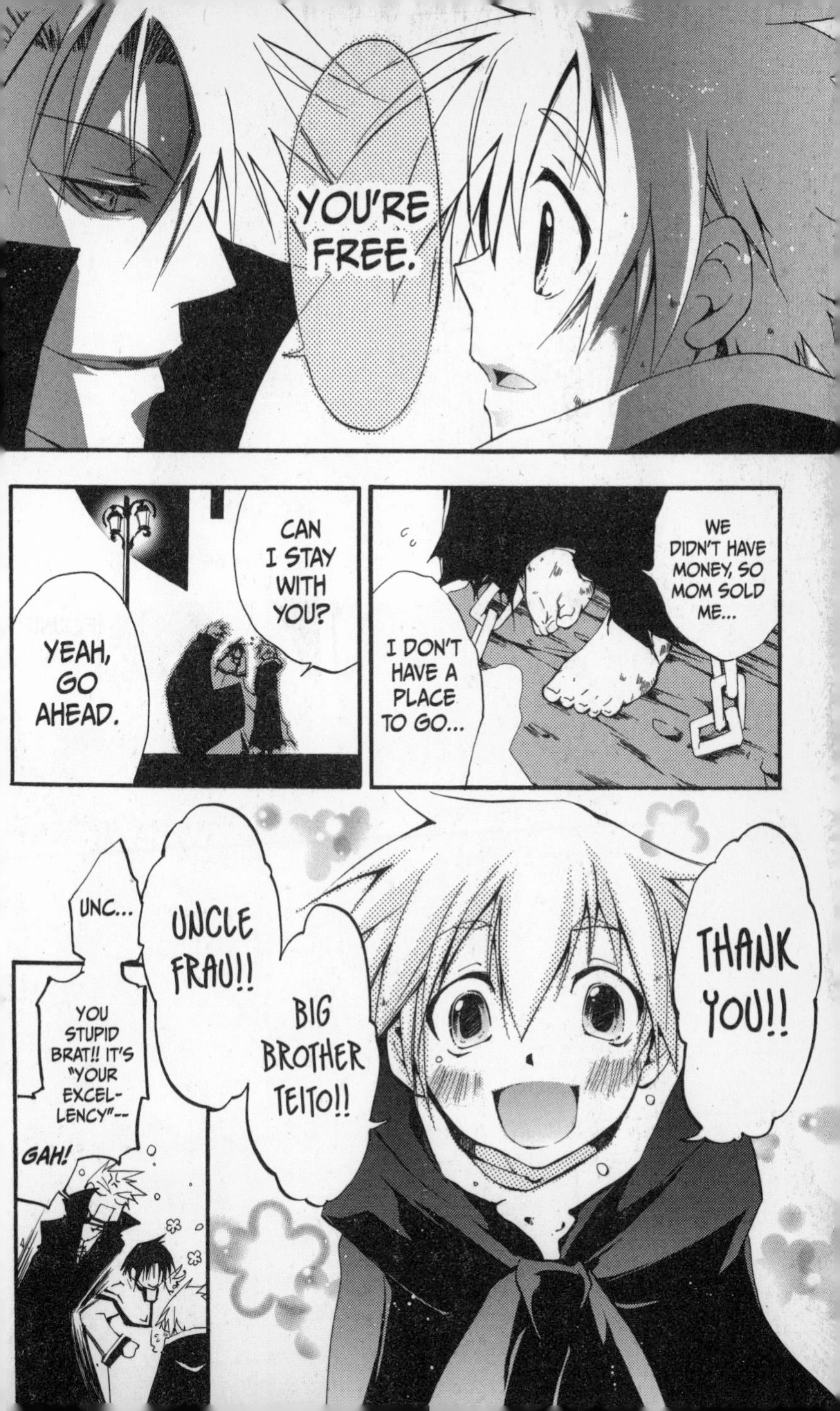
YOU'RE FREE.
WE DIDN'T HAVE MONEY, SO MOM SOLD ME...
I DON'T HAVE A PLACE TO GO...
CAN I STAY WITH YOU?
YEAH, GO AHEAD.
THANK YOU!!
BIG BROTHER TEITO!!
UNCLE FRAU!!
UNC...
YOU STUPID BRAT!! IT'S "YOUR EXCEL-LENCY"--
GAH!

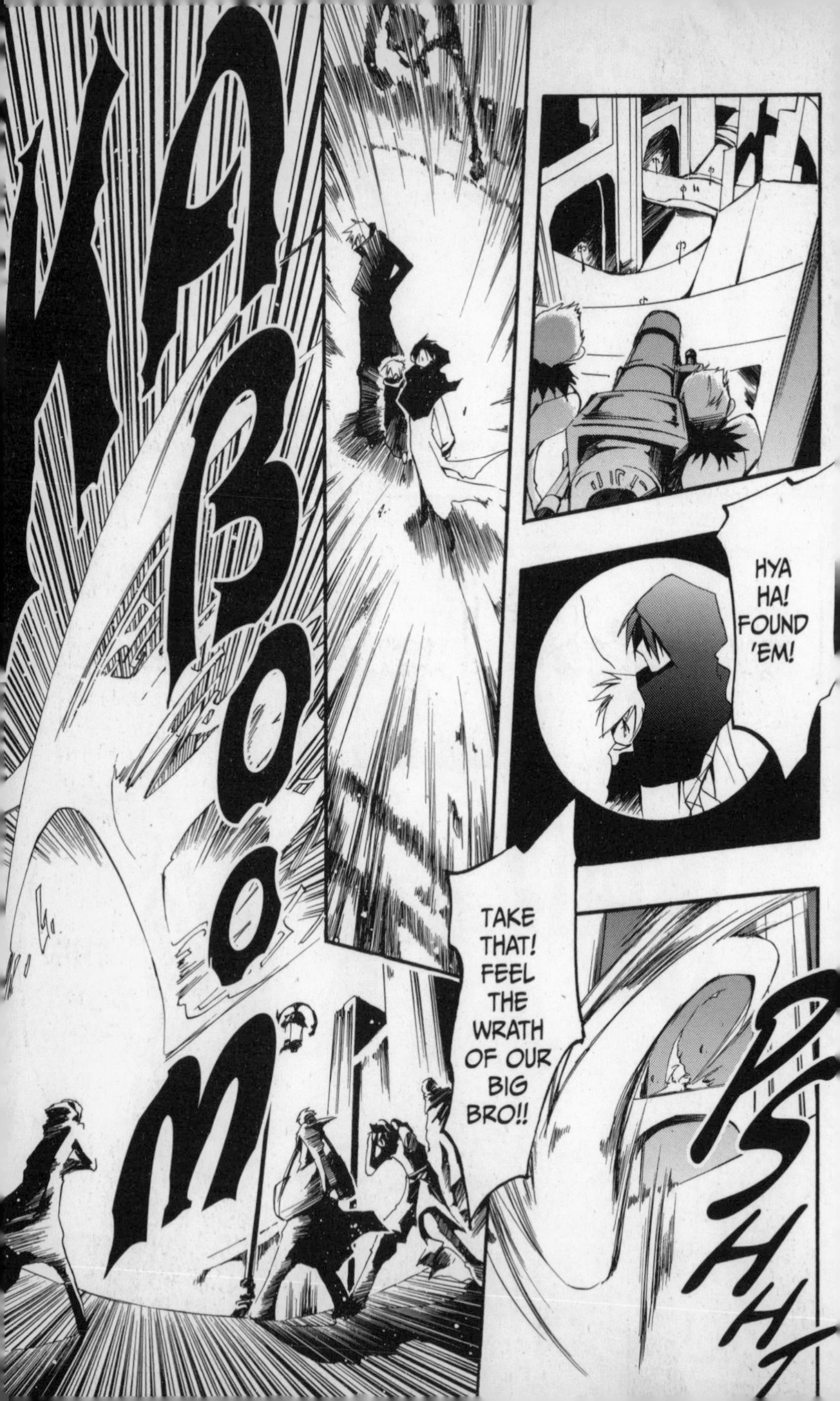
HYA HA! FOUND 'EM!
TAKE THAT! FEEL THE WRATH OF OUR BIG BRO!!
PSHHH
KABOOM

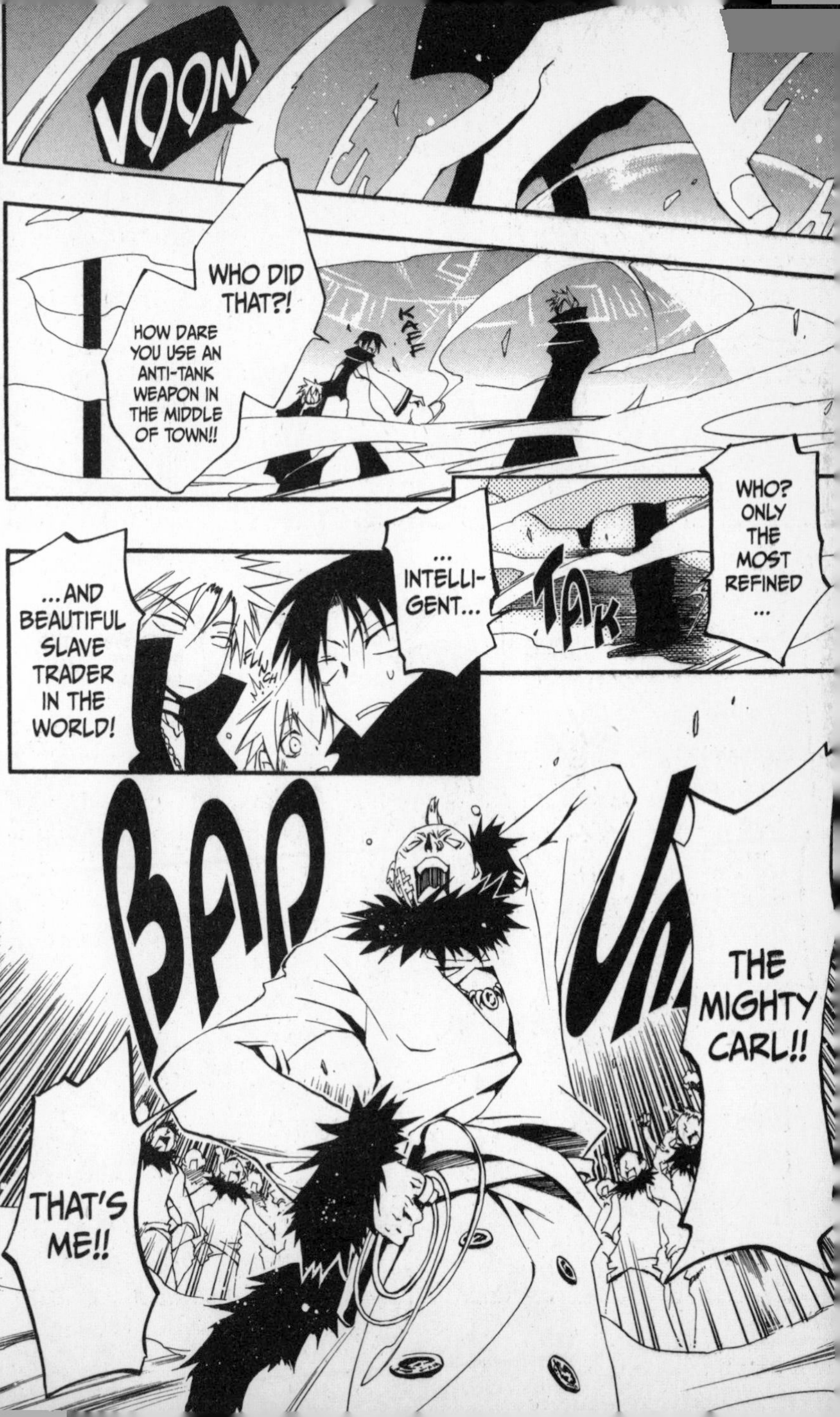
VOOM
KAFF
WHO DID THAT?!
HOW DARE YOU USE AN ANTI-TANK WEAPON IN THE MIDDLE OF TOWN!!
WHO? ONLY THE MOST REFINED...
TAK
...INTELLI-GENT...
...AND BEAUTIFUL SLAVE TRADER IN THE WORLD!
FLINCH
BAM
THE MIGHTY CARL!!
THAT'S ME!!

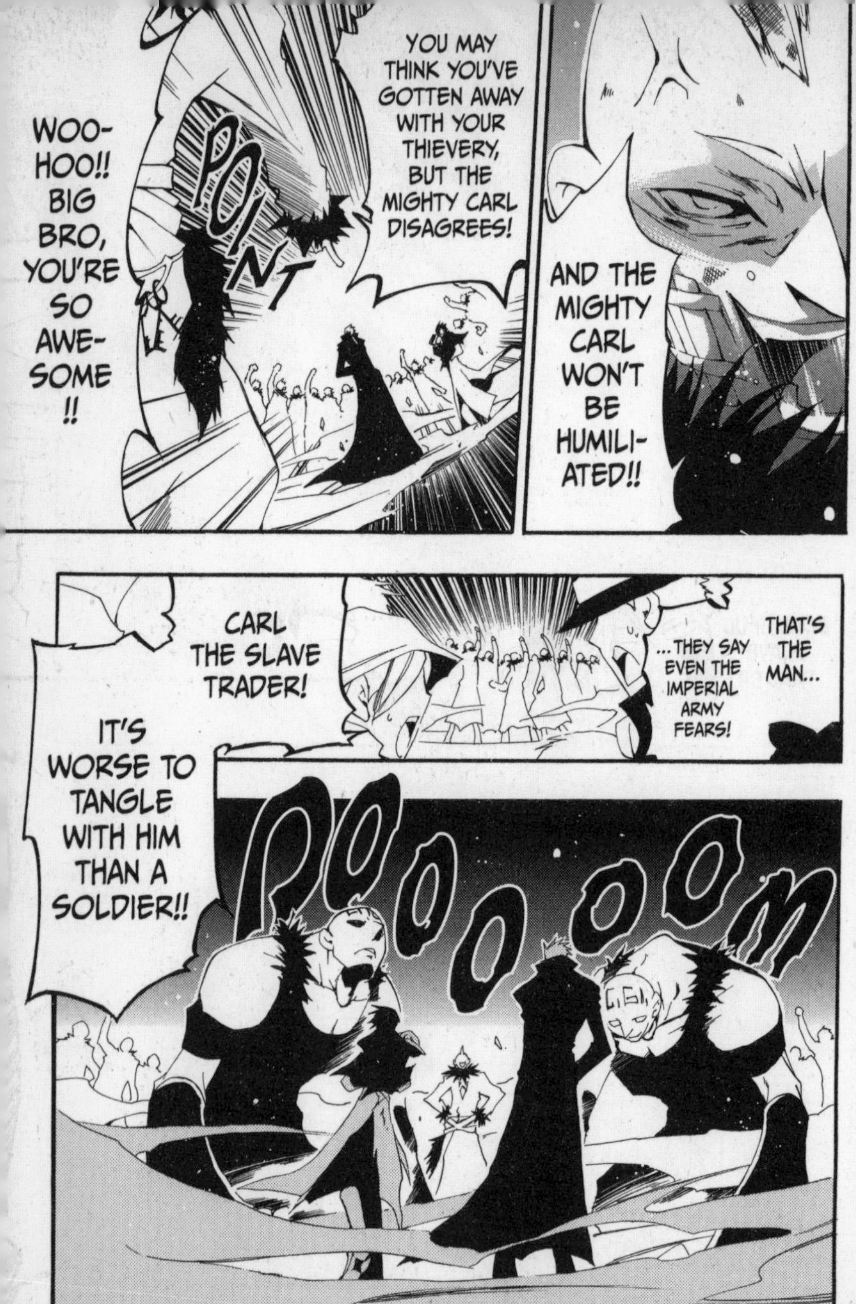
AND THE MIGHTY CARL WON'T BE HUMILIATED!!
YOU MAY THINK YOU'VE GOTTEN AWAY WITH YOUR THIEVERY, BUT THE MIGHTY CARL DISAGREES!
POINT
WOO-HOO!! BIG BRO, YOU'RE SO AWESOME!!
THAT'S THE MAN...
...THEY SAY EVEN THE IMPERIAL ARMY FEARS!
CARL THE SLAVE TRADER!
IT'S WORSE TO TANGLE WITH HIM THAN A SOLDIER!!
DOOOOOOM

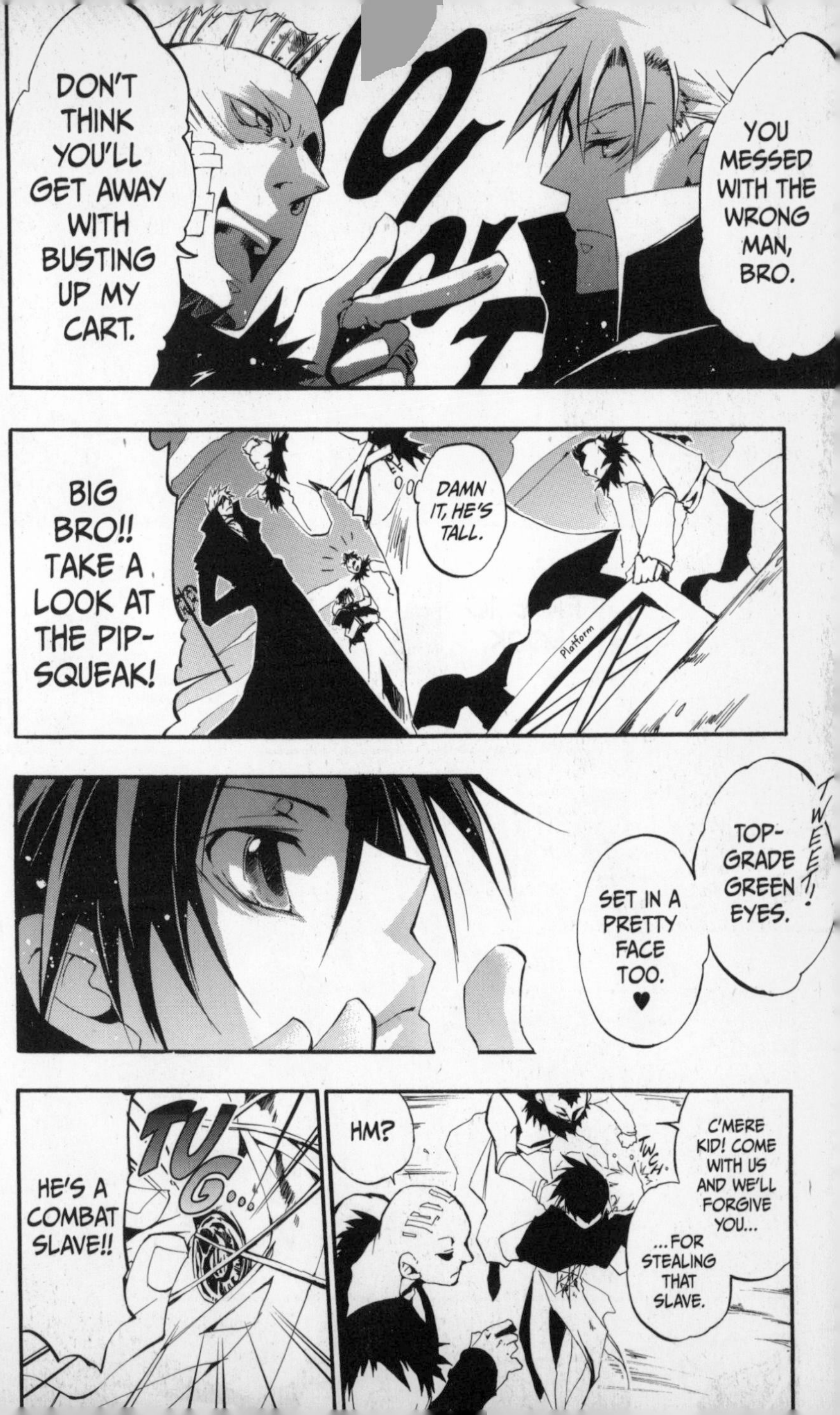
YOU MESSED WITH THE WRONG MAN, BRO.
DON'T THINK YOU'LL GET AWAY WITH BUSTING UP MY CART.
DAMN IT, HE'S TALL.
Platform
BIG BRO!! TAKE A LOOK AT THE PIP-SQUEAK!
TWEET!!
TOP-GRADE GREEN EYES.
SET IN A PRETTY FACE TOO. ♥
C'MERE KID! COME WITH US AND WE'LL FORGIVE YOU...
TWCH
HM?
...FOR STEALING THAT SLAVE.
TUG...
HE'S A COMBAT SLAVE!!

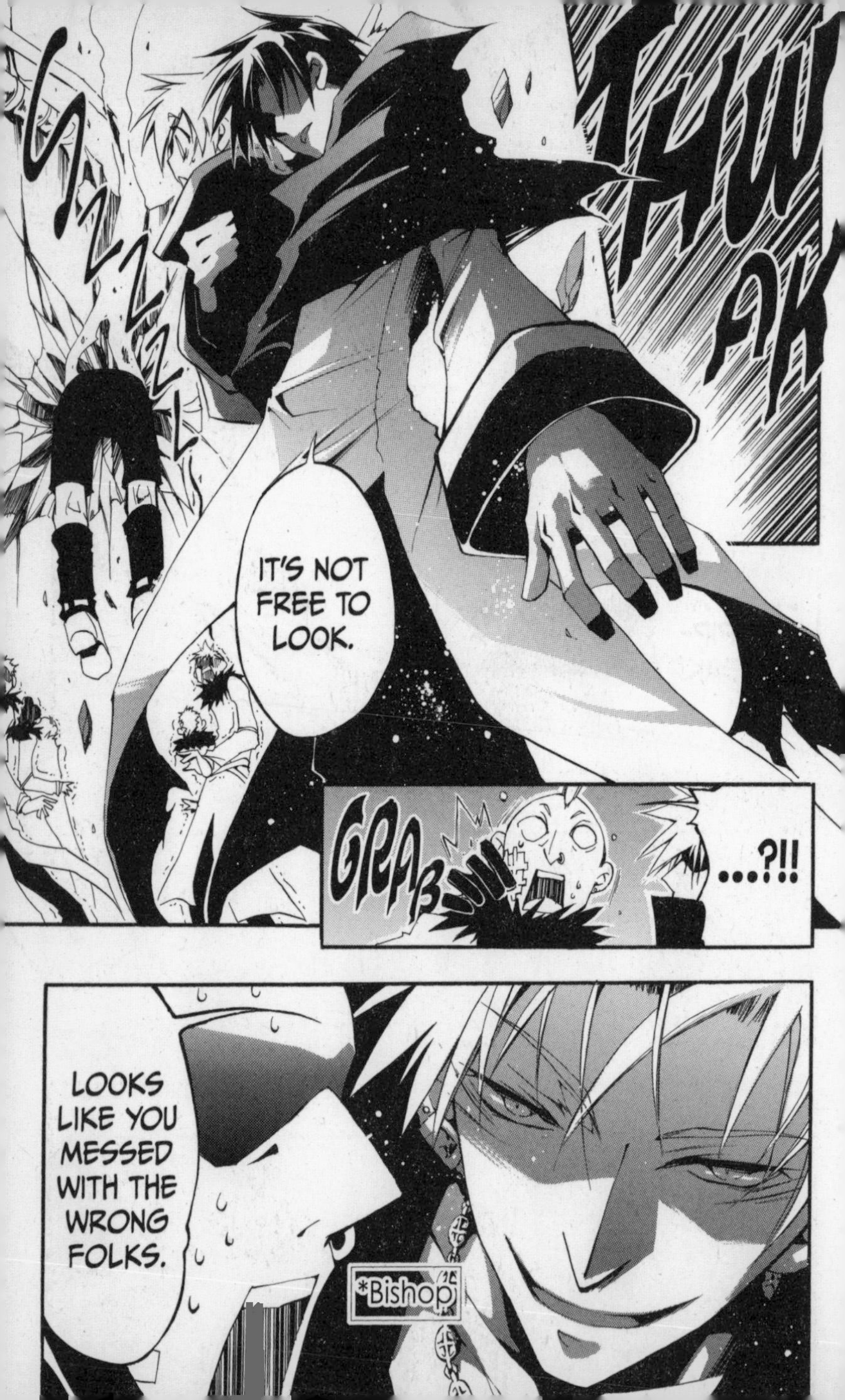
THWAK
SZZZZZ
IT'S NOT FREE TO LOOK.
...?!!
GRAB
LOOKS LIKE YOU MESSED WITH THE WRONG FOLKS.
*Bishop

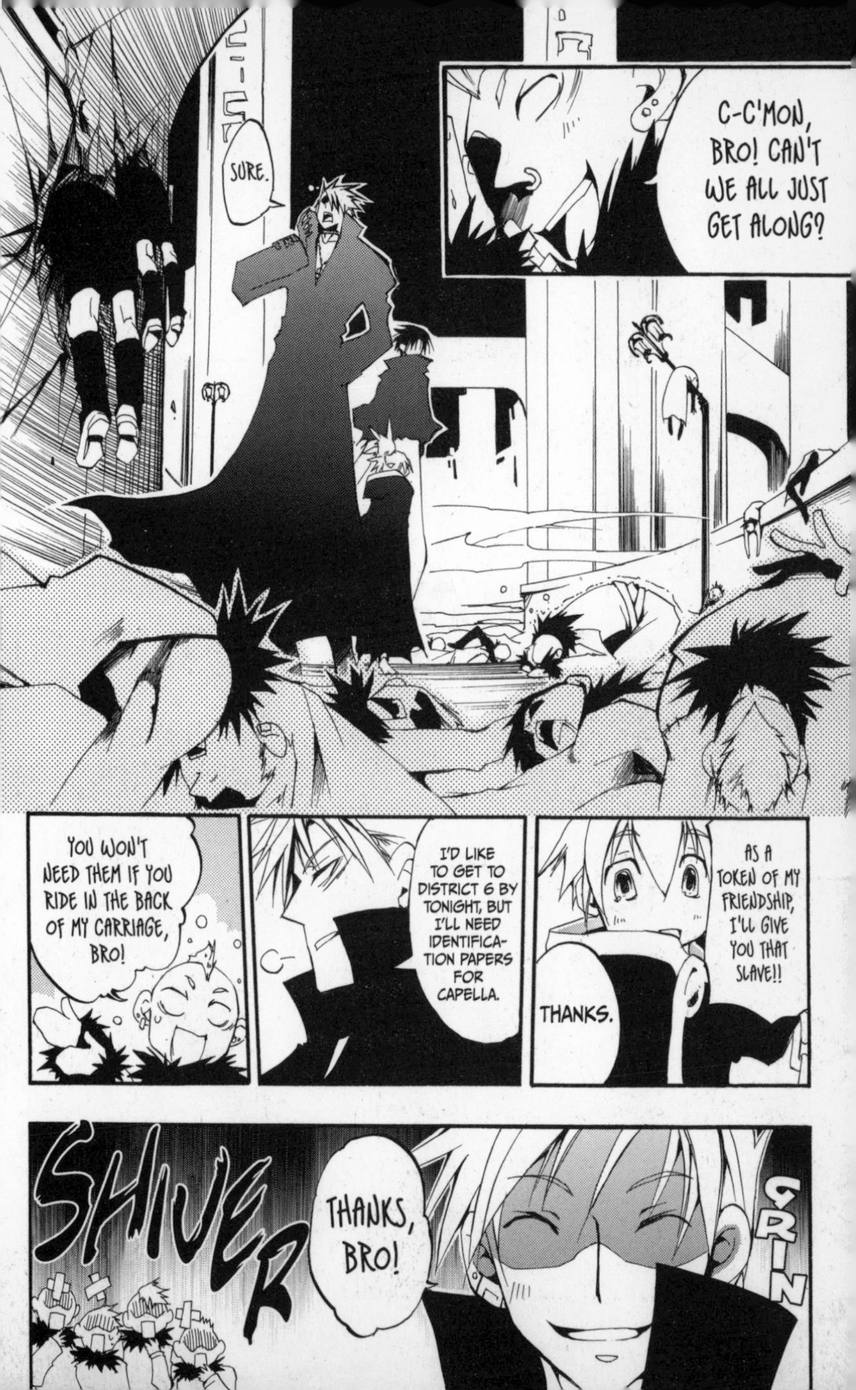
C-C'MON, BRO! CAN'T WE ALL JUST GET ALONG?
SURE.
AS A TOKEN OF MY FRIENDSHIP, I'LL GIVE YOU THAT SLAVE!!
THANKS.
I'D LIKE TO GET TO DISTRICT 6 BY TONIGHT, BUT I'LL NEED IDENTIFICATION PAPERS FOR CAPELLA.
YOU WON'T NEED THEM IF YOU RIDE IN THE BACK OF MY CARRIAGE, BRO!
GRIN
THANKS, BRO!
SHIVER

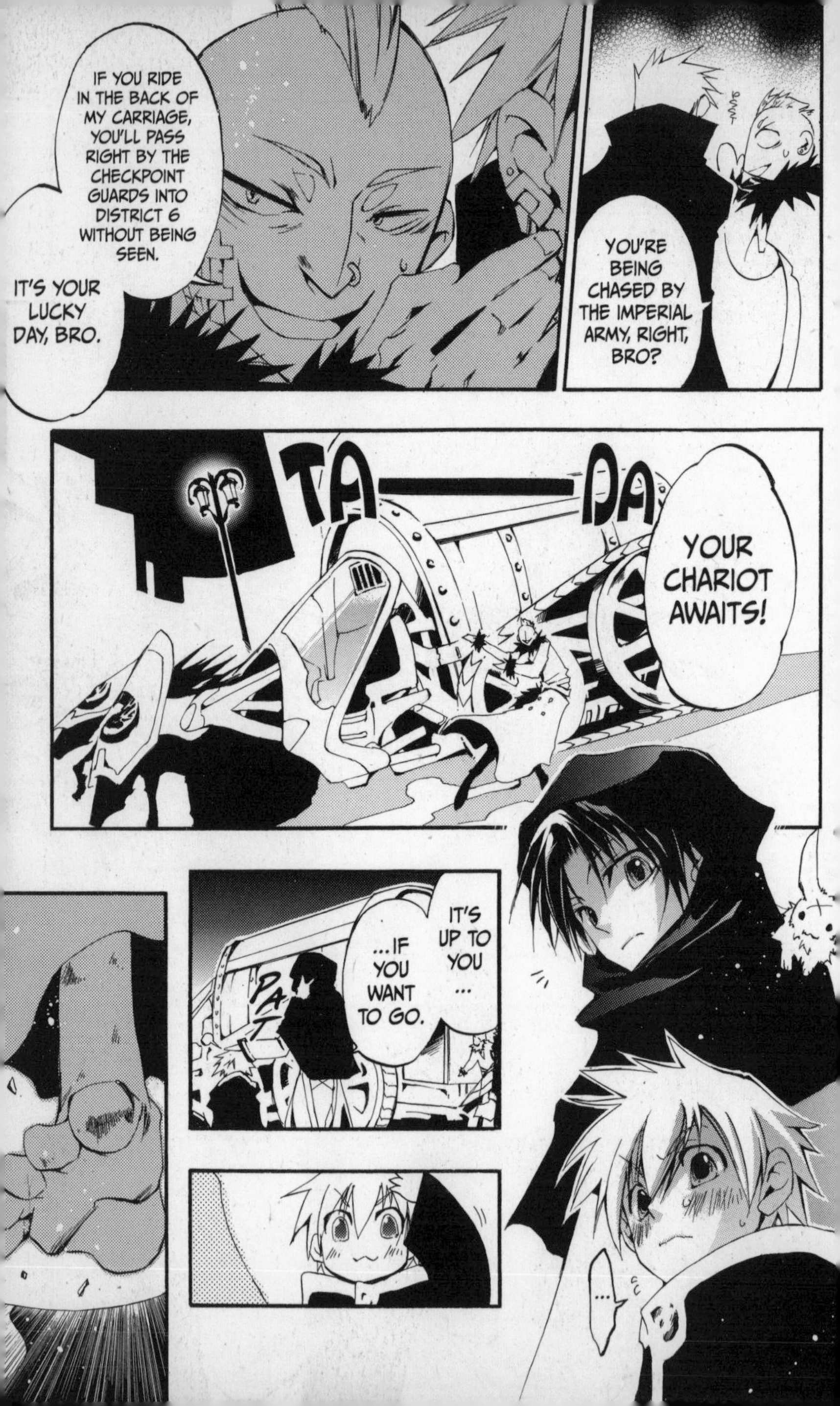
PSST
YOU'RE BEING CHASED BY THE IMPERIAL ARMY, RIGHT, BRO?
IF YOU RIDE IN THE BACK OF MY CARRIAGE, YOU'LL PASS RIGHT BY THE CHECKPOINT GUARDS INTO DISTRICT 6 WITHOUT BEING SEEN.
IT'S YOUR LUCKY DAY, BRO.
TA—DA
YOUR CHARIOT AWAITS!
...
IT'S UP TO YOU ...
...IF YOU WANT TO GO.
PAT

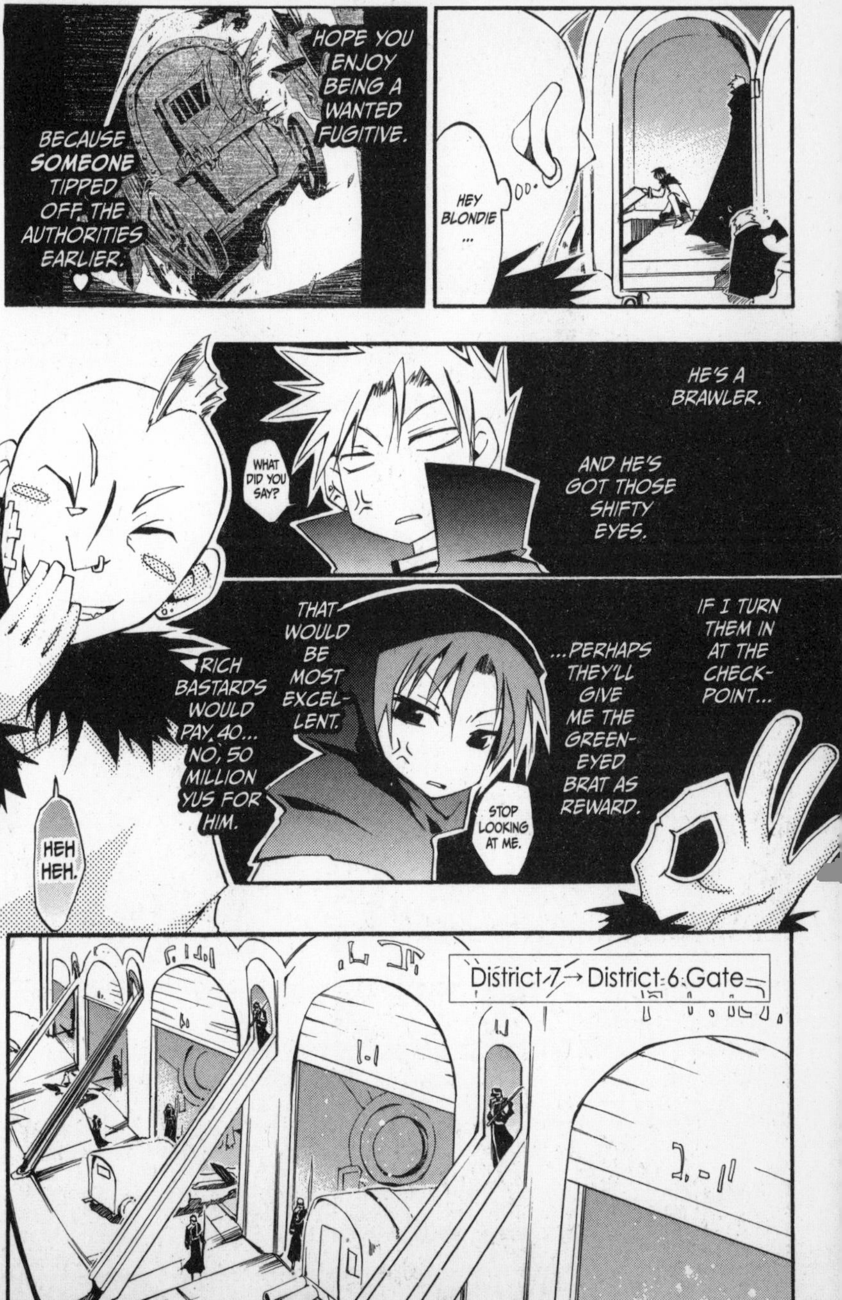
HEY BLONDIE ...
HOPE YOU ENJOY BEING A WANTED FUGITIVE.
BECAUSE SOMEONE TIPPED OFF THE AUTHORITIES EARLIER. ♥
HE'S A BRAWLER.
AND HE'S GOT THOSE SHIFTY EYES.
WHAT DID YOU SAY?
IF I TURN THEM IN AT THE CHECK-POINT...
...PERHAPS THEY'LL GIVE ME THE GREEN-EYED BRAT AS REWARD.
STOP LOOKING AT ME.
THAT WOULD BE MOST EXCEL-LENT.
RICH BASTARDS WOULD PAY 40... NO, 50 MILLION YUS FOR HIM.
HEH HEH.
District 7 → District 6 Gate

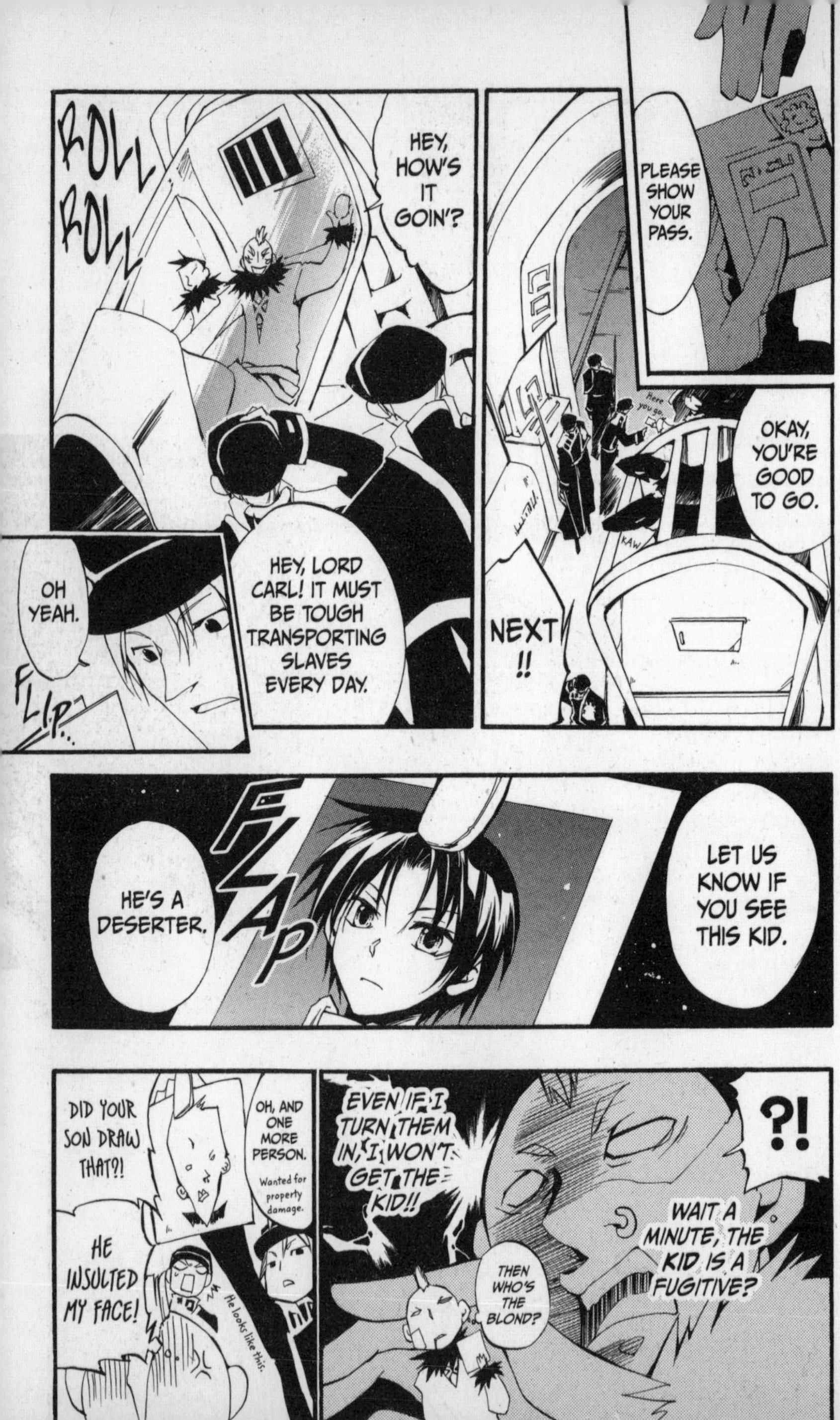
PLEASE SHOW YOUR PASS.
Here you go.
OKAY, YOU'RE GOOD TO GO.
KAW
NEXT!!
HEY, HOW'S IT GOIN'?
ROLL ROLL
HEY, LORD CARL! IT MUST BE TOUGH TRANSPORTING SLAVES EVERY DAY.
OH YEAH.
FLIP...
LET US KNOW IF YOU SEE THIS KID.
FLAP
HE'S A DESERTER.
?!
WAIT A MINUTE, THE KID IS A FUGITIVE?
THEN WHO'S THE BLOND?
EVEN IF I TURN THEM IN, I WON'T GET THE KID!!
OH, AND ONE MORE PERSON.
Wanted for property damage.
DID YOUR SON DRAW THAT?!
HE INSULTED MY FACE!
He looks like this.

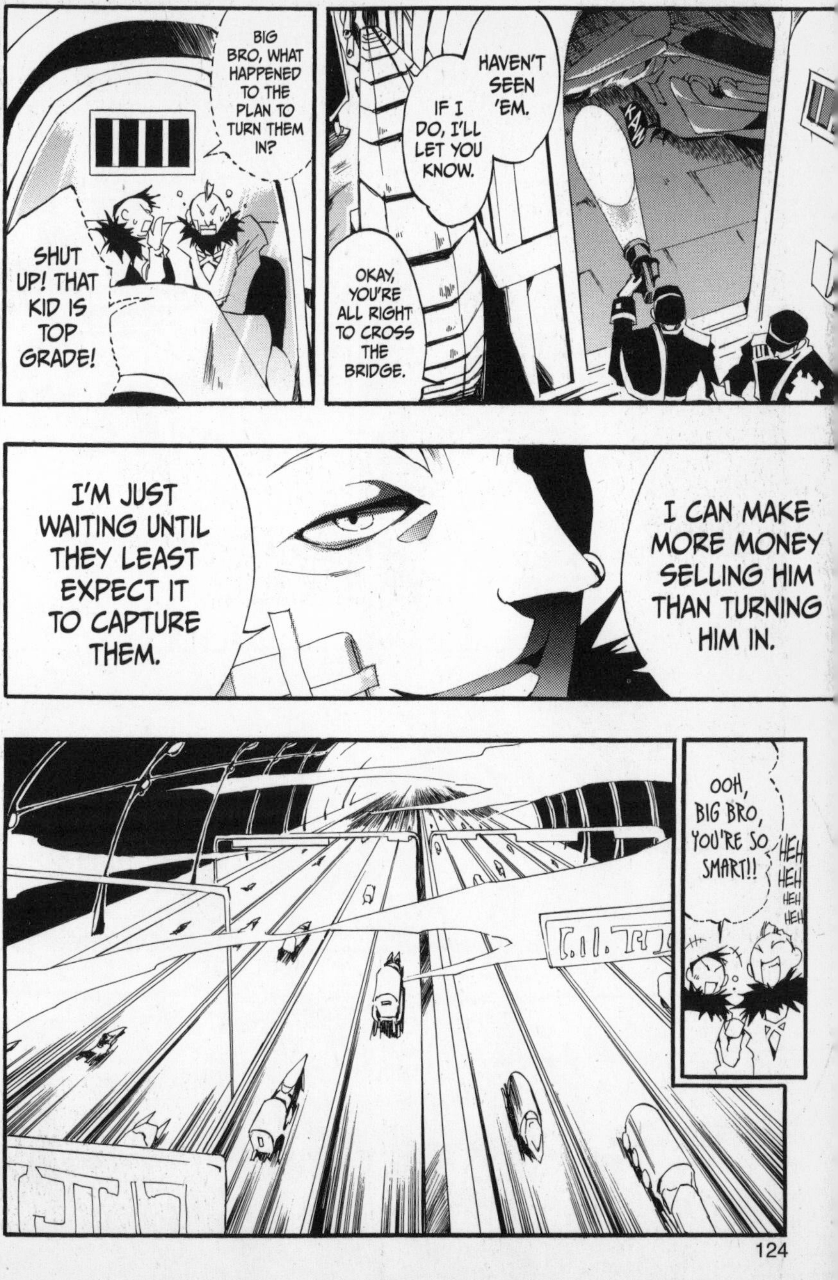
KAW
HAVEN'T SEEN 'EM.
IF I DO, I'LL LET YOU KNOW.
OKAY, YOU'RE ALL RIGHT TO CROSS THE BRIDGE.
BIG BRO, WHAT HAPPENED TO THE PLAN TO TURN THEM IN?
SHUT UP! THAT KID IS TOP GRADE!
I CAN MAKE MORE MONEY SELLING HIM THAN TURNING HIM IN.
I'M JUST WAITING UNTIL THEY LEAST EXPECT IT TO CAPTURE THEM.
OOH, BIG BRO, YOU'RE SO SMART!!
HEH HEH HEH HEH

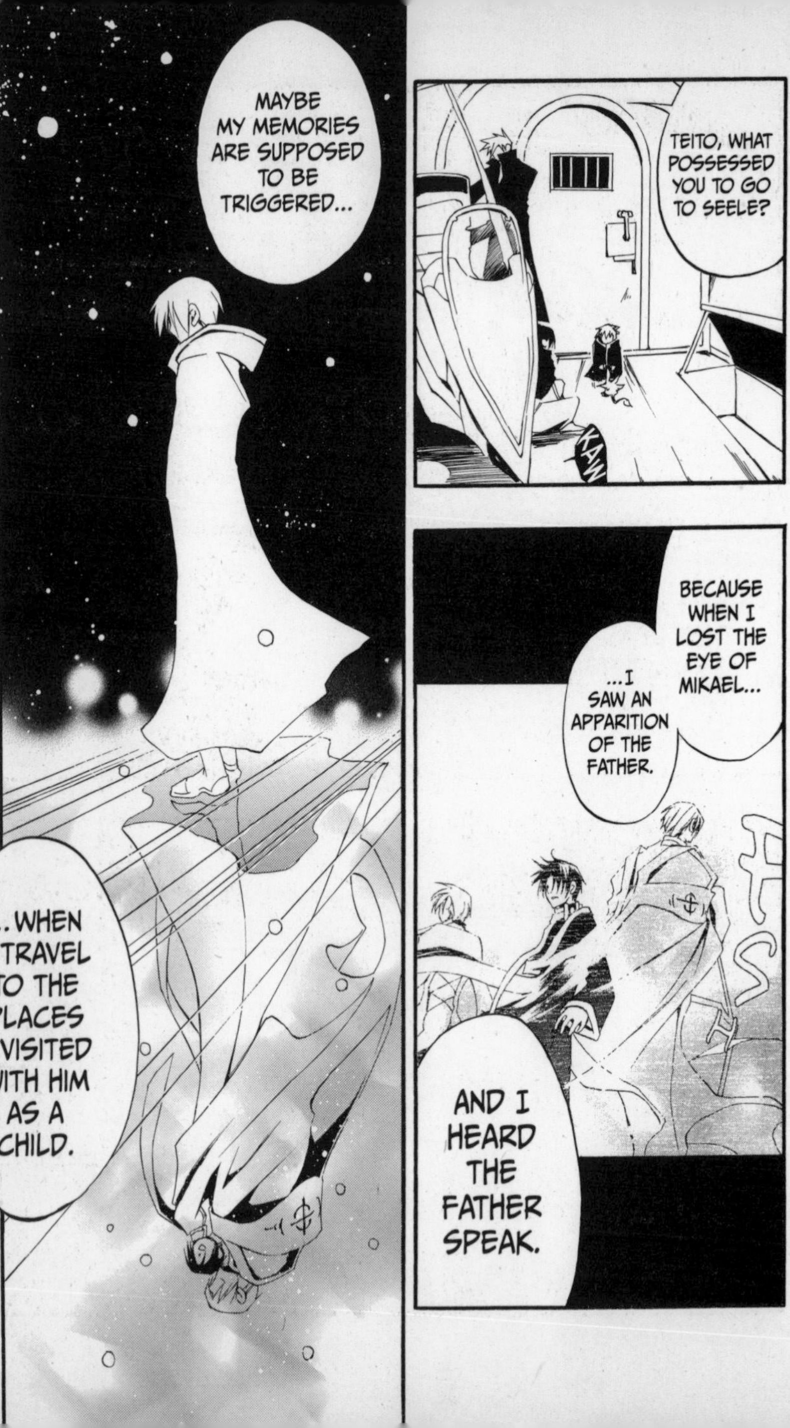
TEITO, WHAT POSSESSED YOU TO GO TO SEELE?
KAW
BECAUSE WHEN I LOST THE EYE OF MIKAEL...
...I SAW AN APPARITION OF THE FATHER.
AND I HEARD THE FATHER SPEAK.
MAYBE MY MEMORIES ARE SUPPOSED TO BE TRIGGERED...
...WHEN I TRAVEL TO THE PLACES I VISITED WITH HIM AS A CHILD.

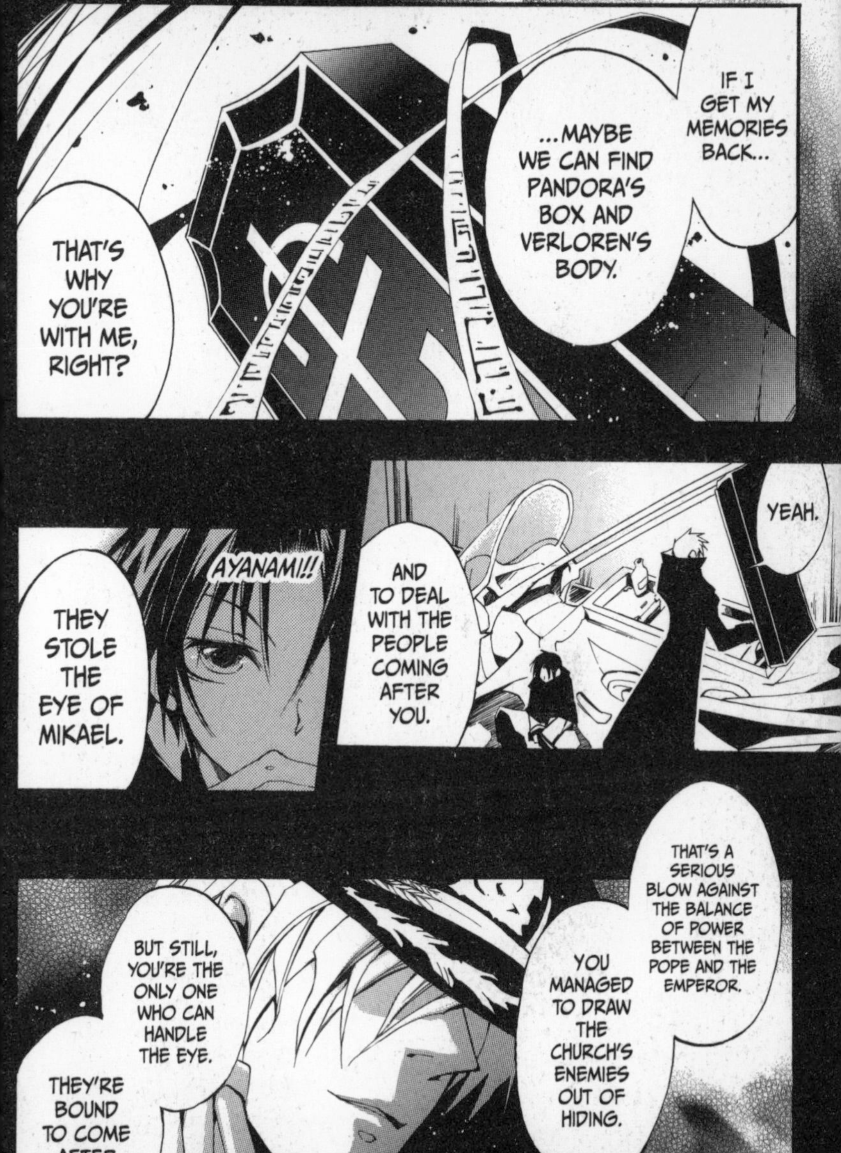
IF I GET MY MEMORIES BACK...
...MAYBE WE CAN FIND PANDORA'S BOX AND VERLOREN'S BODY.
THAT'S WHY YOU'RE WITH ME, RIGHT?
YEAH.
AND TO DEAL WITH THE PEOPLE COMING AFTER YOU.
AYANAMI!!
THEY STOLE THE EYE OF MIKAEL.
THAT'S A SERIOUS BLOW AGAINST THE BALANCE OF POWER BETWEEN THE POPE AND THE EMPEROR.
YOU MANAGED TO DRAW THE CHURCH'S ENEMIES OUT OF HIDING.
BUT STILL, YOU'RE THE ONLY ONE WHO CAN HANDLE THE EYE.
THEY'RE BOUND TO COME AFTER YOU.

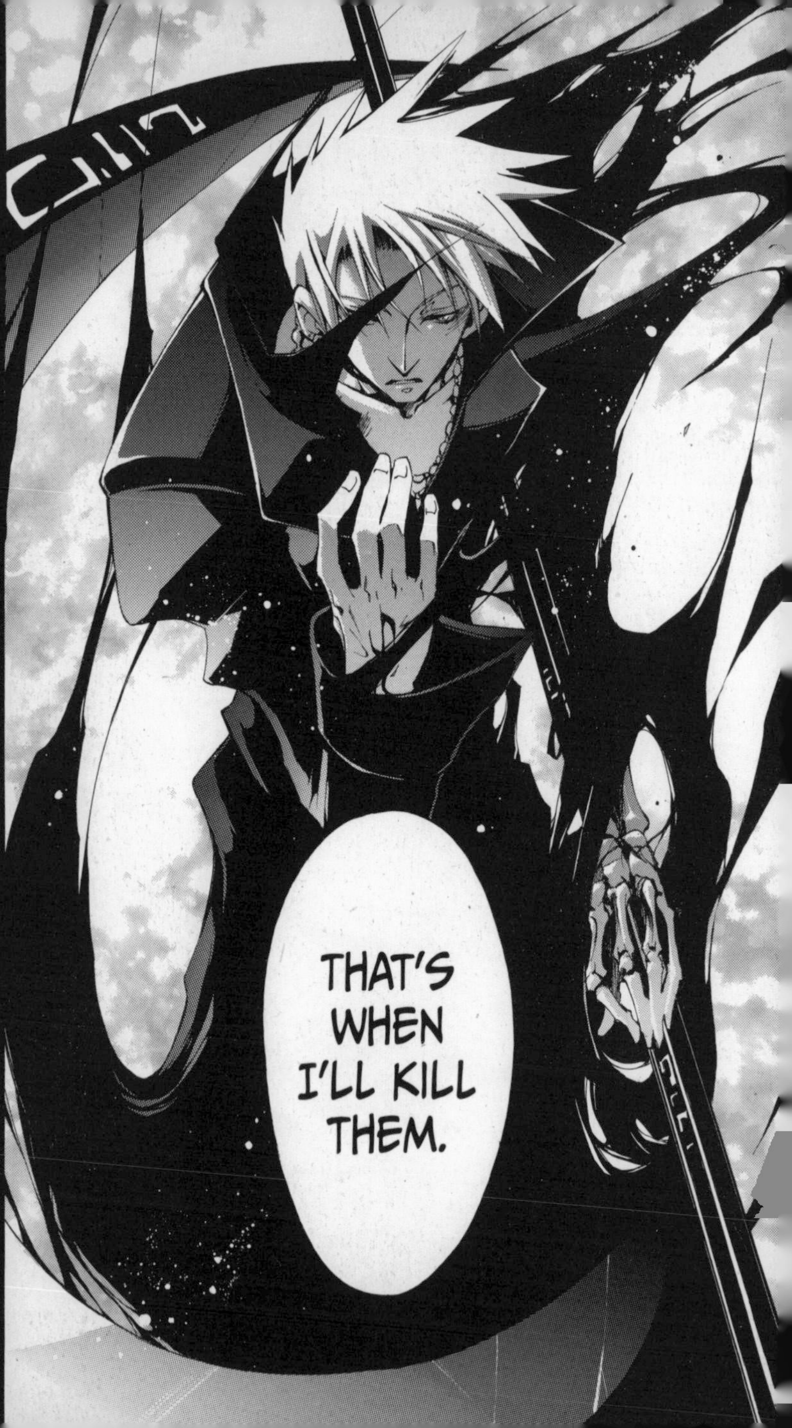
THAT'S WHEN I'LL KILL THEM.

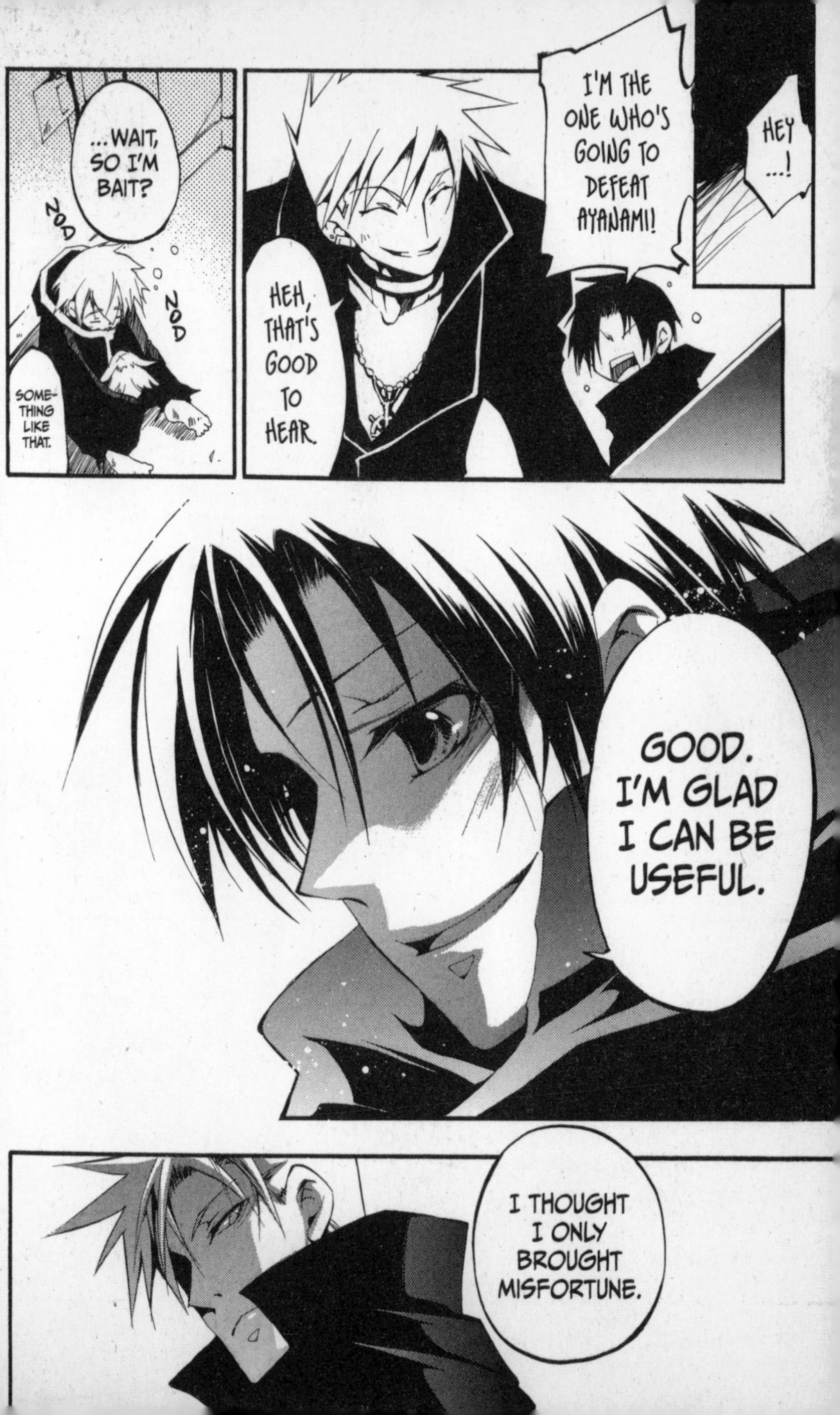
HEY ...!
I'M THE ONE WHO'S GOING TO DEFEAT AYANAMI!
HEH, THAT'S GOOD TO HEAR.
...WAIT, SO I'M BAIT?
NOD NOD
SOMETHING LIKE THAT.
GOOD. I'M GLAD I CAN BE USEFUL.
I THOUGHT I ONLY BROUGHT MISFORTUNE.

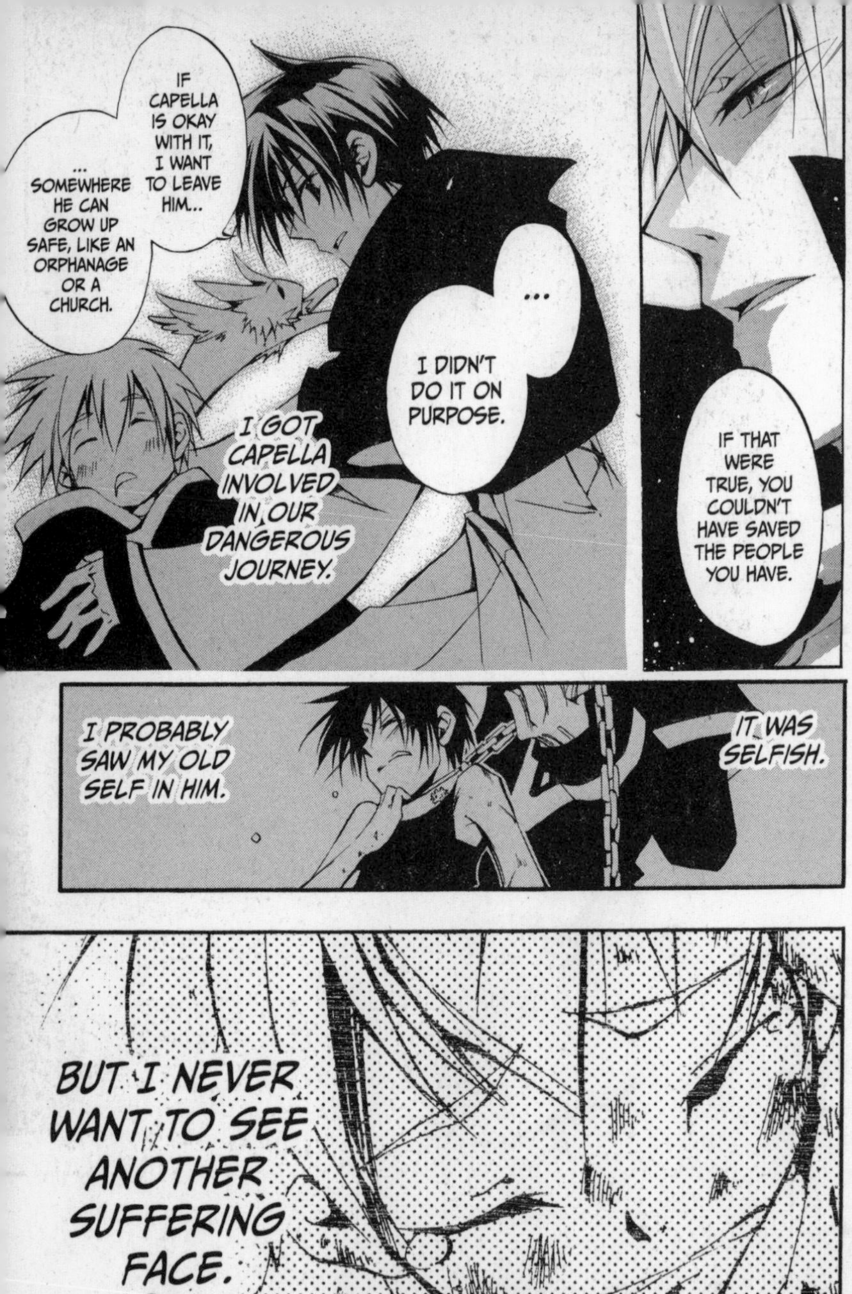
IF THAT WERE TRUE, YOU COULDN'T HAVE SAVED THE PEOPLE YOU HAVE.
IF CAPELLA IS OKAY WITH IT, I WANT TO LEAVE HIM...
... SOMEWHERE HE CAN GROW UP SAFE, LIKE AN ORPHANAGE OR A CHURCH.
...
I DIDN'T DO IT ON PURPOSE.
I GOT CAPELLA INVOLVED IN OUR DANGEROUS JOURNEY.
IT WAS SELFISH.
I PROBABLY SAW MY OLD SELF IN HIM.
BUT I NEVER WANT TO SEE ANOTHER SUFFERING FACE.

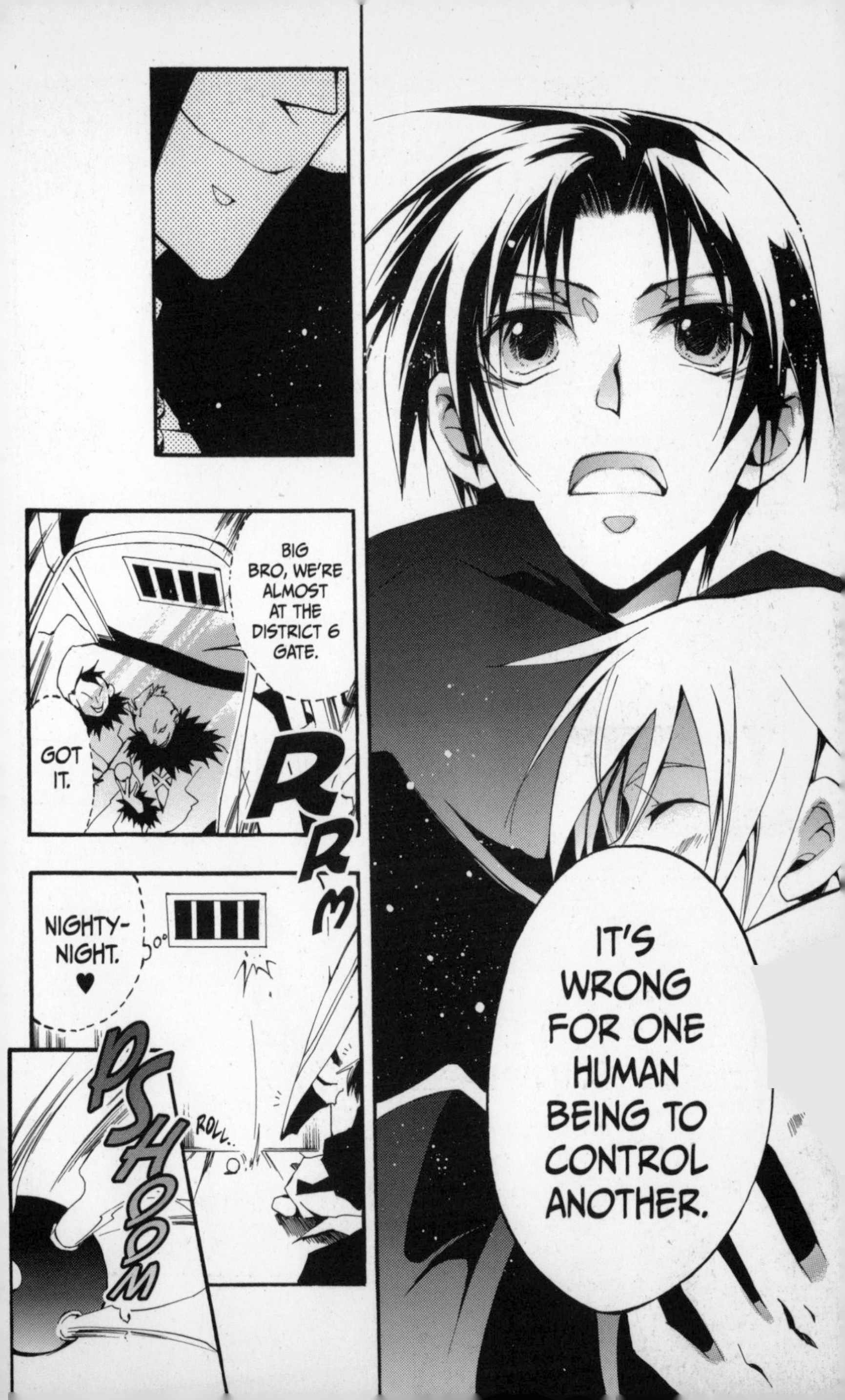
IT'S WRONG FOR ONE HUMAN BEING TO CONTROL ANOTHER.
BIG BRO, WE'RE ALMOST AT THE DISTRICT 6 GATE.
GOT IT.
RRM
NIGHTY-NIGHT. ♥
ROLL..
PSHOOM

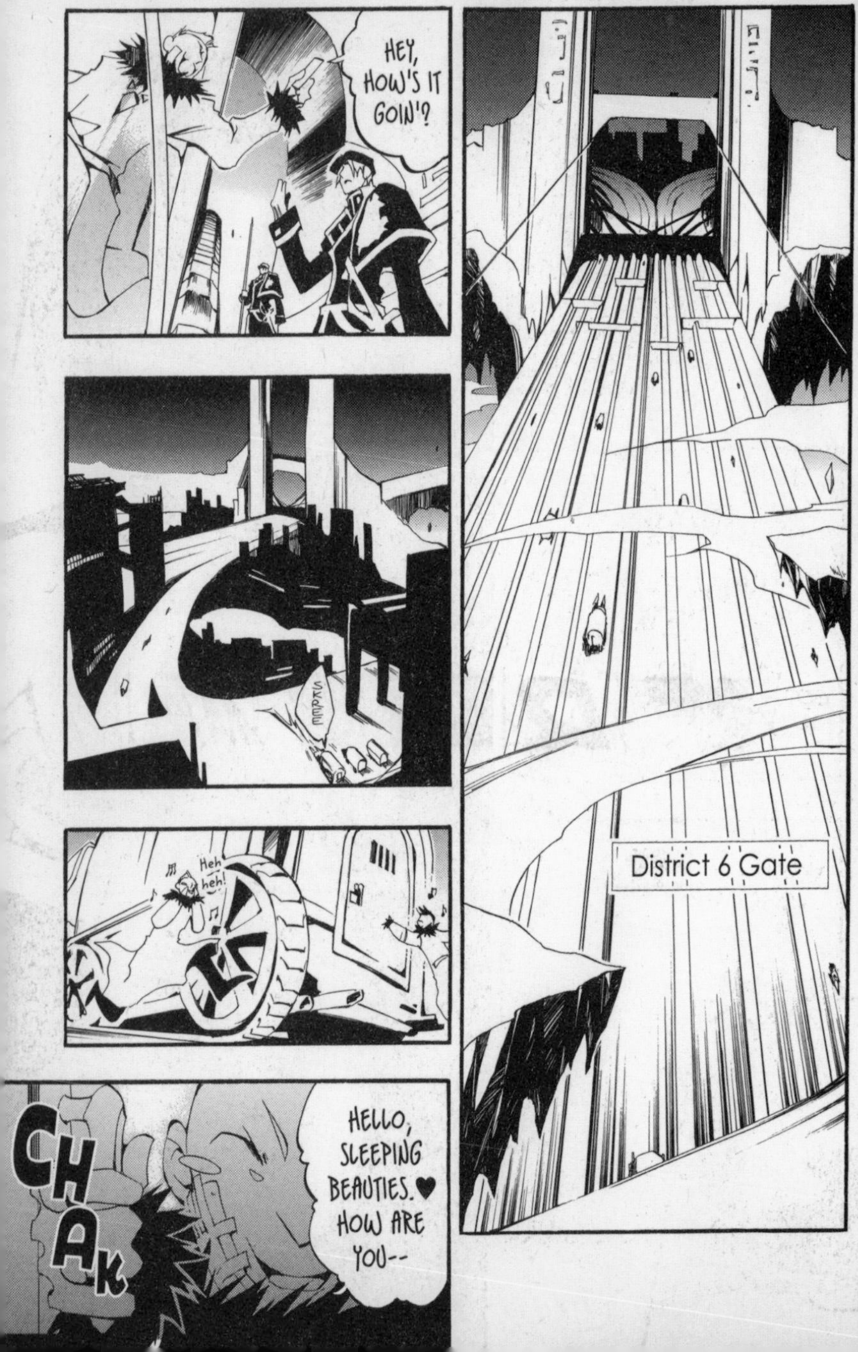
District 6 Gate
HEY, HOW'S IT GOIN'?
SKREE
Heh heh!
HELLO, SLEEPING BEAUTIES.♥ HOW ARE YOU--
CHAK

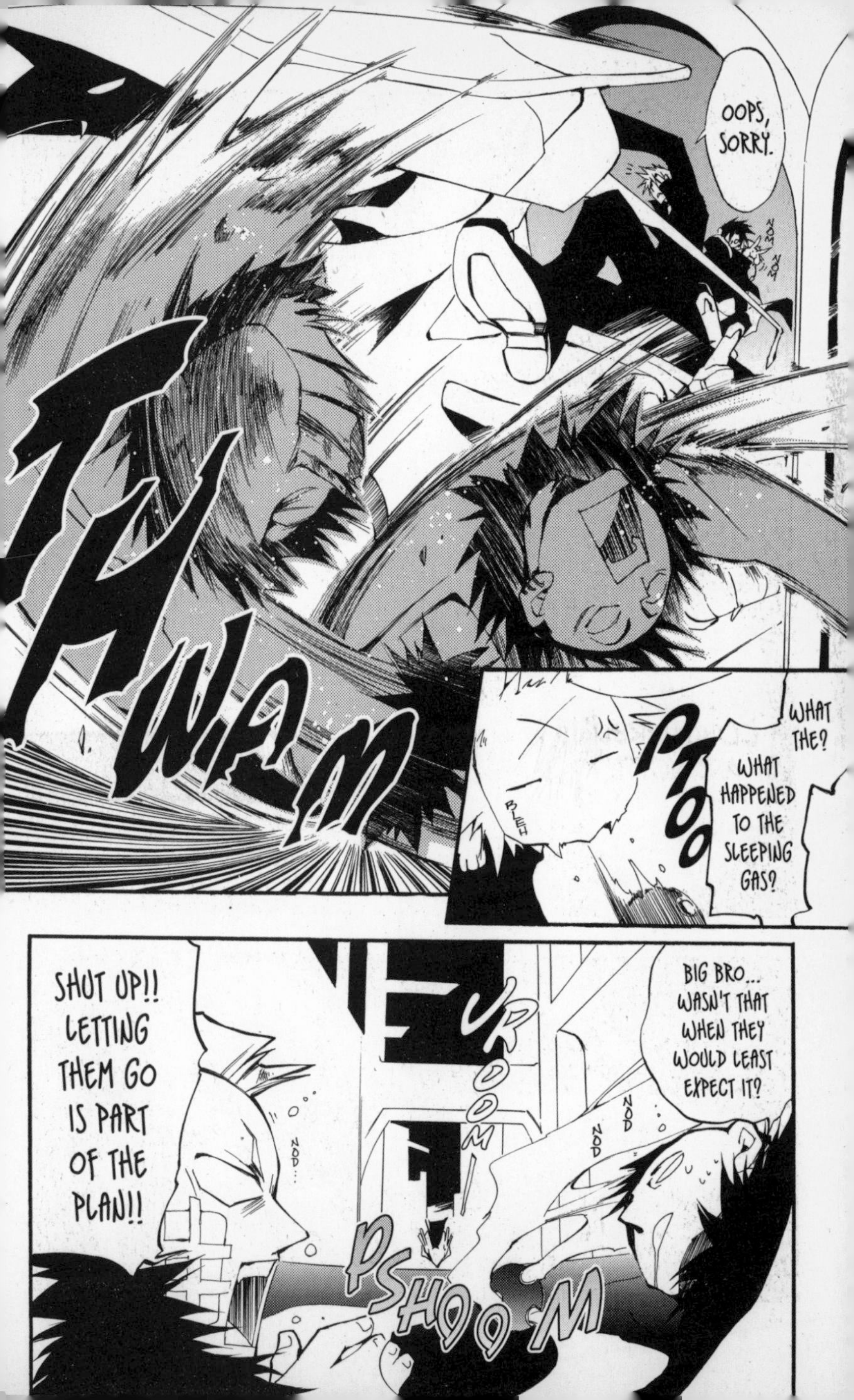
OOPS, SORRY.
NOM NOM
FWAM
WHAT THE?
WHAT HAPPENED TO THE SLEEPING GAS?
PTOO
BLEH
BIG BRO... WASN'T THAT WHEN THEY WOULD LEAST EXPECT IT?
NOD NOD
VROOOM
NOD...
SHUT UP!! LETTING THEM GO IS PART OF THE PLAN!!
PSHOOM

Kapitel.28 "District 6"

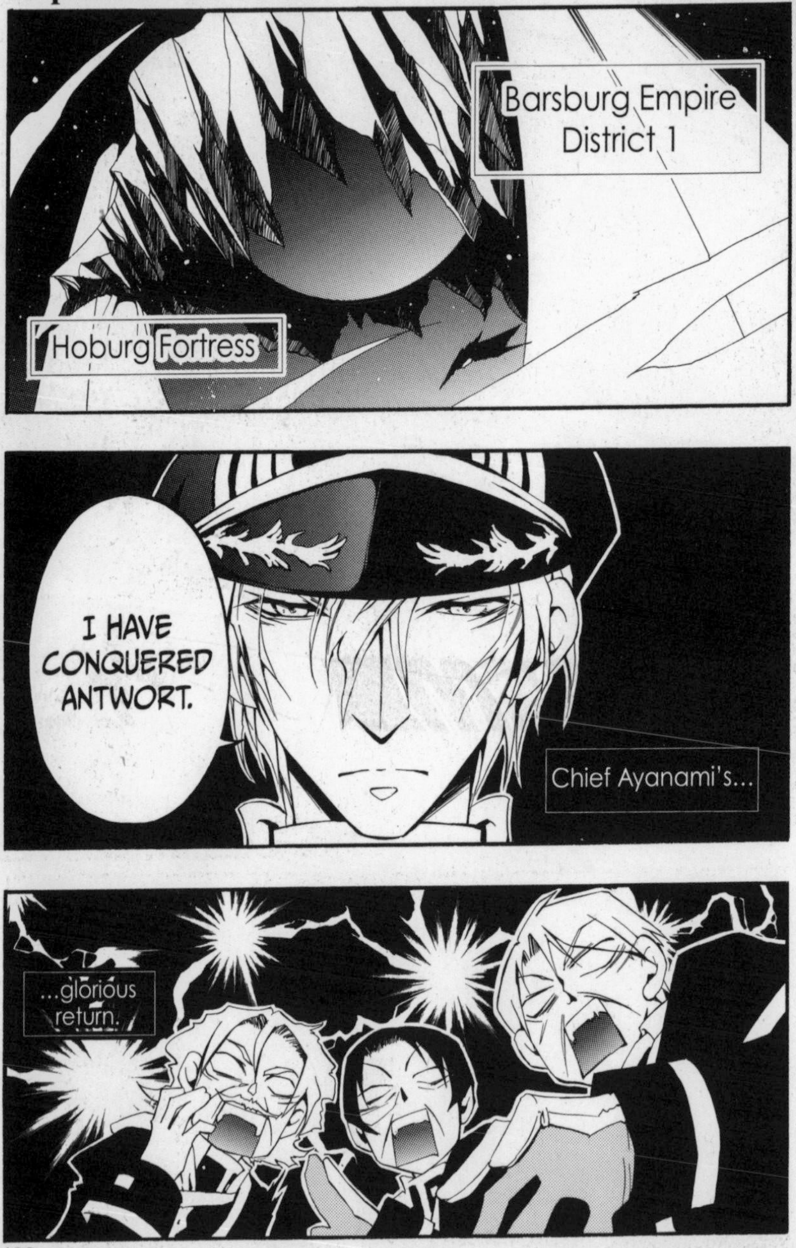
Barsburg Empire District 1
Hoburg Fortress
I HAVE CONQUERED ANTWORT.
Chief Ayanami's...
...glorious return.

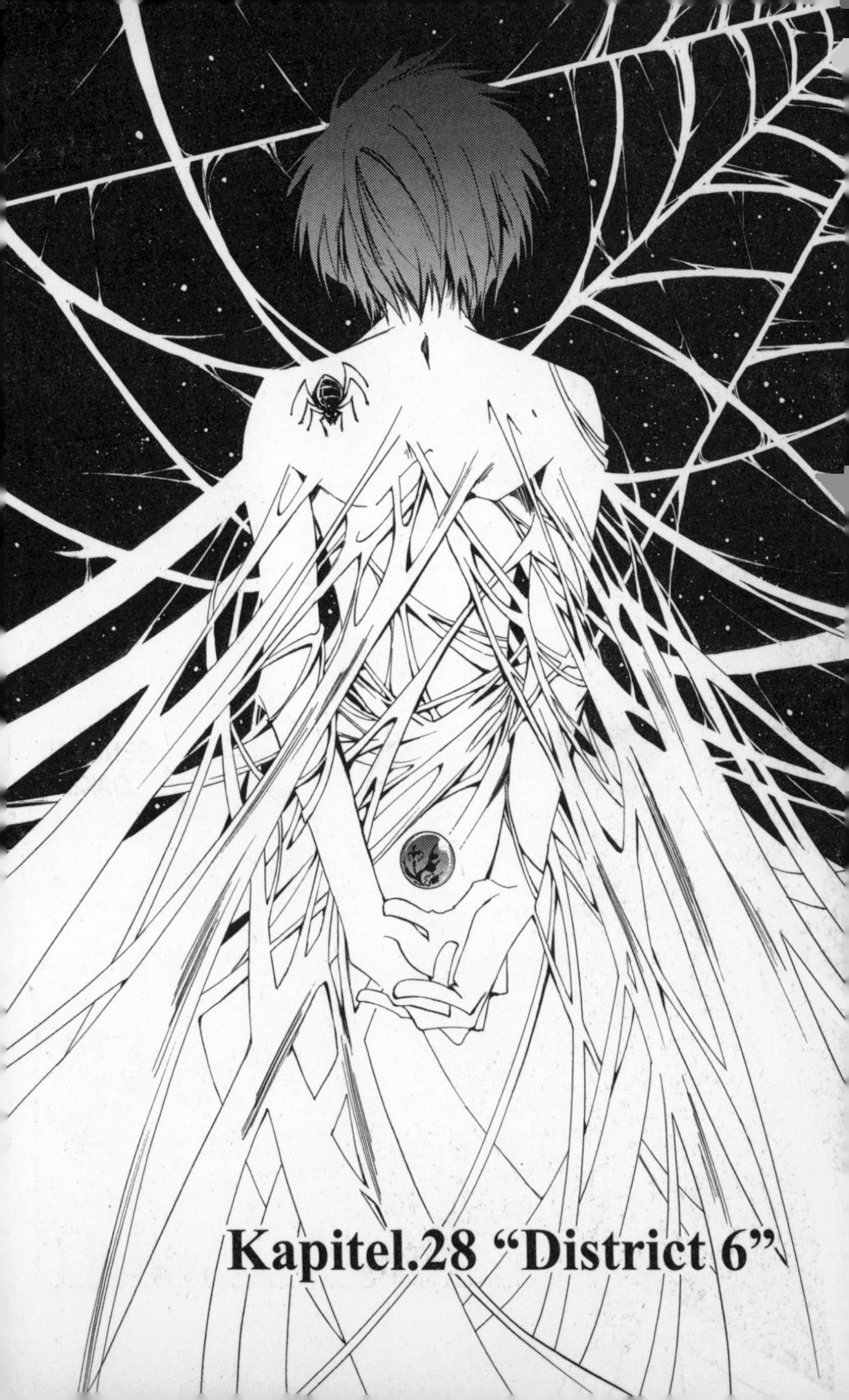

Kapitel.28 “District 6”

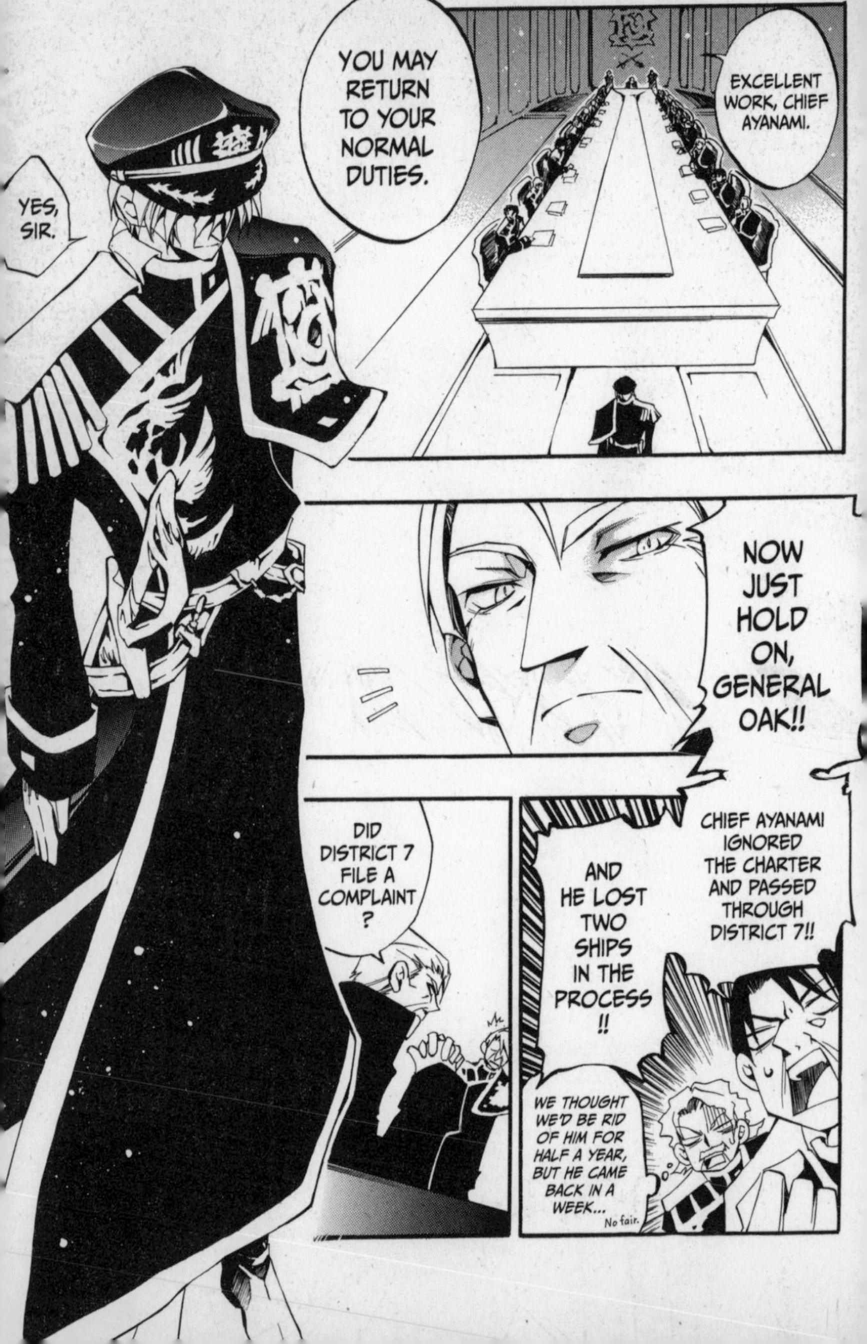
EXCELLENT WORK, CHIEF AYANAMI.
YOU MAY RETURN TO YOUR NORMAL DUTIES.
NOW JUST HOLD ON, GENERAL OAK!!
CHIEF AYANAMI IGNORED THE CHARTER AND PASSED THROUGH DISTRICT 7!!
AND HE LOST TWO SHIPS IN THE PROCESS!!
WE THOUGHT WE'D BE RID OF HIM FOR HALF A YEAR, BUT HE CAME BACK IN A WEEK...
No fair.
DID DISTRICT 7 FILE A COMPLAINT?
YES, SIR.

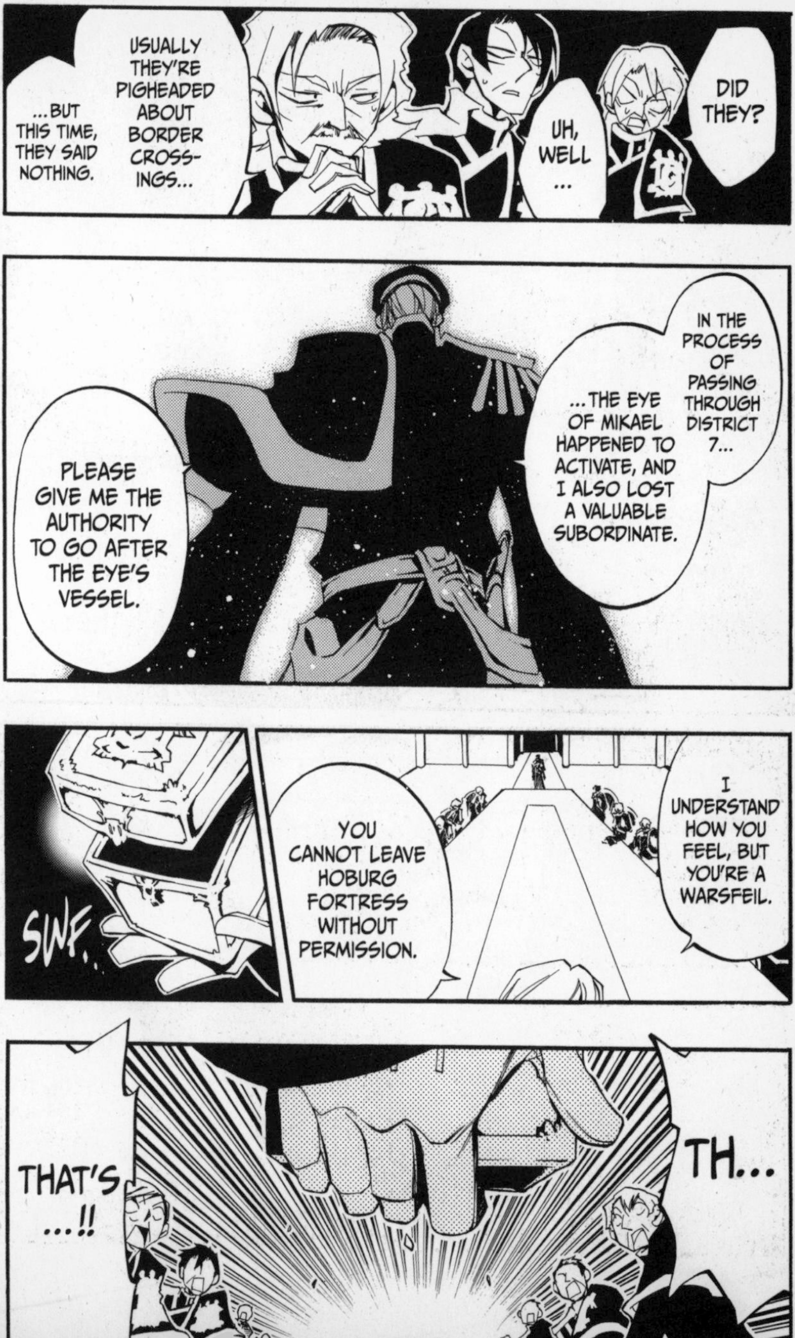
DID THEY?
UH, WELL ...
USUALLY THEY'RE PIGHEADED ABOUT BORDER CROSSINGS...
...BUT THIS TIME, THEY SAID NOTHING.
IN THE PROCESS OF PASSING THROUGH DISTRICT 7...
...THE EYE OF MIKAEL HAPPENED TO ACTIVATE, AND I ALSO LOST A VALUABLE SUBORDINATE.
PLEASE GIVE ME THE AUTHORITY TO GO AFTER THE EYE'S VESSEL.
I UNDERSTAND HOW YOU FEEL, BUT YOU'RE A WARSFEIL.
YOU CANNOT LEAVE HOBURG FORTRESS WITHOUT PERMISSION.
SWF..
TH...
THAT'S ...!!

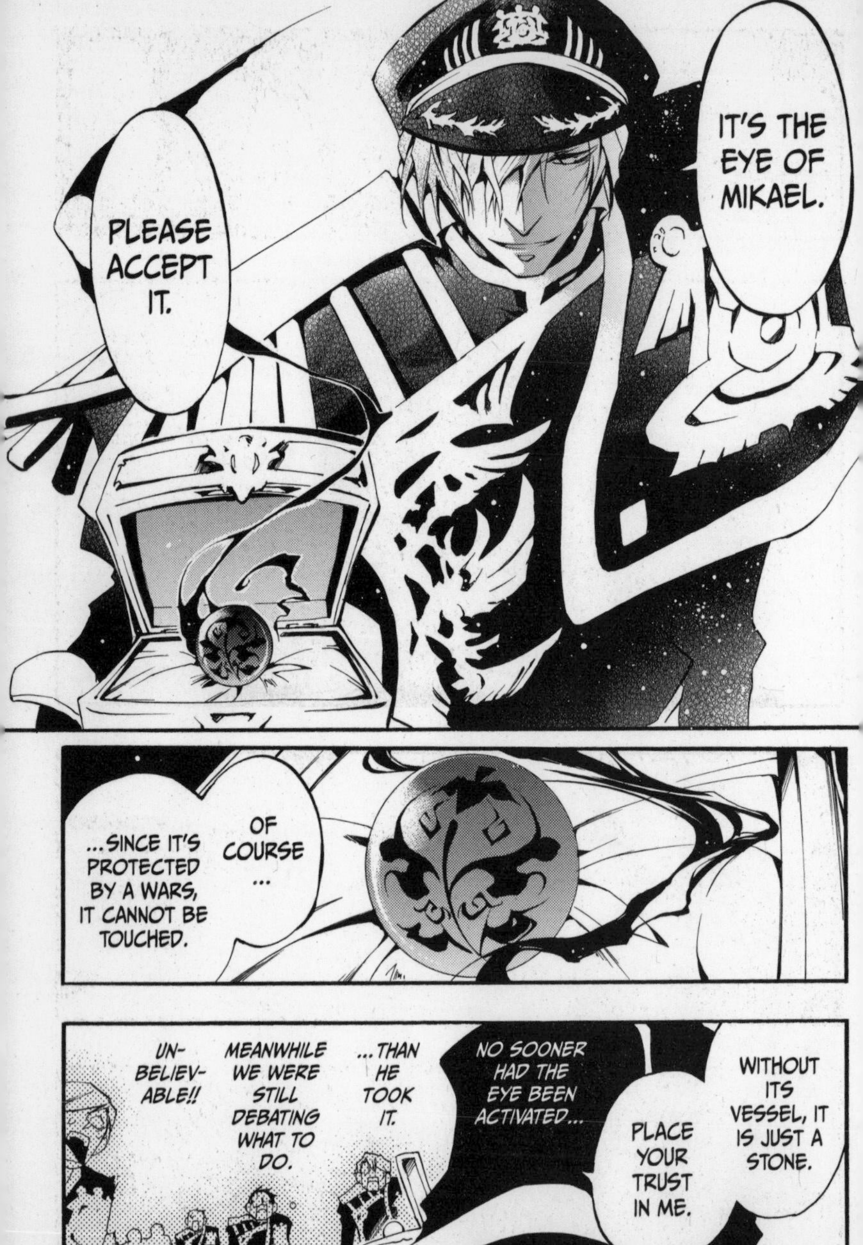
IT'S THE EYE OF MIKAEL.
PLEASE ACCEPT IT.
OF COURSE ...
...SINCE IT'S PROTECTED BY A WARS, IT CANNOT BE TOUCHED.
WITHOUT ITS VESSEL, IT IS JUST A STONE.
PLACE YOUR TRUST IN ME.
NO SOONER HAD THE EYE BEEN ACTIVATED...
...THAN HE TOOK IT.
MEANWHILE WE WERE STILL DEBATING WHAT TO DO.
UN-BELIEV-ABLE!!

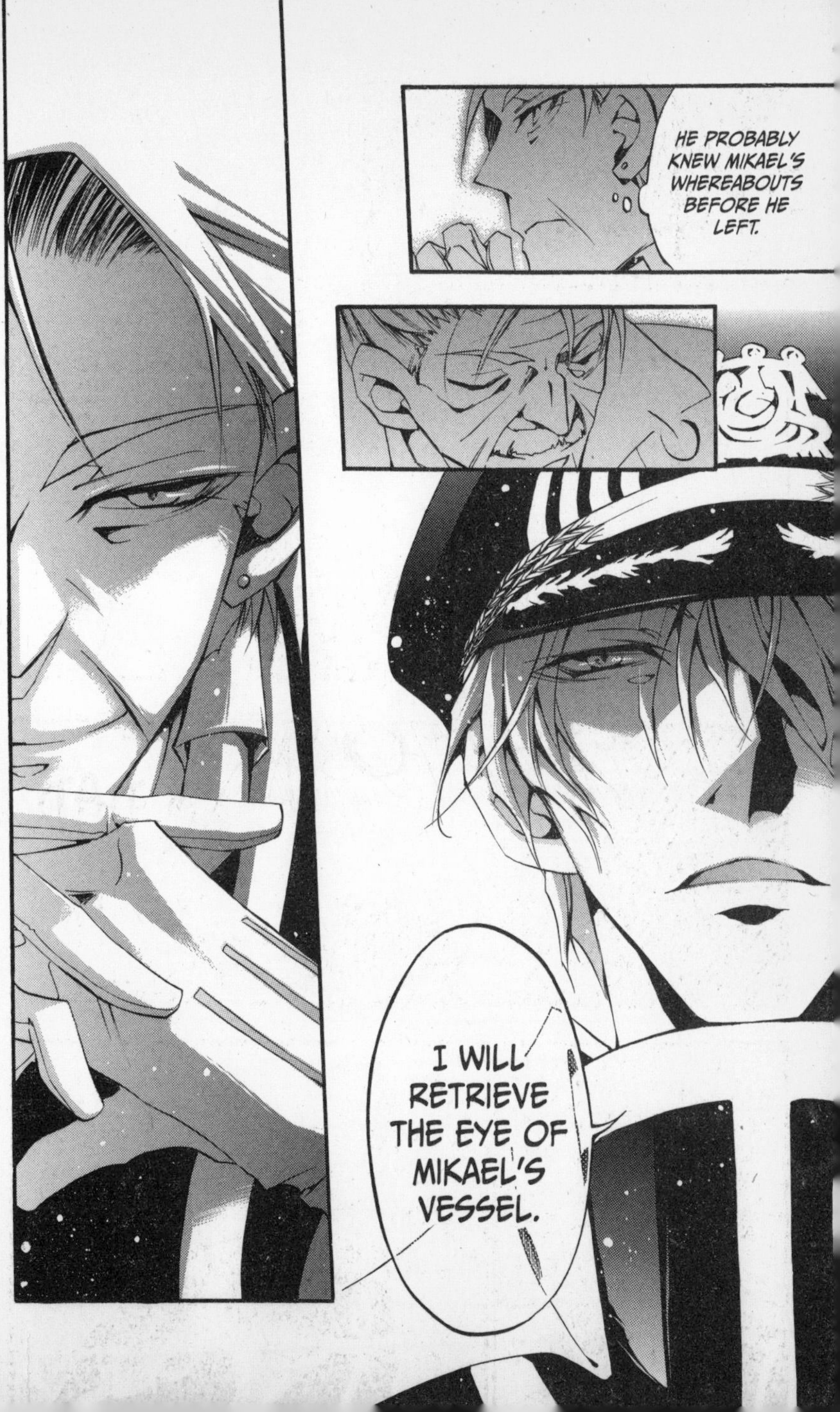
HE PROBABLY KNEW MIKAEL'S WHEREABOUTS BEFORE HE LEFT.
I WILL RETRIEVE THE EYE OF MIKAEL'S VESSEL.

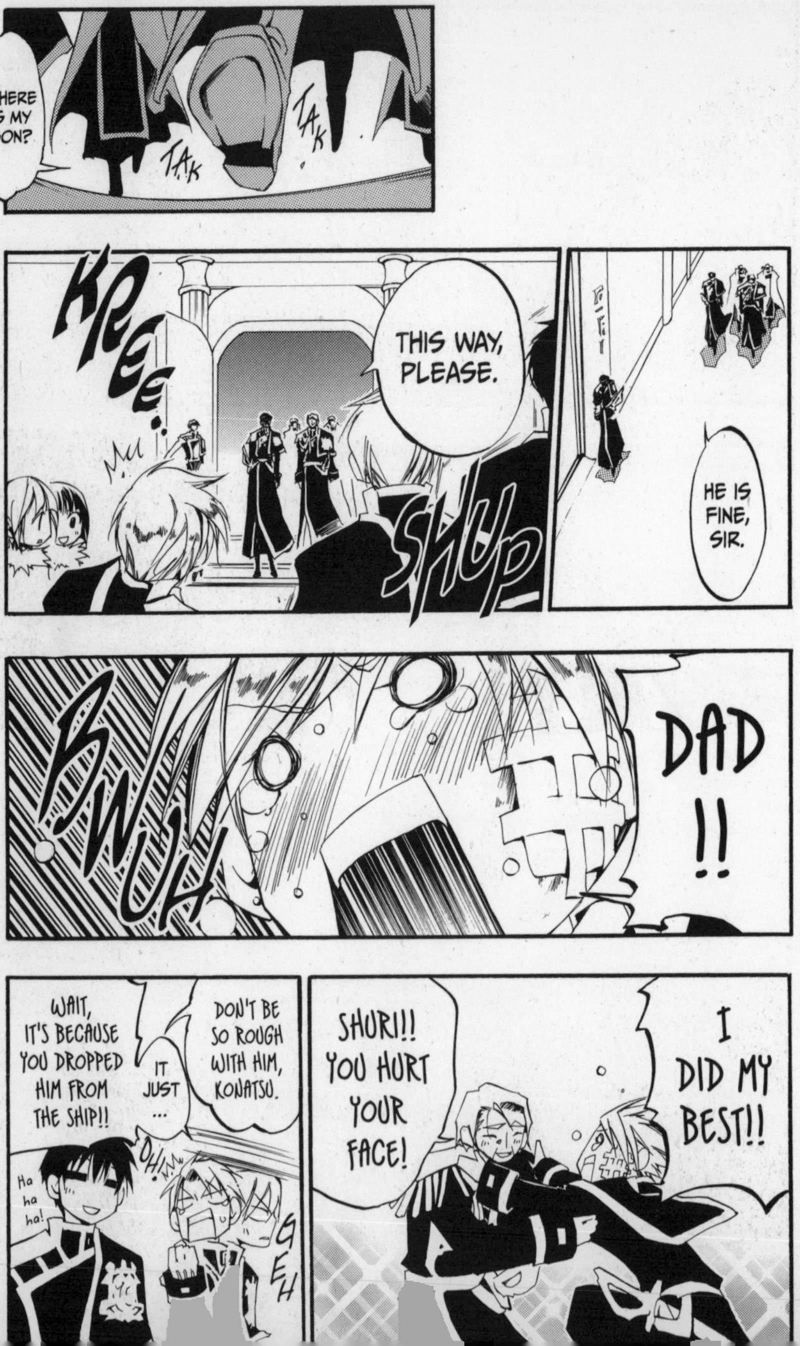
WHERE IS MY SON?
TAK
TAK
HE IS FINE, SIR.
THIS WAY, PLEASE.
KREEE...
SHUP
DAD!!
BWUH
I DID MY BEST!!
SHURI!! YOU HURT YOUR FACE!
DON'T BE SO ROUGH WITH HIM, KONATSU.
IT JUST ...
WAIT, IT'S BECAUSE YOU DROPPED HIM FROM THE SHIP!!
Ha ha ha!
GEH

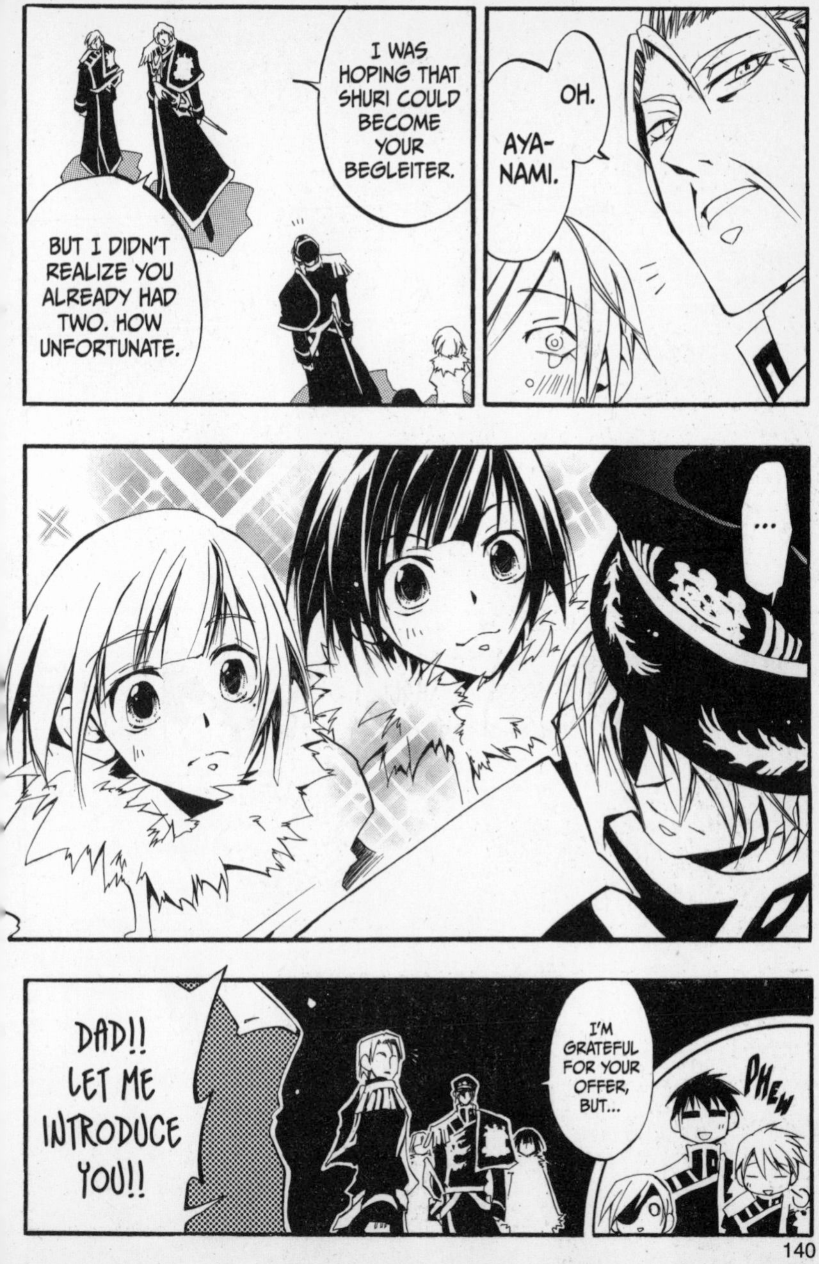
OH.
AYA-NAMI.
I WAS HOPING THAT SHURI COULD BECOME YOUR BEGLEITER.
BUT I DIDN'T REALIZE YOU ALREADY HAD TWO. HOW UNFORTUNATE.
...
I'M GRATEFUL FOR YOUR OFFER, BUT...
PHEW
DAD!! LET ME INTRODUCE YOU!!

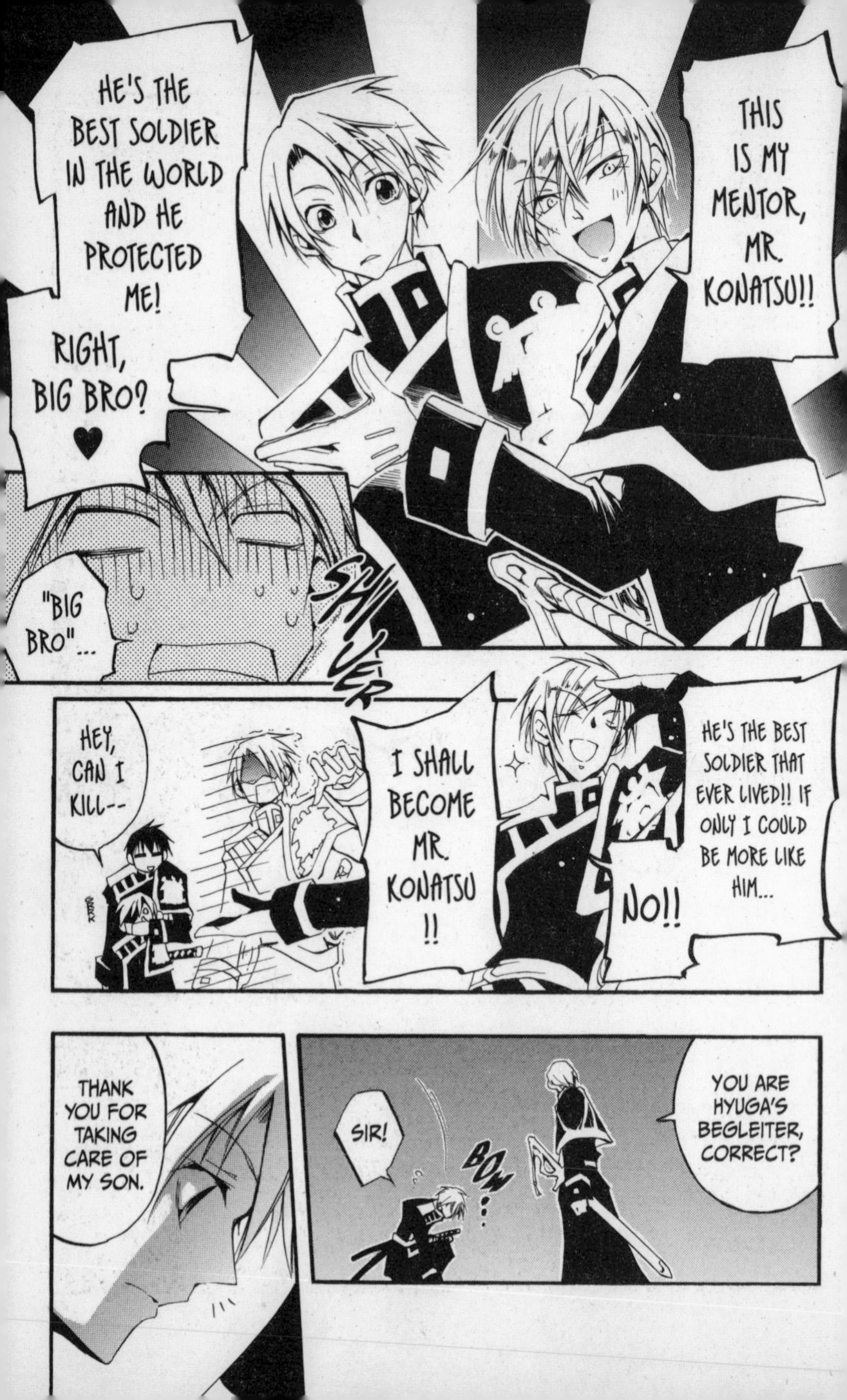
THIS IS MY MENTOR, MR. KONATSU!!
HE'S THE BEST SOLDIER IN THE WORLD AND HE PROTECTED ME!
RIGHT, BIG BRO? ♥
SHIVER
"BIG BRO"...
HE'S THE BEST SOLDIER THAT EVER LIVED!! IF ONLY I COULD BE MORE LIKE HIM...
NO!!
I SHALL BECOME MR. KONATSU!!
HEY, CAN I KILL--
YOU ARE HYUGA'S BEGLEITER, CORRECT?
BOW...
SIR!
THANK YOU FOR TAKING CARE OF MY SON.

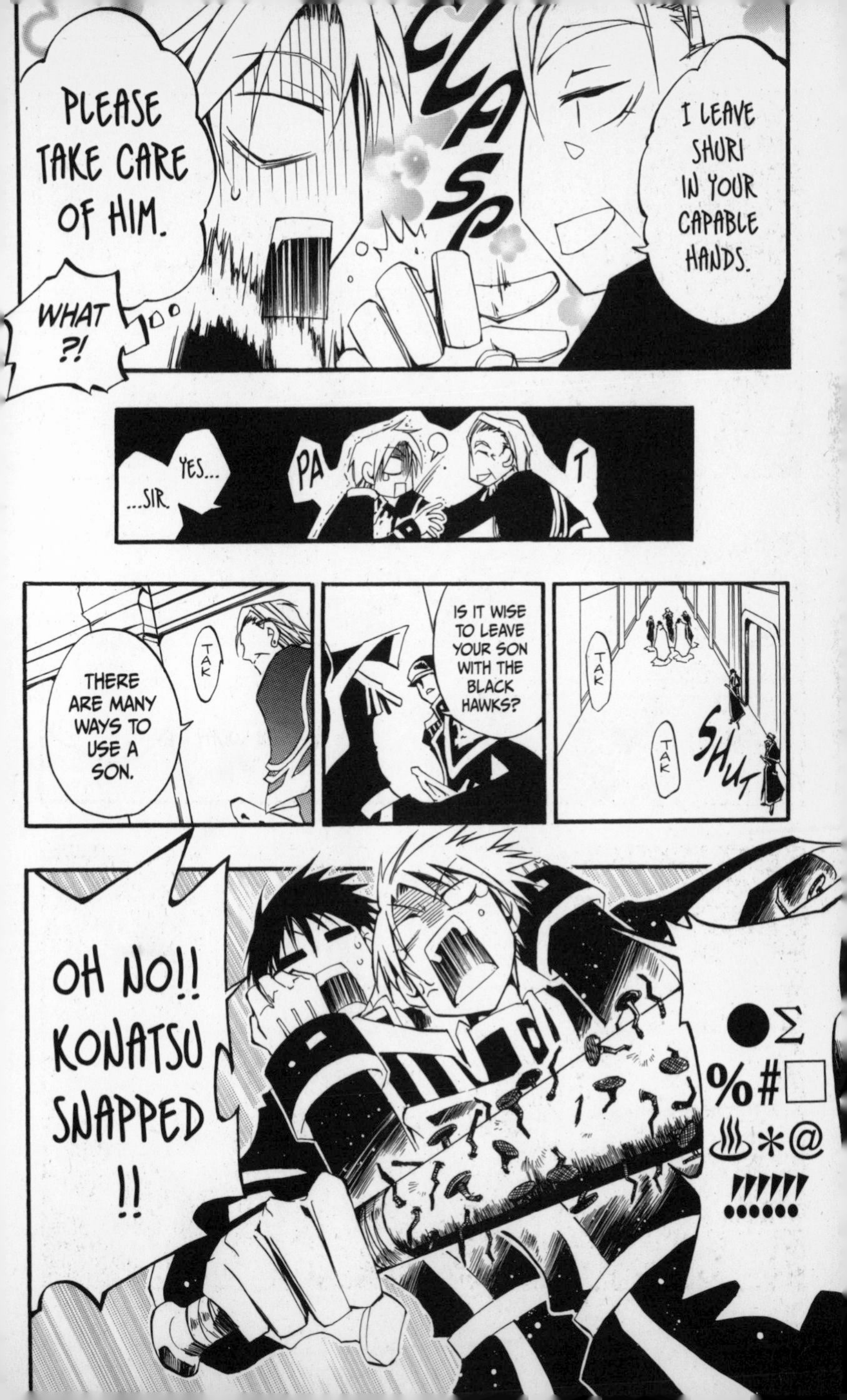
I LEAVE SHURI IN YOUR CAPABLE HANDS.
CLASP
PLEASE TAKE CARE OF HIM.
WHAT ?!
PA T
YES... ...SIR.
TAK
SHUT
TAK
IS IT WISE TO LEAVE YOUR SON WITH THE BLACK HAWKS?
TAK
THERE ARE MANY WAYS TO USE A SON.
●Σ %#□ ♨*@ !!!!!!
OH NO!! KONATSU SNAPPED !!

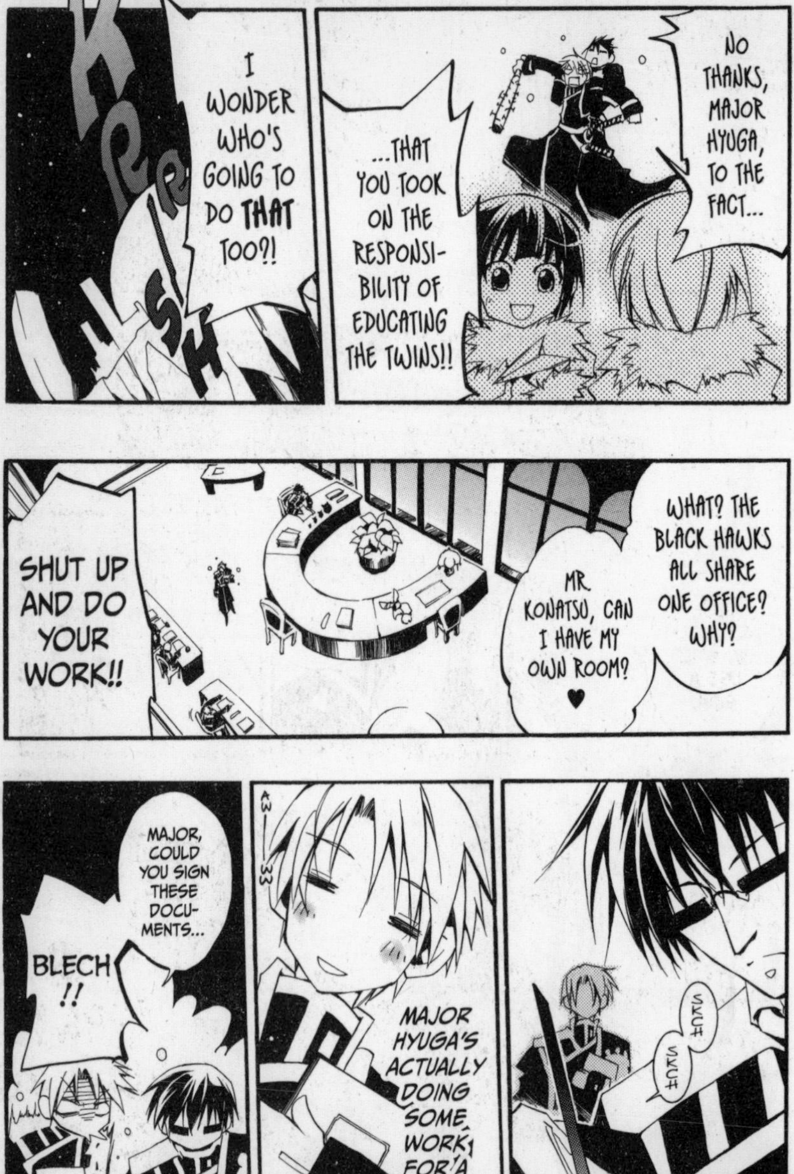
NO THANKS, MAJOR HYUGA, TO THE FACT...
...THAT YOU TOOK ON THE RESPONSIBILITY OF EDUCATING THE TWINS!!
I WONDER WHO'S GOING TO DO **THAT** TOO?!
WHAT? THE BLACK HAWKS ALL SHARE ONE OFFICE? WHY?
MR. KONATSU, CAN I HAVE MY OWN ROOM? ♥
SHUT UP AND DO YOUR WORK!!
MAJOR HYUGA'S ACTUALLY DOING SOME WORK FOR A CHANGE!!
MAJOR, COULD YOU SIGN THESE DOCUMENTS...
BLECH!!

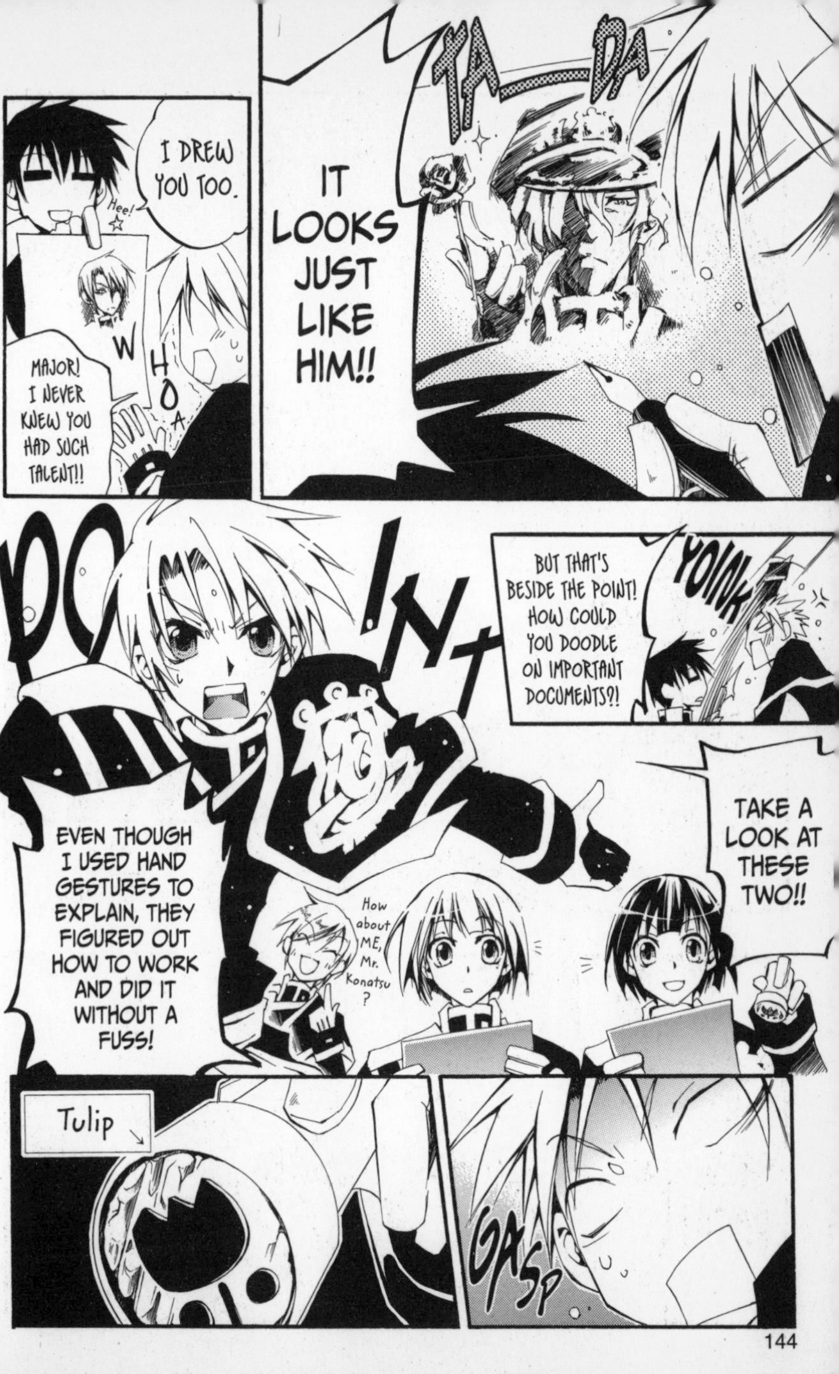

TA-DA
IT LOOKS JUST LIKE HIM!!
I DREW YOU TOO.
Hee! ☆
WHOA
MAJOR! I NEVER KNEW YOU HAD SUCH TALENT!!
YOINK
BUT THAT'S BESIDE THE POINT! HOW COULD YOU DOODLE ON IMPORTANT DOCUMENTS?!
POINT
TAKE A LOOK AT THESE TWO!!
EVEN THOUGH I USED HAND GESTURES TO EXPLAIN, THEY FIGURED OUT HOW TO WORK AND DID IT WITHOUT A FUSS!
How about ME, Mr. Konatsu?
GASP
Tulip

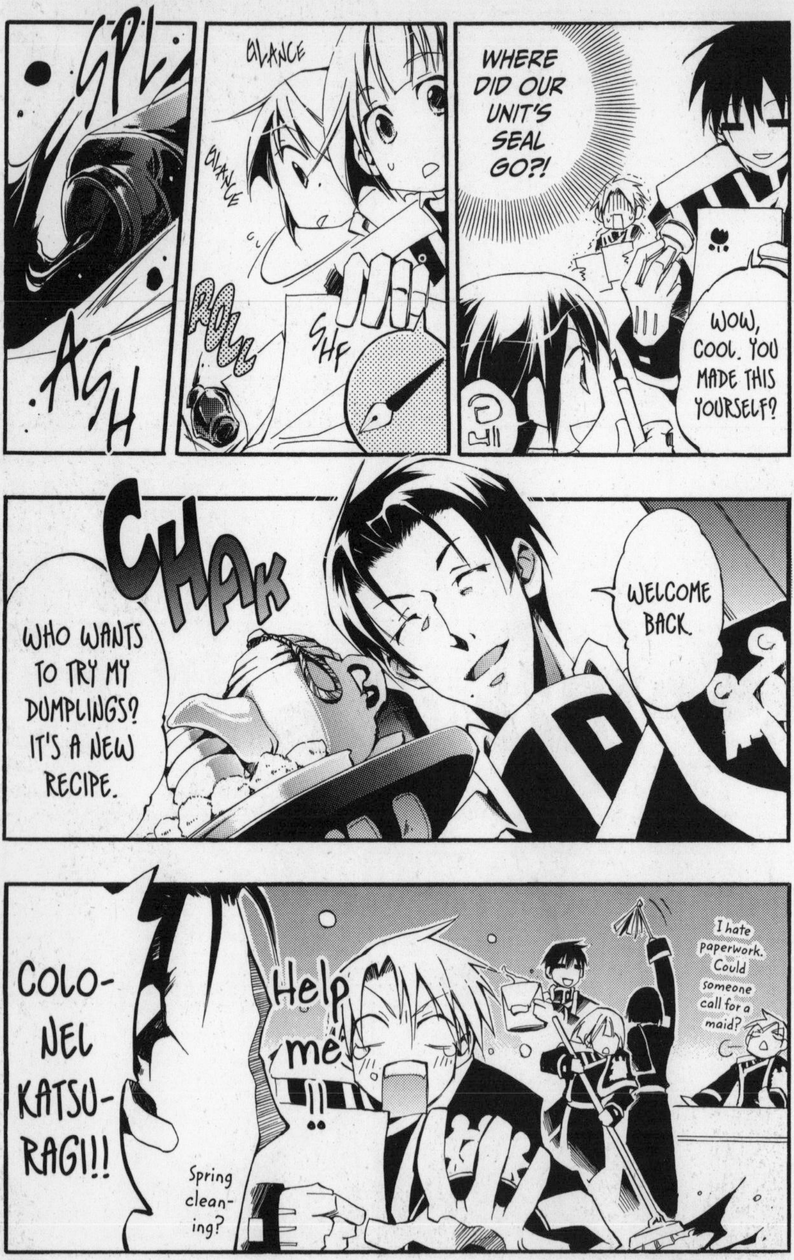
WHERE DID OUR UNIT'S SEAL GO?!
WOW, COOL. YOU MADE THIS YOURSELF?
GLANCE
GLANCE
ROLL
SHF
SPLASH
WELCOME BACK.
CHAK
WHO WANTS TO TRY MY DUMPLINGS? IT'S A NEW RECIPE.
I hate paperwork. Could someone call for a maid?
Help me!!
Spring cleaning?
COLONEL KATSURAGI!!

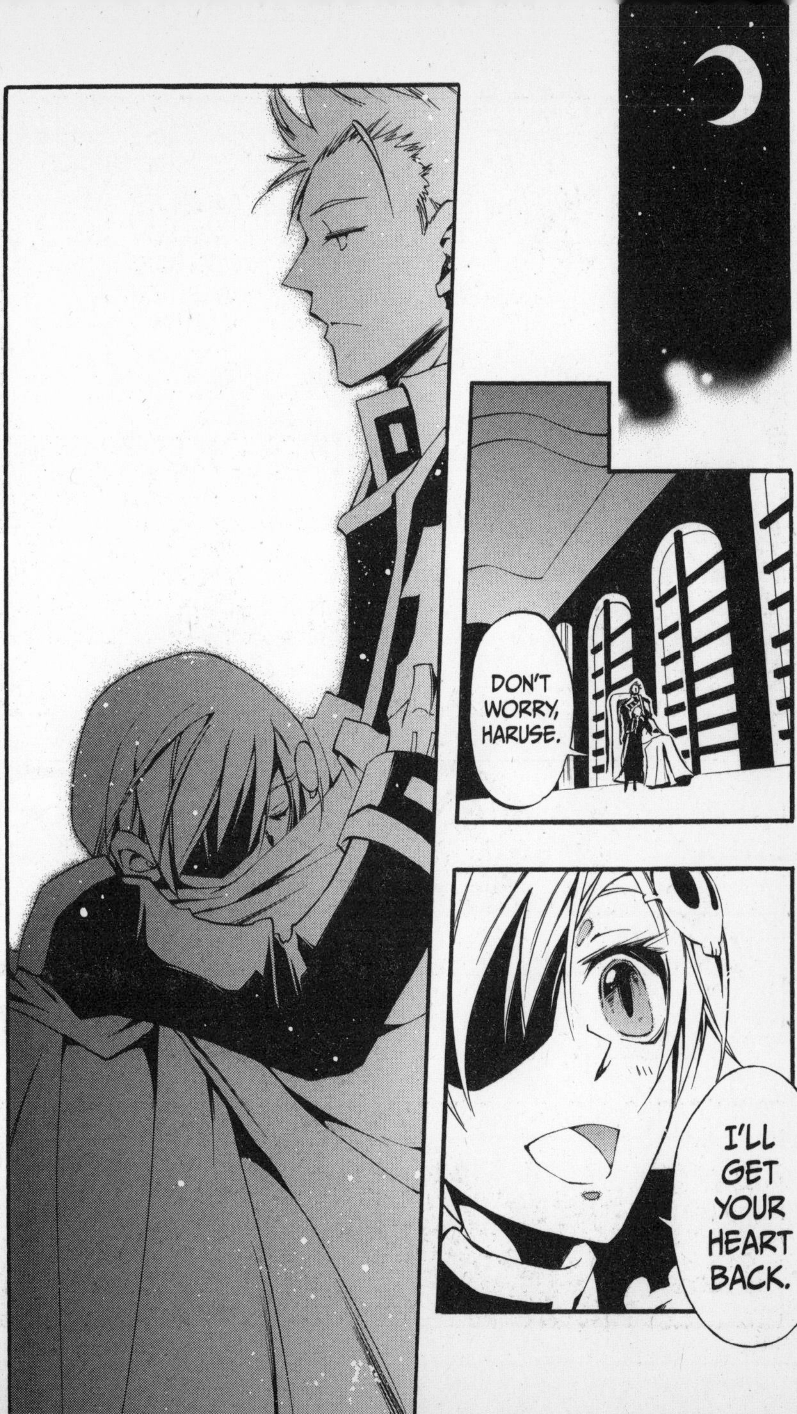
DON'T WORRY, HARUSE.
I'LL GET YOUR HEART BACK.

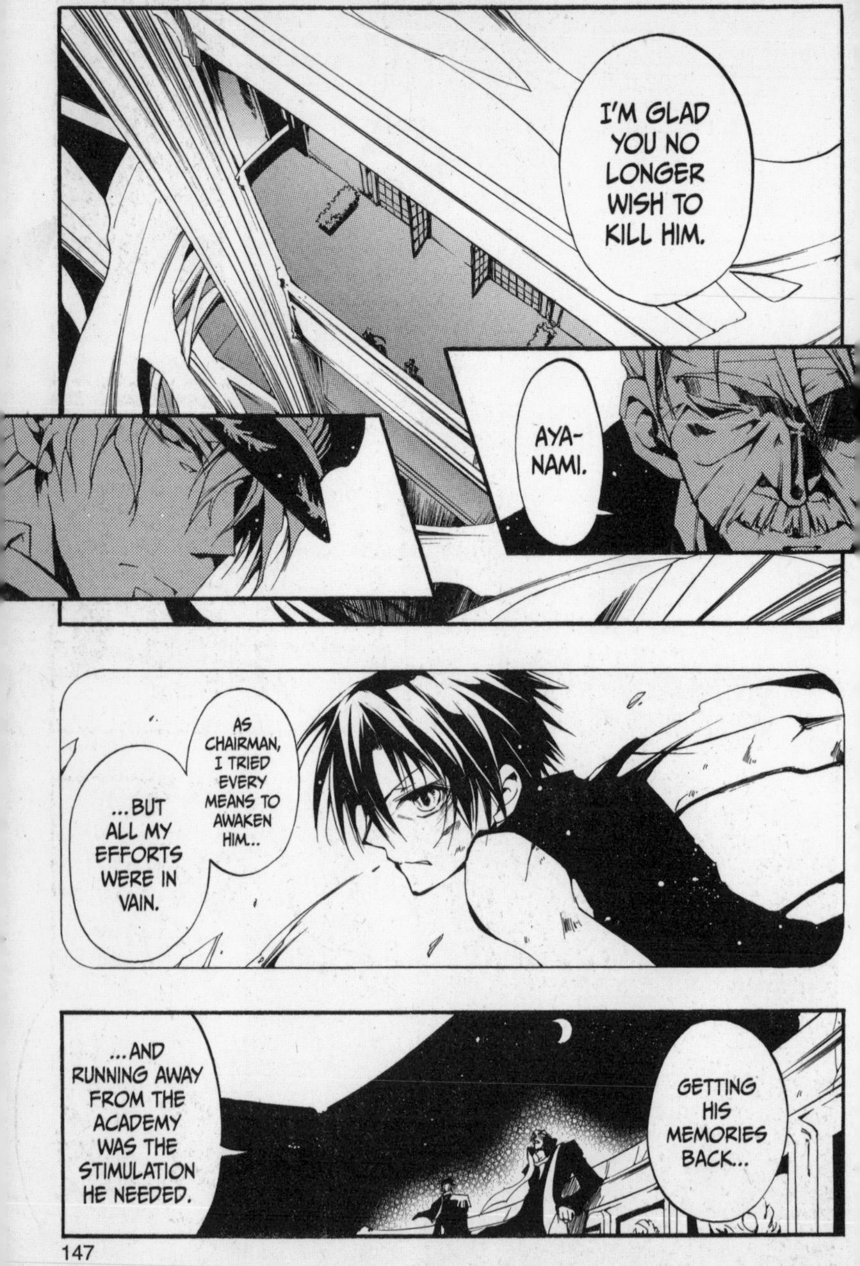
I'M GLAD YOU NO LONGER WISH TO KILL HIM.
AYA-NAMI.
AS CHAIRMAN, I TRIED EVERY MEANS TO AWAKEN HIM...
...BUT ALL MY EFFORTS WERE IN VAIN.
GETTING HIS MEMORIES BACK...
...AND RUNNING AWAY FROM THE ACADEMY WAS THE STIMULATION HE NEEDED.

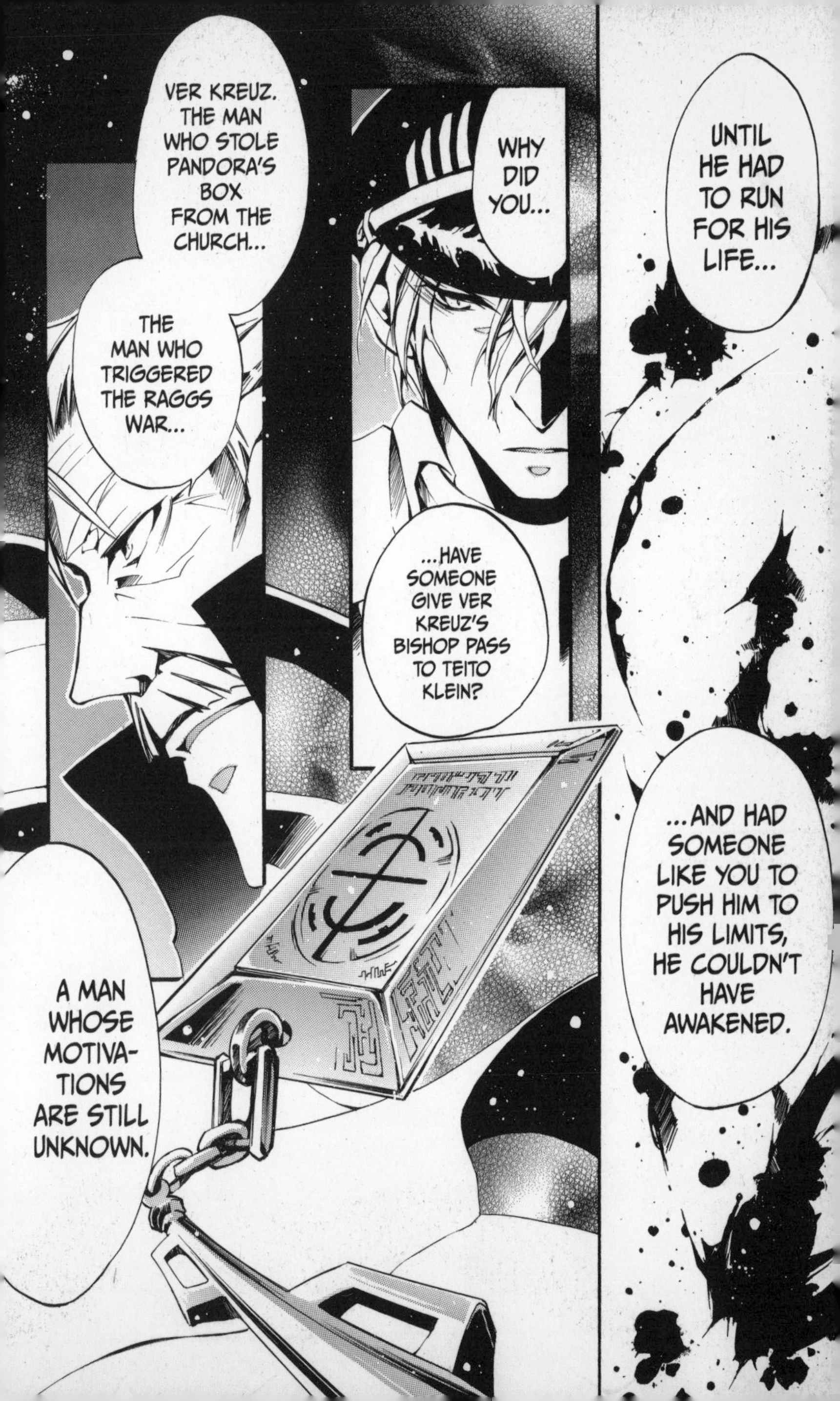
UNTIL HE HAD TO RUN FOR HIS LIFE...
...AND HAD SOMEONE LIKE YOU TO PUSH HIM TO HIS LIMITS, HE COULDN'T HAVE AWAKENED.
WHY DID YOU...
...HAVE SOMEONE GIVE VER KREUZ'S BISHOP PASS TO TEITO KLEIN?
VER KREUZ. THE MAN WHO STOLE PANDORA'S BOX FROM THE CHURCH...
THE MAN WHO TRIGGERED THE RAGGS WAR...
A MAN WHOSE MOTIVA-TIONS ARE STILL UNKNOWN.

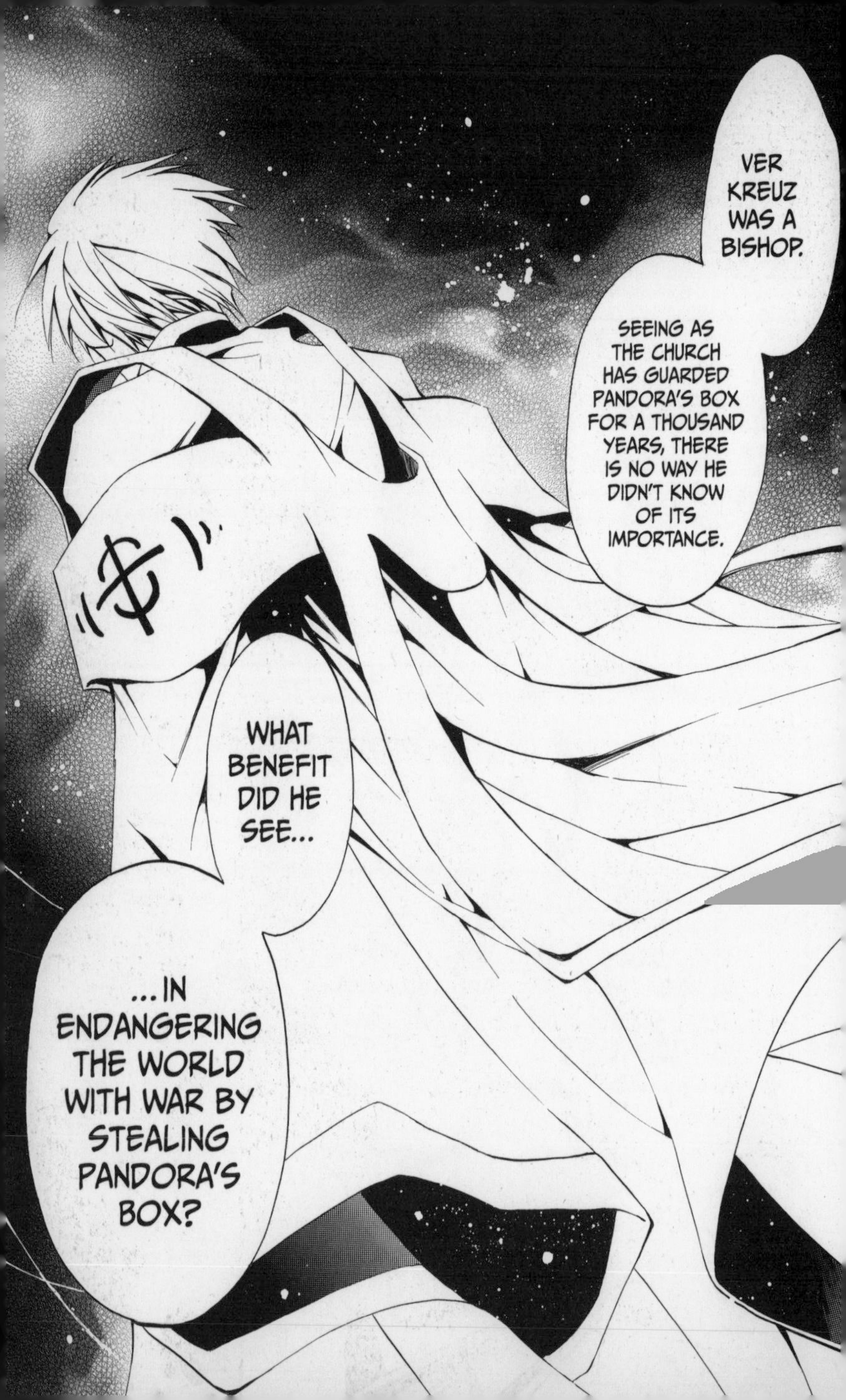
VER KREUZ WAS A BISHOP.
SEEING AS THE CHURCH HAS GUARDED PANDORA'S BOX FOR A THOUSAND YEARS, THERE IS NO WAY HE DIDN'T KNOW OF ITS IMPORTANCE.
WHAT BENEFIT DID HE SEE...
...IN ENDANGERING THE WORLD WITH WAR BY STEALING PANDORA'S BOX?

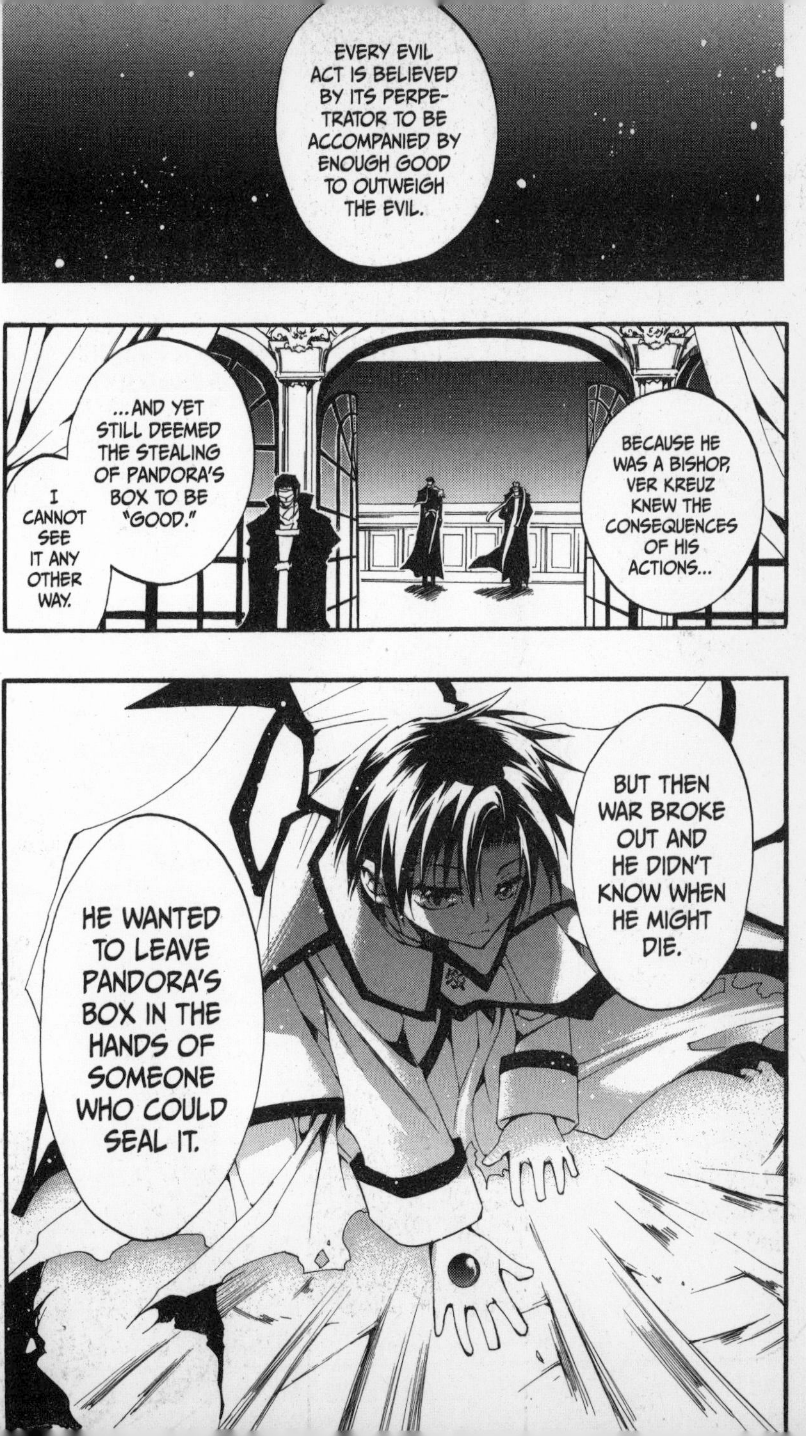
EVERY EVIL ACT IS BELIEVED BY ITS PERPETRATOR TO BE ACCOMPANIED BY ENOUGH GOOD TO OUTWEIGH THE EVIL.
BECAUSE HE WAS A BISHOP, VER KREUZ KNEW THE CONSEQUENCES OF HIS ACTIONS...
...AND YET STILL DEEMED THE STEALING OF PANDORA'S BOX TO BE "GOOD."
I CANNOT SEE IT ANY OTHER WAY.
BUT THEN WAR BROKE OUT AND HE DIDN'T KNOW WHEN HE MIGHT DIE.
HE WANTED TO LEAVE PANDORA'S BOX IN THE HANDS OF SOMEONE WHO COULD SEAL IT.

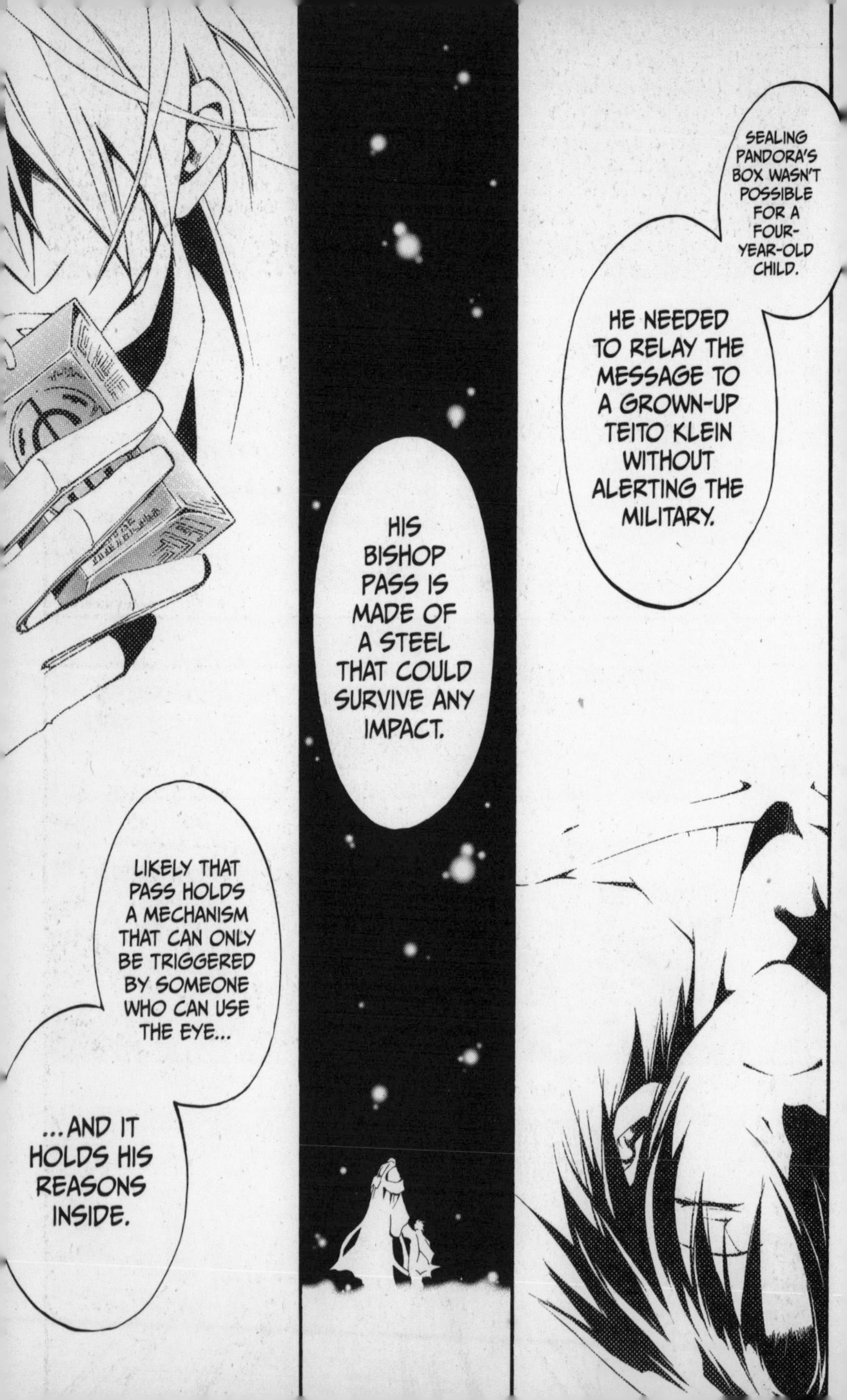
SEALING PANDORA'S BOX WASN'T POSSIBLE FOR A FOUR-YEAR-OLD CHILD.
HE NEEDED TO RELAY THE MESSAGE TO A GROWN-UP TEITO KLEIN WITHOUT ALERTING THE MILITARY.
HIS BISHOP PASS IS MADE OF A STEEL THAT COULD SURVIVE ANY IMPACT.
LIKELY THAT PASS HOLDS A MECHANISM THAT CAN ONLY BE TRIGGERED BY SOMEONE WHO CAN USE THE EYE...
...AND IT HOLDS HIS REASONS INSIDE.

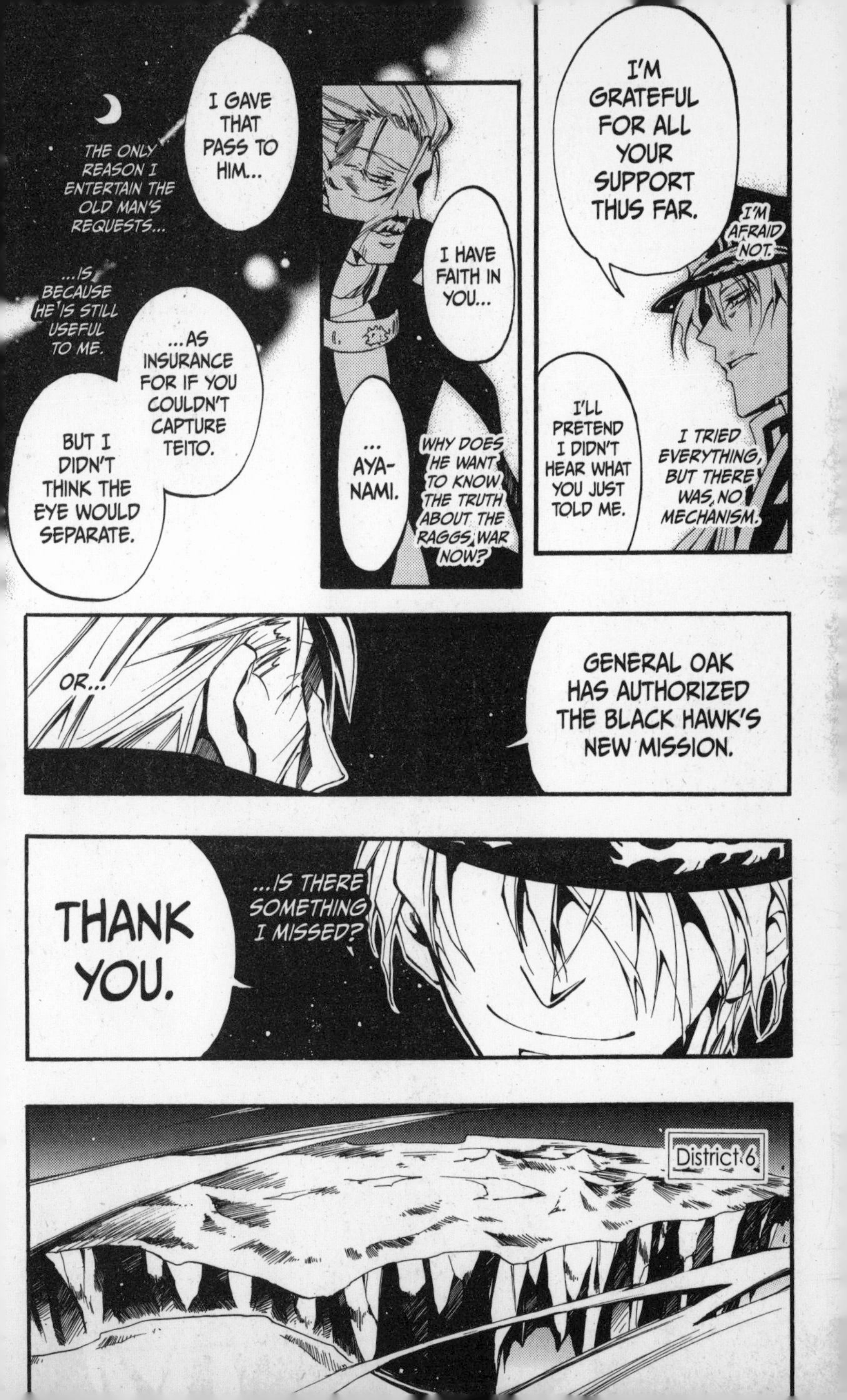
I'M GRATEFUL FOR ALL YOUR SUPPORT THUS FAR.
I'M AFRAID NOT.
I TRIED EVERYTHING, BUT THERE WAS NO MECHANISM.
I'LL PRETEND I DIDN'T HEAR WHAT YOU JUST TOLD ME.
I HAVE FAITH IN YOU...
WHY DOES HE WANT TO KNOW THE TRUTH ABOUT THE RAGGS WAR NOW?
...AYANAMI.
I GAVE THAT PASS TO HIM...
THE ONLY REASON I ENTERTAIN THE OLD MAN'S REQUESTS...
...IS BECAUSE HE IS STILL USEFUL TO ME.
...AS INSURANCE FOR IF YOU COULDN'T CAPTURE TEITO.
BUT I DIDN'T THINK THE EYE WOULD SEPARATE.
GENERAL OAK HAS AUTHORIZED THE BLACK HAWK'S NEW MISSION.
OR...
...IS THERE SOMETHING I MISSED?
THANK YOU.
District 6

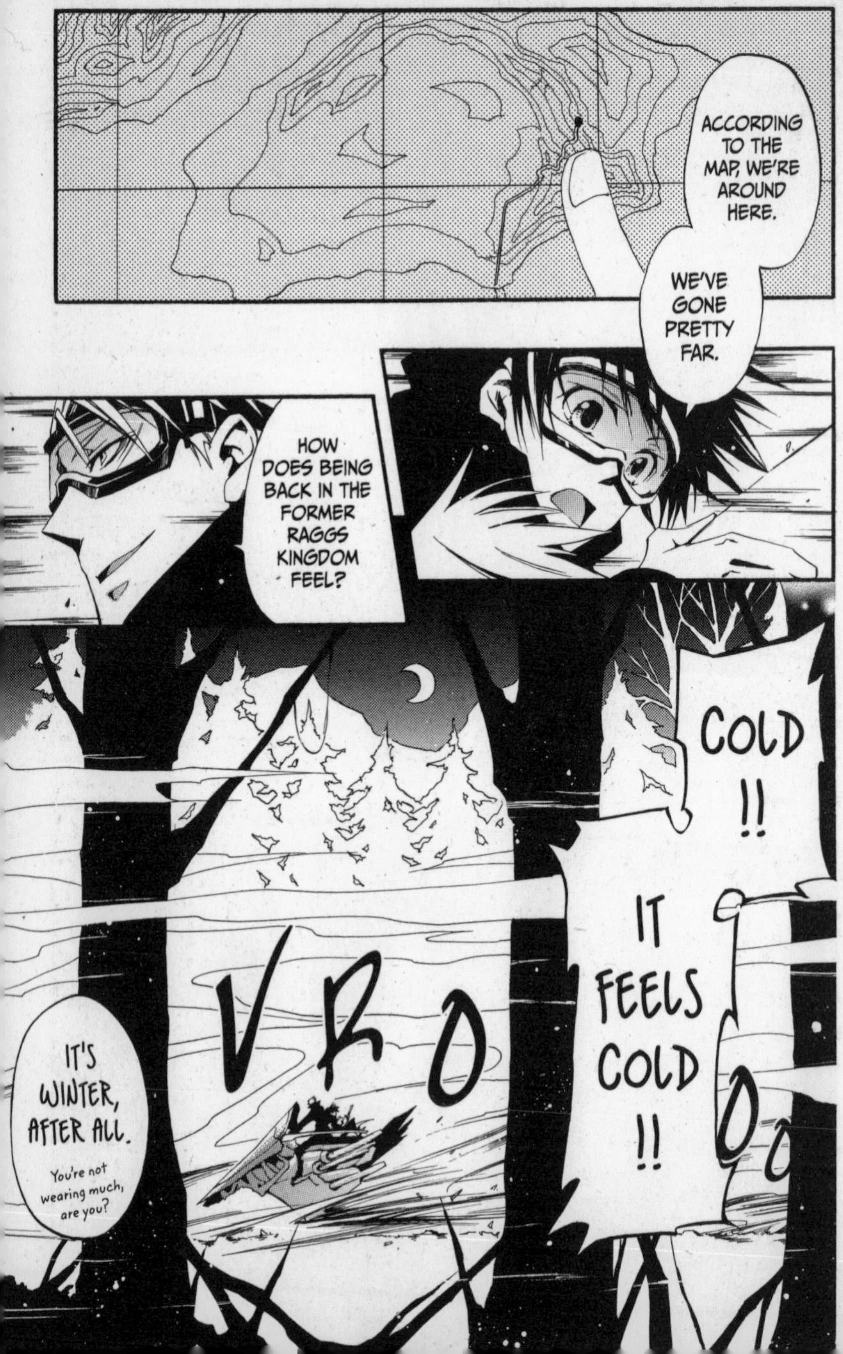
ACCORDING TO THE MAP, WE'RE AROUND HERE.
WE'VE GONE PRETTY FAR.
HOW DOES BEING BACK IN THE FORMER RAGGS KINGDOM FEEL?
COLD!!
IT FEELS COLD!!
VROOO
IT'S WINTER, AFTER ALL.
You're not wearing much, are you?

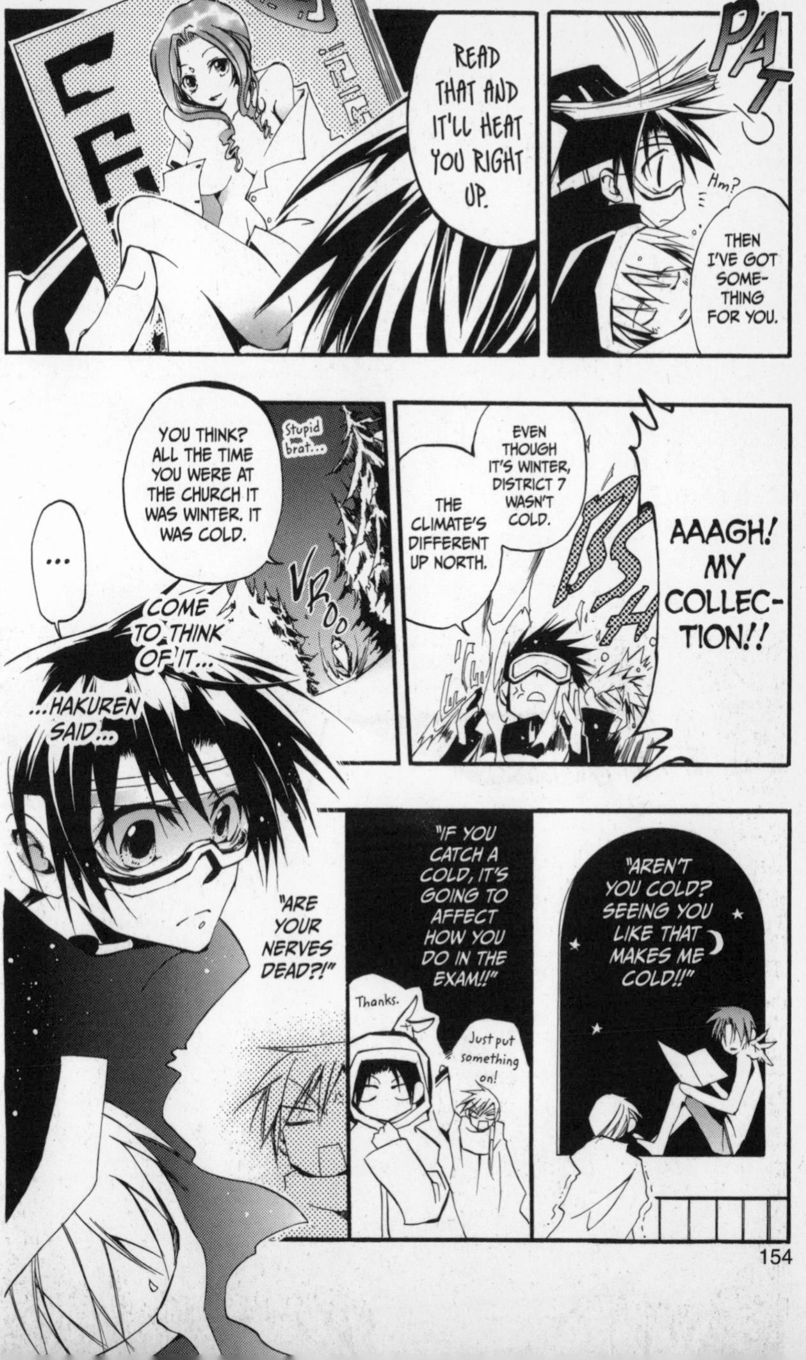
PAT
Hm?
THEN I'VE GOT SOME-THING FOR YOU.
READ THAT AND IT'LL HEAT YOU RIGHT UP.
AAAGH! MY COLLEC-TION!!
EVEN THOUGH IT'S WINTER, DISTRICT 7 WASN'T COLD.
THE CLIMATE'S DIFFERENT UP NORTH.
Stupid brat...
YOU THINK? ALL THE TIME YOU WERE AT THE CHURCH IT WAS WINTER. IT WAS COLD.
VROOO
...
COME TO THINK OF IT...
...HAKUREN SAID...
"AREN'T YOU COLD? SEEING YOU LIKE THAT MAKES ME COLD!!"
"IF YOU CATCH A COLD, IT'S GOING TO AFFECT HOW YOU DO IN THE EXAM!!"
Thanks.
Just put something on!
"ARE YOUR NERVES DEAD?!"

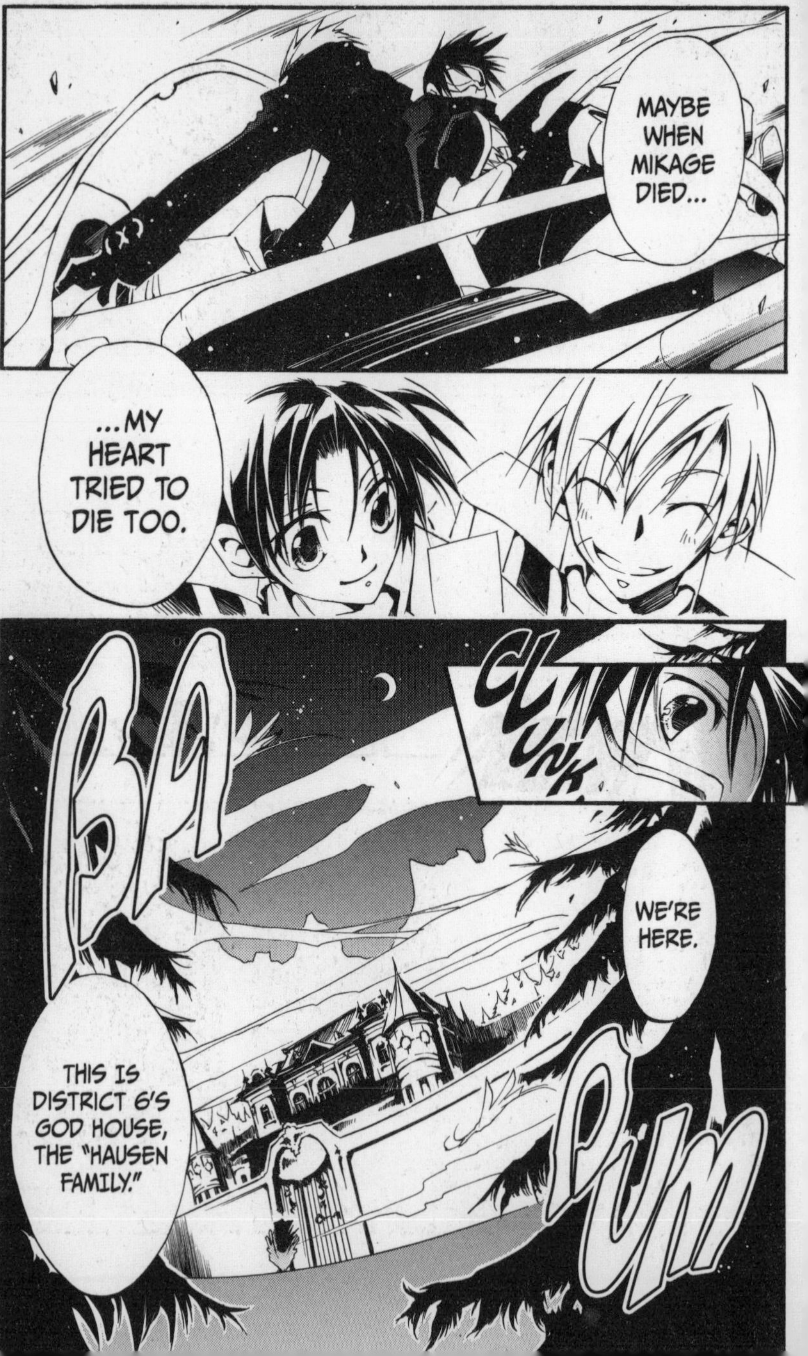
MAYBE WHEN MIKAGE DIED...
...MY HEART TRIED TO DIE TOO.
CLUNK
WE'RE HERE.
BA
THIS IS DISTRICT 6'S GOD HOUSE, THE "HAUSEN FAMILY."

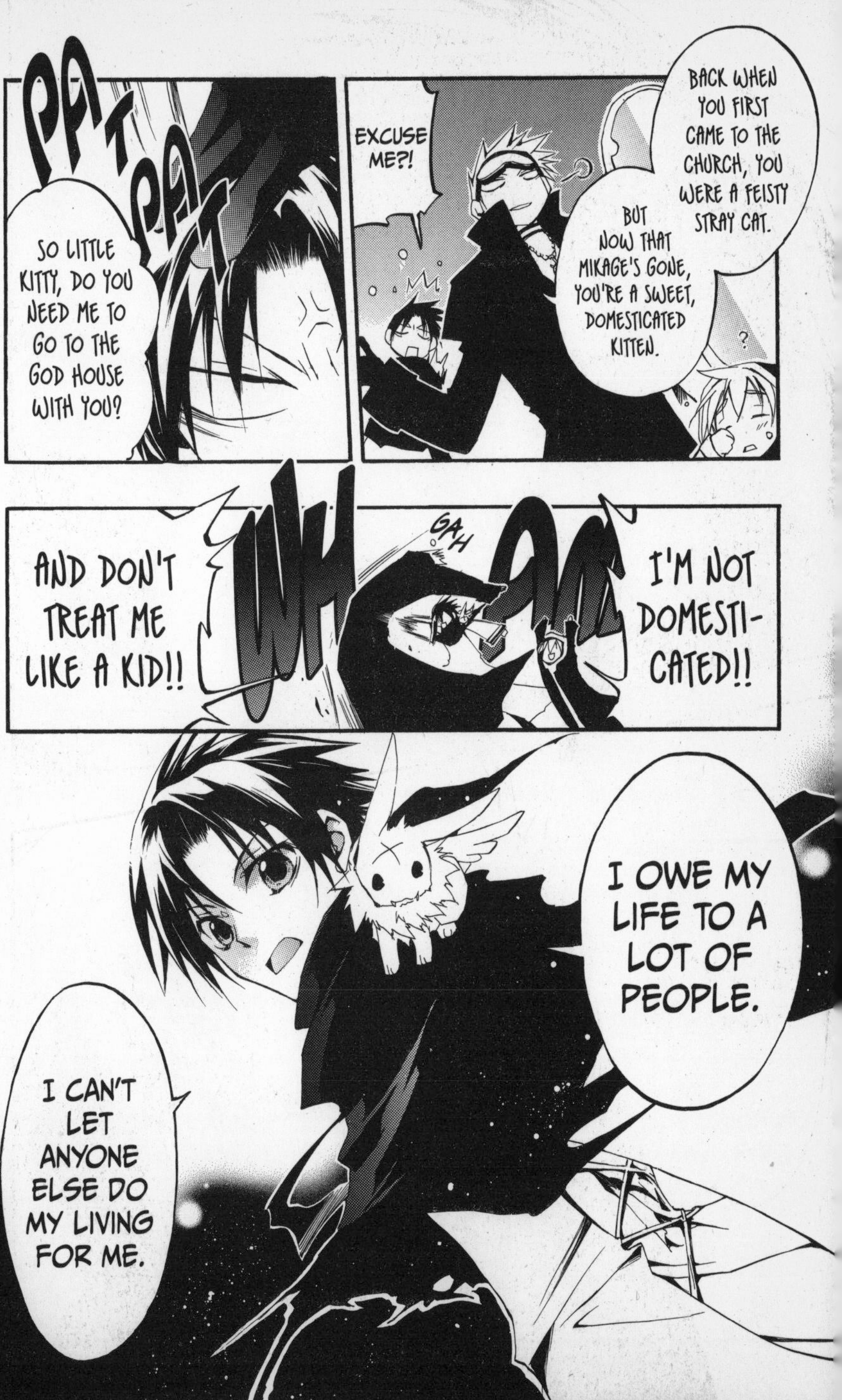
BACK WHEN YOU FIRST CAME TO THE CHURCH, YOU WERE A FEISTY STRAY CAT.
BUT NOW THAT MIKAGE'S GONE, YOU'RE A SWEET, DOMESTICATED KITTEN.
EXCUSE ME?!
?
PAT PAT
SO LITTLE KITTY, DO YOU NEED ME TO GO TO THE GOD HOUSE WITH YOU?
I'M NOT DOMESTICATED!!
GAH
AND DON'T TREAT ME LIKE A KID!!
I OWE MY LIFE TO A LOT OF PEOPLE.
I CAN'T LET ANYONE ELSE DO MY LIVING FOR ME.

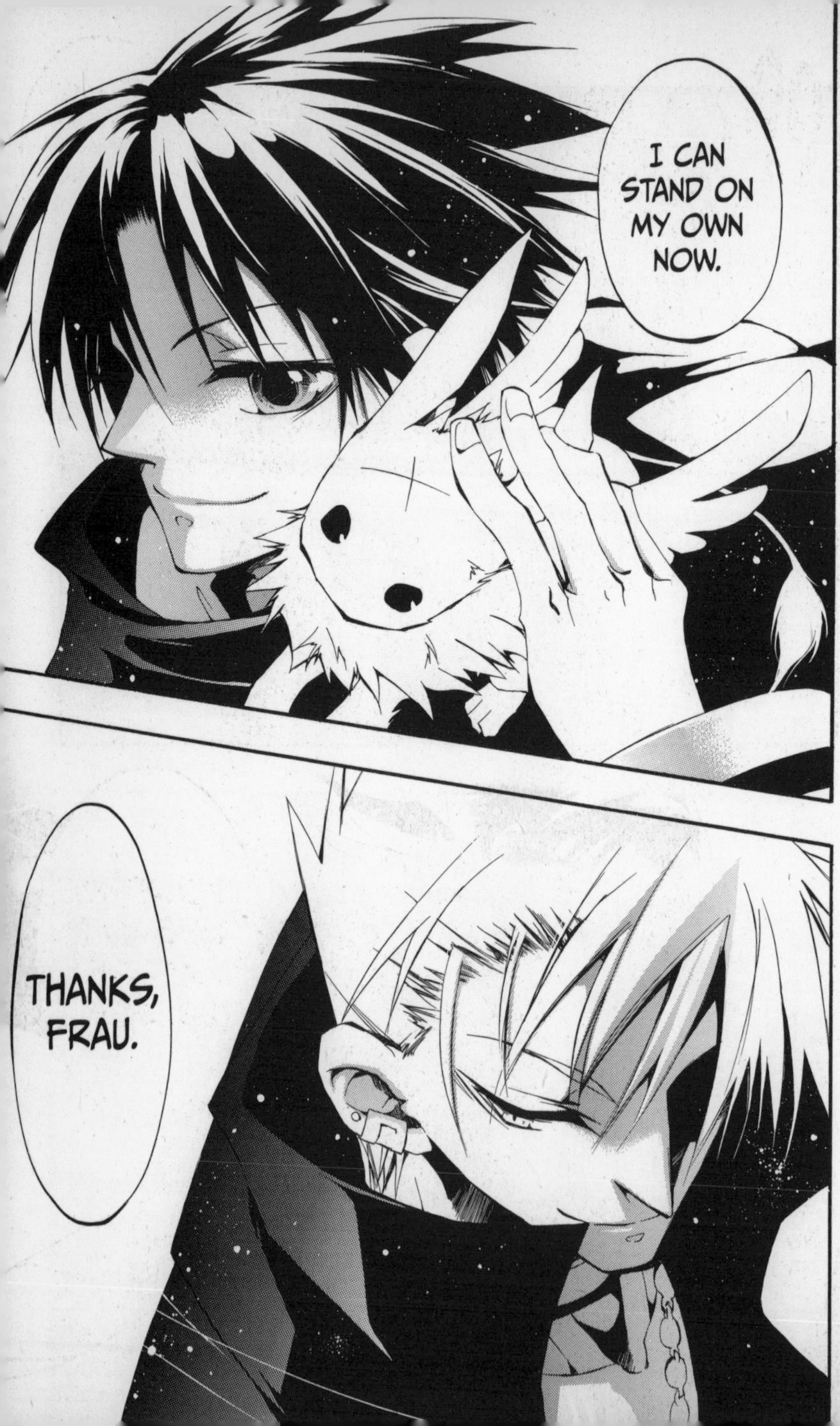
I CAN STAND ON MY OWN NOW.
THANKS, FRAU.

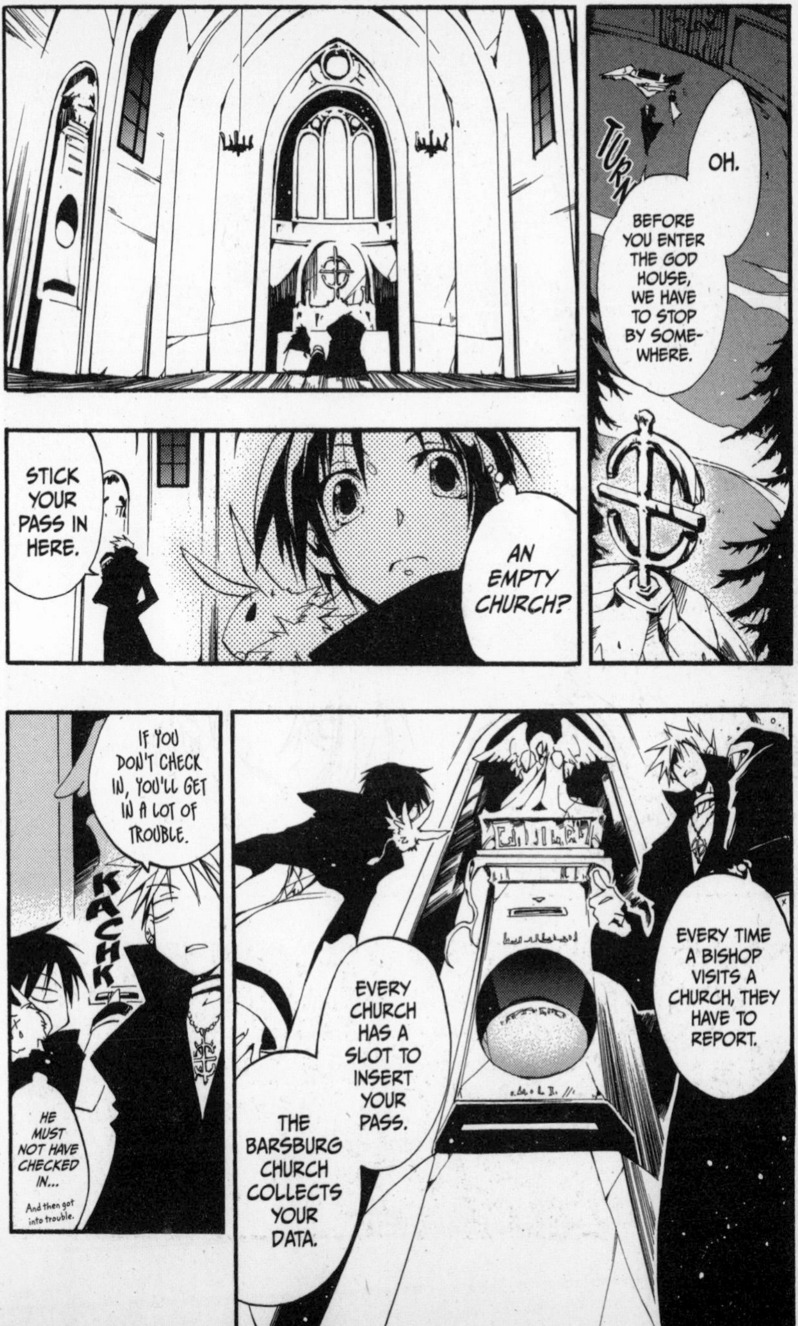
TURN
OH.
BEFORE YOU ENTER THE GOD HOUSE, WE HAVE TO STOP BY SOME-WHERE.
AN EMPTY CHURCH?
STICK YOUR PASS IN HERE.
EVERY TIME A BISHOP VISITS A CHURCH, THEY HAVE TO REPORT.
EVERY CHURCH HAS A SLOT TO INSERT YOUR PASS.
THE BARSBURG CHURCH COLLECTS YOUR DATA.
IF YOU DON'T CHECK IN, YOU'LL GET IN A LOT OF TROUBLE.
KACHK
HE MUST NOT HAVE CHECKED IN...
And then got into trouble.

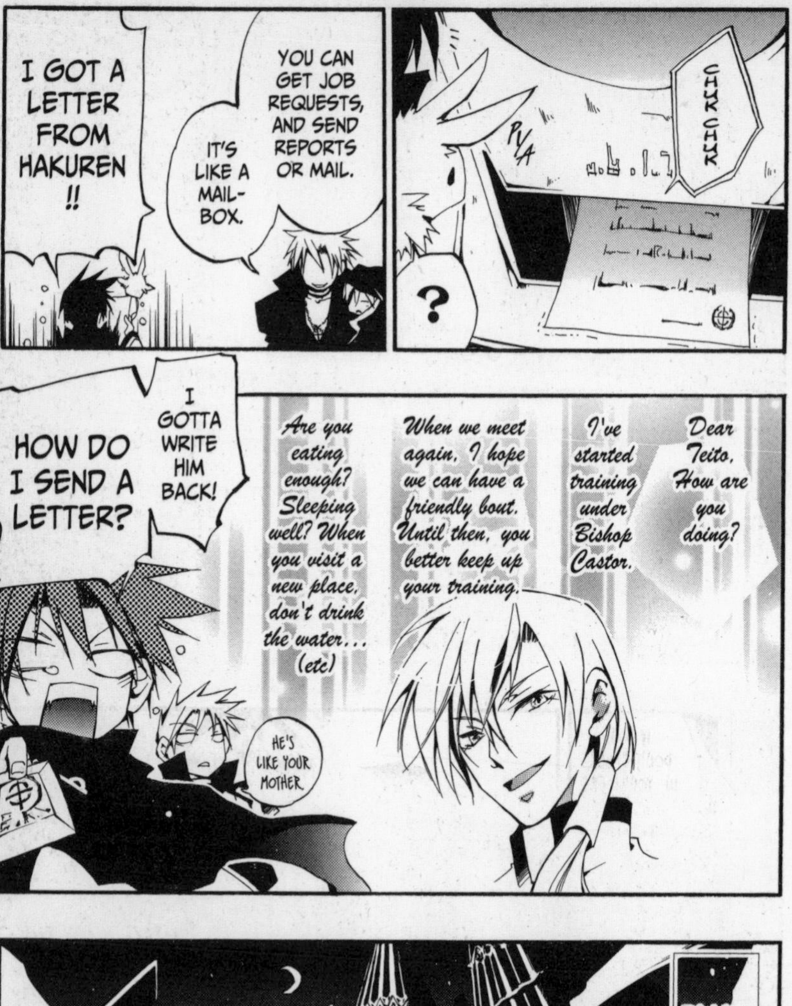
CHUK CHUK
PYA
?
YOU CAN GET JOB REQUESTS, AND SEND REPORTS OR MAIL.
IT'S LIKE A MAILBOX.
I GOT A LETTER FROM HAKUREN !!
Dear Teito, How are you doing?
I've started training under Bishop Castor.
When we meet again, I hope we can have a friendly bout. Until then, you better keep up your training.
Are you eating enough? Sleeping well? When you visit a new place, don't drink the water... (etc)
HE'S LIKE YOUR MOTHER.
I GOTTA WRITE HIM BACK!
HOW DO I SEND A LETTER?
District 7 Barsburg Church

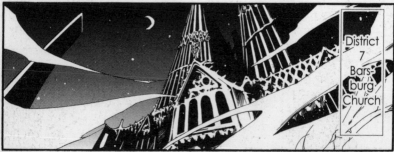

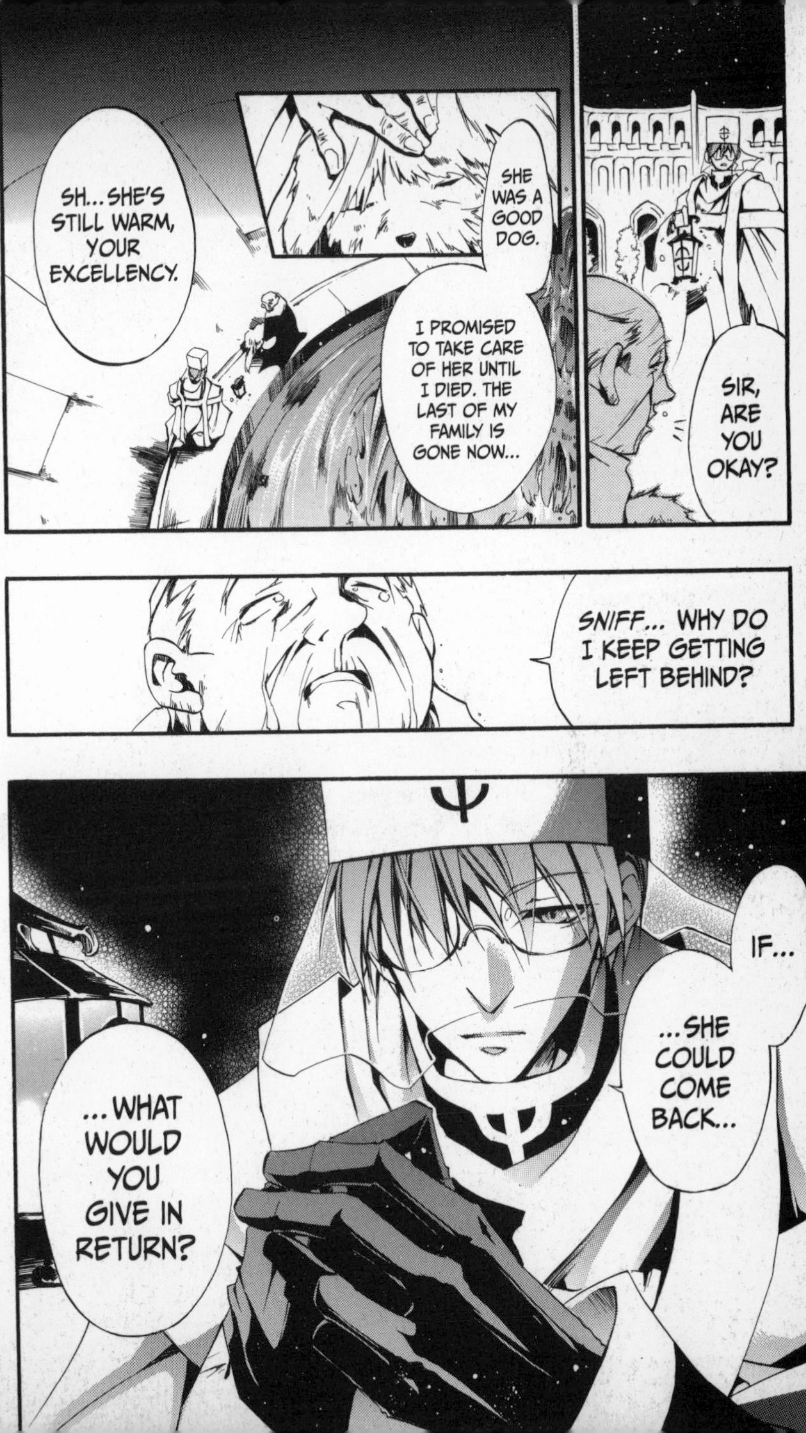
SIR, ARE YOU OKAY?
SH... SHE'S STILL WARM, YOUR EXCELLENCY.
SHE WAS A GOOD DOG.
I PROMISED TO TAKE CARE OF HER UNTIL I DIED. THE LAST OF MY FAMILY IS GONE NOW...
SNIFF... WHY DO I KEEP GETTING LEFT BEHIND?
IF...
...SHE COULD COME BACK...
...WHAT WOULD YOU GIVE IN RETURN?

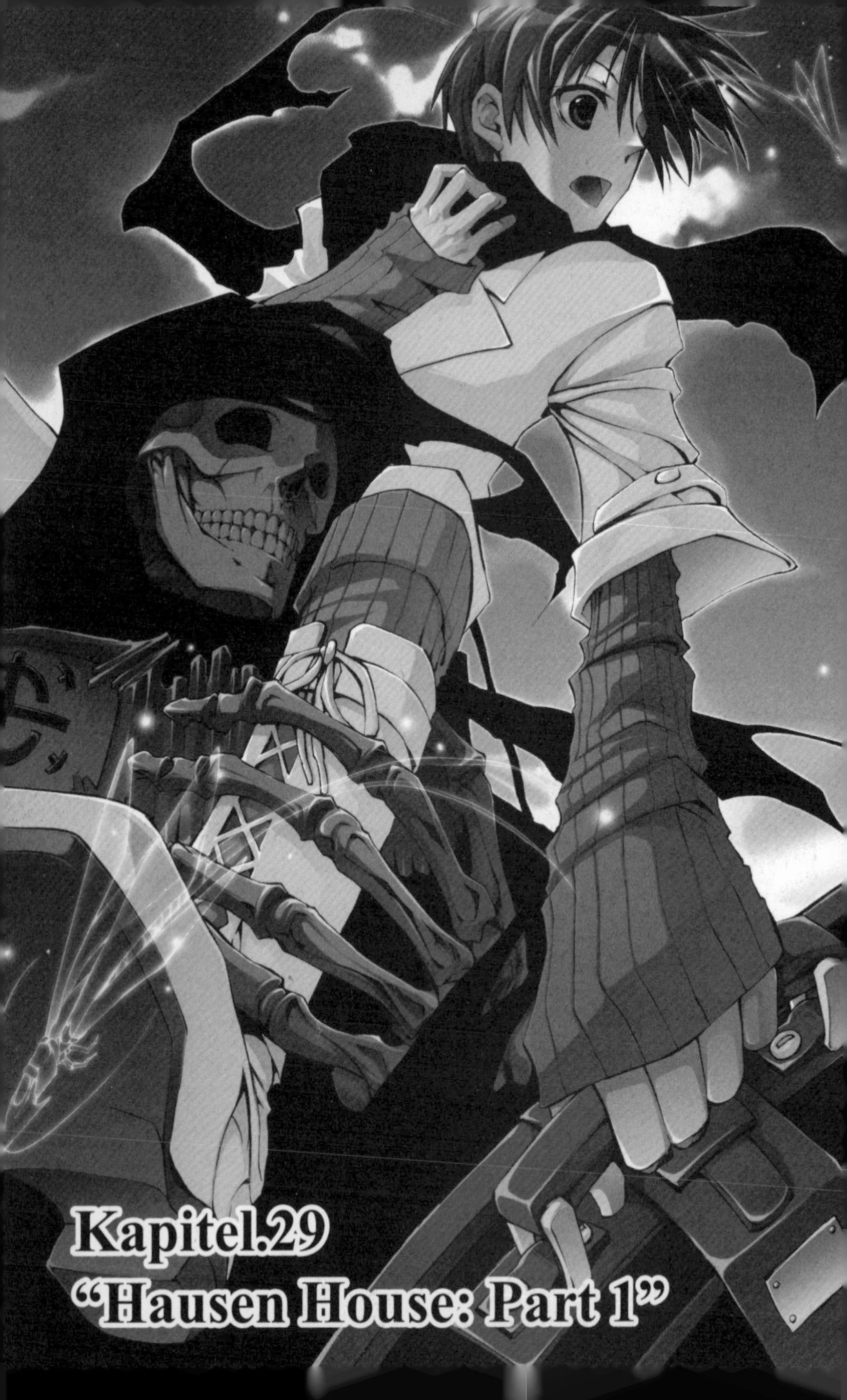

Kapitel.29
"Hausen House: Part 1"

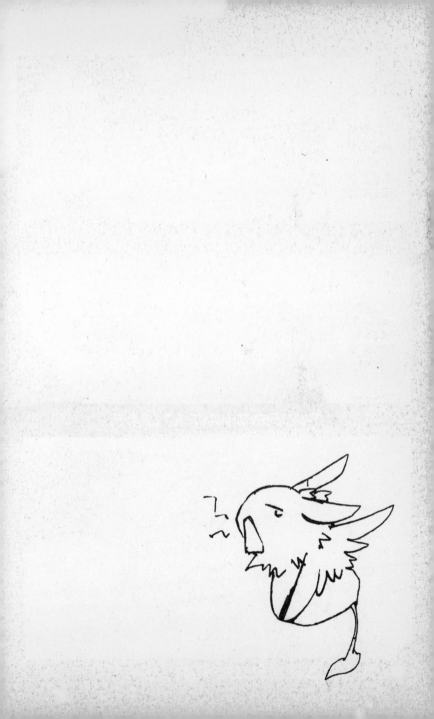

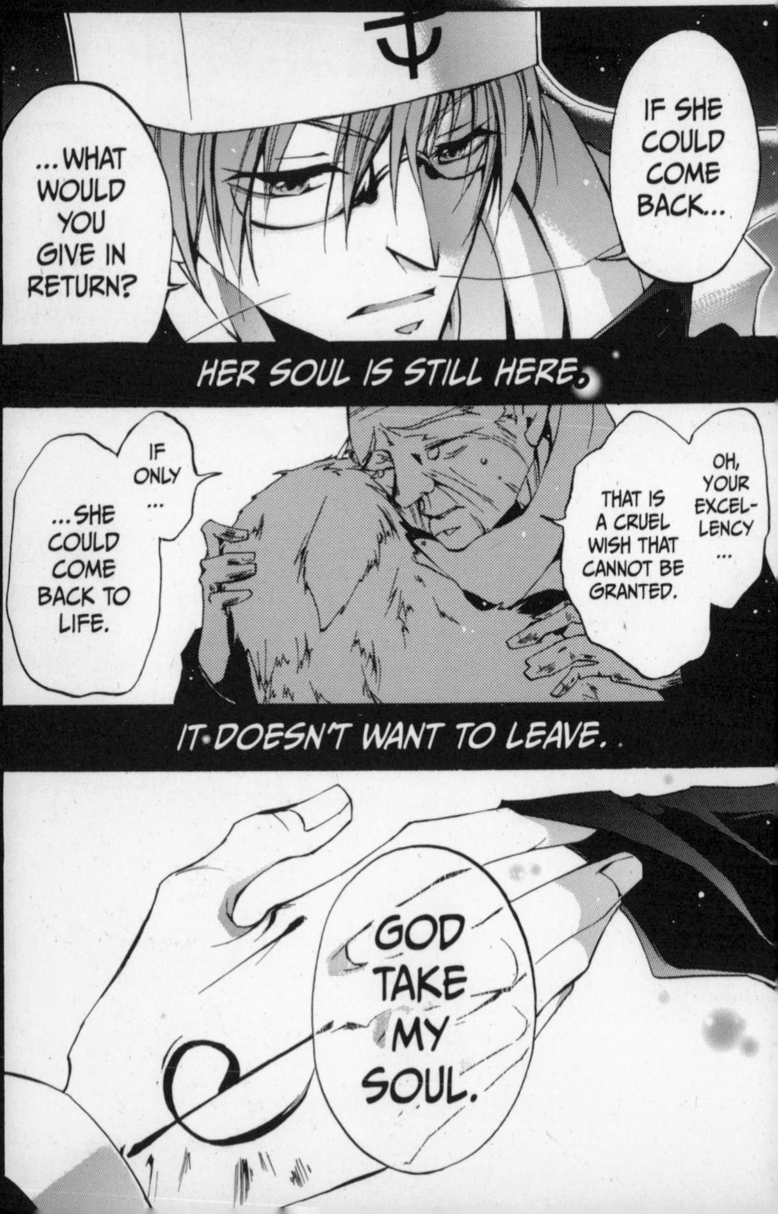
IF SHE COULD COME BACK...
...WHAT WOULD YOU GIVE IN RETURN?
HER SOUL IS STILL HERE.
OH, YOUR EXCEL-LENCY ...
THAT IS A CRUEL WISH THAT CANNOT BE GRANTED.
IF ONLY ...
...SHE COULD COME BACK TO LIFE.
IT DOESN'T WANT TO LEAVE.
GOD TAKE MY SOUL.

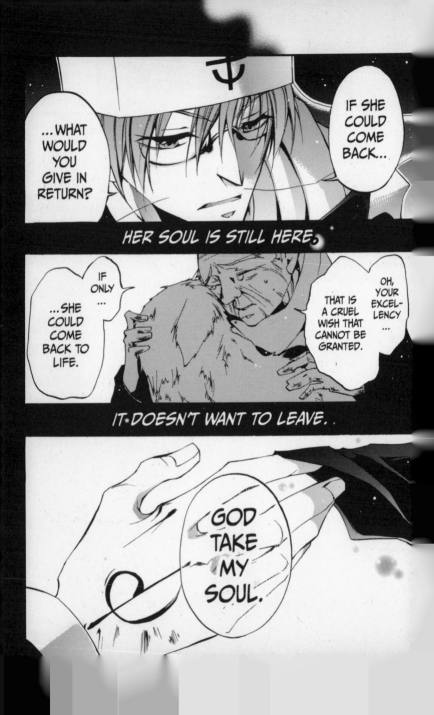

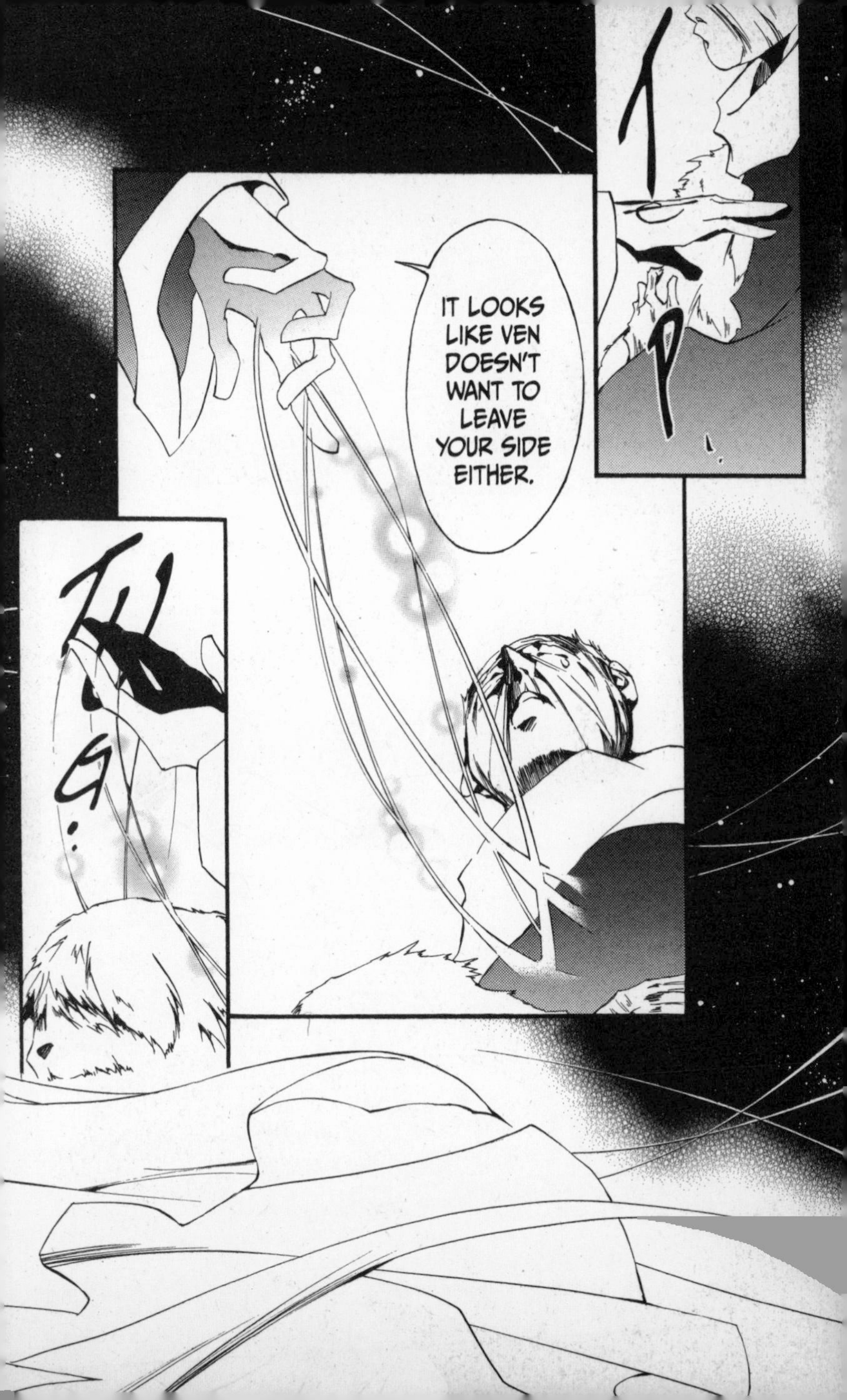
IT LOOKS LIKE VEN DOESN'T WANT TO LEAVE YOUR SIDE EITHER.

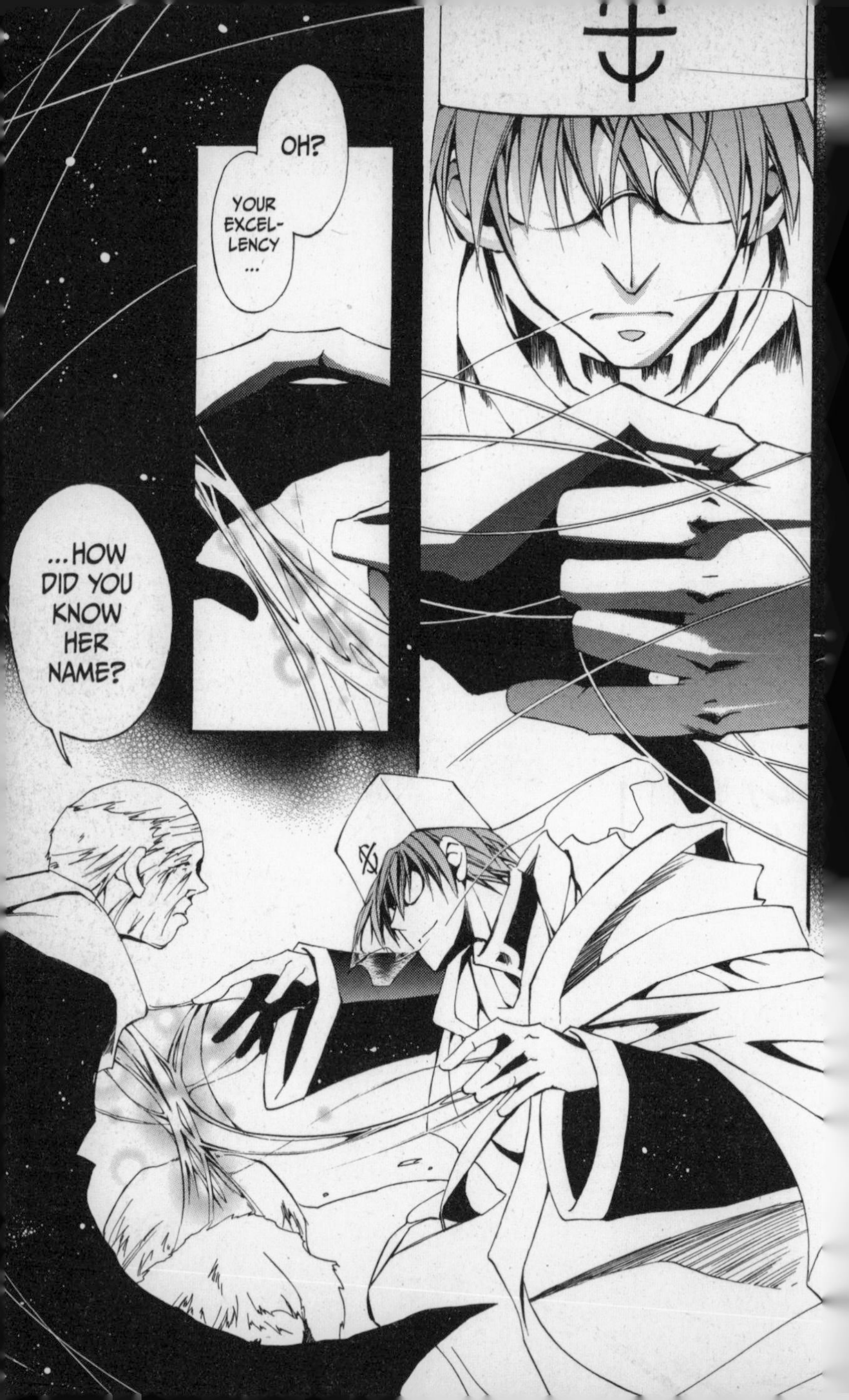
OH?
YOUR EXCEL- LENCY ...
...HOW DID YOU KNOW HER NAME?

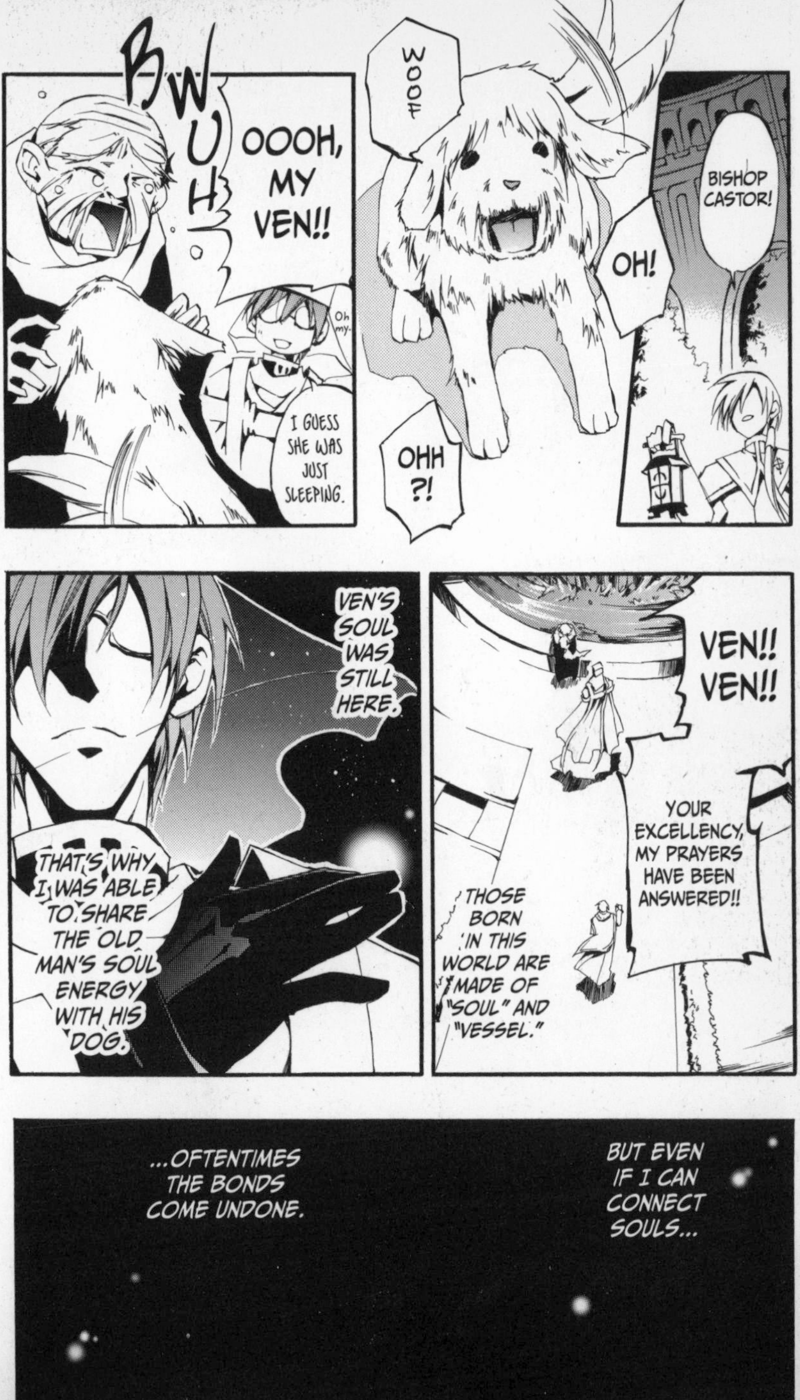
BISHOP CASTOR!
OH!
WOOF
OHH ?!
BWUH
OOOH, MY VEN!!
Oh my.
I GUESS SHE WAS JUST SLEEPING.
VEN!! VEN!!
YOUR EXCELLENCY, MY PRAYERS HAVE BEEN ANSWERED!!
THOSE BORN IN THIS WORLD ARE MADE OF "SOUL" AND "VESSEL."
VEN'S SOUL WAS STILL HERE.
THAT'S WHY I WAS ABLE TO SHARE THE OLD MAN'S SOUL ENERGY WITH HIS DOG.
BUT EVEN IF I CAN CONNECT SOULS...
...OFTENTIMES THE BONDS COME UNDONE.

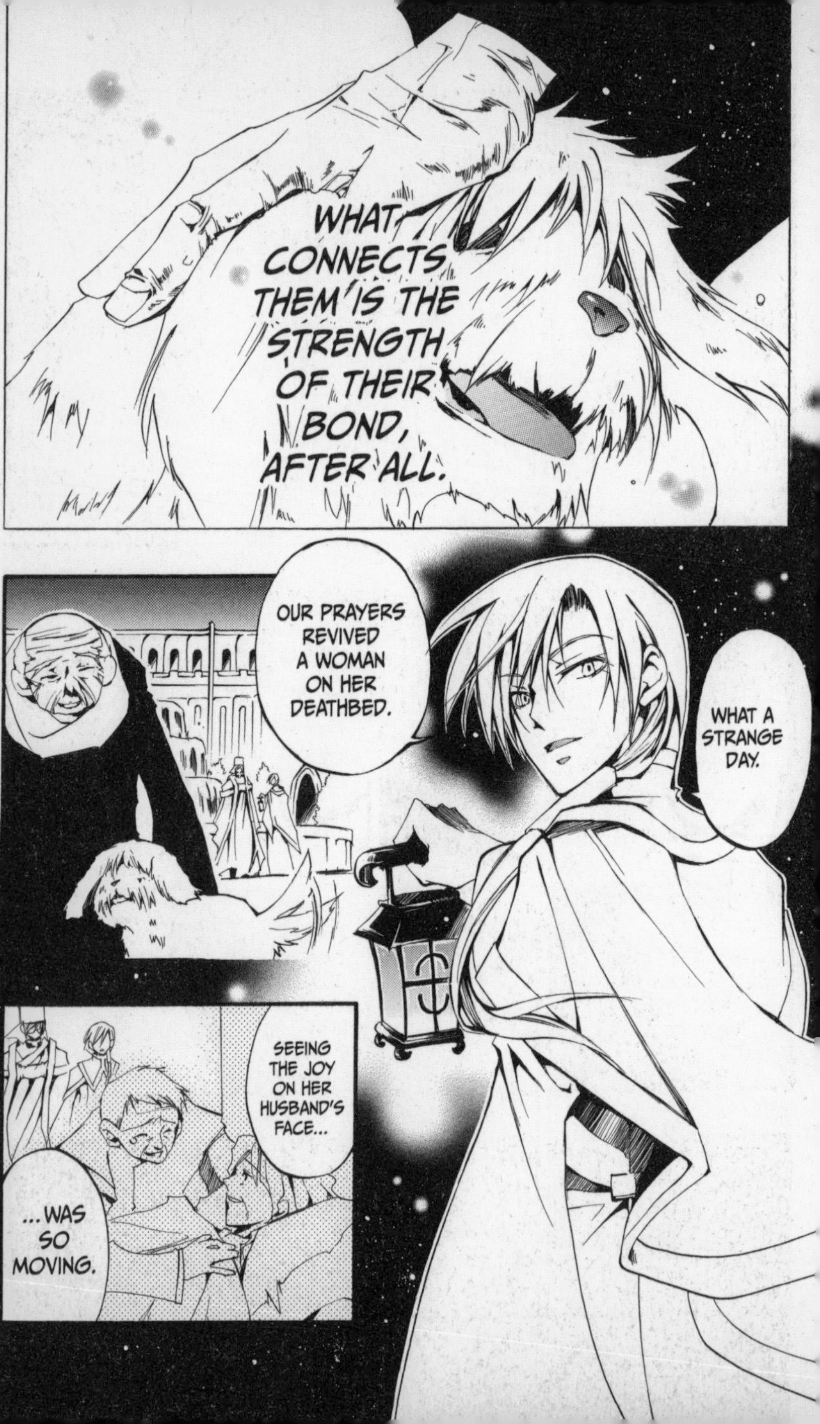
WHAT CONNECTS THEM IS THE STRENGTH OF THEIR BOND, AFTER ALL.
WHAT A STRANGE DAY.
OUR PRAYERS REVIVED A WOMAN ON HER DEATHBED.
SEEING THE JOY ON HER HUSBAND'S FACE...
...WAS SO MOVING.

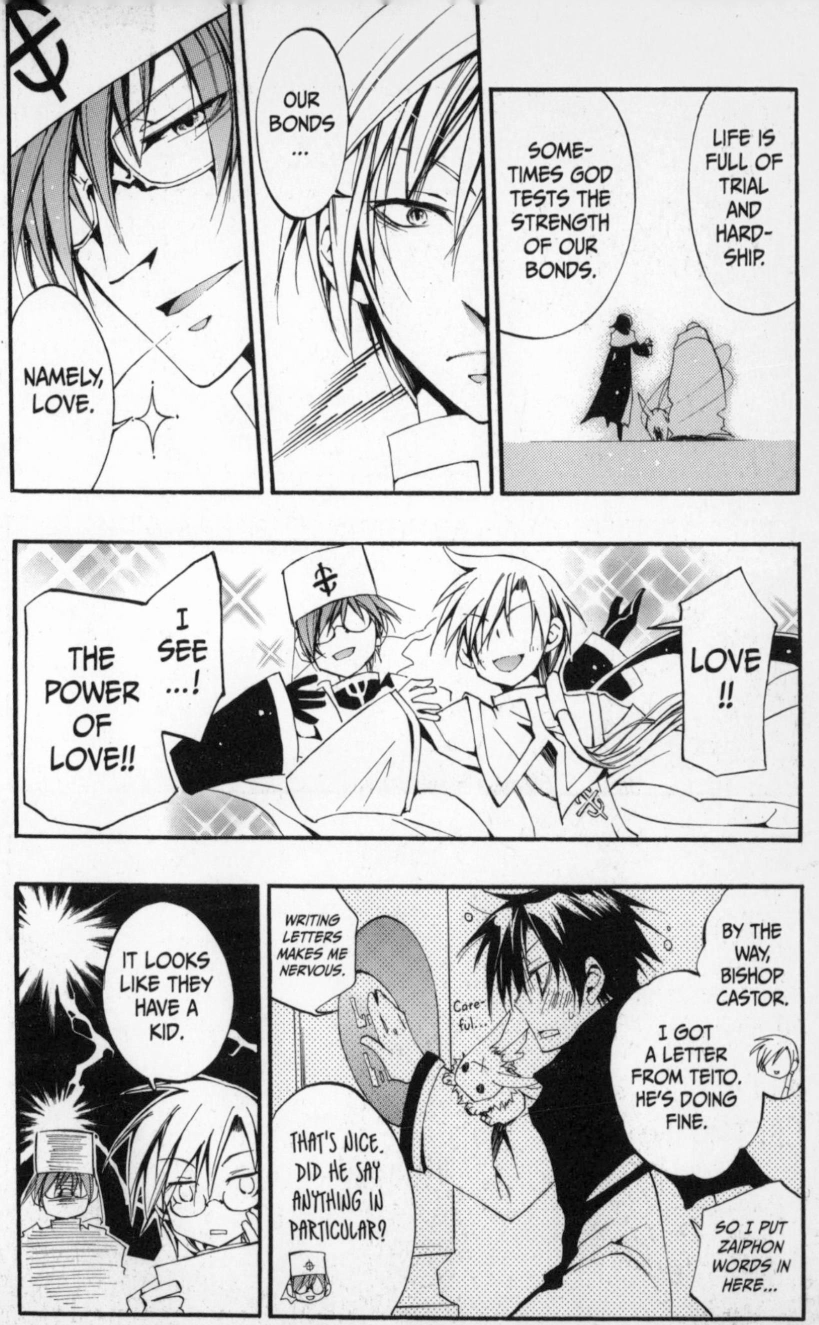
LIFE IS FULL OF TRIAL AND HARDSHIP.
SOMETIMES GOD TESTS THE STRENGTH OF OUR BONDS.
OUR BONDS...
NAMELY, LOVE.
LOVE!!
I SEE...!
THE POWER OF LOVE!!
BY THE WAY, BISHOP CASTOR.
I GOT A LETTER FROM TEITO. HE'S DOING FINE.
WRITING LETTERS MAKES ME NERVOUS.
Careful...
THAT'S NICE. DID HE SAY ANYTHING IN PARTICULAR?
SO I PUT ZAIPHON WORDS IN HERE...
IT LOOKS LIKE THEY HAVE A KID.

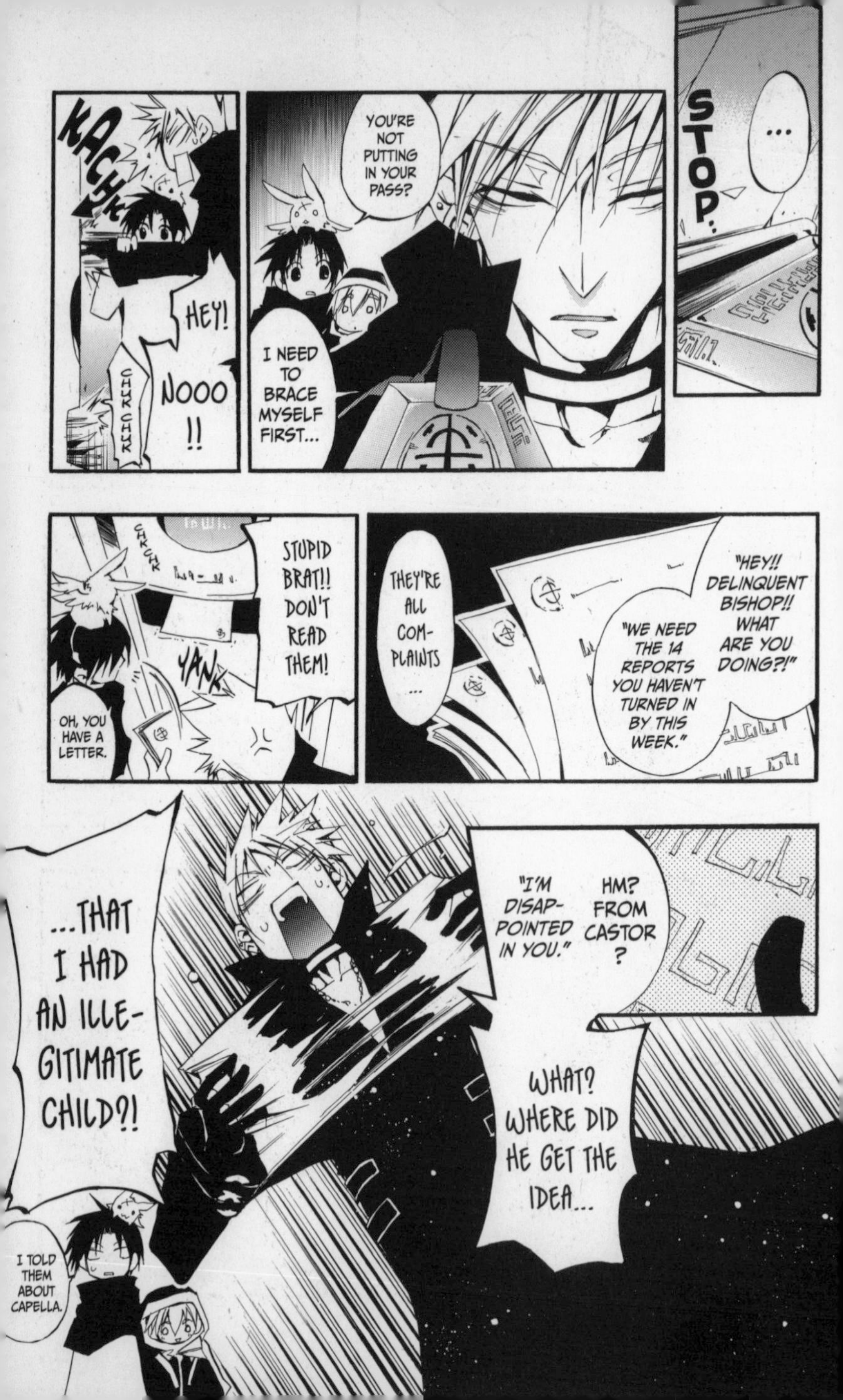
...
STOP...
YOU'RE NOT PUTTING IN YOUR PASS?
I NEED TO BRACE MYSELF FIRST...
KACHK
HEY!
NOOO!!
CHUK CHUK
"HEY!! DELINQUENT BISHOP!! WHAT ARE YOU DOING?!"
"WE NEED THE 14 REPORTS YOU HAVEN'T TURNED IN BY THIS WEEK."
THEY'RE ALL COMPLAINTS...
STUPID BRAT!! DON'T READ THEM!
CHK CHK
YANK
OH, YOU HAVE A LETTER.
HM? FROM CASTOR?
"I'M DISAPPOINTED IN YOU."
WHAT? WHERE DID HE GET THE IDEA...
...THAT I HAD AN ILLEGITIMATE CHILD?!
I TOLD THEM ABOUT CAPELLA.

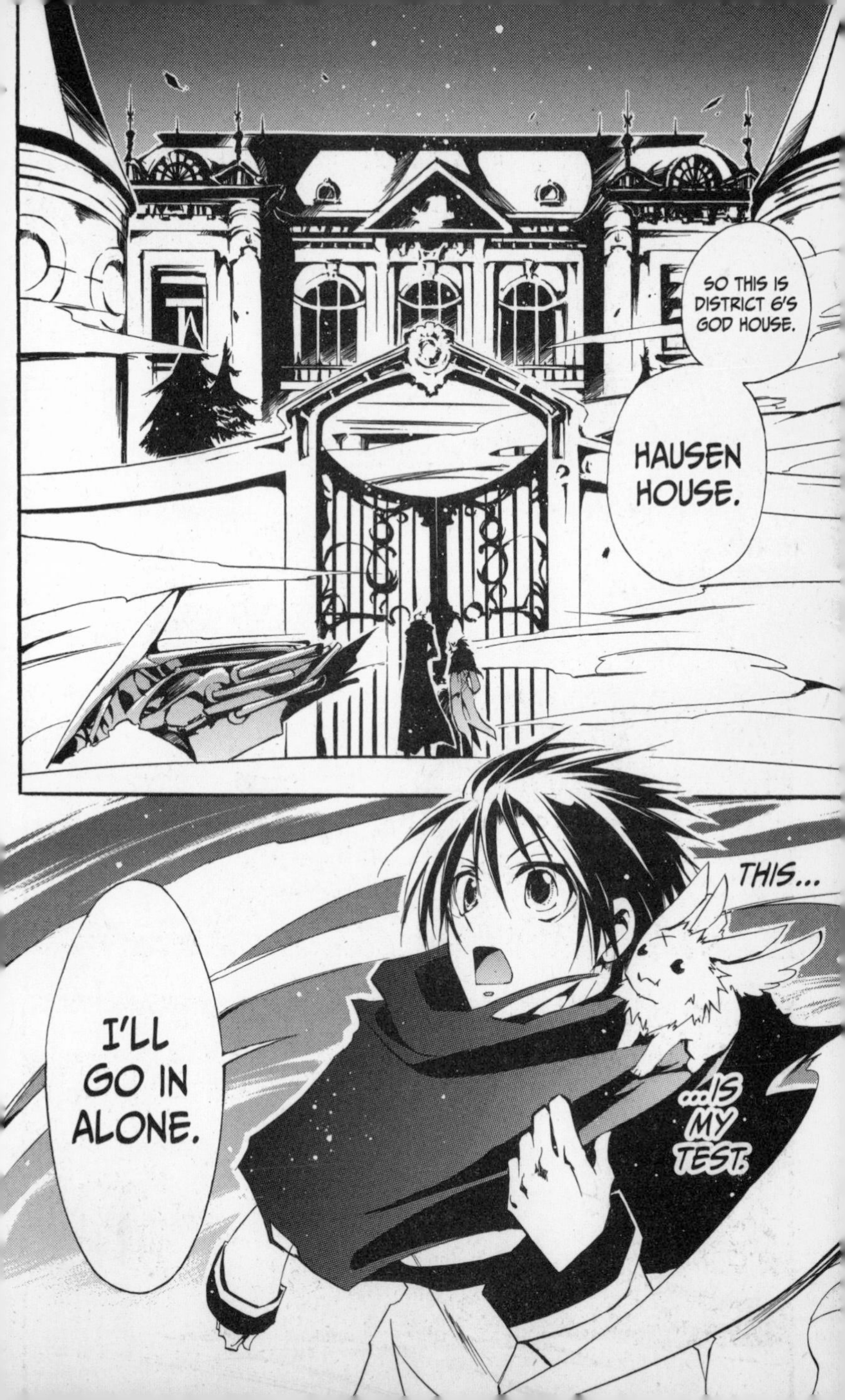
SO THIS IS DISTRICT 6'S GOD HOUSE.
HAUSEN HOUSE.
THIS...
...IS MY TEST.
I'LL GO IN ALONE.

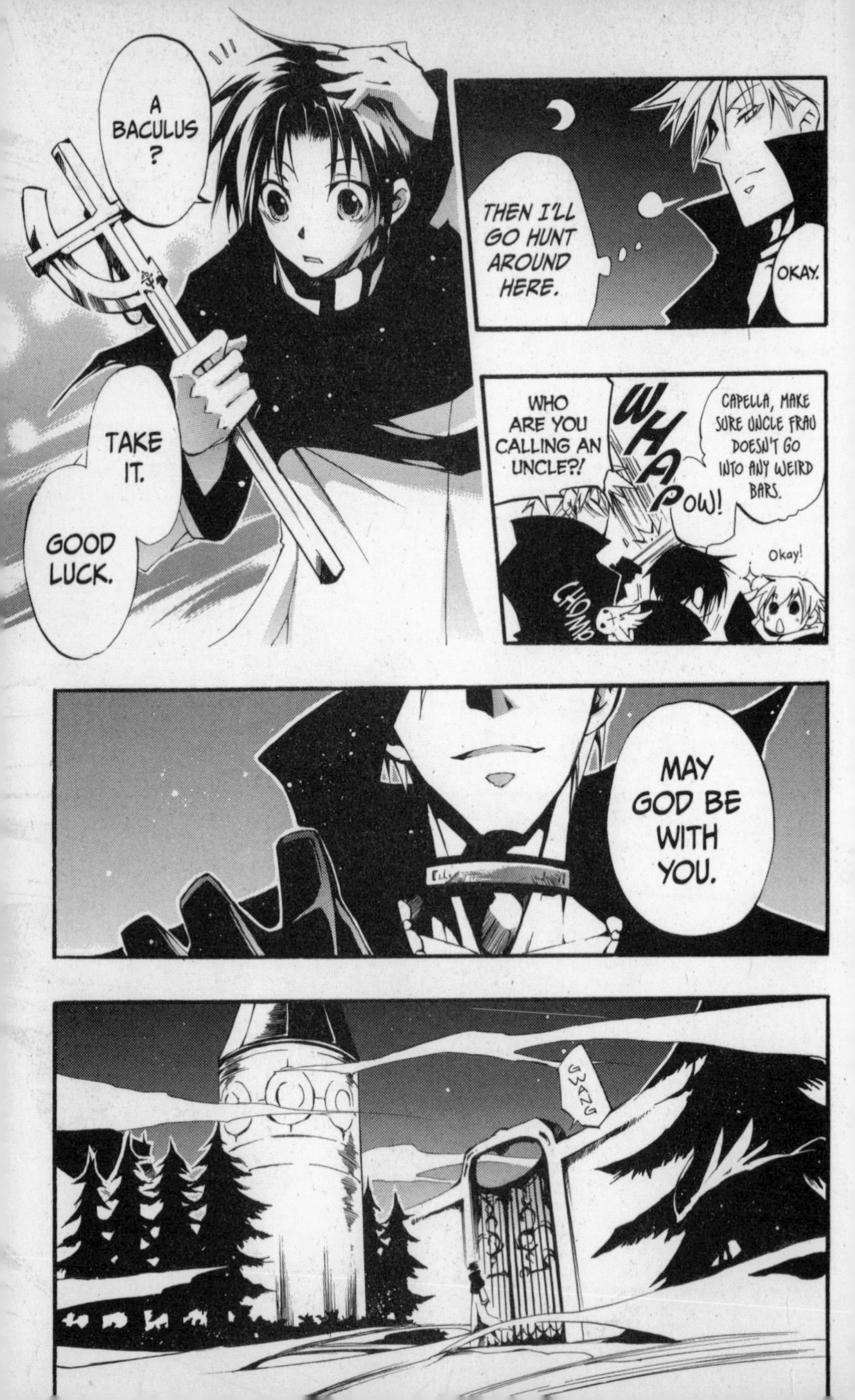
THEN I'LL GO HUNT AROUND HERE.
OKAY.
CAPELLA, MAKE SURE UNCLE FRAU DOESN'T GO INTO ANY WEIRD BARS.
WHAPOW!
WHO ARE YOU CALLING AN UNCLE?!
Okay!
CHOMP
A BACULUS?
TAKE IT.
GOOD LUCK.
MAY GOD BE WITH YOU.
GWANG

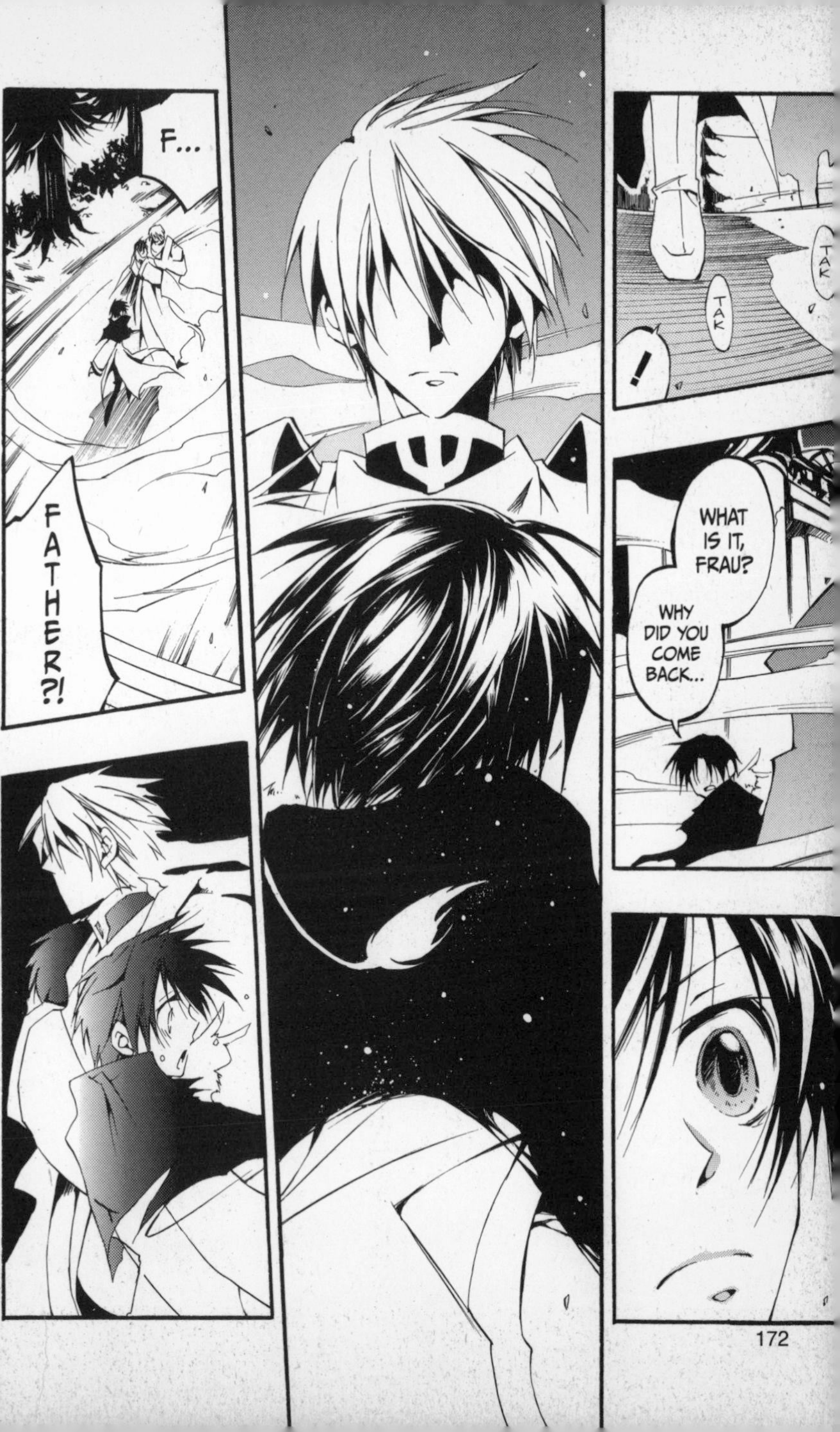
TAK
TAK
!
WHAT IS IT, FRAU?
WHY DID YOU COME BACK...
F...
FATHER?!

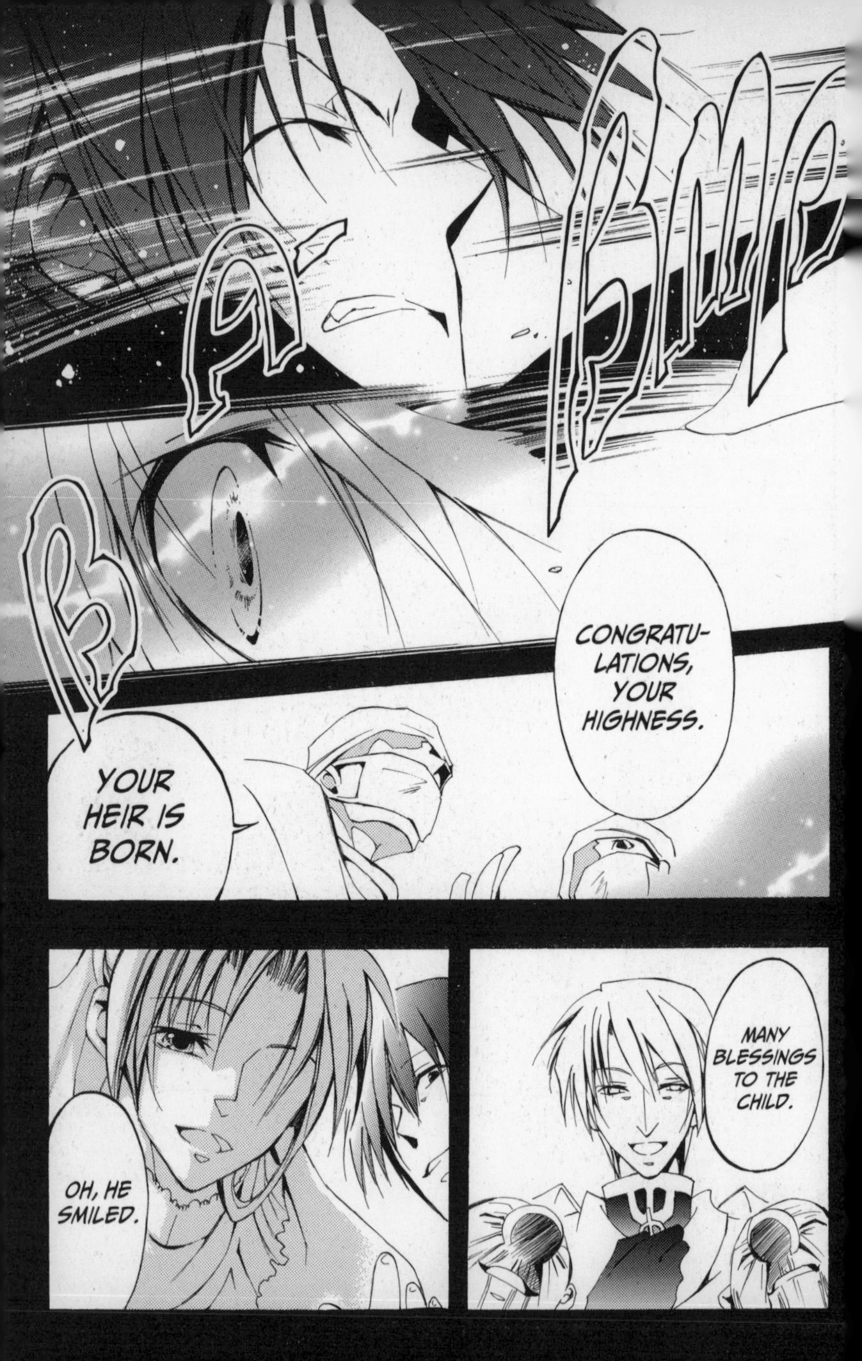
CONGRATU-LATIONS, YOUR HIGHNESS.
YOUR HEIR IS BORN.
MANY BLESSINGS TO THE CHILD.
OH, HE SMILED.

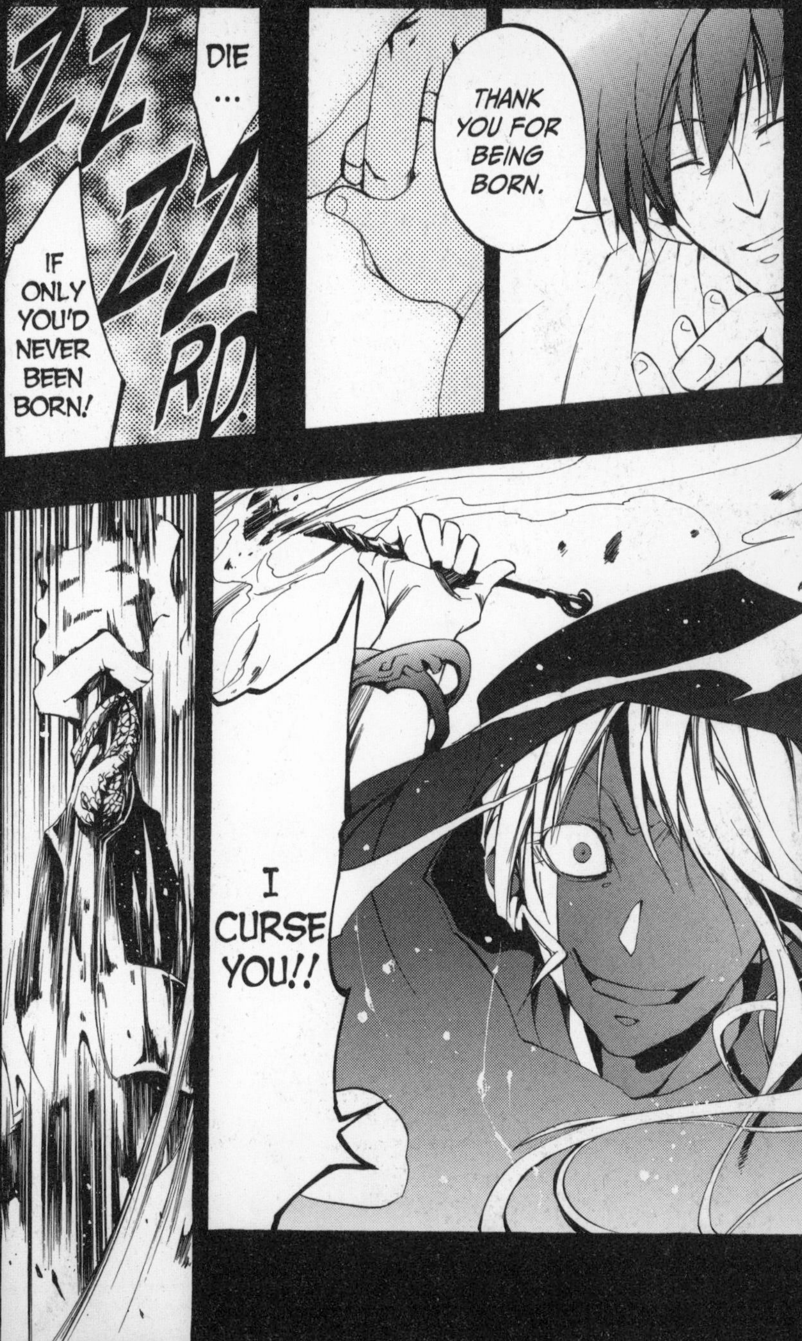
THANK YOU FOR BEING BORN.
DIE ...
IF ONLY YOU'D NEVER BEEN BORN!
I CURSE YOU!!

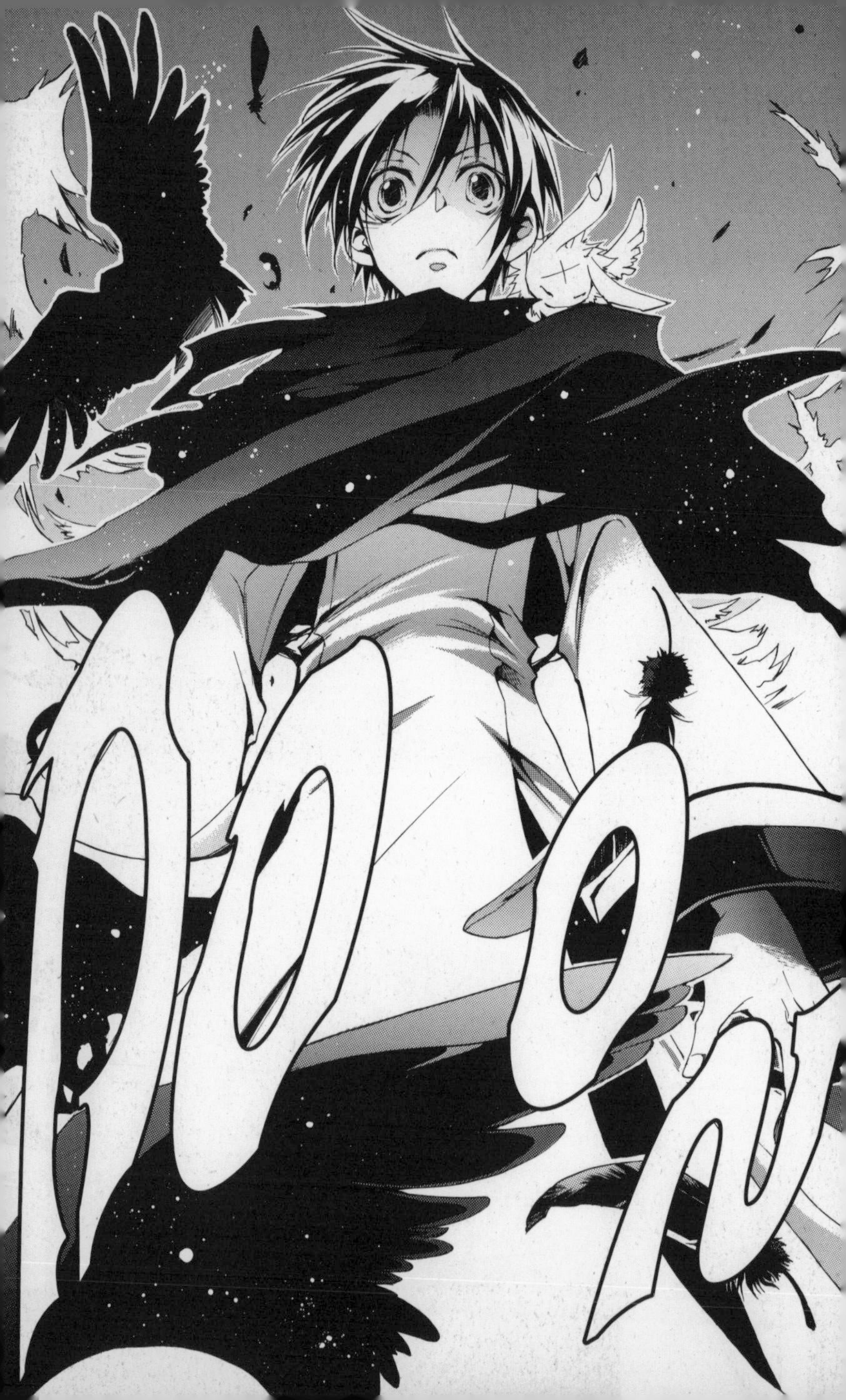
!

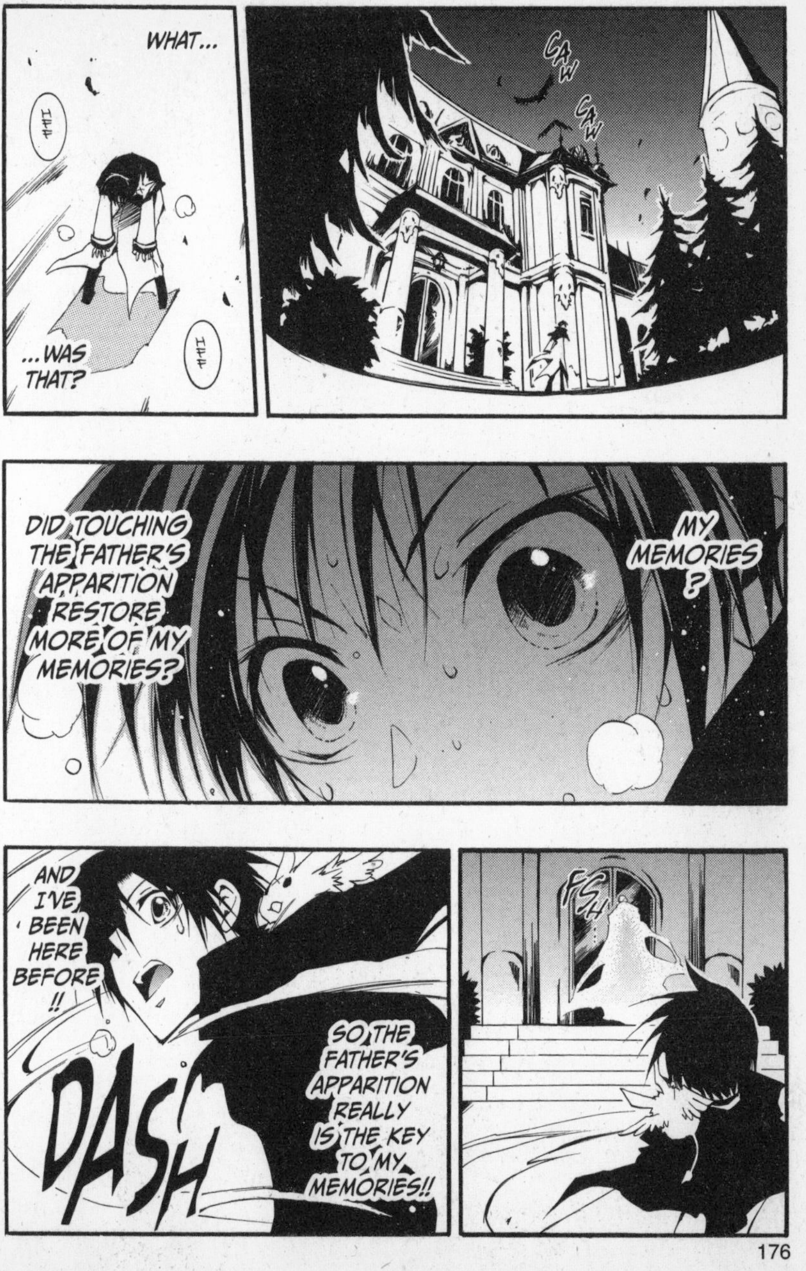
CAW
CAW
WHAT...
HFF
HFF
...WAS THAT?
MY MEMORIES?
DID TOUCHING THE FATHER'S APPARITION RESTORE MORE OF MY MEMORIES?
FSH
AND I'VE BEEN HERE BEFORE!!
SO THE FATHER'S APPARITION REALLY IS THE KEY TO MY MEMORIES!!
DASH

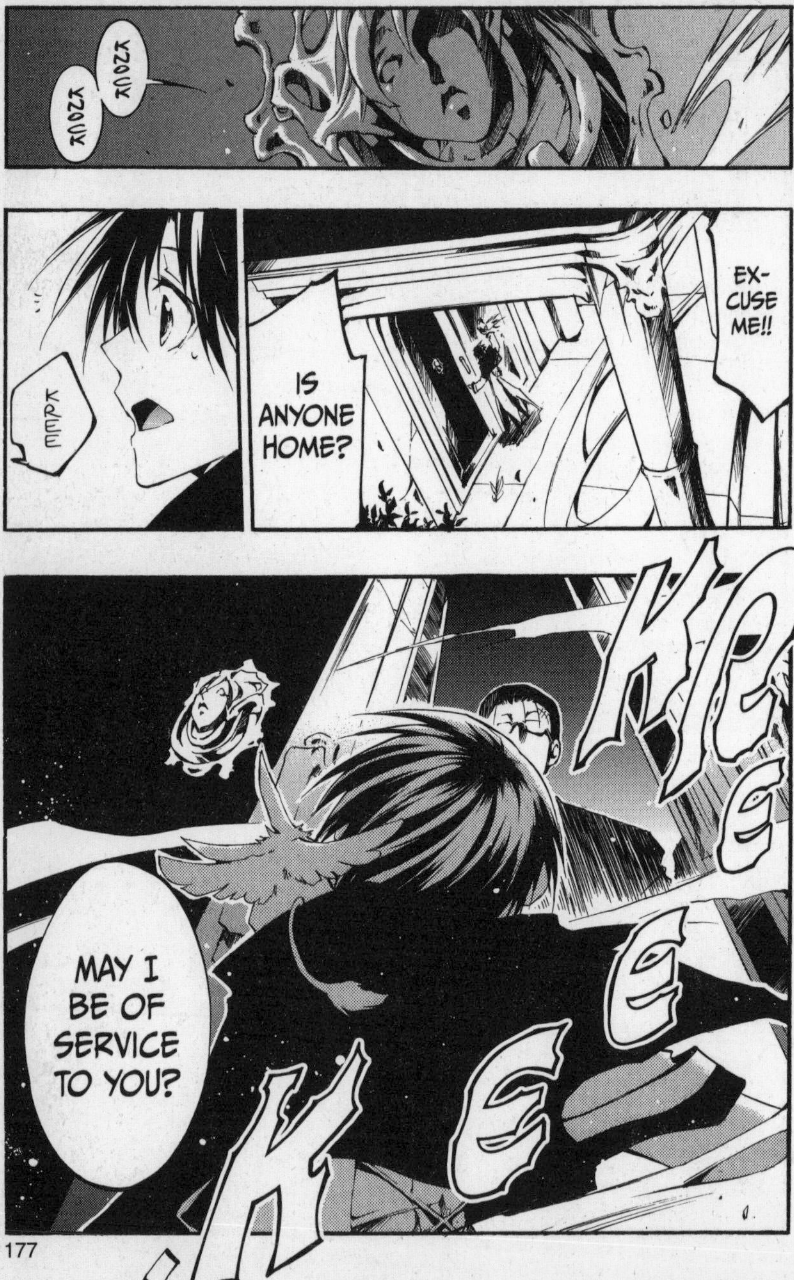
KNOCK
KNOCK
EX-CUSE ME!!
IS ANYONE HOME?
KREE
KREEEK
MAY I BE OF SERVICE TO YOU?

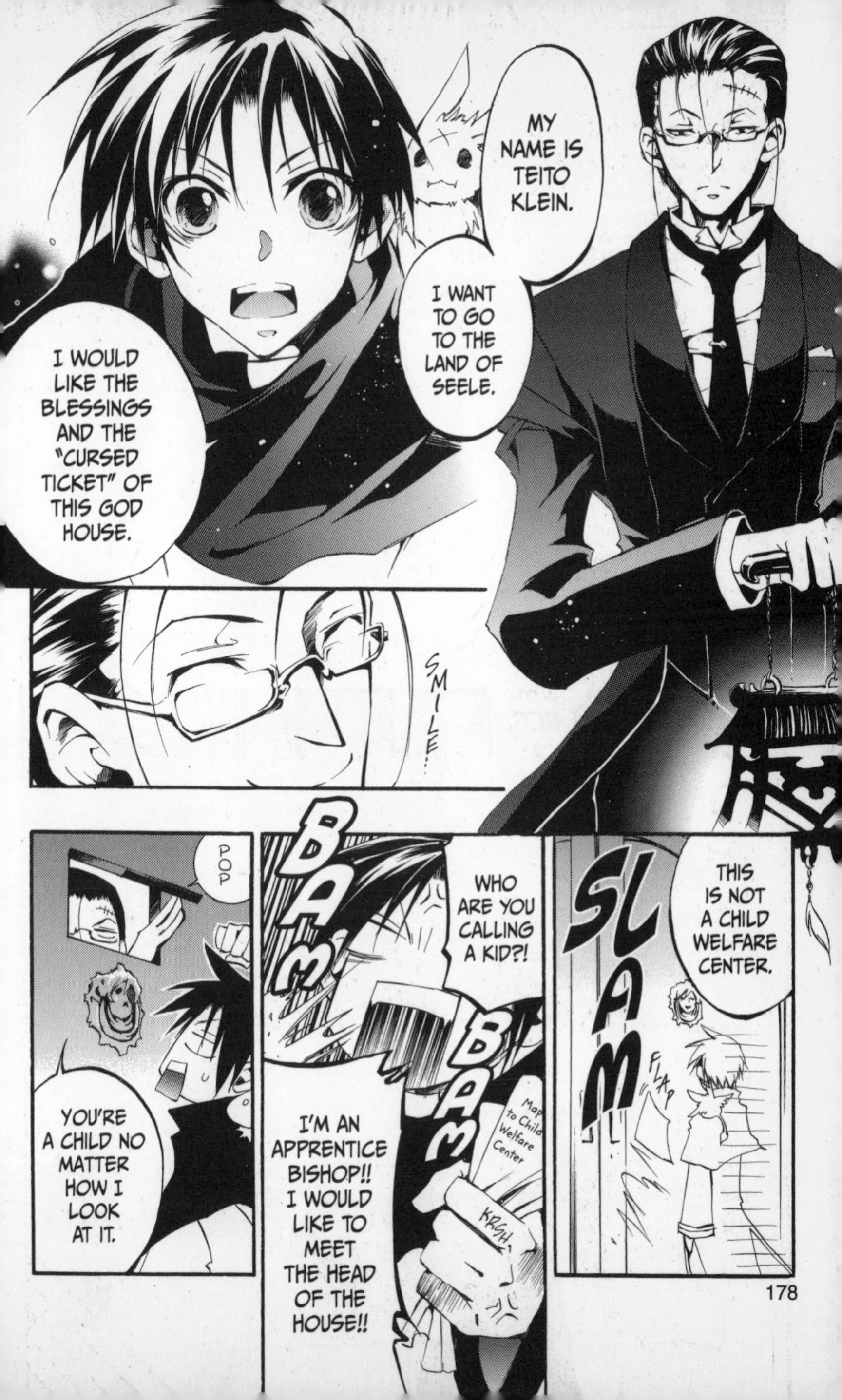
MY NAME IS TEITO KLEIN.
I WANT TO GO TO THE LAND OF SEELE.
I WOULD LIKE THE BLESSINGS AND THE "CURSED TICKET" OF THIS GOD HOUSE.
SMILE...
THIS IS NOT A CHILD WELFARE CENTER.
SLAM
FLAP
Map to Child Welfare Center
WHO ARE YOU CALLING A KID?!
BAM BAM BAM
KRSH
I'M AN APPRENTICE BISHOP!! I WOULD LIKE TO MEET THE HEAD OF THE HOUSE!!
POP
YOU'RE A CHILD NO MATTER HOW I LOOK AT IT.

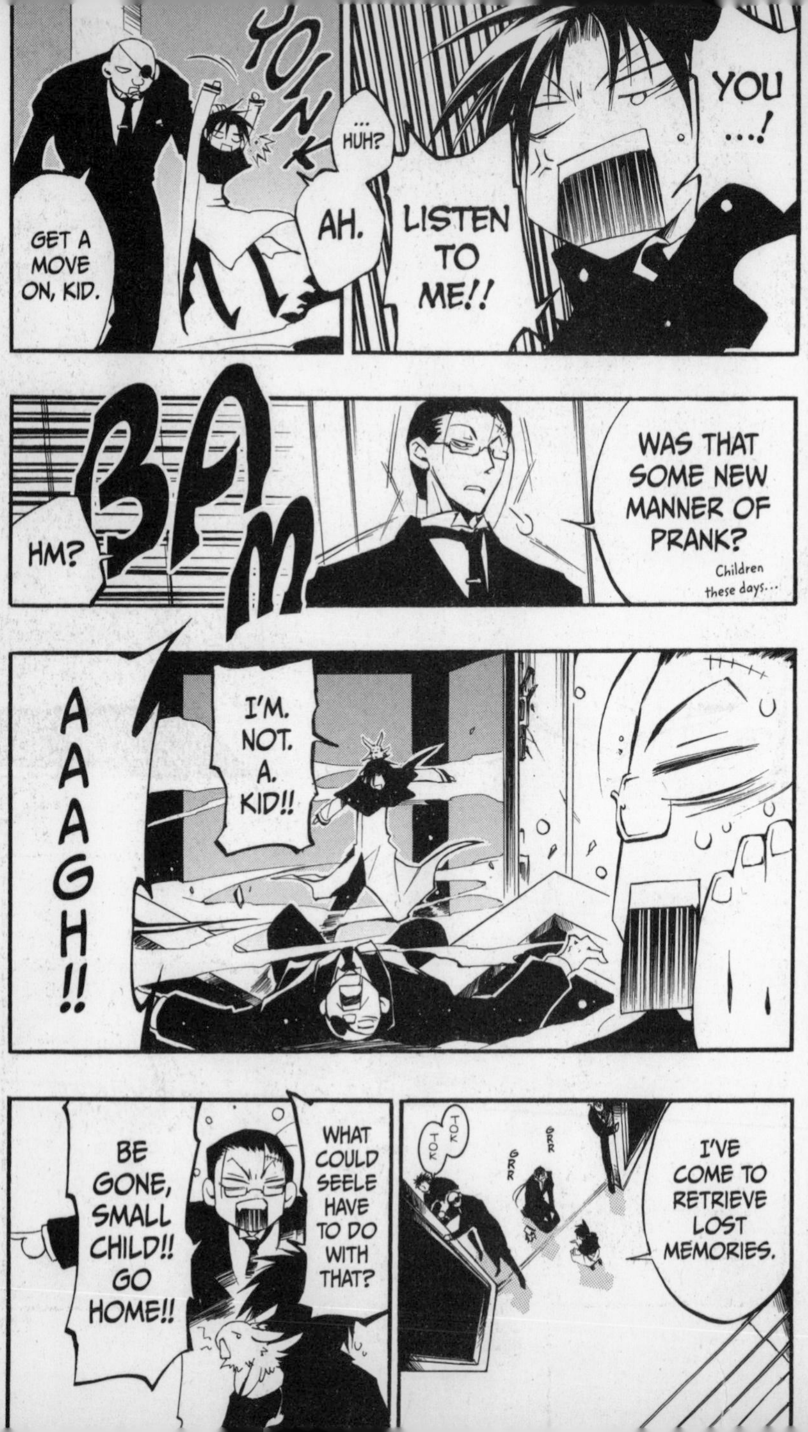
YOU ...!
LISTEN TO ME!!
... HUH?
AH.
YOINK
GET A MOVE ON, KID.
WAS THAT SOME NEW MANNER OF PRANK?
Children these days...
HM?
I'M. NOT. A. KID!!
AAAGH!!
I'VE COME TO RETRIEVE LOST MEMORIES.
GRR
GRR
TOK TOK
WHAT COULD SEELE HAVE TO DO WITH THAT?
BE GONE, SMALL CHILD!! GO HOME!!

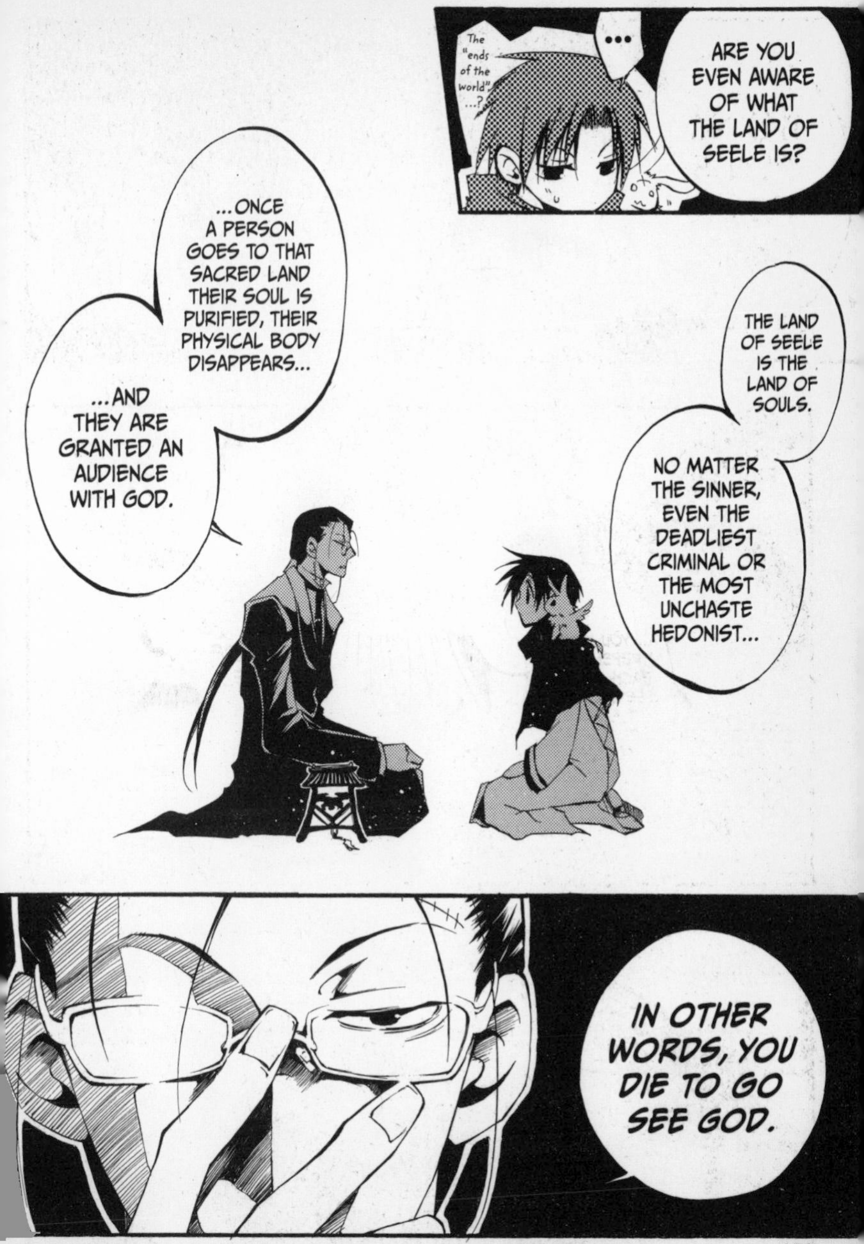
ARE YOU EVEN AWARE OF WHAT THE LAND OF SEELE IS?
...
The "ends of the world"...?
THE LAND OF SEELE IS THE LAND OF SOULS.
NO MATTER THE SINNER, EVEN THE DEADLIEST CRIMINAL OR THE MOST UNCHASTE HEDONIST...
...ONCE A PERSON GOES TO THAT SACRED LAND THEIR SOUL IS PURIFIED, THEIR PHYSICAL BODY DISAPPEARS...
...AND THEY ARE GRANTED AN AUDIENCE WITH GOD.
IN OTHER WORDS, YOU DIE TO GO SEE GOD.

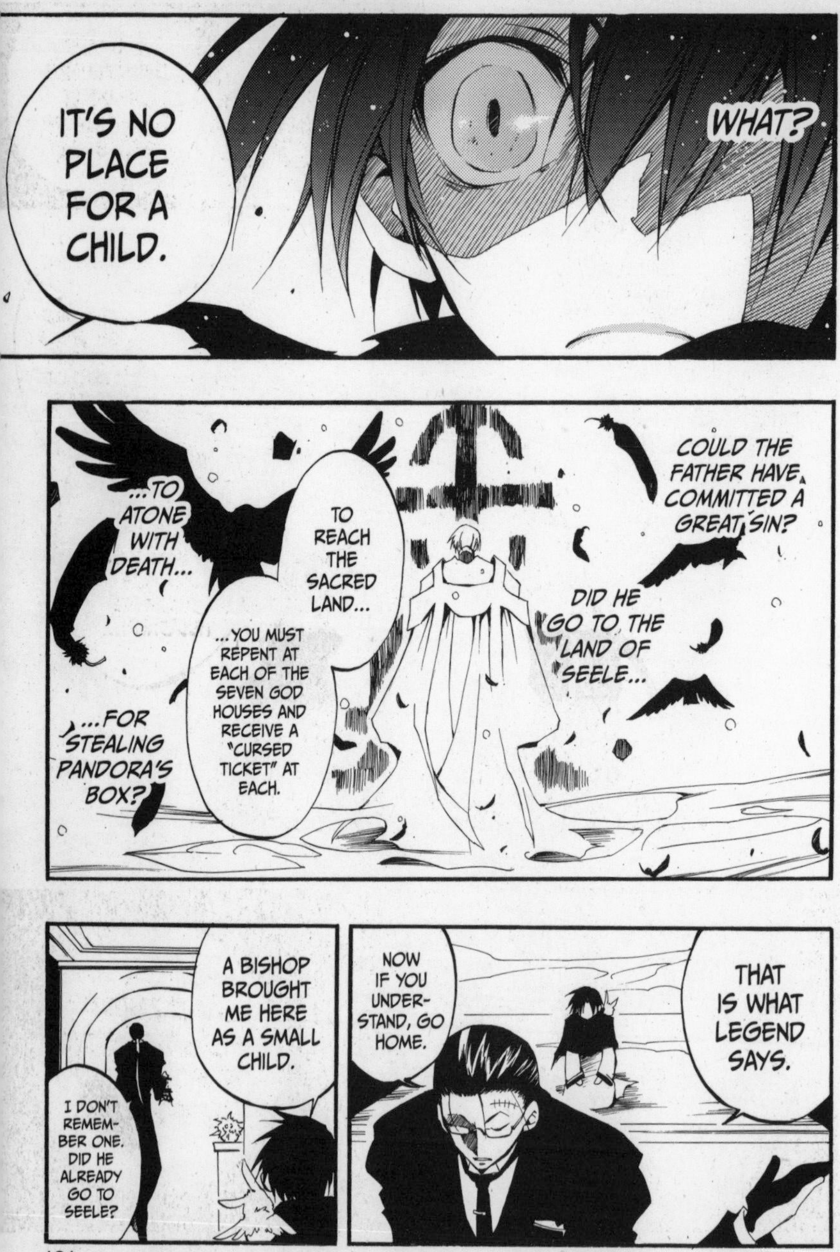
WHAT?
IT'S NO PLACE FOR A CHILD.
COULD THE FATHER HAVE COMMITTED A GREAT SIN?
DID HE GO TO THE LAND OF SEELE...
TO REACH THE SACRED LAND...
...YOU MUST REPENT AT EACH OF THE SEVEN GOD HOUSES AND RECEIVE A "CURSED TICKET" AT EACH.
...TO ATONE WITH DEATH...
...FOR STEALING PANDORA'S BOX?
THAT IS WHAT LEGEND SAYS.
NOW IF YOU UNDER-STAND, GO HOME.
A BISHOP BROUGHT ME HERE AS A SMALL CHILD.
I DON'T REMEM-BER ONE. DID HE ALREADY GO TO SEELE?

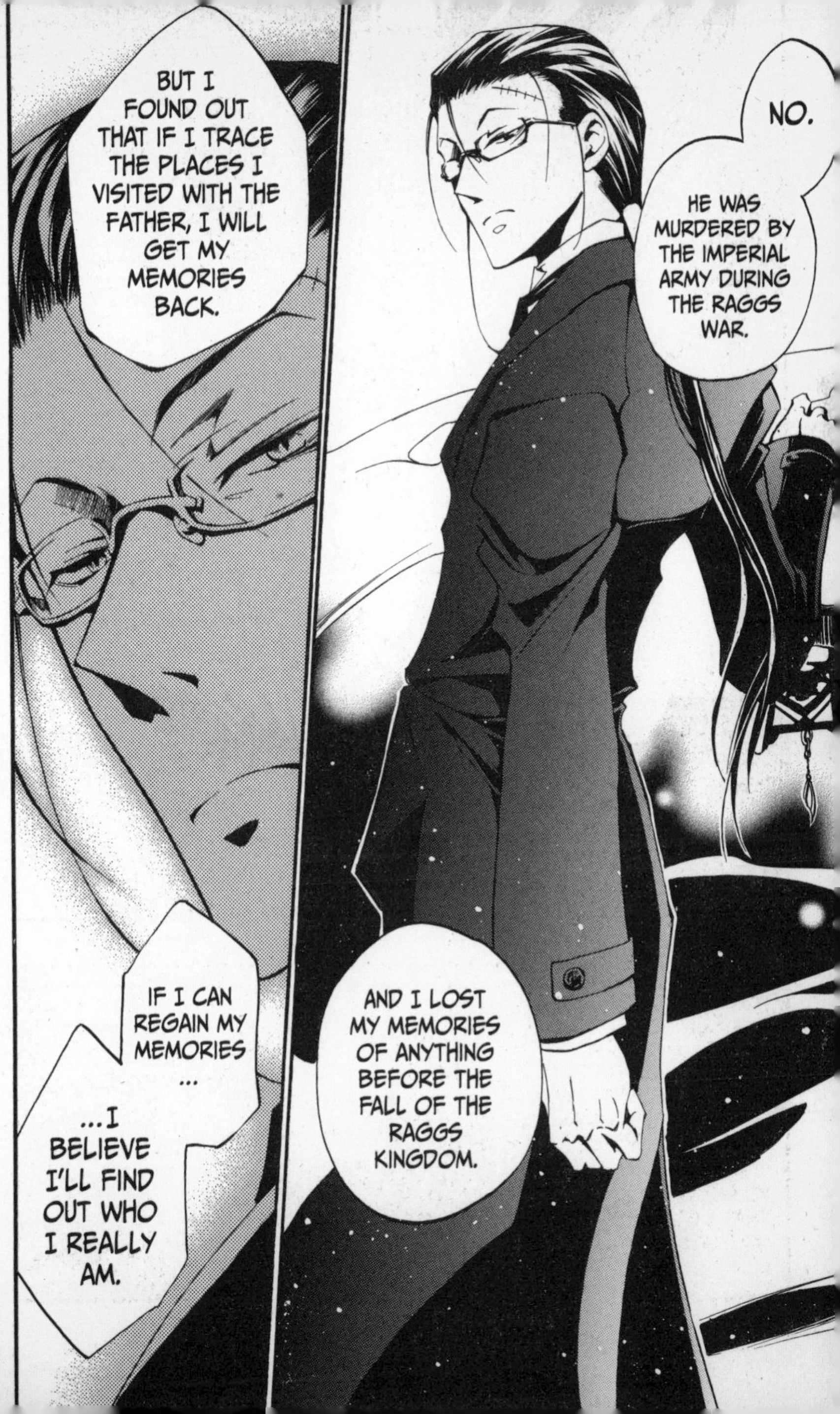
NO.
HE WAS MURDERED BY THE IMPERIAL ARMY DURING THE RAGGS WAR.
AND I LOST MY MEMORIES OF ANYTHING BEFORE THE FALL OF THE RAGGS KINGDOM.
BUT I FOUND OUT THAT IF I TRACE THE PLACES I VISITED WITH THE FATHER, I WILL GET MY MEMORIES BACK.
IF I CAN REGAIN MY MEMORIES ...
...I BELIEVE I'LL FIND OUT WHO I REALLY AM.

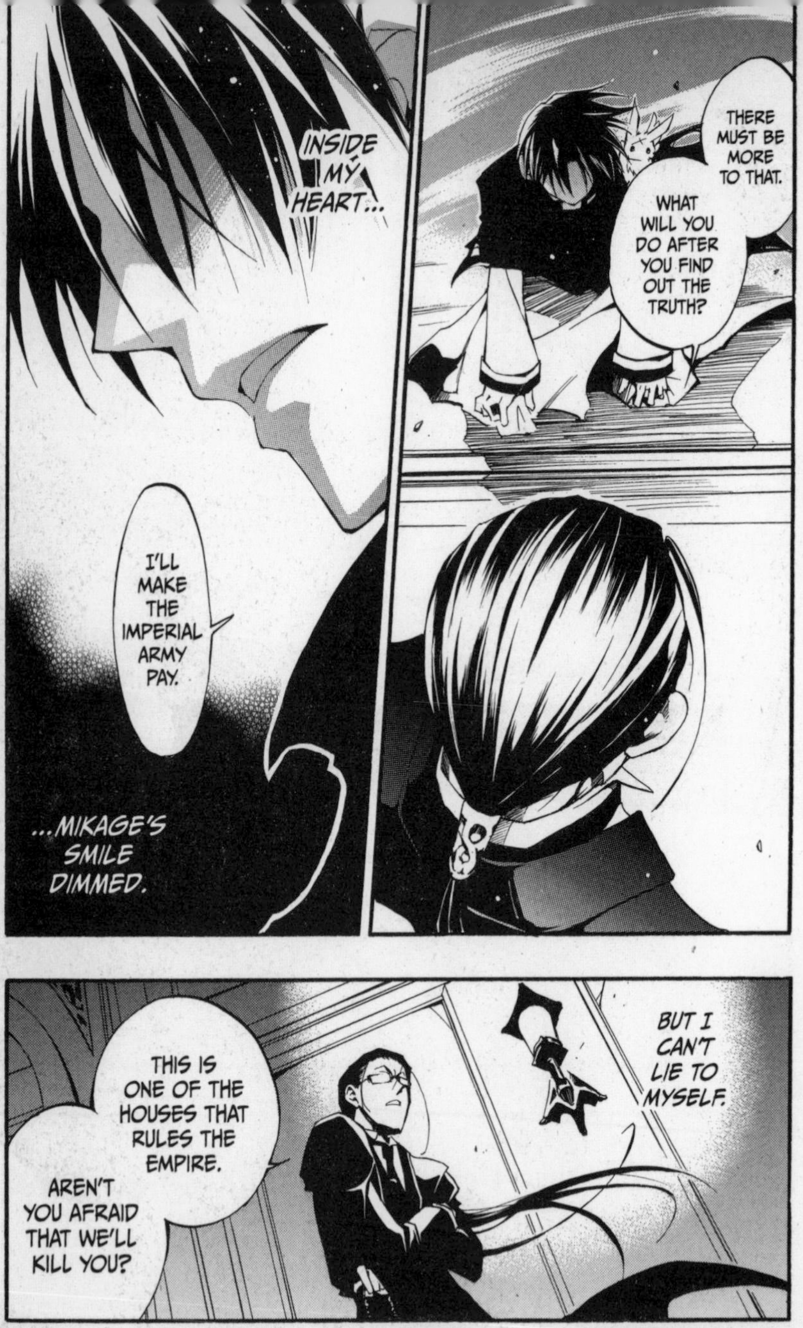
THERE MUST BE MORE TO THAT.
WHAT WILL YOU DO AFTER YOU FIND OUT THE TRUTH?
INSIDE MY HEART...
I'LL MAKE THE IMPERIAL ARMY PAY.
...MIKAGE'S SMILE DIMMED.
BUT I CAN'T LIE TO MYSELF.
THIS IS ONE OF THE HOUSES THAT RULES THE EMPIRE.
AREN'T YOU AFRAID THAT WE'LL KILL YOU?

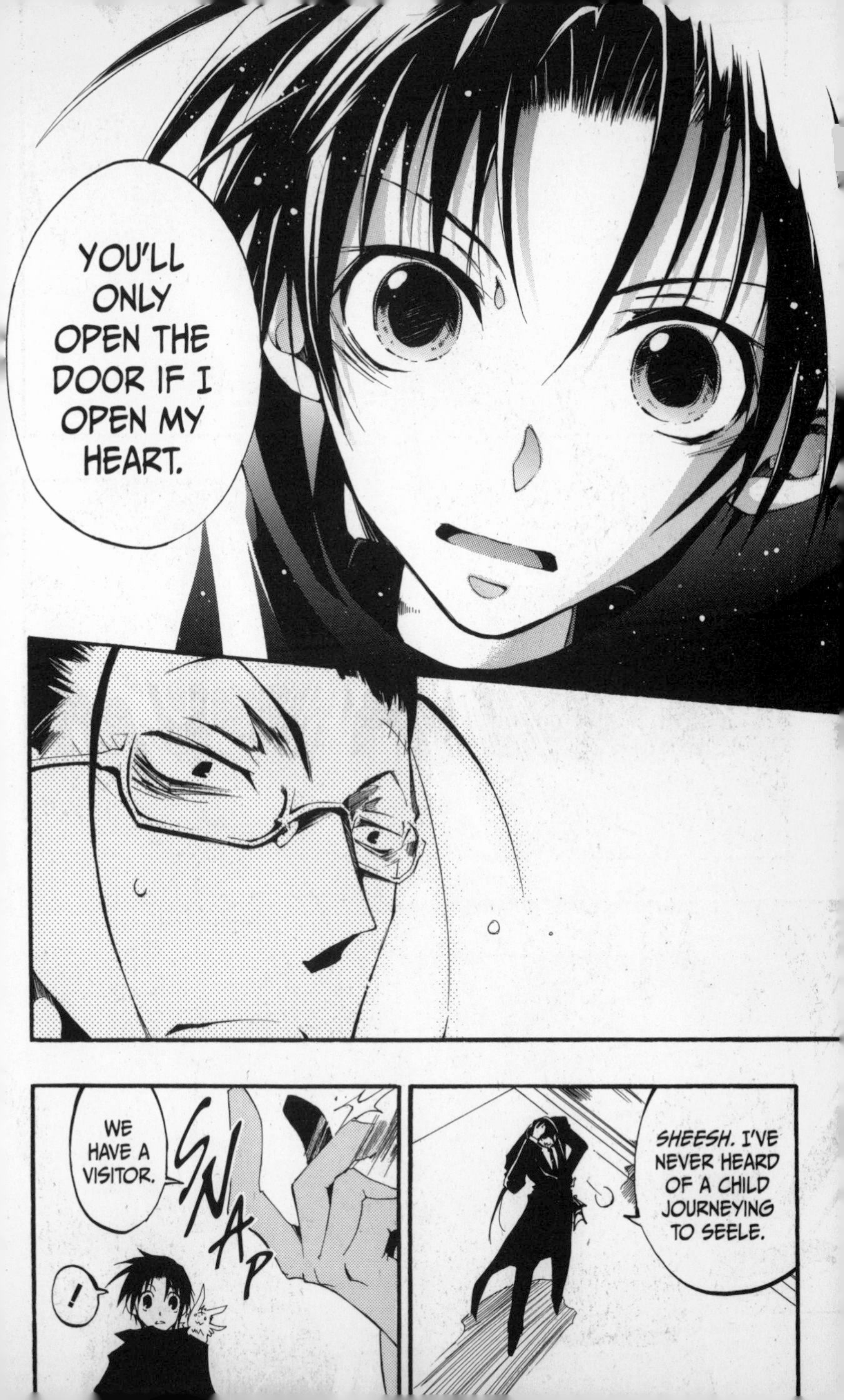
YOU'LL ONLY OPEN THE DOOR IF I OPEN MY HEART.
SHEESH. I'VE NEVER HEARD OF A CHILD JOURNEYING TO SEELE.
WE HAVE A VISITOR.
SNAP
!

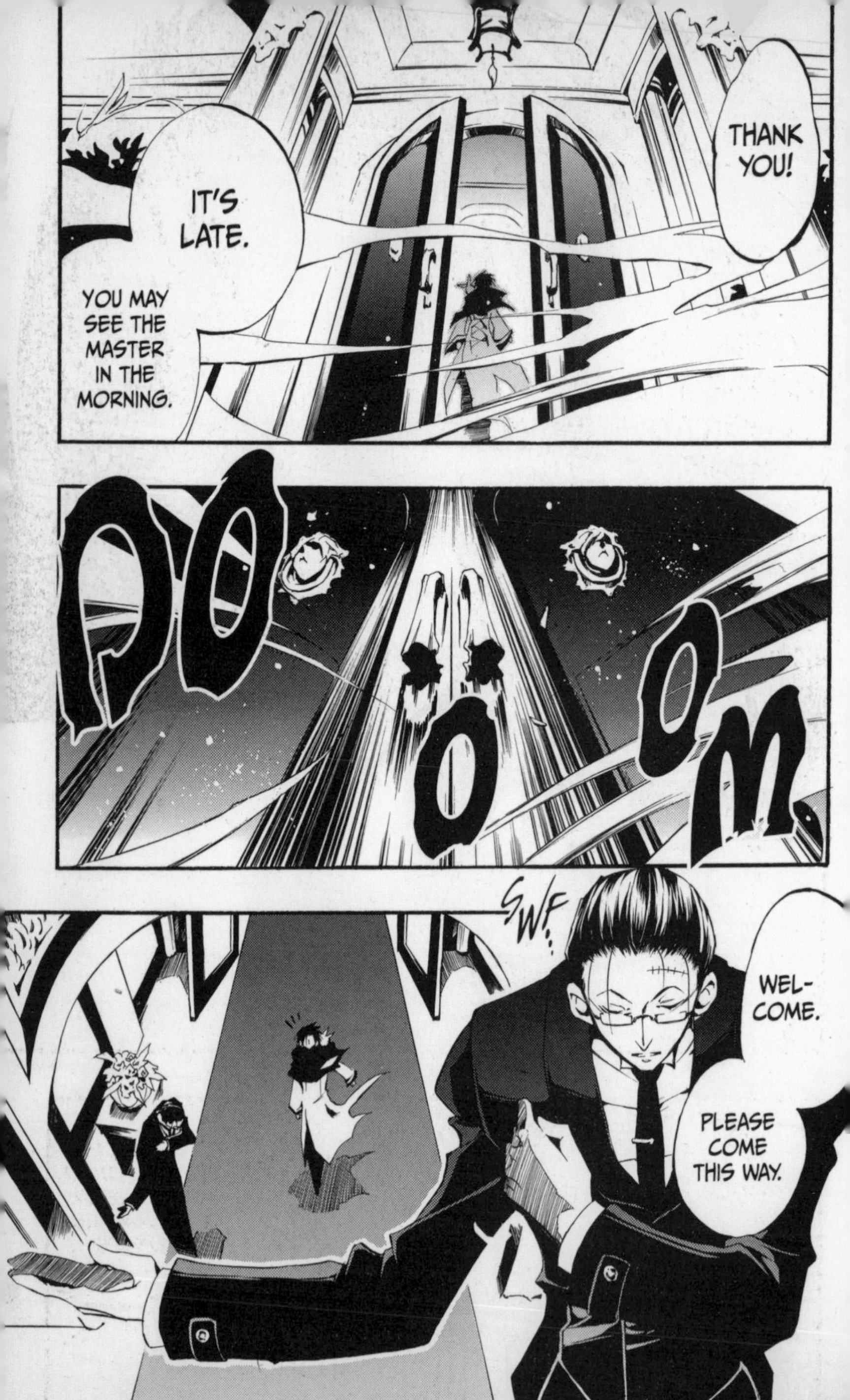
THANK YOU!
IT'S LATE.
YOU MAY SEE THE MASTER IN THE MORNING.
DOOOOM
SWF
WEL-COME.
PLEASE COME THIS WAY.

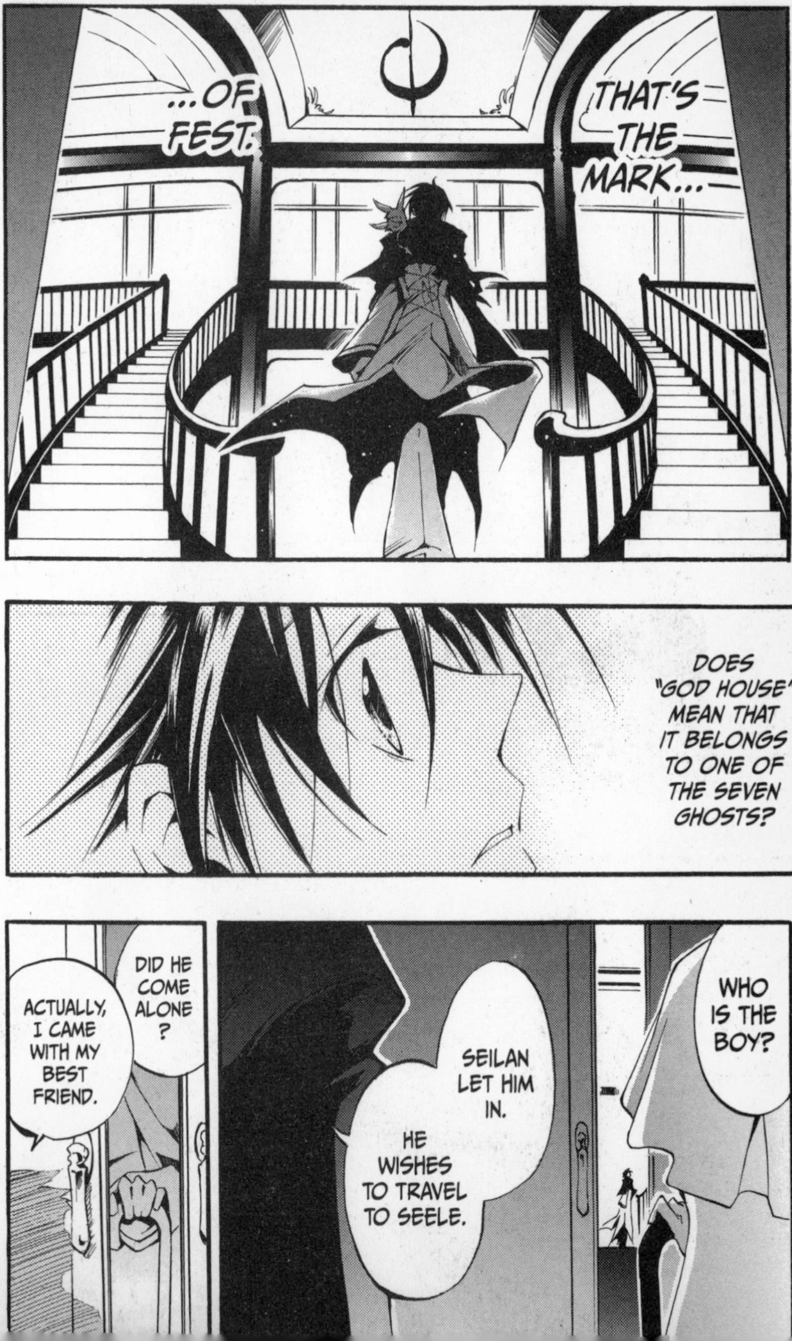
THAT'S THE MARK...
...OF FEST.
DOES "GOD HOUSE" MEAN THAT IT BELONGS TO ONE OF THE SEVEN GHOSTS?
WHO IS THE BOY?
SEILAN LET HIM IN.
HE WISHES TO TRAVEL TO SEELE.
DID HE COME ALONE ?
ACTUALLY, I CAME WITH MY BEST FRIEND.

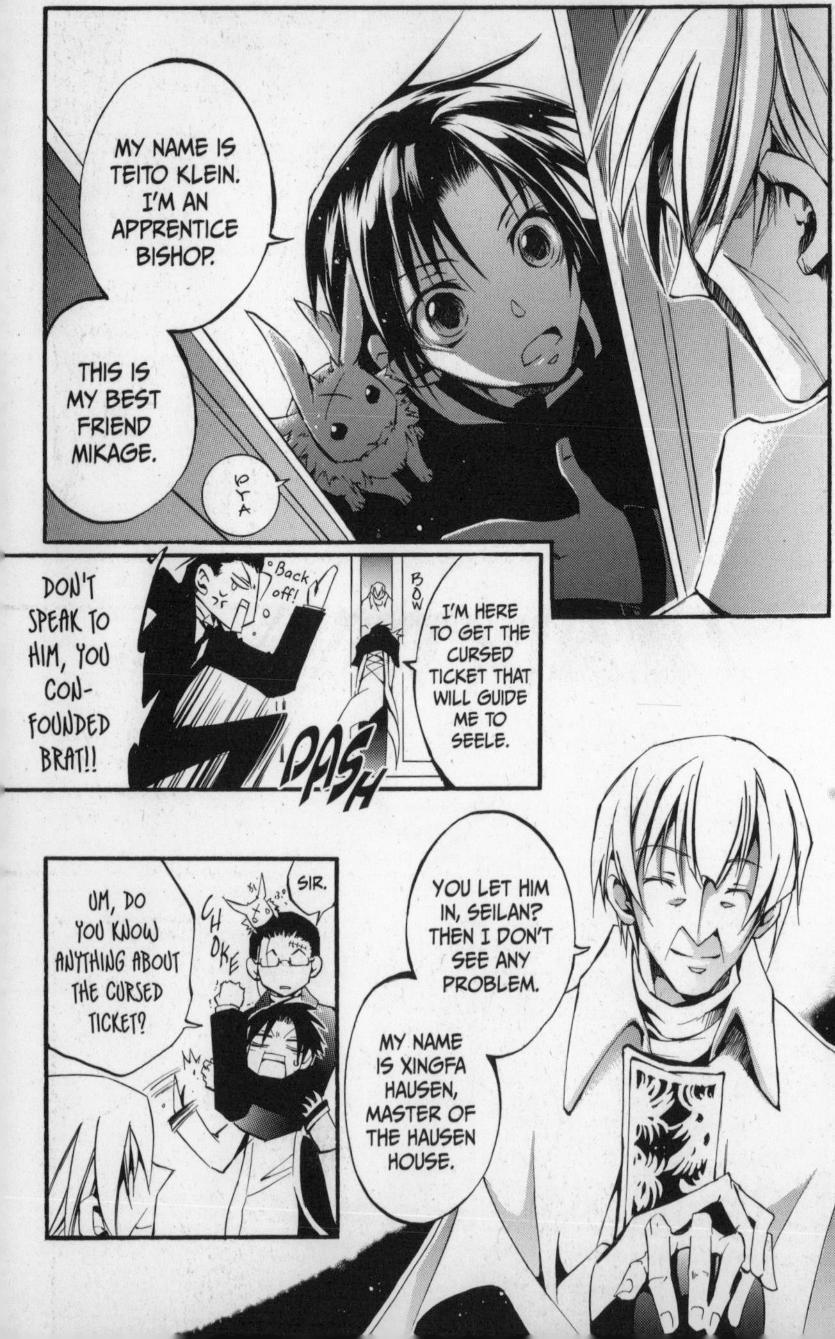
MY NAME IS TEITO KLEIN. I'M AN APPRENTICE BISHOP.
THIS IS MY BEST FRIEND MIKAGE.
PYA
BOW
I'M HERE TO GET THE CURSED TICKET THAT WILL GUIDE ME TO SEELE.
Back off!
DON'T SPEAK TO HIM, YOU CON-FOUNDED BRAT!!
DASH
YOU LET HIM IN, SEILAN? THEN I DON'T SEE ANY PROBLEM.
MY NAME IS XINGFA HAUSEN, MASTER OF THE HAUSEN HOUSE.
SIR.
CHOKE
UM, DO YOU KNOW ANYTHING ABOUT THE CURSED TICKET?

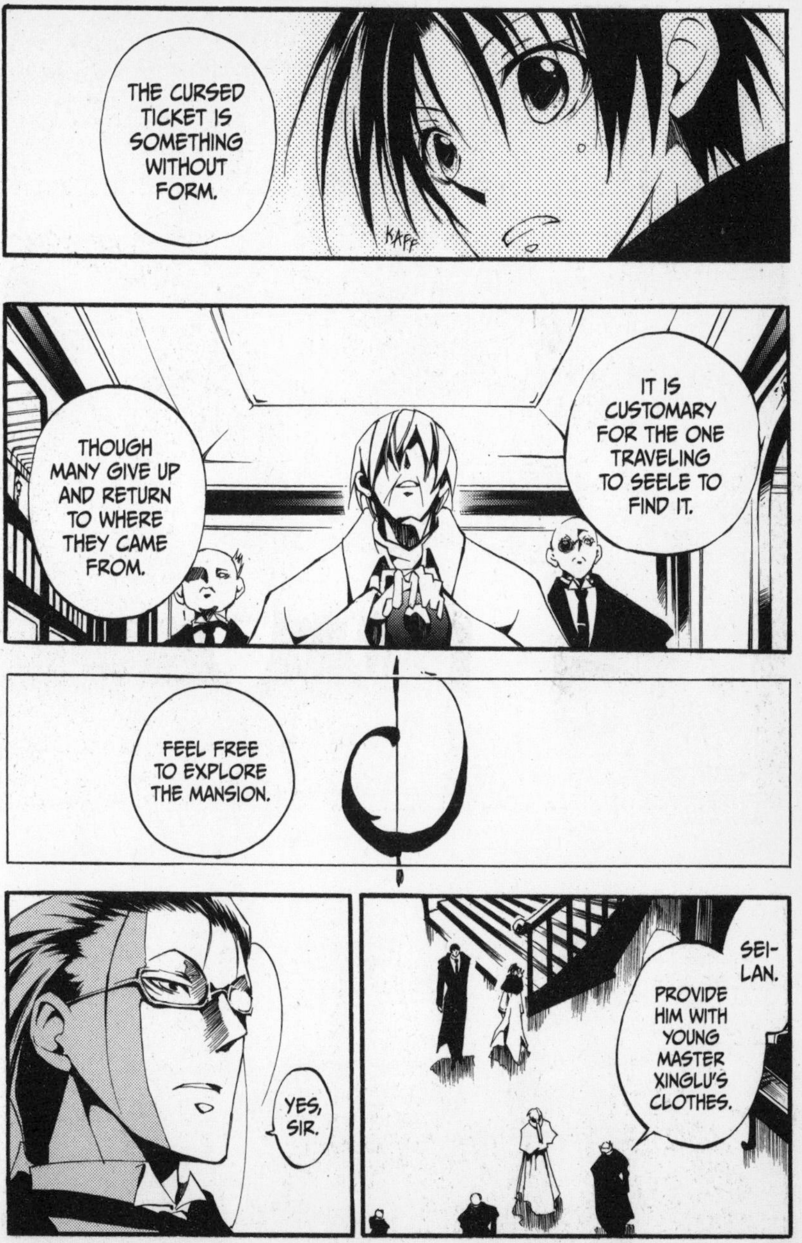
THE CURSED TICKET IS SOMETHING WITHOUT FORM.
KAFF
IT IS CUSTOMARY FOR THE ONE TRAVELING TO SEELE TO FIND IT.
THOUGH MANY GIVE UP AND RETURN TO WHERE THEY CAME FROM.
FEEL FREE TO EXPLORE THE MANSION.
SEI-LAN.
PROVIDE HIM WITH YOUNG MASTER XINGLU'S CLOTHES.
YES, SIR.

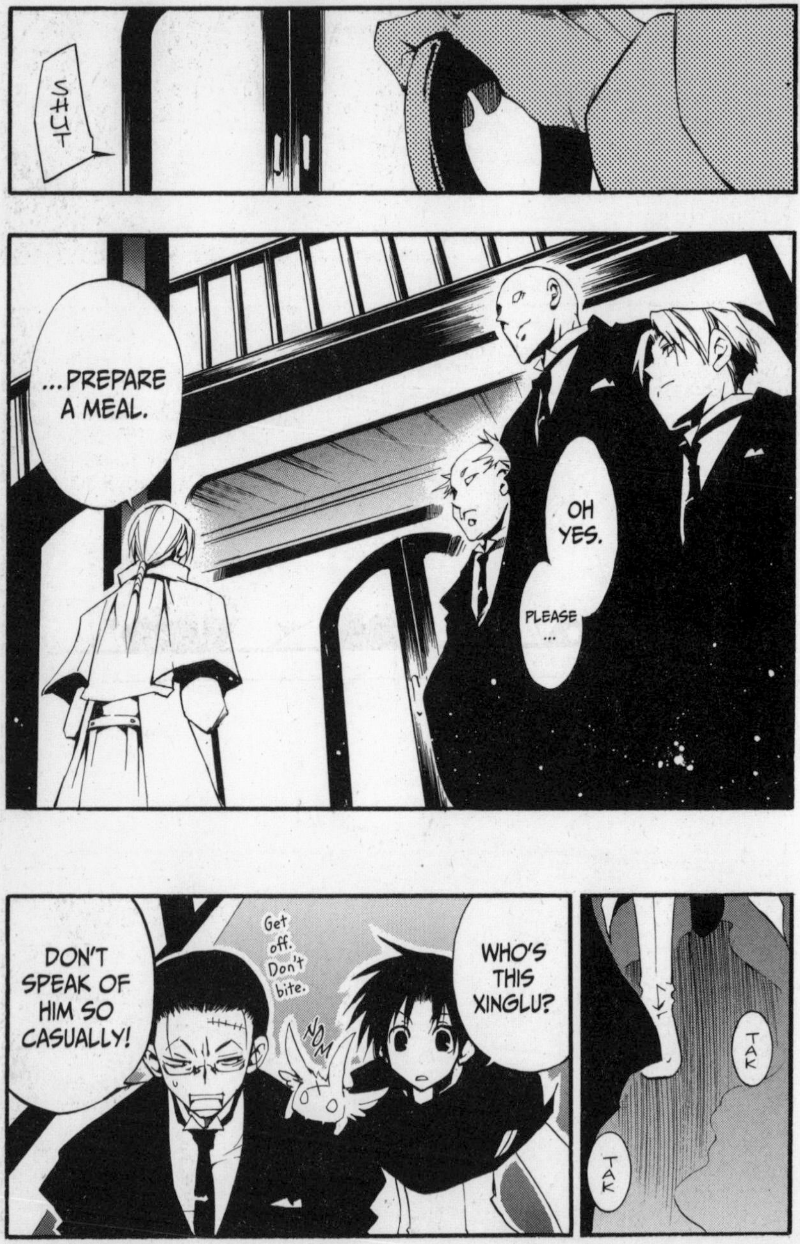
SHUT
OH YES.
PLEASE ...
...PREPARE A MEAL.
TAK
TAK
WHO'S THIS XINGLU?
Get off. Don't bite.
NOM
DON'T SPEAK OF HIM SO CASUALLY!

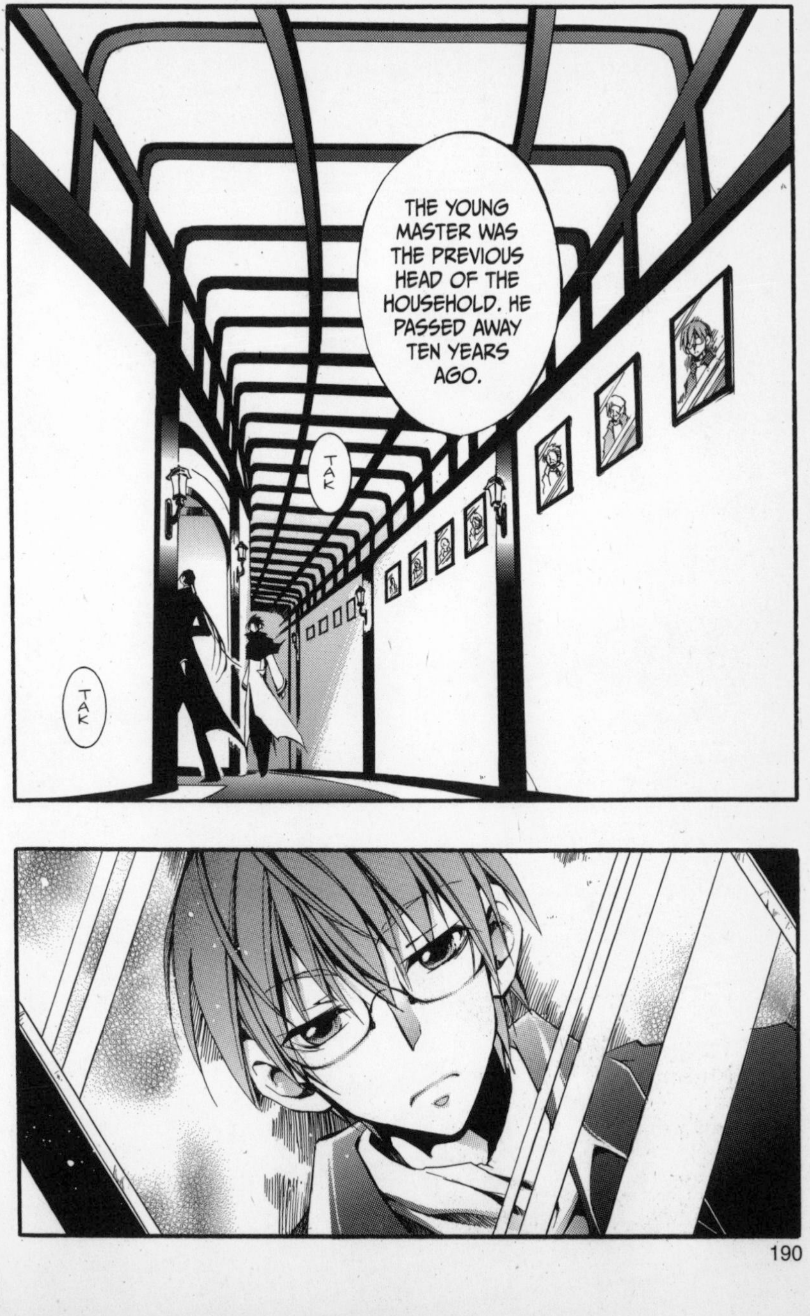
THE YOUNG MASTER WAS THE PREVIOUS HEAD OF THE HOUSEHOLD. HE PASSED AWAY TEN YEARS AGO.
TAK
TAK

Okay!

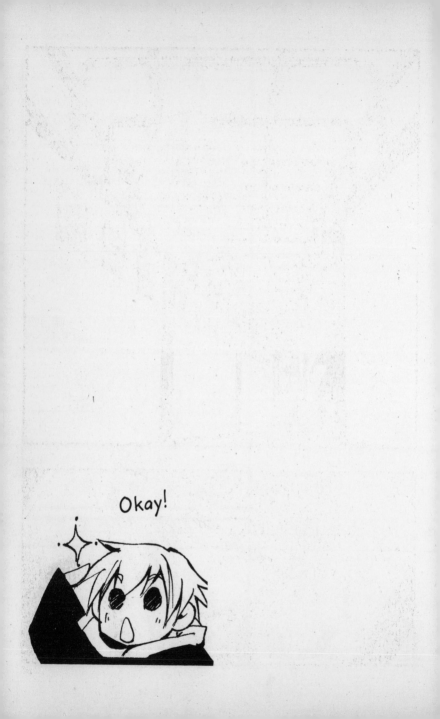

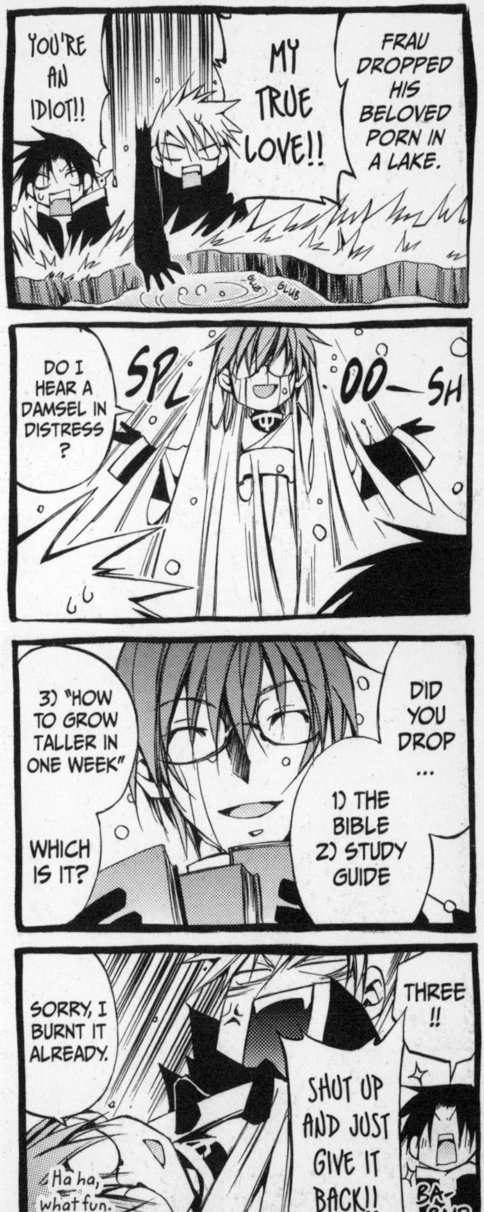

FRAU DROPPED HIS BELOVED PORN IN A LAKE.
MY TRUE LOVE!!
YOU'RE AN IDIOT!!
GLUB GLUB
SPLOO-SH
DO I HEAR A DAMSEL IN DISTRESS?
DID YOU DROP...
1) THE BIBLE 2) STUDY GUIDE
3) "HOW TO GROW TALLER IN ONE WEEK" WHICH IS IT?
THREE!!
SHUT UP AND JUST GIVE IT BACK!!
BA-BMP
SORRY, I BURNT IT ALREADY.
Ha ha, what fun.

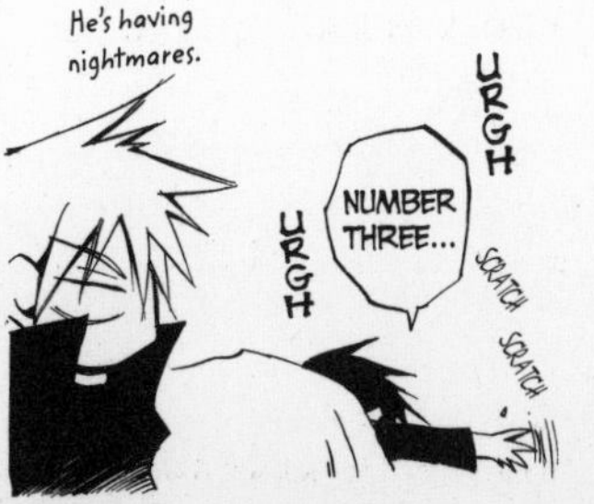

He's having nightmares.
URGH
NUMBER THREE...
URGH
SCRATCH
SCRATCH

Afterword

Thank you, everyone, for making volume 5 happen. Thank you so much for picking it up.

Originally, Teito was supposed to start on his journey around volume 3, but we thought of so much stuff that we wanted to include that he didn't leave until this volume.

From now on, the story will be told against the back-drop of the God Houses. We're going to have a lot of fun drawing it, so we hope you stick around and watch the story unfold. ♥

To everyone who has sent letters or email, thank you so much for your kindness! There's a lot of Teito and Frau fans out there, but Ayanami is popular too. Thank you, guys, we're sure the Chief is happy too...

Hope to see you again in volume 6.

Thank you! ♥♥ Ichihara & Amemiya
11.2007

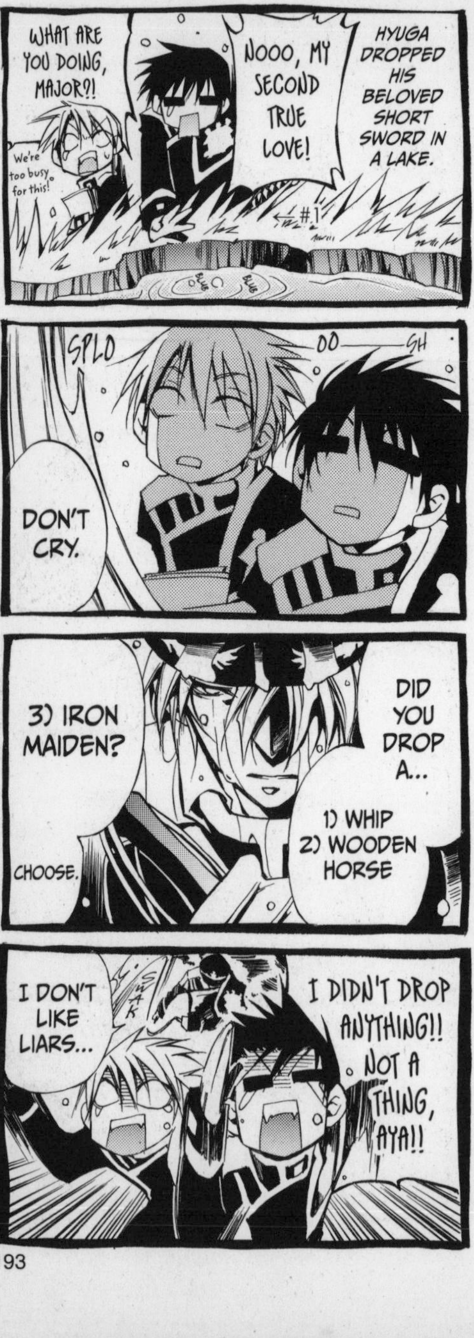

HYUGA DROPPED HIS BELOVED SHORT SWORD IN A LAKE.
NOOO, MY SECOND TRUE LOVE!
WHAT ARE YOU DOING, MAJOR?!
We're too busy for this!
#1
SPLO
OO
SH
DON'T CRY.
DID YOU DROP A...
1) WHIP
2) WOODEN HORSE
3) IRON MAIDEN?
CHOOSE.
I DIDN'T DROP ANYTHING!! NOT A THING, AYA!!
I DON'T LIKE LIARS...

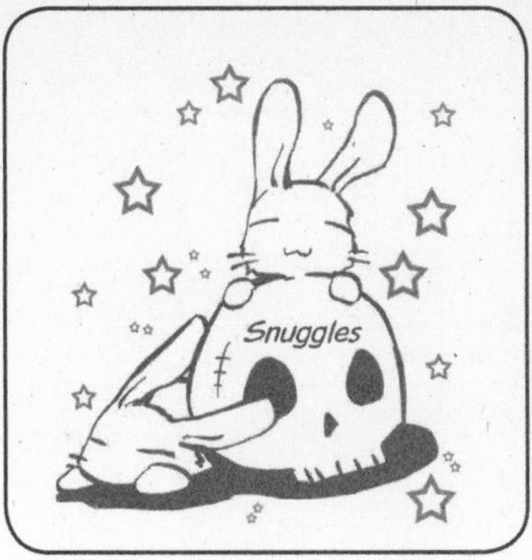
Snuggles

Whenever work gets crazy, for some reason we start checking out travel sites or real estate sites. After letting our imaginations take a vacation, we return to our work feeling refreshed.

—Yuki Amemiya & Yukino Ichihara, 2007

Yuki Amemiya was born in Miyagi, Japan, on March 25. Yukino Ichihara was born in Fukushima, Japan, on November 24. Together they write and illustrate *07-Ghost*, the duo's first series. Since its debut in 2005, *07-Ghost* has been translated into a dozen languages, and in 2009 it was adapted into a TV anime series.

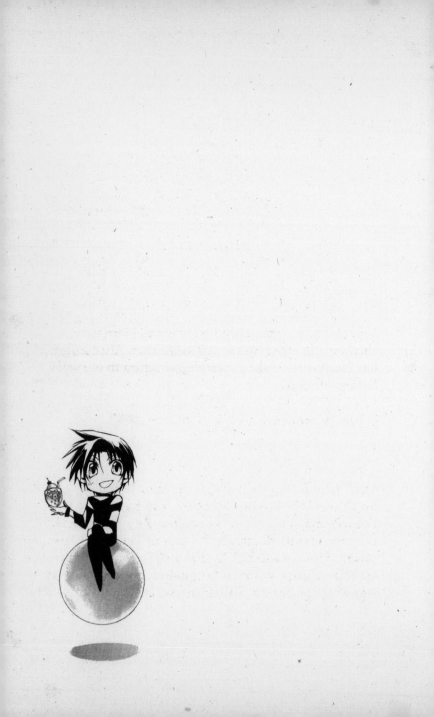

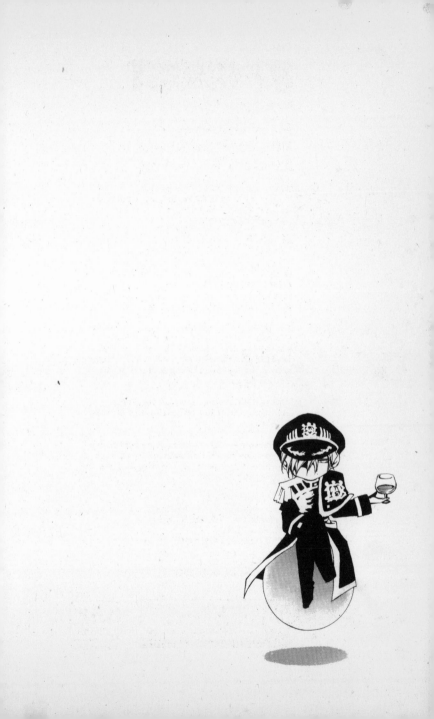

07-GHOST

Volume 5

STORY AND ART BY
YUKI AMEMIYA and YUKINO ICHIHARA

Translation/Satsuki Yamashita
Touch-up Art & Lettering/Vanessa Satone
Design/Shawn Carrico
Editor/Hope Donovan

07-GHOST © 2007
by Yuki Amemiya/Yukino Ichihara
All rights reserved.
Original Japanese edition published by
ICHIJINSHA, INC., Tokyo.
English translation rights arranged with
ICHIJINSHA, INC.

The rights of the author(s) of the work(s) in
this publication to be so identified have been
asserted in accordance with the Copyright,
Designs and Patents Act 1988. A CIP catalogue
record for this book is available from the
British Library.

The stories, characters and incidents
mentioned in this publication are entirely
fictional.

No portion of this book may be reproduced
or transmitted in any form or by any
means without written permission from the
copyright holders.

Printed in Canada

Published by VIZ Media, LLC
P.O. Box 77010
San Francisco, CA 94107

10 9 8 7 6 5 4 3 2 1
First printing, July 2013

PARENTAL ADVISORY
07-GHOST is rated T for Teen and is
recommended for ages 13 and up. This
volume contains realistic and fantasy violence.
ratings.viz.com

www.viz.com

Enter_the_world_of_

LOVELESS

story_+_art_by_YUN_KOUGA

2-in-1 EDITIONS

Each 2-in-1 edition includes
6 color pages and
50 pages of
never-before-seen
BONUS comics,
artist commentary
and interviews!

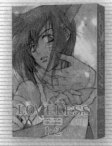

only $14.99!
($16.99 CAN / £9.99 UK)

Available at your local book store,
comic book shop or library, or online at:

store.viz.com

Loveless © Yun Kouga/ICHIJINSHA

RATED
T
FOR
TEEN
ratings.viz.com

viz
media
www.viz.com

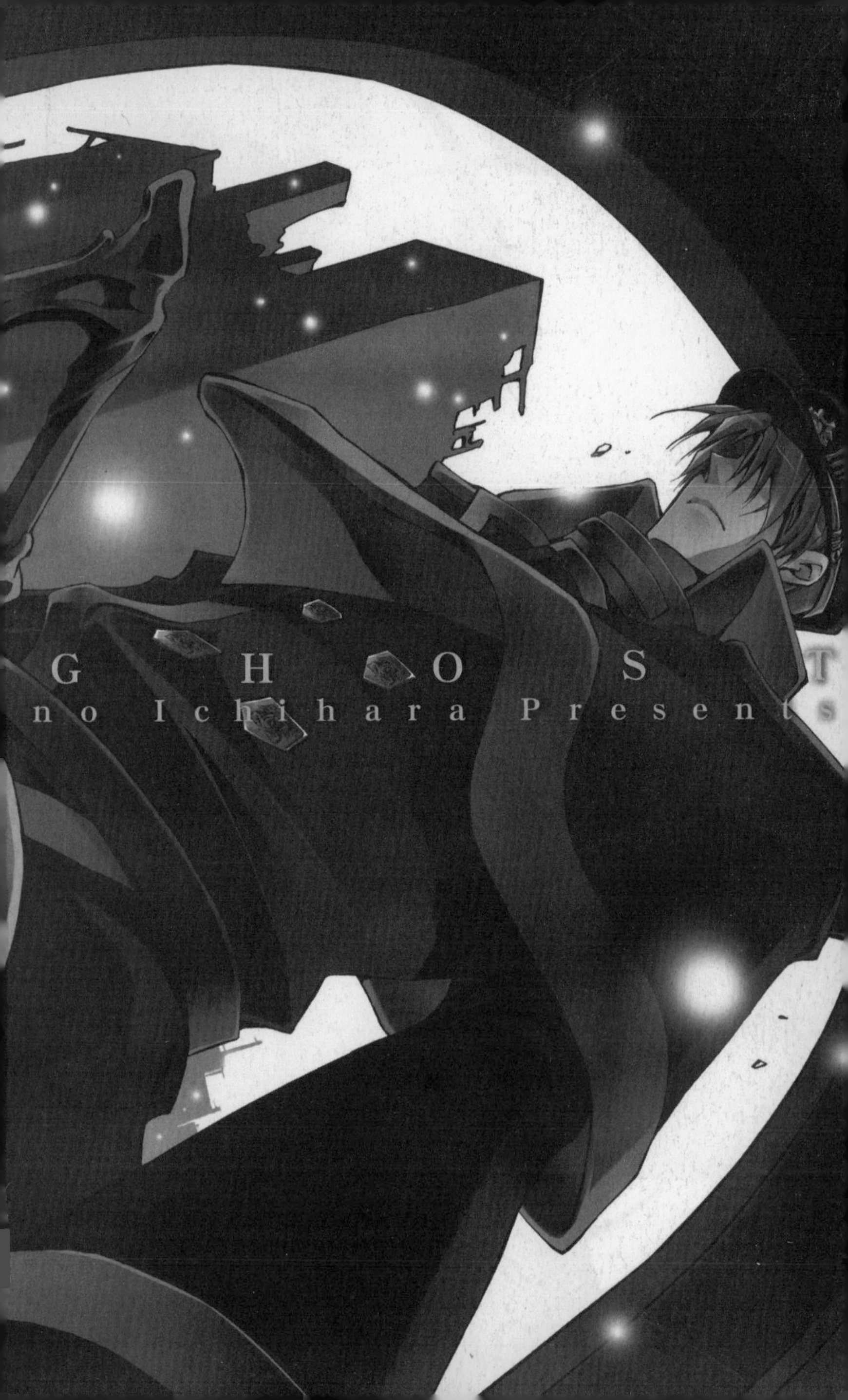
G H O S T
no Ichihara Presents

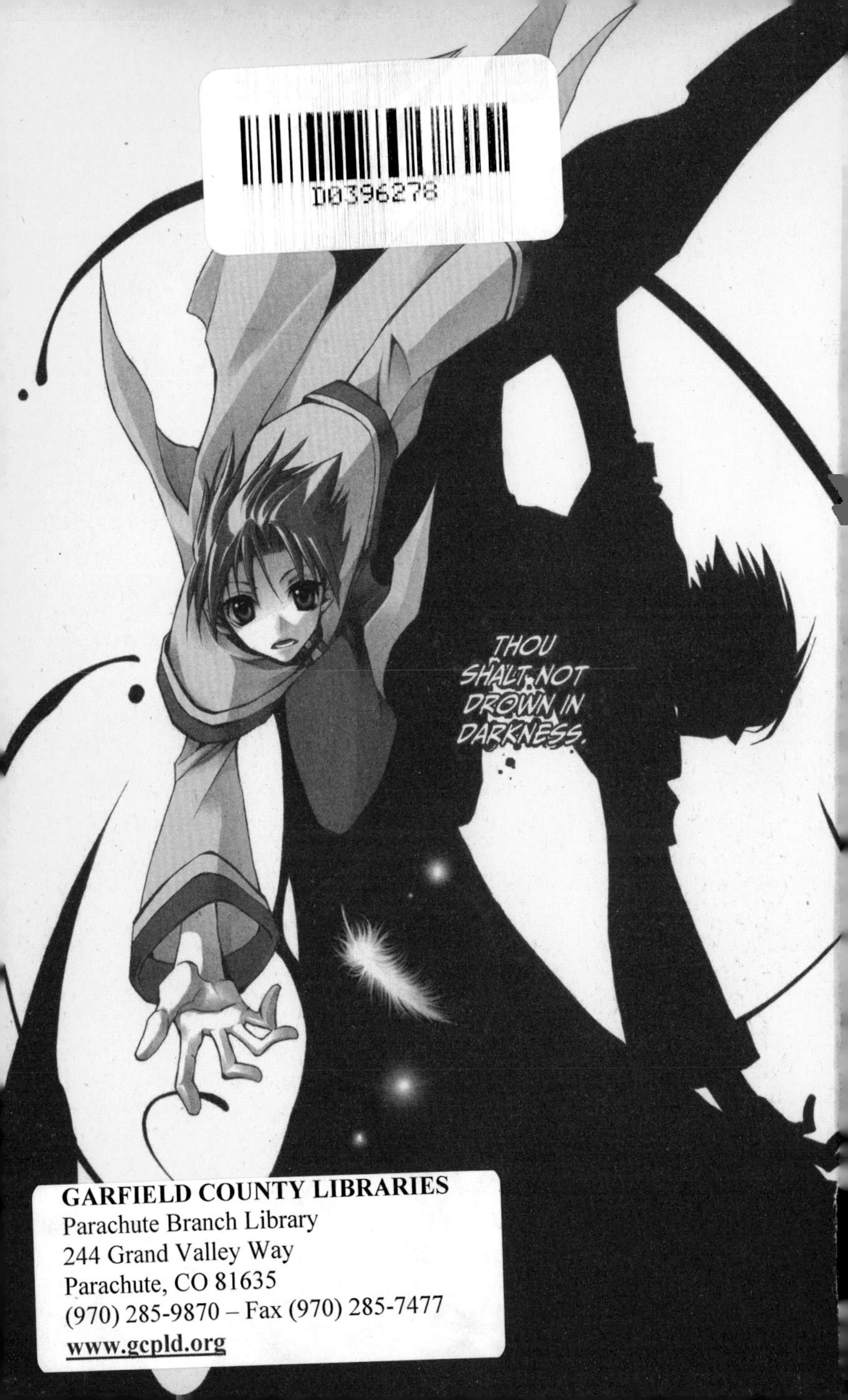
THOU SHALT NOT DROWN IN DARKNESS.